ACCOUNTING IN CENTRAL AND EASTERN EUROPE

RESEARCH IN ACCOUNTING IN EMERGING ECONOMIES

Series Editors: Mathew Tsamenyi and Shahzad Uddin

Recent Volumes:

Volume 1:	Research in Third World Accounting – Edited by R. S. Olusegun Wallace
Volume 2:	Research in Third World Accounting – Edited by R. S. Olusegun Wallace
Volume 3:	Research in Accounting in Emerging Economies – Edited by R. S. Olusegun Wallace
Supplement 1:	Accounting and Development – A Special Case for Africa – Edited by R. S. Olusegun Wallace and Shabani Nzinge (Guest Editor)
Volume 4:	Research in Accounting in Emerging Economies – Edited by R. S. Olusegun Wallace, John M. Samuels, Richard J. Briston and Shahrokh M. Saudagaran
Volume 5:	Research in Accounting in Emerging Economies – Edited by R. S. Olusegun Wallace, John M. Samuels, Richard J. Briston and Shahrokh M. Saudagaran
Volume 6:	Accounting and Accountability in Emerging and Transition Economies – Edited by Trevor Hopper and Zahirul Hoque (Guest Editors)
Volume 7:	Accounting, Banking and Corporate Financial Management in Emerging Economies – Edited by Victor Murinde (Guest Editor)
Volume 8:	Corporate Governance in Less Developed and Emerging Economies – Edited by Professor Mathew Tsamenyi and Dr Shahzad Uddin
Volume 9:	Accounting in Emerging Economies – Edited by Professor Mathew Tsamenyi and Dr Shahzad Uddin
Volume 10:	Research in Accounting in Emerging Economiers – Edited by Professor Mathew Tsamenyi and Dr Shahzad Uddin
Volume 11:	Accounting in Asia – Edited by S. Susela Devi and Keith Hooper
Volume 12A:	Accounting in Africa – Edited by Venancio Tauringana and Musa Mangena
Volume 12B:	Finance and Development in Africa – Edited by Kojo Menyah and Joshua Abor

RESEARCH IN ACCOUNTING IN EMERGING ECONOMIES
VOLUME 13

ACCOUNTING IN CENTRAL AND EASTERN EUROPE

EDITED BY

CĂTĂLIN NICOLAE ALBU

Faculty of Accounting and Management Information Systems,
The Bucharest University of Economic Studies,
Bucharest, Romania

RĂZVAN V. MUSTAŢĂ

Faculty of Economics and Business Administration,
Babeş-Bolyai University, Cluj-Napoca, Romania

Emerald

United Kingdom – North America – Japan
India – Malaysia – China

Emerald Group Publishing Limited
Howard House, Wagon Lane, Bingley BD16 1WA, UK

First edition 2013

British Library Cataloguing in Publication Data
A catalogue record for this book is available from the British Library

ISBN: 978-1-78190-938-6
ISSN: 1479-3563 (Series)

CONTENTS

LIST OF CONTRIBUTORS

Cătălin Nicolae Albu	The Bucharest University of Economic Studies, Bucharest, Romania
Nadia Albu	The Bucharest University of Economic Studies, Bucharest, Romania
David Alexander	University of Birmingham, Birmingham, UK
Jaan Alver	Tallinn University of Technology, Tallinn, Estonia
Lehte Alver	Tallinn University of Technology, Tallinn, Estonia
Cagnur Kaytmaz Balsari	Dokuz Eylul University, Turkey
Carmen Giorgiana Bonaci	Babeş-Bolyai University, Cluj-Napoca, Romania
Chiraţa Caraiani	The Bucharest University of Economic Studies, Bucharest, Romania
Cornelia Dascălu	The Bucharest University of Economic Studies, Bucharest, Romania
Tatiana A. Garanina	St. Petersburg University, Russia
Olesea Ghedrovici	Academy of Economic Studies of Moldova, Chisinau, Moldova
Ionel-Alin Ienciu	Babeş-Bolyai University, Cluj-Napoca, Romania
Nicoleta Maria Ienciu	Babeş-Bolyai University, Cluj-Napoca, Romania

Mateja Jerman	University of Primorska, Koper, Slovenia
Polina S. Kormiltseva	St. Petersburg University, Russia
Camelia Iuliana Lungu	The Bucharest University of Economic Studies, Bucharest, Romania
Dumitru Matiș	Babeş-Bolyai University, Cluj-Napoca, Romania
Cristina Maria Morariu	The Bucharest University of Economic Studies, Bucharest, Romania
Răzvan V. Mustaţă	Babeş-Bolyai University, Cluj-Napoca, Romania
Alexandra Muţiu	Babeş-Bolyai University, Cluj-Napoca, Romania
Sergeja Slapničar	University of Ljubljana, Ljubljana, Slovenia
Jiří Strouhal	University of Economics, Prague, Czech Republic
Neža Štumberger	JECOM, LLC, Cerklje na Gorenjskem, Slovenia
Liis Talpas	Tallinn University of Technology, Tallinn, Estonia
Secil Varan	Dokuz Eylul University, Turkey
Maja Zaman Groff	University of Ljubljana, Ljubljana, Slovenia

ABOUT THE EDITORS

Cătălin Nicolae Albu is an associate professor of accounting with the Bucharest University of Economic Studies, Romania, from which he obtained his PhD in 2005. His current research and teaching areas are management accounting, internal auditing, IFRS, and the true and fair view. He is 2011 senior Fulbright grantee at the University of Dayton, USA and KPMG Romania fellow. His research has recently been published in *Critical Perspectives on Accounting*, *Australian Accounting Review*, *Journal of International Financial Management & Accounting*, *Journal of Accounting in Emerging Economies* and *Accounting in Europe*.

Răzvan V. Mustaţă holds a PhD from the Babeş-Bolyai University, being an associate professor within the Accounting and Audit Department of the same University. He is currently vice dean of the Faculty of Economics and Business Administration, former member of the Babeş-Bolyai University Senate, of the University Administration Council, Faculty Council and also former students' Chancellor and *Prefectum Studiorum* within the University. He is a current member of the European Accounting Association and co-organizer of the *AAC 2013 Convention*, *AAC 2011 Convention*, *AAC 2009 Convention*, *3rd AAC 2008 Annual Conference* and *Luca Paciolo Seminar*.

INTRODUCTION

We would like to begin by saying that we are extremely honoured and pleased to have been invited to guest co-edit a special issue of the book series *Research in Accounting in Emerging Economies* dedicated to accounting in Central and Eastern European (CEE) countries. With so many countries being referred to as transitional, emerging or developing, research to date was only able to provide significant insights in a limited number of instances.

Transition and emerging economies have attracted an increased interest from researchers, international organisations, money lenders and other investors over the course of the last decades. CEE countries, most of them former components of the communist bloc, have suffered diverse influences over time. Historically, the advent of communism in the 1940s and 1950s has stopped the economic and political development of these countries. Its fall during the late 1980s and early 1990s triggered severe changes in the economic and social environment of these countries, with profound consequences on the countries' accounting and business models.

The accounting regulatory process in these countries has mostly been a public one, although some countries also involved private sector and professional bodies. The main user of accounting information was reported to be the state. The accounting model was reformed, sometimes in successive steps and not always quite consistent with each other, to follow the model(s) of more advanced countries such as France, Germany or the United States. Additionally, the need to present the countries as modern ones, with a view to attract foreign investors, raised the regulators' interest in the International Accounting Standards/International Financial Reporting Standards (IASs/IFRSs). Thus, IASs/IFRSs and IASC's conceptual framework were considered at various times and in different approaches as model to reform financial reporting in these countries. Additionally, the countries' political will to join the European Union (EU) compelled the national regulators to ensure a high level of harmonisation with the European Directives even before these countries joined the EU, and concluded with their enactment subsequently (for the ones that in the end became full members).

Also, CEE economies do not make exception to findings in other emerging economies: a lower level of development of the accounting profession, lower focus on professional judgment, and lesser quality of financial reporting, than in more developed countries. Although it is not well enough researched in the region, managerial accounting seems to be in an incipient stage of development, with historically less focus on decision-making, especially during the communist period. Audit is a fairly recent profession. The market capitalisation of stock exchanges in these countries is understandably smaller than that of western economies, hence corporate governance institutions and practices are still developing.

It is in the midst of these processes of change and reform that we called for theoretical and empirical chapters that will further our understanding of accounting issues in CEE countries. We have thus collected a total of 12 chapters representative of various themes within the accounting field, from six countries of the region, namely Estonia, Moldova, Slovenia, Romania, Turkey and Russia (the latter was selected for geographical and historical closeness with the other countries represented). Various methodologies are used for the purposes of their respective chapters by the 26 authors representing eight countries, thus satisfying a wide range of reader interests.

We have divided the chapters in five large themes. The first theme is the very topical issue of consequences of IFRSs application. We start off thus this issue with two chapters addressing these matters, in Turkey and in Russia respectively. We continue with the context and challenges of the process of accounting harmonisation in the region. Namely, we have included in this theme three chapters addressing the case of Romania, Estonia and Moldova. We go on by dealing with reporting and disclosure issues related to intangible assets and intellectual capital, with three chapters on Romania and Slovenia. Two chapters addressing corporate social responsibility and environmental reporting issues follow, both of them on the case of Romania. We conclude by including two more chapters studying the matters related to the accounting profession at large; one is situated in Slovenia, and the other in Romania. A brief description of each article follows.

The first chapter in the issue is Varan and Balsari (2013), an empirical chapter investigating the adoption of IFRS and loss avoidance in Turkey. The authors measure loss avoidance in an earnings distribution approach, for all non-financial firms listed on the Istanbul Stock Exchange for the period 1998–2010. Results reported include lower loss aversion in the post-IFRS period, more significant for large firms compared to high leverage firms, and for mandatory adopters compared to voluntary adopters.

Further, loss aversion is not affected by IFRS adoption in the case of highly leveraged firms and voluntary adopters.

The second chapter in the issue is Garanina and Kormiltseva (2013), the second empirical chapter selected. The chapter investigates the effect of IFRS adoption on the value relevance of financial reporting in Russia. The authors do not find any evidence of increased value relevance to external users of financial information after IFRS adoption when comparing and evaluating the Russian Accounting Standards and IFRS, across the entire population of firms listed on the Russian financial market. The authors explain this finding by the so-called mock compliance with IFRS undergoing in their sample firms.

Albu, Albu, and Alexander (2013) is the first qualitative chapter included in the special issue. They address the matters related to the application and use of the True and Fair View (TFV) concept within the Romanian context, as a case study of concept transferability. TFV originates in the United Kingdom, and was imposed in the EU via the European Directives. However, by investigating all accounting legal sources, and by interviewing key representatives of major stakeholders involved in the process of financial reporting in Romania, the authors report on different perceptions of the concept held by various stakeholders within the country under study, and on the difficulty of assuming that concept transferability works when the host country features other characteristics from the ones where the concept originated.

The fourth chapter included is Alver, Alver, and Talpas (2013). They investigate the institutional pressures and the role of the state in designing the financial accounting and reporting model in Estonia. This is the first conceptual chapter of the special issue, looking in a literature review approach at the coercive, normative and mimetic institutional pressures shaping the development of the Estonian accounting model. The authors highlight the role of IFRS in this evolution, but also point out to the opportunity Estonia now has to take lead in designing an accounting model that would better suit its needs.

Alexander and Ghedrovici (2013) is the fifth chapter in the special issue, and the second conceptual chapter. The authors reflect on the importance of the historical and cultural factors of the evolution of Moldovan accounting within its broader economic, political and social context. By analysing the content of national accounting regulations and economic conditions in the country, the authors highlight the pervasiveness of some features related to people's mentality, formed over a long period of time as a result of the political and cultural closeness individualistic and independent thinking values, in the occurrence of many contemporaneous spheres, including accounting.

The following two chapters address disclosures of intellectual capital in Romania. Thus, the sixth chapter is Ienciu and Matiş (2013), an empirical chapter examining voluntary intellectual capital disclosures of Romanian listed firms, via content analysis. The authors show that the key components of intellectual capital are relatively poorly reported by the companies in their sample. The main areas of intellectual capital disclosures relate firstly to the structural capital, secondly to the relational capital and finally to the human capital. As a general statement, the authors conclude to the indifference with which most Romanian companies handle this matter.

Morariu (2013) is the issue's seventh chapter, and the second addressing intellectual capital disclosure, more specifically the determinants of this disclosure in Romania. The author reports on the findings of her in-depth analyses (construction of a disclosure index and correlation and regression analyses). She finds that the industry and the firm size do not influence the intellectual capital disclosure practices of Romanian firms in her sample, but their combination seems to significantly predict such practices. The author advances as an explanation for this state of affairs the novelty of the intellectual capital concept and disclosures in Romania.

The eighth chapter selected is Jerman (2013). She explores the reporting practices of Slovene listed firms by analysing the obligatory and voluntary disclosures related to intangibles in the firms' annual reports. This is another qualitative piece of research, studying the required and voluntary IFRS disclosures by selected companies from 2007 to 2011. The author finds a reduced level of mandatory disclosures, despite being better represented than the voluntary ones. However, the author finds deficiencies even in the reporting practices of some sample companies related to mandatory disclosures.

Lungu, Caraiani, and Dascălu (2013) is the ninth chapter in the special issue, and the first one to address the very important issue of corporate and social responsibility. Thus, the authors investigate the scope of social and environmental reporting by Romanian listed entities, from the perspective of integrating it in financial reporting, and develop on a novel approach to the presentation of social and environmental information in the annual reports. Among the chapter's findings are the initial stage of development of such social and environmental focus of Romanian companies, and the tendency of such companies to report on the mandatory framework rather than a voluntary one.

The following chapter addresses the environmental disclosure practices of listed Romanian firms. Ienciu (2013) is the tenth chapter in the issue, and analyses the environmental reporting practices of Romanian listed companies, through the lens of the legitimacy theory. The author finds evidence of a weak quality and quantity of environmental information disclosed by the companies in his sample. Also, he finds that large more exposed firms tend to have better environmental disclosures, in an attempt to answer the pressure of the stakeholders and to maintain their legitimacy. None of the firms in the sample prepare a separate environmental or sustainability report. Finally, the reported environmental information is not correlated with firms' environmental performance.

The eleventh chapter in this special issue is Slapničar, Groff, and Štumberger (2013). The authors set out to investigate in the Slovene context whether professional accounting qualification matters for the provision of accounting services, via estimating a structural equation model. They find that professional qualification is positively associated with competences, which are in turn positively associated with knowledge and larger service product mix, but not with customer loyalty and litigation risk. The authors conclude that in the Slovenian context, professional qualification matters for the provision of accounting services. Finally, they believe that price of the services is also a significant factor in customer loyalty.

The twelfth and final chapter in this issue is Bonaci, Mustaţă, Muţiu, and Strouhal (2013). They aim to assess Romanian accounting students' academic performance in the context of a specific class, and to place that in the context of the particularities of the Romanian accounting environment. They employ a questionnaire-based survey administered to senior undergraduate accounting students, and then compared the self-assessed performance with the actual performance as assessed via students' grades for the same subject. The authors find that such students would benefit from an improvement in their abilities to self-assess their work. Finally, regarding Bloom's taxonomy of educational objectives, Romanian undergraduate students seem to prefer questions pertaining to the application and analysis levels, rather than evaluation-type of questions.

We hope that you will enjoy our selection of chapters addressing various issues related to accounting in CEE countries. We recommend this issue to all readers interested in better understanding the context of emerging economies in Central and Eastern Europe.

Cătălin Nicolae Albu
Răzvan V. Mustaţa
Editors

REFERENCES

Albu, C. N., Albu, N., & Alexander, D. (2013). The true and fair view concept in Romania: A case study of concept transferability. In C. N. Albu & R. V. Mustaţă (Eds.), *Accounting in Central Eastern Europe*. Bingley, UK: Emerald.

Alexander, D., & Ghedrovici, O. (2013). Evolution of accounting in Moldova: Some reflections about the importance of historical and cultural factors. In C. N. Albu & R. V. Mustaţă (Eds.), *Accounting in Central Eastern Europe*. Bingley, UK: Emerald.

Alver, L., Alver, J., & Talpas, L. (2013). Institutional pressures and the role of the state in designing the financial accounting and reporting model in Estonia. In C. N. Albu & R. V. Mustaţă (Eds.), *Accounting in Central Eastern Europe*. Bingley, UK: Emerald.

Bonaci, C. G., Mustaţă, R. V., Muţiu, A., & Strouhal, J. (2013). Assessing accounting students' academic performance: A case study on Romania. In C. N. Albu & R. V. Mustaţă (Eds.), *Accounting in Central Eastern Europe*. Bingley, UK: Emerald.

Garanina, T. A., & Kormiltseva, P. (2013). The effect of international financial reporting standards (IFRS) adoption on the value relevance of financial reporting: A case of Russia. In C. N. Albu & R. V. Mustaţă (Eds.), *Accounting in Central Eastern Europe*. Bingley, UK: Emerald.

Ienciu, I.-A. (2013). Environmental disclosure of Romanian listed entities. In C. N. Albu & R. V. Mustaţă (Eds.), *Accounting in Central Eastern Europe*. Bingley, UK: Emerald.

Ienciu, N. M., & Matiş, D. (2013). Intellectual capital disclosure of Romanian listed companies. In C. N. Albu & R. V. Mustaţă (Eds.), *Accounting in Central Eastern Europe*. Bingley, UK: Emerald.

Jerman, M. (2013). Intangible assets and their reporting practices: Evidence from Slovenia. In C. N. Albu & R. V. Mustaţă (Eds.), *Accounting in Central Eastern Europe*. Bingley, UK: Emerald.

Lungu, C. I., Caraiani, C., & Dascălu, C. (2013). Reconsidering financial reporting from the perspective of corporate social and environmental responsibility. Romanian companies' approach. In C. N. Albu & R. V. Mustaţă (Eds.), *Accounting in Central Eastern Europe*. Bingley, UK: Emerald.

Morariu, C. M. (2013). The determinants of intellectual capital disclosure: evidence from Romania. In C. N. Albu & R. V. Mustaţă (Eds.), *Accounting in Central Eastern Europe*. Bingley, UK: Emerald.

Slapničar, S., Groff, M. Z., & Štumberger, N. (2013). Does professional accounting qualification matter for the provision of accounting services? In C. N. Albu & R. V. Mustaţă (Eds.), *Accounting in Central Eastern Europe*. Bingley, UK: Emerald.

Varan, S., & Balsari, K. (2013). The adoption of international financial reporting standards (IFRS) and loss avoidance in Turkey. In C. N. Albu & R. V. Mustaţă (Eds.), *Accounting in Central Eastern Europe*. Bingley, UK: Emerald.

THE ADOPTION OF INTERNATIONAL FINANCIAL REPORTING STANDARDS (IFRS) AND LOSS AVOIDANCE IN TURKEY

Secil Varan and Cagnur Kaytmaz Balsari

ABSTRACT

Purpose – *The purpose of the study is to present evidence on the International Financial Reporting Standards (IFRS) adoption and earnings quality relationship on an emerging country context focusing on firm characteristics.*

Design/methodology/approach – *To measure loss avoidance, the earnings distribution approach is followed. Data includes all the nonfinancial firms listed on the Borsa Istanbul (BIST) for the period covering 1998–2010. The sample is divided into subsegments according to size and leverage, considering the potential impact of different financial reporting incentives. Furthermore, mandatory and voluntary adopters are examined separately.*

Accounting in Central and Eastern Europe
Research in Accounting in Emerging Economies, Volume 13, 1–25

ISSN: 1479-3563/doi:10.1108/S1479-3563(2013)0000013006

Findings – *The results indicate lower loss aversion in the post-IFRS period. Furthermore, we found that incentives dominate accounting standards in determining financial reporting quality. The decrease in loss aversion after IFRS adoption is more significant for large firms compared to small firms, low leverage firms compared to high leverage firms, and for mandatory IFRS adopter firms compared to voluntary IFRS adopters.*

Originality/Value – *Research provides inconsistent evidence on the relationship between IFRS adoption and earnings quality. Turkey represents an interesting environment to test the impact of IFRS adoption, as the Turkish accounting system has followed a historical path from a Continental European accounting system to an Anglo-Saxon accounting system. The current Turkish accounting system exhibits features of both these systems. Additionally, IFRS adoption was optional in 2003 and mandatory in 2005 in line with EU regulations, and the changes in the reporting environment are supported by the regulatory developments and institutional changes in Turkey.*

Keywords: Accounting; IFRS; loss avoidance; financial reporting incentives; Turkey; statistical evidence

INTRODUCTION

Theory suggests that adopting higher quality standards enhances earnings quality. International Financial Reporting Standards (IFRS) is viewed as a high quality accounting standard by regulators and empirical research confirms this argument. However, there is inconsistent evidence on the relationship between IFRS adoption and earnings quality. Besides IFRS adoption, literature suggests that investor protection, audit quality, regulatory enforcement, financial system, and business culture are all relevant for earnings quality (Demirguc-Kunt & Levine, 1999; Jeanjean & Stolowy, 2008; Soderstrom & Sun, 2007). Hence, differences in earnings quality exist among countries sharing common standards for financial reporting. Additionally, financial reporting behavior may vary among firms, as firms with different characteristics may have different financial reporting incentives (Jeanjean & Stolowy, 2008; Leuz & Oberholzer-Gee, 2006).

Therefore, the purpose of the study is to present evidence on the IFRS adoption and earnings quality relationship on an emerging country context focusing on firm characteristics. Consistent with the prior literature, we expect that incentives dominate accounting standards in determining financial reporting quality. Turkey represents an interesting environment to test the impact of IFRS adoption, as the Turkish accounting system has followed a historical path from a Continental European accounting system to an Anglo-Saxon accounting system; the current Turkish accounting system therefore exhibits features of both these systems. Additionally, IFRS was optional in 2003, in line with the European Union (EU), and mandatory in 2005 for firms listed on Borsa Istanbul (BIST) in line with EU regulations, and the changes in the reporting environment are supported by the regulatory developments and institutional changes in Turkey. Finally, SMEs still applying the Turkish GAAP (Generally Accepted Accounting Principles) are in a transitional phase to IFRS.

One of the measures of earnings quality is the level of earnings management. Earnings management is related to firm reporting incentives which are the function of firm characteristics. Measuring earnings quality is a challenging task and all methodologies applied in the literature have pros and cons. Leuz, Nanda, and Wysocki (2003) found that European and Asian firms exhibit a higher degree of earnings management measured by loss avoidance than Anglo-American firms. This study uses loss avoidance as an incentive-based earnings management measure as a proxy for earnings quality, following Burgstahler and Dichev (1997). Durak (2010) examined the accrual quality as an earnings management measure of the listed nonfinancial firms prior to and after IFRS adoption in Turkey, and found increased accrual quality for these firms after IFRS adoption. However, in literature, although there are multicountry studies examining Turkish data, no evidence has been detected regarding the impact of IFRS adoption on loss aversion practices of Turkish nonfinancial firms.

To compare the earnings management practices of the listed firms prior to and after mandatory IFRS adoption, we follow the methodology of Burgstahler and Dichev (1997), Degeorge, Patel, and Zeckhauser (1999), and more recently Jeanjean and Stolowy (2008), which investigate loss avoidance.

Data includes all the nonfinancial listed firms on BIST covering the period of 1998–2010 with 2,167 observations. Financial institutions and holdings are excluded from the sample as these firms operate in different regulatory environments.

Besides reporting environments, firm characteristics are also relevant for earnings quality (Gaio, 2010). For this reason, the sample firms are divided into subsegments in terms of size and leverage, considering the potential impact of different financial reporting incentives. Since the early and mandatory adoption of IFRS also reflects different incentives, the sample firms are additionally examined as voluntary and mandatory IFRS adopters. The graphical and statistical evidence shows that for all subsegments, the results indicate lower loss aversion in the post-IFRS period. Furthermore, loss aversion is not affected by IFRS adoption for highly leveraged firms and voluntary adopters. The results for highly leveraged firms indicate that bank monitoring seems to be more effective than the standards used in financial reporting for a bank oriented institutional setting. Regarding the voluntary IFRS adopters, the necessity of transparency and financial reporting quality based on the incentive of external orientation may affect the results.

The rest of the chapter is organized as follows: the second section presents the Turkish accounting environment, the third section gives a brief overview of the relevant literature and develops the hypotheses, the fourth section describes data and methodology; the fifth section presents the results and the sixth section concludes.

TURKISH ACCOUNTING ENVIRONMENT

Turkey represents an interesting environment to test the impact of IFRS adoption for three reasons. First, the Turkish accounting system has followed a historical path from a Continental European accounting system to an Anglo-Saxon accounting system; the current Turkish accounting system therefore exhibits features of both these systems (Yildiz, Elitas, & Uc, 2011). The Turkish accounting system was first influenced by the French system and the German system, and then by the US accounting system due to the economic and political relationship between the US and Turkey in the 1950s (Terzi, Oktem, & Sen, 2013). The listed firms in BIST reported their financial statements in accordance with the Turkish GAAP until 2005 in Turkey, in compliance with the Uniform Chart of Accounts in Turkey, which was issued in 1994 (Terzi et al., 2013). The Turkish Commercial Code is derived from the French Commercial Code and influenced by the German and Italian Commercial Codes (Balsari, Ozkan, & Secer, 2009). It determines the fundamental accounting requirements for the local GAAP. However, the accounting rules are mainly established by the Tax Law. Consequently, the Turkish GAAP is a tax-based accounting system. The main differences in the accounting treatments between the local GAAP and IFRS are the measurement, classification and disclosure requirements for assets, liabilities, revenue and expenses. For instance, the Turkish GAAP does not allow impairment of assets and, contrary to IFRS, expenses are classified as ordinary and extraordinary in the income statement.

Second, IFRS was optional in 2003, in line with the EU, and mandatory in 2005 for firms listed on BIST in line with EU regulations (Yildiz et al., 2011). The mandatory adopters have applied inflation accounting in the 2003–2005 period, which was in line with IAS 29. Thus the difference between voluntary and mandatory adopters may also be attributed to the choice of inflation accounting.

Third, the changes in the reporting environment are supported by the regulatory developments and institutional changes in Turkey. The Turkish Accounting Standards Board (TASB) which was established for improving the quality of financial reporting began its operations in 2002. The Board first published Turkish Accounting Standards and then Turkish Financial Reporting Standards, by directly translating the complete set of IFRS developed by IASB (Akyuz, Bulca, & Uc, 2008). The Capital Markets Board of Turkey (CMB) issued the communiqué on Accounting Standards in 2003, requiring the mandatory application of IFRS, and encouraged the firms listed on BIST for early adoption. CMB additionally issued the communiqué on Independent Audit in Capital Markets in 2002, which was effective by 2006. Following the changes on the financial reporting requirements of listed firms, CMB issued the Corporate Governance (CG) Principles based on the CG Principles of OECD. The issuance of these principles supported the changes in the financial reporting environment, as the agency theory argues that CG and accounting information are linked, and the most important function of CG is to ensure the quality of the financial reporting process (Cohen, Krishnamoorthy, & Wright, 2004). The CMB CG Principles were set in line with the "Comply" or "Explain" approach, thus by 2005, CMB required all listed firms on BIST to disclose their "CG Compliance Report" in annual reports. As a bank-based country with high concentrated ownership, the consensus in Turkey on the significance of CG principles is mainly reflected by the new Commercial Code No. 6102, which came into effect on July 1, 2012. Consistent with the new Commercial Code, some private companies are also required to apply IFRS in their financial statements as of January 1, 2013 under the Turkish Commercial Code (Terzi et al., 2013).

LITERATURE REVIEW AND HYPOTHESES DEVELOPMENT

Consistent with the view that the use of high quality standards leads to high quality financial reporting, Barth, Landsman, and Lang (2008) find that firms which adopt IFRS exhibit lower earnings management compared to the local GAAP for an international sample of firms. Many other studies found contradictory results in single or multicountry setting for the effect of IFRS adoption on earnings management (e.g., Aubert & Grudnitski, 2012). The differences in findings may be attributable to the differences in reporting environments in different countries such as law orientation, previous accounting orientation, investor protection, ownership structure, culture, financial system, and firm-level differences (Demirguc-Kunt & Levine, 1999; Jeanjean & Stolowy, 2008; Leuz et al., 2003; Morais & Curto, 2008).

The conflicting findings of these studies may also be attributable to the methodological differences. Although we eliminated country-level differences by focusing on a single country, the change in earnings quality prior to and after IFRS adoption, as Barth et al. (2008) highlights, may also be affected by the changes in firms' incentives and the economic environment. In addition, earnings management is difficult to measure as it may be applied in different forms (Leuz et al., 2003). Total and specific accrual models are widely used to capture EM practices. However, Kaplan (1985) states that the level of accruals may fluctuate due to economic conditions, therefore a high level of accruals does not necessarily mean higher earnings smoothing.

Additionally, using accrual models and other methodologies to test earnings management led to contradictory results in some studies. Ahmed, Neel, and Wang (2010) found that firms that adopted IAS/IFRS standards in 2005 exhibit greater loss avoidance relative to the benchmark control firms in the post-adoption period. However, they also found that both IFRS adopters and control firms exhibit a significantly lower likelihood of reporting small positive earnings in the post-adoption period relative to the pre-adoption period, which is inconsistent with greater earnings management.

Barth et al. (2008) examines the effects of adopting IFRS on earnings management, and uses an indicator variable that equals one if net income scaled by total assets is between 0 and 0.01. Their findings indicate that non-IFRS firms manage earnings toward small positive amounts more frequently than firms that adopted IFRS.

Christensen, Lee, and Walker (2008) use two kinds of earnings management measures, earnings smoothing and loss avoidance for German firms, and report that incentives dominate accounting standards in determining accounting quality. Christensen et al. (2008) found that mandatory IFRS adopters have higher leverage and a lower analyst following, implying that these firms confront less demand for transparency.

Durak (2010) examined the accrual quality of the listed nonfinancial firms prior to and after IFRS adoption, and found increased accrual quality for these firms after IFRS adoption in Turkey. However, in literature, although Turkish data are included in some multicountry studies (Leuz et al., 2003), there is no evidence on the impact of IFRS adoption on loss aversion practices of Turkish nonfinancial firms. Additionally, Leuz et al. (2003) provides evidence of earnings management differences across 31 countries, and detect loss aversion. Leuz et al. (2003) found that European and Asian firms exhibit a higher degree of earnings management measured by loss avoidance than Anglo-American firms.

Therefore, we use loss avoidance in this study as an incentive-based earnings management measure following Burgstahler and Dichev (1997). One other reason to use this methodology is the study of Jeanjean and Stolowy (2008) which uses the loss avoidance measure of EM in a three country study to investigate the impact of IFRS adoption. Jeanjean and Stolowy (2008) consider the firm level differences in their research design, and build an aggregate measure instead of analyzing different firm characteristics separately.

Thus, we focus on firm characteristics in our analysis and apply sensitivity tests on the change in the economic environment. We first analyze whether certain firm characteristics that indicate different financial reporting incentives explain the differences in earnings quality in the pre-IFRS period. Then, we investigate whether earnings quality increased with the adoption of IFRS in an emerging civil-law country context. We analyze loss aversion as an attribute of earnings quality. Leuz et al. (2003) find that earnings management is more pronounced in non-common law countries. Since Turkey is a civil-law country, we expect higher loss avoidance before the adoption of IFRS. Furthermore, Turkey has a bank-based financial system, high ownership concentration, tax-based previous accounting system, and low investor protection rights, which all point toward lower accounting quality. Ball (2001) argues that changing accounting standards without changing institutional setting and enforcement may have little impact on financial reporting behavior. Since the changes in the reporting environment are supported by the regulatory developments and institutional changes in Turkey as explained in the second section, our first hypothesis is developed as:

Hypothesis 1. *Loss avoidance will be lower after IFRS adoption.*

Besides reporting environment, firm characteristics are also relevant for earnings quality (Gaio, 2010). Financial reporting incentives, thus the degree of managerial discretion, varies with firm characteristics (Narktabtee & Patpanichchot, 2011). Therefore, the effect of the IFRS adoption on earnings quality, specifically on loss avoidance may differ across firms with different characteristics. Ball, Robin, and Wu (2003) argue that the quality of accounting information is related to incentives which are driven by the institutional setting of the firm. It is also possible to have different reporting incentives depending on firm characteristics, despite the use of common standards. This raises concern that IFRS adoption may not always lead to equivalent effect in quality of accounting information for all firms, even in the same institutional setting.

Aubert and Grudnitski (2012) find that earnings management decreases with IFRS adoption using the incentive-based earnings management measure in a multicountry setting. However, as they used analyst forecast as their earnings management threshold, the companies in their sample are likely to consist of large firms in Europe which analysts follow. Firm size is viewed as an important factor for earnings management practices. However, according to Kim, Liu, and Rhee (2003) there are two conflicting expectations for the relationship between size and earnings management. First, large firms are expected to have better internal control and are likely to have better audit quality and a higher reputation cost, thus they are expected to exhibit less earnings management. On the other hand, large firms have higher incentives to meet the earnings thresholds due to the higher analyst following. More complex transactions create an opportunity to manage earnings and utilize a higher negotiating power over auditors, thus they might be expected to have higher earnings management. Regarding IFRS adoption, it is expected that large firms have more resources and systems to adopt IFRS thoroughly, relative to the small firms. Because of these two different views, the expectation for large firms is not clear. Therefore, hypothesis two is developed as follows:

Hypothesis 2. *The decrease in earnings management will be more pronounced for large firms after IFRS adoption.*

Management incentives to manage earnings are higher for avoiding violating debt covenants and highly leveraged firms are expected to be involved in more earnings management practices. On the other hand, the monitoring level is higher for highly leveraged firms. Literature also suggests that voluntary and mandatory adoption of IFRS reflects different incentives, and voluntary adoption is driven by the level of external orientation. Christensen et al. (2008) found that mandatory IFRS adopters have higher leverage and lower analyst following. Particularly in a bank-based financial system (such as in Turkey), bank monitoring in highly leveraged firms would be stronger, which may lower earnings management regardless of standards used. Thus, we predict that the impact of IFRS adoption, together with the regulations on audit requirements on earnings quality, would be more pronounced for mandatory adopters and low leverage firms.

Therefore, hypothesis three is developed as follows:

Hypothesis 3. *The level of the decrease in loss avoidance will be more pronounced for mandatory adopters and low leverage firms after IFRS adoption.*

We investigate whether the impact of IFRS adoption is different for firms with different characteristics. Specifically, we analyze differences among small and large firms, high and low leverage firms, and voluntary and mandatory IFRS adopters. To perform the analysis for testing our hypothesis, we subdivide our sample into pre- and post-IFRS periods and then divide the data into groups according to variable means of size, leverage, and voluntary and mandatory IFRS adopters.

DATA AND METHODOLOGY

Data includes all the nonfinancial listed firms on the BIST covering the period of 1998–2010 with 2,167 observations. Financial institutions and holdings are excluded from the sample as these firms operate in different regulatory environments. Table 1 shows the number of nonfinancial firms used in the sample by years. FINNET database is used for gathering data.

In Turkey, IFRS adoption was mandatory by 2005. However, voluntary adoption was enabled in 2003–2004. Moreover, in 2004, financial statements were adjusted for high inflation rates. Thus, to avoid estimation

Table 1. Sample Generation.

Pre-IFRS Period			Post-IFRS Period		
Year	Total numberof firms (listed on BIST)	Number of nonfinancial firms	Year	Total number of firms (listed on BIST)	Number of nonfinancial firms
1998	277	169	2005	304	203
1999	285	182	2006	316	206
2000	315	185	2007	319	212
2001	310	204	2008	317	210
2002	288	199	2009	315	207
			2010	331	212
Total		939			1,250
Unavailable		22			
Remaining		917			1,250

errors, we define pre-IFRS period as 1998–2002, and post-IFRS period as 2005 onward.

To compare the loss avoidance practices of listed firms prior to and after mandatory IFRS adoption, we follow Burgstahler and Dichev (1997) and Degeorge et al. (1999), which investigate the behavior of earnings based on the prospect theory (Kahneman & Tversky, 1979). Prospect theory implies that agents feel losses more deeply than gains of the same value, thus the tendency toward loss aversion leads to the argument that "the largest gains in utility, and hence the largest incentives to manage earnings, occur when moving from a relative or absolute loss to a gain" (Burgstahler & Dichev, 1997). Therefore, we analyze the graphical distribution of earnings to determine any discontinuities around the behavioral threshold of reporting positive earnings.

To investigate the threshold of loss avoidance or reporting positive earnings, the graphical distribution of earnings per share ratio (EPS) is used, and the discontinuities around zero are examined. First, the histograms of earnings distributions prior to and after 2005 are compared for the complete sample.

Second, the sample firms are divided into subsegments according to size and leverage, considering the potential impact of differential financial reporting incentives.

The suggestion of Degeorge et al. (1999) is followed to calculate the bin width of the histograms of the EPS, as twice the interquartile range of the variable multiplied by the negative cube root of the sample. According to Eq. (1), the bin widths are computed as 0.002 for the pre-IFRS period, and 0.02 for the post-IFRS period.

$$\text{Bin width: } 2(\text{IQR})n^{-1/3} \tag{1}$$

where

IQR = Sample interquartile range
n = the number of available observations.

To measure earnings management, the ratio of the frequency of small profits to small losses are computed (Burgstahler & Dichev, 1997; Leuz et al., 2003; Shen & Chih, 2005), revealing the extent to which insiders manage earnings to avoid reporting losses (Leuz et al., 2003). If greater than unity, the ratio of small profits to small losses indicates earnings management, and higher ratios signify more earnings management (Shen & Chih, 2005). The actual number of observations just before and after zero are used for the calculation according to the bin widths (EM_1) as well as twice the bin widths (EM_2) on the histograms of EPS (Beatty, Ke, & Petroni, 2002).

For more statistical evidence, we test the null hypothesis for earnings smoothing, which suggests that the distributions of earnings levels and changes are smooth; therefore the expected number of observations in any given interval of the distribution is the average of the number of observations in the two immediately adjacent intervals (Shen & Chih, 2005). We follow Burgstahler and Dichev (1997) and Shen and Chih (2005) and define EM_3 as Eq. (2), the difference between the actual and expected number of observations for the interval immediately to the right of zero:

$$EM_3 = \frac{AQ_i - EQ_i}{SD_i} \tag{2}$$

where

AQ_i = Actual number of observations in interval i (the first interval on the right of zero)
EQ_i = Expected number of observations in interval i (the average of the number of observations in the two immediately adjacent intervals)
SD_i = estimated standard deviation of the difference between the actual and expected numbers of observations around interval i as estimated by Eq. (3).

$$SD_i = [Np_i(1 - p_i) + (1/4)N(p_{i-1} + p_{i+1})(1 - p_{i-1} - p_{i+1})]^{1/2} \tag{3}$$

where

N = fiscal years
p_i = the proportion of the actual number of observations for interval i to the years.

Following Jeanjean and Stolowy (2008), we calculate the odds ratios for small profits to small losses ratio using the Stata software's "tabodds" command which tabulates the odds of failure against a categorical explanatory variable (post-IFRS observations), and applies a test for the linear trend of the log odds against the numerical code used for the categories of IFRS adoption period. This test shows whether the change in the odds (decrease or increase) is significant with increasing application of IFRS.

RESULTS

The descriptive statistics and the definitions of the variables are presented in Table 2, which reveals that on average, EPS ratios are negative for listed

Table 2. Descriptive Statistics.

	Pre-IFRS Period			Post-IFRS Period		
Variables[a]	*N*	Mean	Standard deviation	*N*	Mean	Standard deviation
LNASSETS	917	17.4	1.35	1,250	19.07	1.57
LEVERAGE	916	0.66	0.56	1,209	0.53	0.63
TOTAL	916	−.02	0.01	1,250	−0.05	0.02
SMALL	458	−0.03	0.22	640	−0.13	0.75
LARGE	458	−0.02	0.15	610	0.03	0.26
LOWLEV	580	0.01	0.02	690	0.05	0.17
HIGHLEV	335	−0.08	0.31	554	−0.18	0.82
VOLUNT	256	−0.01	0.10	313	−0.02	0.41
MANDAT	660	−0.04	0.22	931	−0.06	0.62

[a]LNASSETS: Natural log of total assets;
LEVERAGE: The ratio of total liabilities to total assets (debt ratio);
TOTAL: EPS ratio, the ratio of net income to the number of shares outstanding for all sample firms;
SMALL: EPS for firms that have lower total assets than the mean of LNASSETS;
LARGE: EPS for firms that have higher total assets than the mean of LNASSETS;
LOWLEV: EPS for firms that have lower debt ratios than the mean of LEVERAGE;
HIGHLEV: EPS for firms that have higher debt ratios than the mean of LEVERAGE;
VOLUNT: EPS for firms that have voluntarily adopted IFRS in years 2003–2004;
MANDAT: EPS for mandatory IFRS adopters.

firms prior to and after IFRS adoption. It can be observed that in both pre- and post-IFRS periods, firms that have lower leverage ratios are the most profitable, whereas higher leveraged firms are the largest in terms of earnings losses. Yet the losses on average rise up to −0.18 in post-IFRS period from −0.09.

Graphical Evidence

Figure 1 shows the EPS distributions of the listed firms in BIST in 1998–2010. The bin width we apply in the histogram according to the Eq. (1) is 0.01. The frequency of small losses that are in the range [−0.01, 0.00] is 459; and the frequency of small profits that are in the range [0.00, 0.01] is 172. Thus, the ratio of small profits to losses is computed as 2.67, which shows that the listed firms in BIST report small declines in earnings less often than small increases in earnings, suggesting EM to exceed the zero threshold of reporting positive profits. Figure 2 presents the earnings distributions of the listed firms for the pre- and post-IFRS adoption. Bin

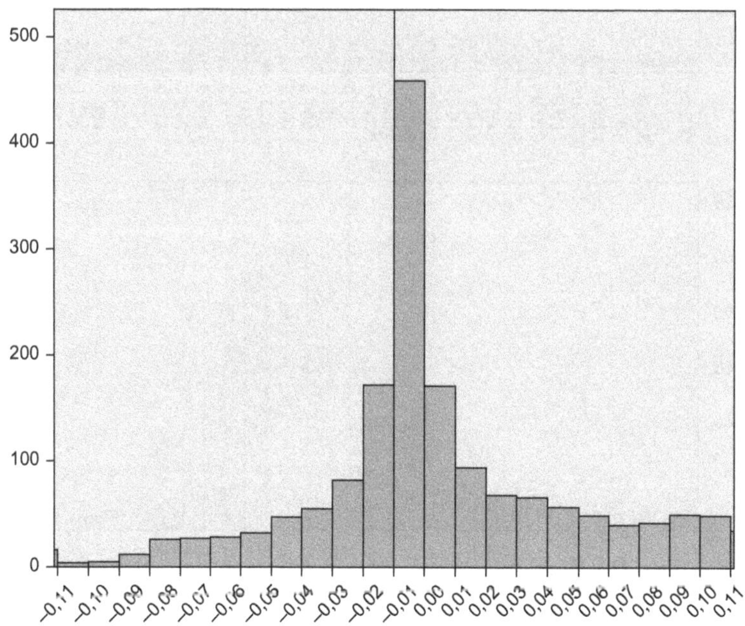

Fig. 1. EPS Distributions of the Listed Firms in ISE in 1998–2010.

widths are 0.002 for the pre-IFRS period and 0.02 for the post-IFRS period. According to Fig. 2, EM to exceed zero thresholds alleviates after IFRS adoption. The frequencies of the distributions just before and after zero according to the bin widths are 133 and 45 for EPS pre-IFRS, and 105 and 73 for EPS post-IFRS. Therefore the ratio of small profits to losses declines from 2.95 to 1.44 after IFRS adoption (Table 2). In Figs. 3, 4, 5, 6, 7, and 8 the sample firms are divided into subsegments in terms of size, leverage, and voluntary and mandatory IFRS adopters. The figures show

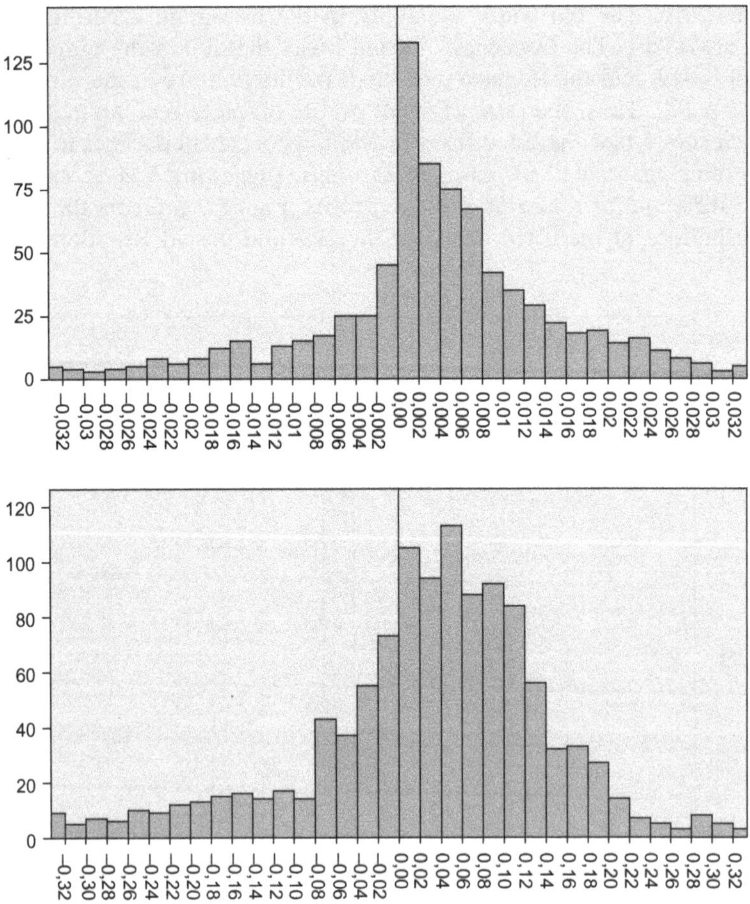

Fig. 2. EPS Distribution Pre–Post-IFRS for Nonfinancial Listed Firms.

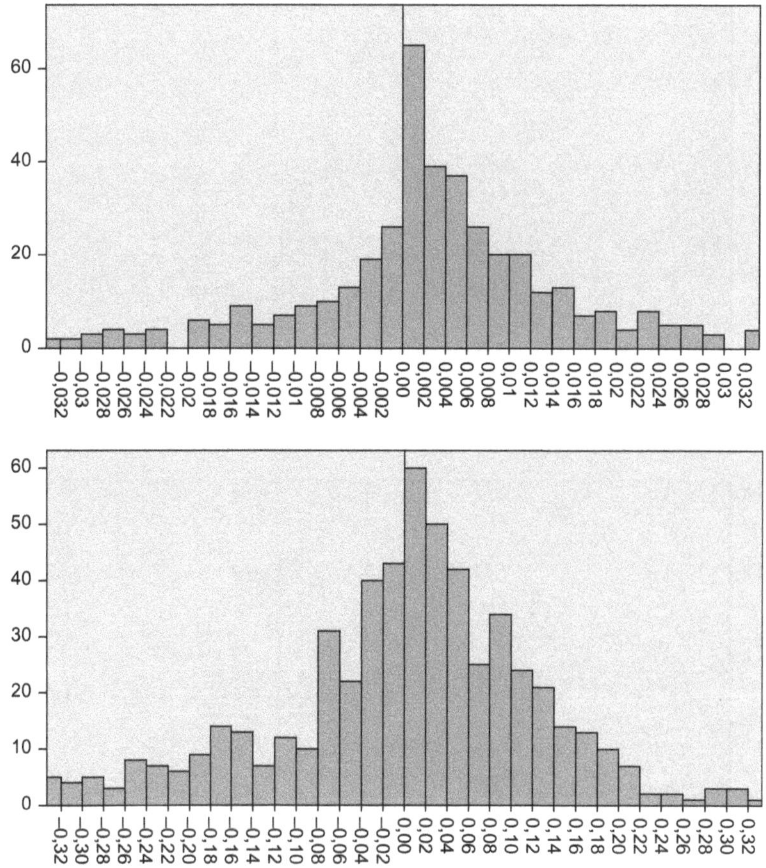

Fig. 3. EPS Distribution Pre–Post-IFRS for Small Firms.

that the earnings distributions show lower discontinuities around zero threshold in the post-IFRS period. Figures 3 and 4 show the graphical evidence for the pre- and post-IFRS periods separately for small and large firms. It can be observed that both small and large firms exhibit high loss avoidance in the pre-IFRS period. However, large firm difference is much more pronounced between small profits and small losses in comparison to small firms. Additionally, it can be observed that loss avoidance decreased for both types of firms in the post-IFRS period. Yet the decrease is higher for large firms. Figures 5 and 6 show graphical evidence for the pre- and

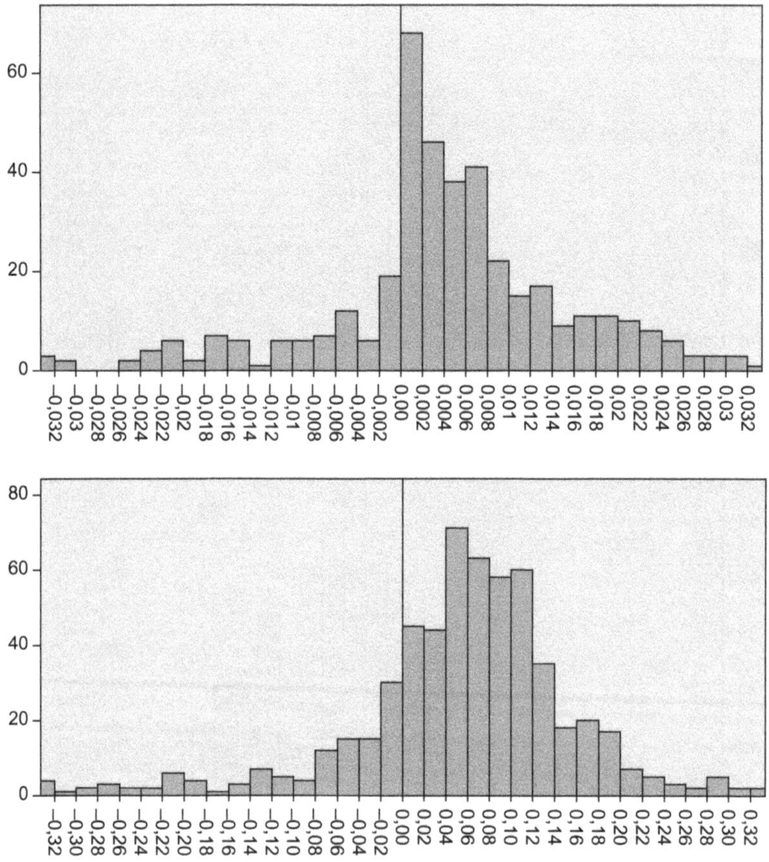

Fig. 4. EPS Distribution Pre–Post-IFRS for Large Firms.

post-IFRS period separately for low and high leverage firms. It can be seen from the graphical evidence that low leverage firms exhibit higher loss avoidance in comparison to high leverage firms. Additionally, decrease in loss avoidance of low leverage firms for the post-IFRS period is higher. The results for the voluntary and mandatory IFRS adopters as shown in Figs. 7 and 8 show that mandatory adopters exhibit higher loss avoidance in comparison to voluntary adopters in the pre-IFRS period.

Graphical evidence provides a visual tool to detect earnings smoothing to exceed thresholds for sample firms. Yet, graphical evidence should

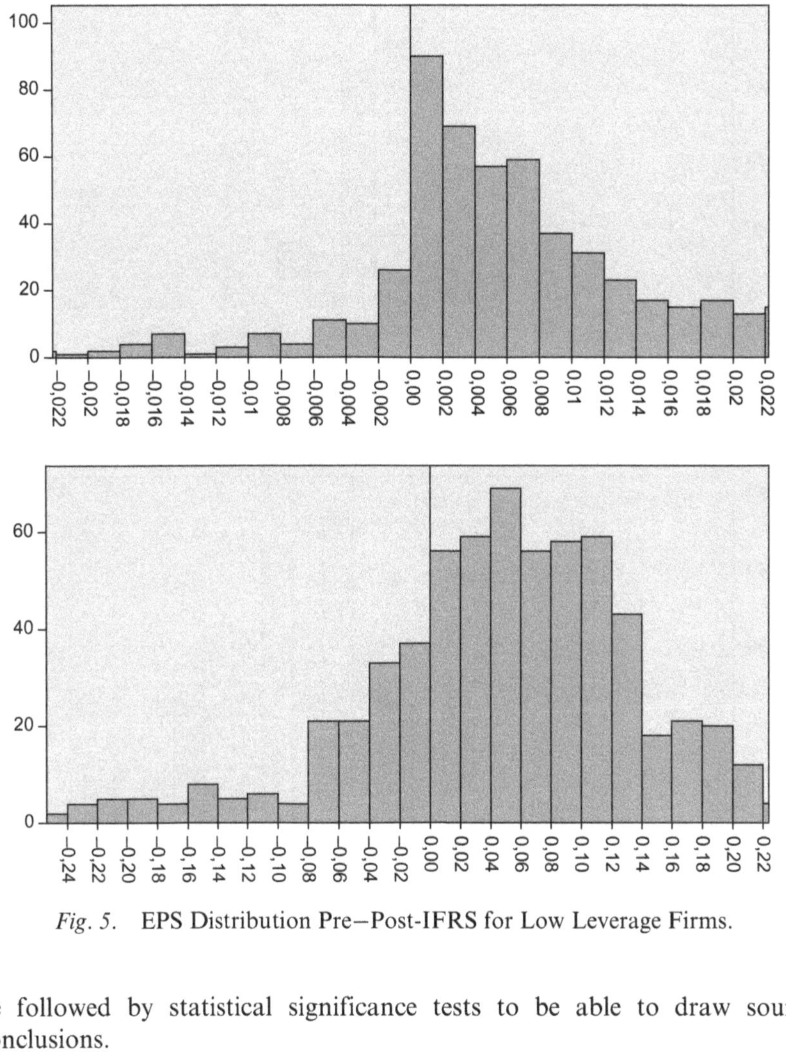

Fig. 5. EPS Distribution Pre–Post-IFRS for Low Leverage Firms.

be followed by statistical significance tests to be able to draw sound conclusions.

Statistical Evidence

The ratios of small profits to losses are presented in Table 3. According to Table 3, regardless of firm specific characteristics, listed firms in BIST have become less likely to engage in earnings smoothing in the post-IFRS

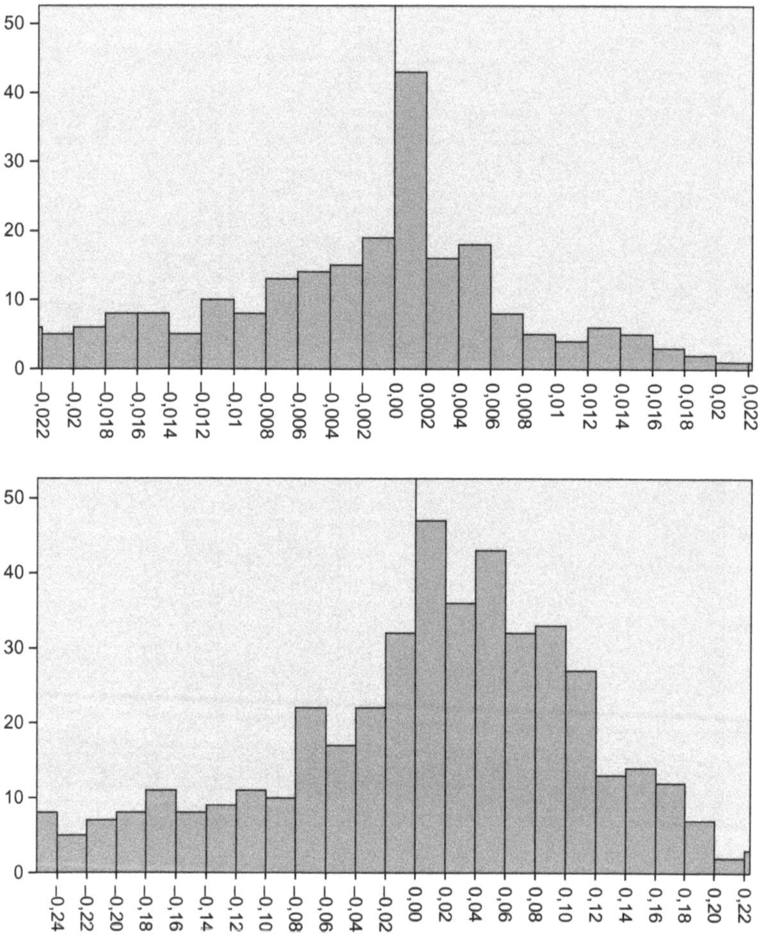

Fig. 6. EPS Distribution Pre–Post-IFRS for High Leverage Firms.

period. Regarding EM_3, the results show that small positive earnings and small increases in earnings are significantly higher than expected, indicating loss aversion except for the voluntary IFRS adopters in the pre-IFRS period. For the post-IFRS period however, the null hypothesis of no loss avoidance cannot be rejected for LARGE, LEVLOW, and VOLUNT variables. This result provides evidence for the impact of high quality standards to financial reporting quality where a tax-based previous local accounting

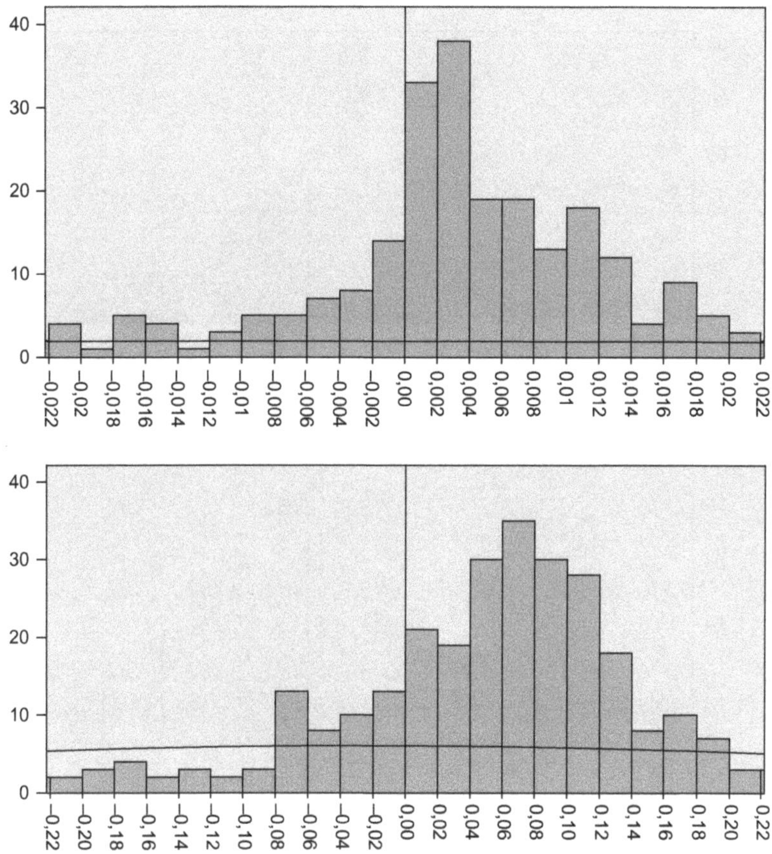

Fig. 7. EPS Distribution Pre–Post-IFRS for Voluntary Adopters.

system has been in place. This evidence points to the importance of other countrywide factors such as local GAAP and investor protection level. The evidence related to the large firms supports the view that large firms have higher incentives to meet earnings thresholds due to the higher analyst following. Complex transactions create an opportunity to manage earnings and utilize a higher negotiating power over auditors. The evidence related to leverage and voluntary IFRS adopters is interesting. Even though high leverage firms are expected to have more incentives to manage earnings, loss avoidance is higher for low leverage firms in the pre-IFRS period which shows the importance of the monitoring provided by banks in the

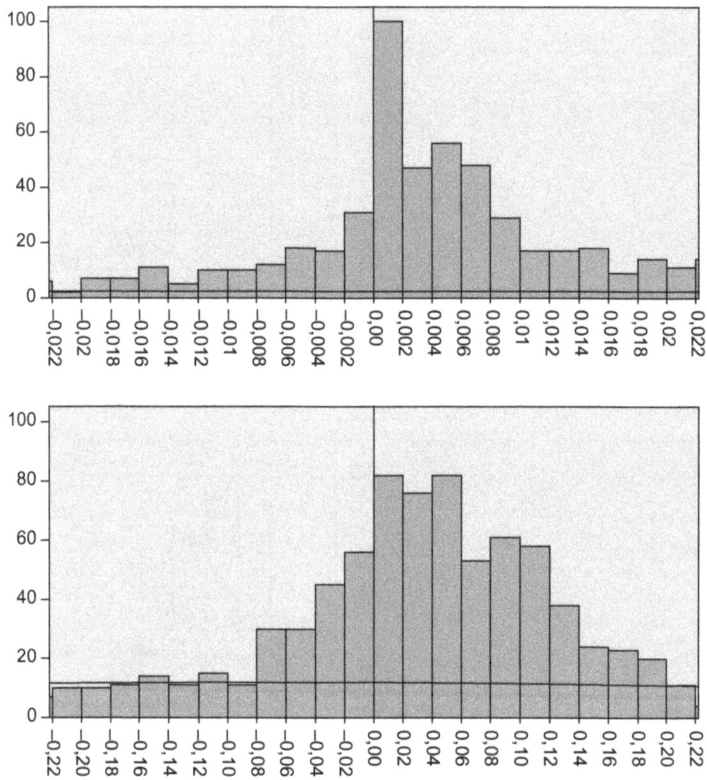

Fig. 8. EPS Distribution Pre–Post-IFRS for Mandatory Adopters.

economy. The results regarding the early adopters of IFRS show that firms which have voluntarily adopted IFRS exhibit less loss avoidance prior to and after IFRS adoption in comparison with the other subsamples. Voluntary adopters also are the sole subsample that EM_3 measure is insignificant for both periods.

The test results showing the significance of difference in loss avoidance for the pre- and post-IFRS periods are presented in Table 4. The odds ratios and results for the score test for trend of odds ratios are provided respectively. We found significant results for the TOTAL sample, LARGE firms sample, and more significant results for LEVLOW firms, and the MANDAT sample at the 1% level. These findings show that the practice

Table 3. Ratios of Small Profits to Losses Pre–Post-IFRS Adoption.

	Pre-IFRS Period			Post-IFRS Period		
	EM_1	EM_2	EM_3	EM_1	EM_2	EM_3
TOTAL	2.95	3.11	6.04**	1.44	1.56	1.82*
SMALL	2.50	2.29	4.02**	1.40	1.33	1.57*
LARGE	3.58	4.56	4.19**	1.50	1.98	1.05
LEVLOW	3.46	4.42	4.34**	1.54	1.66	1.16
LEVHIGH	2.26	1.74	3.79**	1.47	1.54	1.71*
VOLUNT	2.36	3.23	1.12	1.62	1.74	0.96
MANDAT	3.23	3.06	6.04**	1.46	1.56	1.58*

*Significant at the 0.5% level.
**Significant at the 0.1% level.
TOTAL: EPS ratio, the ratio of net income to the number of shares outstanding for all sample firms;
SMALL: EPS for firms that have lower total assets than the mean of LNASSETS;
LARGE: EPS for firms that have higher total assets than the mean of LNASSETS;
LOWLEV: EPS for firms that have lower debt ratios than the mean of LEVERAGE;
HIGHLEV: EPS for firms that have higher debt ratios than the mean of LEVERAGE;
VOLUNT: EPS for firms that have voluntarily adopted IFRS in years 2003–2004;
MANDAT: EPS for mandatory IFRS adopters.

of loss aversion is not affected by IFRS adoption for voluntary IFRS adopters and highly leveraged firms.

Sensitivity Tests

Since the Turkish economy was severely impacted by the financial crises of 2001–2002, the EPS distributions for the pre-crises and crises periods are also analyzed. No significant differences are detected. Additionally, we examine the voluntary and mandatory adopters in terms of size and leverage. As presented in Table 5, voluntary IFRS adopters are larger in size, however they have lower leverage in both the pre- and post-IFRS periods consistent with the findings of Christensen et al. (2008). This fact suggests that the results found for large firms and low leverage firms are even stronger if we exclude the voluntary adopters. Therefore, the results of firm characteristics are robust to the preference of early IFRS adoption.

Table 4. Odds Ratios Pre–Post-IFRS Adoption.

Variables	Cases	Controls	Odds	Score test for trend of odds
	Small profits	Small losses	Ratios	χ^2
TOTAL				
Pre-IFRS	133	45	2.95	
Post-IFRS	105	73	1.44	9.91**
SMALL				
Pre-IFRS	65	26	2.50	
Post-IFRS	60	43	1.40	3.64
LARGE				
Pre-IFRS	68	19	3.58	
Post-IFRS	45	30	1.50	6.26*
LEVLOW				
Pre-IFRS	90	26	3.46	
Post-IFRS	57	37	1.54	7.07**
LEVHIGH				
Pre-IFRS	43	19	2.26	
Post-IFRS	47	32	1.47	1.45
VOLUNT				
Pre-IFRS	33	14	2.36	0.63
Post-IFRS	21	13	1.62	
MANDAT				
Pre-IFRS	100	31	3.23	8.47**
Post-IFRS	82	56	1.46	

*Significant at the 0.5% level.
**Significant at the 0.1% level.
TOTAL: EPS ratio, the ratio of net income to the number of shares outstanding for all sample firms;
SMALL: EPS for firms that have lower total assets than the mean of LNASSETS;
LARGE: EPS for firms that have higher total assets than the mean of LNASSETS;
LOWLEV: EPS for firms that have lower debt ratios than the mean of LEVERAGE;
HIGHLEV: EPS for firms that have higher debt ratios than the mean of LEVERAGE;
VOLUNT: EPS for firms that have voluntarily adopted IFRS in years 2003–2004;
MANDAT: EPS for mandatory IFRS adopters.

Table 5. Mean Values of LNASSETS and LEVERAGE for Voluntary and Mandatory IFRS Adopters.

	Pre-IFRS		Post-IFRS	
	LNASSETS	LEVERAGE	LNASSETS	LEVERAGE
VOLUNT	17.82	0.59	19.69	0.45
MANDAT	17.17	0.69	18.88	0.55

CONCLUSIONS AND DISCUSSION

The purpose of the study is to present evidence on the IFRS adoption and earnings quality relationship on an emerging country context focusing on firm characteristics. Consistent with Barth et al. (2008) and Durak (2010), the results show higher earnings quality in the post-IFRS period compared to the pre-IFRS period, for the overall sample. This result indicates that using high quality standards increases earnings quality in a civil law, bank oriented, low investor protection country with a previous tax-based accounting practice, and shows the importance of the quality of reporting standards in a less than perfect institutional setting.

Consistent with Ball et al. (2003), Christensen et al. (2008), Gaio (2010), Narktabtee and Patpanichchot (2011), and Soderstrom and Sun (2007), we found that incentives dominate accounting standards in determining financial reporting quality, and that management incentives are crucial in determination of earnings quality consistent with Jeanjean and Stolowy (2008). The decrease in loss aversion after IFRS adoption is more significant for large firms compared to small firms, low leverage firms compared to high leverage firms, and for mandatory IFRS adopters firms compared to early IFRS adopters. These findings imply that large firms have more successfully adopted the standards than small firms, resulting in a more significant impact on their earnings quality. This finding provides insight for the regulators in their decision to adopt IFRS by SMEs. As the resources of the SMEs are limited in terms of infrastructure and human capital, IFRS adoption might not produce the desired results for SMEs. Second, for high leverage firms and voluntary adopters, loss aversion is not affected by IFRS adoption. This result may be attributable to the high level of bank monitoring for high leverage firms in the pre-IFRS period. Bank monitoring seems to be more effective than the standards used in financial reporting for a bank oriented institutional setting. This result shows the importance of effective monitoring mechanisms for achieving high quality financial reporting. Regarding the voluntary IFRS adopters, the necessity of transparency and financial reporting quality based on the incentive of external orientation may affect the results.

This study has two major limitations. The first of these is the use of a single-country sample that consists of the nonfinancial listed firms. Thus, the generalizability of the results to other economic environments and financial institutions is limited. Second, this study focuses on one of the main tools of earnings management as loss aversion. However, firms may engage in earnings management practices via various tools. This study does not examine earnings management through total and specific accruals.

Further research may analyze the IFRS adoption and earnings quality relationship in the financial sector of the emerging countries, as these institutions are vital for economies, and may play major roles in the financial crises.

ACKNOWLEDGMENTS

We would like to express our gratitude toward the editors of the book, Cătălin Nicolae Albu and Răzvan V. Mustaţă for their support and encouragement during the process, and to anonymous referees for their valuable suggestions and insight which helped us in completion of this chapter.

REFERENCES

Ahmed, S. A., Neel, M., & Wang, D. (2010). Does mandatory adoption of IFRS improve accounting quality? Preliminary evidence. *Contemporary Accounting Research*, doi: 10.1111/j.1911-3846.2012.01193.x

Akyuz, Y., Bulca, H., & Uc, M. (2008). *The activities of Turkish accounting standards board (TASB) for improving the quality of the financial knowledge and general view on Turkish financial reporting standards (TFRS)*. ICME, Tirana, Albania, March 1, 2008, Epoka University Icme'08, March 28–29, Tirana.

Aubert, F., & Grudnitski, G. (2012). Analysts' estimates: What they could be telling us about the impact of IFRS on earnings manipulation in Europe. *Review of Accounting and Finance*, *11*, 53–72.

Ball, R. (2001). *Infrastructure requirements for an economically efficient system of public financial reporting and disclosure*. Brookings-Wharton Papers on Financial Services, pp. 127–182.

Ball, R., Robin, A., & Wu, J. S. (2003). Incentives versus standards: Properties of accounting income in four East Asian countries. *Journal of Accounting and Economics*, *36*, 235–270.

Balsari, C. K., Ozkan, S., & Secer, C. (2009). Financial statement effects of adopting IFRS in Turkey: The mediating effect of Inflation Accounting. *Journal of International Finance and Economics*, *9*, 55–68.

Barth, M., Landsman, W., & Lang, M. (2008). International Accounting Standards and accounting quality. *Journal of Accounting Research*, *46*, 467–498.

Beatty, A., Ke, B., & Petroni, K. (2002). Earnings management to avoid earnings declines across publicly and privately held banks. *The Accounting Review*, *3*, 547–570.

Burgstahler, D., & Dichev, I. (1997). Earnings smoothing to avoid earnings decreases and losses. *Journal of Accounting and Economics*, *1*, 99–126.

Cohen, J., Krishnamoorthy, G., & Wright, A. (2004). The corporate governance mosaic and financial reporting quality. *Journal of Accounting Literature*, *23*, 87–152.

Christensen, H. B., Lee, E., & Walker M., (2008). *Incentives or standards: What determines accounting quality changes around IFRS adoption?* AAA 2008 Financial Accounting and Reporting Section (FARS) Paper. Retrieved from http://ssrn.com/abstract = 1013054

Degeorge, F., Patel, J., & Zeckhauser, R. (1999). Earnings smoothing to exceed thresholds. *Journal of Business*, *1*, 1–33.

Demirguc-Kunt, A., & Levine, R. (1999). *Bank-based and market-based financial systems – Cross-country comparisons*. Policy Research Working Paper Series Number 2143. Retrieved from http://www-wds.worldbank.org/servlet/WDSContentServer/WDSP/IB/1999/09/14/000094946_99072307505320/Rendered/PDF/multi_page.pdf

Durak, M. G. (2010). *Türkiye'de Uluslararası Finansal Raporlama Standartları'na Geçişin Tahakkukların Güvenilirliği Ve Kazançların Süreğenliği Üzerindeki Etkileri: Istanbul Menkul Kıymetler Borsası (IMKB) Uygulamaları*. Unpublished doctoral thesis, Dokuz Eylul University, Izmir.

Gaio, C. (2010). The relative importance of firm and country characteristics for earnings quality around the world. *European Accounting Review*, *19*, 693–738.

Jeanjean, T., & Stolowy, H. (2008). Do accounting standards matter? An exploratory analysis of earnings smoothing before and after IFRS adoption. *Journal of Accounting & Public Policy*, *27*, 480–494.

Kahneman, D., & Tversky, A. (1979). Prospect theory: An analysis of decision under risk. *Econometrica*, *47*, 263–292.

Kaplan, R. (1985). Comments on Paul Healy: Evidence on the effect of bonus schemes on accounting procedures and accrual decisions. *Journal of Accounting and Economics*, *7*, 109–113.

Kim, Y., Liu, C., & Rhee, S. G. (2003). *The effect of firm size on earnings smoothing*. Working Paper. College of Business Administration, University of Hawaii. Retrieved from http://www2.hawaii.edu/~fima/PDF/Finance_Seminar/EarningsMgmt.pdf

Leuz, C., Nanda, D., & Wysocki, P. D. (2003). Earnings smoothing and investor protection: An international comparison. *Journal of Financial Economics*, *69*, 91–124.

Leuz, C., & Oberholzer-Gee, F. (2006). Political relationships, global financing, and corporate transparency: Evidence from Indonesia. *Journal of Financial Economics*, *81*, 411–439.

Morais, A., & Curto, J. (2008). Accounting quality and the adoption of IASB standards – Portuguese evidence. *Rev. contab. Finanç.*, 19 (September/December), 103–111 (São Paulo).

Narktabtee, K., & Patpanichchot, S. (2011). The impact of country-level vs firm-level factors on the effectiveness of IFRS adoption: The case of European Union. *International Business & Economics Research Journal*, *10*, 79–92.

Shen, C., & Chih, H. (2005). Investor protection, prospect theory, and earnings management: An international comparison of the banking industry. *Journal of Banking & Finance*, *29*, 2675–2697.

Soderstrom, N. S., & Sun, K. J. (2007). IFRS adoption and accounting quality: A review. *European Accounting Review*, *16*, 675–702.

Terzi, S., Oktem, R., & Sen, I. K. (2013). Impact of adopting ınternational financial reporting standards: Empirical evidence from Turkey. *International Business Research*, *6*, 55–66.

Yildiz, F., Elitas, C., & Uc, M. (2011). Classification of Turkish accounting system. *International Journal of Business and Social Science*, *2*, 108–118.

THE EFFECT OF INTERNATIONAL FINANCIAL REPORTING STANDARDS (IFRS) ADOPTION ON THE VALUE RELEVANCE OF FINANCIAL REPORTING: A CASE OF RUSSIA

Tatiana A. Garanina and Polina S. Kormiltseva

ABSTRACT

Purpose – *The purpose of this study is to empirically examine the influence of International Financial Reporting Standards (IFRS) adoption by Russian public companies on the value relevance of financial reporting in Russia.*

Design/methodology/approach – *We selected 67 Russian public companies that reported both under Russian Accounting Standards (RAS) and IFRS for four consecutive years (2006–2009).*

Research limitations – *The main limitation of the chapter is the sample, but this can be explained by the fact that only 67 companies in Russia*

Accounting in Central and Eastern Europe
Research in Accounting in Emerging Economies, Volume 13, 27–60

ISSN: 1479-3563/doi:10.1108/S1479-3563(2013)0000013007

report under the two standards (RAS and IFRS). So the sample could not be increased as there were no other companies that fulfilled the characteristics of the sample.

Findings – *The results obtained show that on the Russian market there is no evidence of increased value relevance of financial reporting to external users of financial information after adopting IFRS when comparing and evaluating the two regimes (RAS and IFRS) unconditionally. Such results can be explained by the notion of mock compliance which originated due to the institutional differences between the RAS and IFRS development environments.*

Originality/value – *Adoption of IFRS by companies in emerging markets has been a subject of interest for lots of researchers, but this is the first research of its kind in the field of value relevance of adoption of IFRS on the Russian market.*

Keywords: IFRS; Russian accounting standards; adoption; value relevance

INTRODUCTION

The emergence and development of multinational concerns, growth of international financial markets and changes in investor behavior have contributed to the internationalization of economic activity. As a result financial reporting has spread beyond national borders. However, interpretation and understanding of financial information at the international level is hindered by a multitude of factors, including the diversity of the accounting principles and rules governing the preparation of reports in different countries.

Thus, since the 1970s considerable efforts have been made by various bodies, such as International Accounting Standards Board (IASB), to harmonize accounting and financial reporting standards in different countries in order to improve the usefulness and comparability of financial information in the international context. In 2002, such initiatives resulted in the approval of the regulation which provides for the mandatory application of International Financial Reporting Standards (IFRS) by companies listed on the European regulated stock markets as of January 2005. This regulatory change did not only affect the equity financing initiatives by putting additional pressure on issuers to adopt new reporting standards but also on the debt finance raising activities as more international, especially Europe-based banks started requiring their clients to comply with IFRS in order to be able to obtain syndicated loans.

The results of the IFRS campaign are quite astonishing. In 2009 more than 100 countries adopted IFRS[1] (in a form of requiring, permitting or converging with IFRS), and a number of other economically important countries, including Japan and Canada, had programs in place to converge their national standards with IFRS. The most impressive breakthrough in the international convergence debate took place in 2007, when the US Securities and Exchange Commission announced its adoption of rules under which it will accept filings from foreign private issuers containing financial statements prepared in accordance with IFRS without requiring reconciliation to United States generally accepted accounting principles, US GAAP. This change eliminated what had historically been one of the main obstacles for foreign private issuers to enter and to remain in the US public markets.

The emergence and adoption of IFRS has particular consequences for transition economies too. Since these countries do not possess the financial reporting infrastructure that developed countries already enjoy, the lack of credibility of reported financial information adversely affects these countries' ability to attract foreign capital. Adopting IFRS is seen as one way to overcome this barrier and many transitioning economies are adopting IFRS as a means of giving credibility to corporate financial statements. On one hand, adopting IFRS in these circumstances can be seen as an economic decision aimed at reducing the cost of acquired capital and increasing its amount for the large national enterprises. On the other hand, it can be assessed as a political decision aimed at "joining the club" of developed and well established countries. Some authors including Walter (2008) see the IFRS adoption by emerging countries much more as a politics-based rather than economics-based decision due to the fact that most of the emerging economies lack the institutional infrastructure (i.e., law enforcement structures, accounting educational institutions, professional associations, etc.) which limits the full-scale IFRS adoption in those countries.

Russian Federation is one of the emerging countries that has outlined a plan for gradual IFRS adoption with a number of accounting reforms taking place during the last decade. The current plan aims to achieve the full-scale IFRS adoption by 2015 by means of evolutionary convergence of the Russian Accounting Standards (RAS) with IFRS. Currently, there are over 200 Russian public companies that report under IFRS, which is slightly more than 50% of all Russian listed companies. In addition, since 2007 the main Russian stock exchange, the Russian Trade Systems (RTS), requires IFRS filings for all the listed companies. The other stock exchange in Russia – MICEX does not require IFRS from the companies listed there. In this chapter we will investigate voluntary adoption of IFRS. Voluntary adoption in this case is considered from the perspective that is not required by state's law. Considering that Russia has two stock exchanges and only one requires IFRS, any company applying IFRS to get public applies it voluntarily as it can choose from any of the two platforms to trade on. Another valid point is that now more companies in Russia have started to report under IFRS consequently from year to year that also has lead us to the research question discussed in this chapter.

Taking into consideration all the aspects of IFRS adoption in transition economies outlined above, the convergence between the RAS and the IFRS poses a few research questions involving the comparative value relevance of these two reporting standards and the potential ability of IFRS to fulfill its role of providing relevant and reliable information in the Russian institutional environment.

In these circumstances, the IFRS application cannot fully embrace its function of providing financial reporting users with relevant and reliable information on the company's performance, and thus national reporting standards in conjunction with existing institutional framework might provide more relevant and adequate information representation rather than IFRS. If the last statement is true, then the company's stakeholders are better off relying on the information provided in accordance with the national financial reporting standards.

The main research objective of the present study is to explore the influence of IFRS adoption by Russian public companies on the value relevance of financial reporting in Russia. In pursuance of the above, this study focuses on the following research question (mainly derived from the analysis of previous studies of the issue carried out mostly in European countries): Does the voluntary adoption of IFRS in Russia increase the value relevance of financial reporting?

The chapter consists of several parts. The first three parts represent information about the adoption of IFRS in emerging markets and specific situation of implementation of IFRS in Russia. The main definitions of quality of financial reporting and value relevance are also represented over there. Then, the hypothesis is outlined and the sample is defined. The main results and steps for further research are represented at the last parts of the chapter.

The obtained results show that on the Russian market, there is no evidence of increased value relevance of financial reporting to external users of financial information after adopting IFRS when comparing and evaluating the two regimes (RAS and IFRS) unconditionally. Such results can be explained by the notion of mock compliance which originates due to the institutional differences between the RAS and IFRS development environments.

This study focuses on the needs of external users of financial information reported by the companies, mainly non-majority shareholders and potential investors, who do not have access to private information channels in the so called "insider" economy of the Russian Federation.

CONSEQUENCES OF IFRS ADOPTION: EMERGING MARKETS

Currently, since the advent of the mandatory IFRS application by the EU countries, there is an ongoing debate over the process, scale, and consequences of IFRS adoption over the world, especially in the emerging economies. In most cases they do not share the historical development and institutional background of the Anglo-Saxon countries, and more generally that of the developed countries also. With regard to this discrepancy, our further investigation is devoted to the main benefits associated with IFRS adoption, and the explanatory factors of the decision to adopt or not to adopt the IFRS, both on the country and business level. Let us now look more closely into the main challenges faced by the IFRS adoption in the emerging economies and the reasons for the "two-standard" approach, and superficial compliance.

Scholars questioning the positive effect of IFRS relates it to the following obstacles usually associated with IFRS implementation in any emerging country: the lack of expertise and the underdeveloped accounting profession; the questionable practices of professionals; the lack of resources for regulation and enforcement; the need to educate the business environment about IFRS implications (including tax authorities, investors, and analysts); the culture of secrecy and fraud; the link between financial reporting and tax laws; the lack of IFRS knowledge; and the need to change the mindset of finance personnel (Ali, Ahmed, & Eddie, 2009). More often than not, these institutional obstacles and differences have led to the IFRS implementation which is successful only on the surface and may cover up real differences and accounting figures' manipulations under a veneer of international convergence.

It is also important to note that the group of developing countries is not homogeneous, because they have a different historical background, different stages in their economical development and different levels of development of the groups interested in accounting (i.e., accounting profession, stock exchange, auditors, users, etc.). Albu, Albu, Bunea, Calu, and Gîrbină (2011) in their literature review point out that there are four distinguished groups, one of them being the European communist bloc countries. Previous studies in ex-communist countries (such as Poland, Hungary, Czech Republic, and Romania) show that even if the changes toward substance over form and a focus on investor interests have been attempted, the emphasis on proper bookkeeping and on adhering to tax regulations has continued to persist (Albu et al., 2011). Also, due to problems associated with lack of clarity in the fiscal law, a variable level of understanding of IFRS by the regulators and preparers, the persistence of the communist mentality among accountants who gained their knowledge and skills prior to the transition, the accountants' preference for more prescriptive regulation and less choice of accounting treatments were also documented.

These remarks are extremely interesting for the purpose of the current study as the process and consequences of IFRS adoption in Russia will be examined further.

Most of the literature devoted to the adoption of IFRS focuses on the consequences of accounting principles transition and the determinants of accounting quality that are likely to influence the transition. Thus, numerous empirical studies investigate whether the adoption of IFRS has caused significant changes to consolidated financial statements. These studies investigate *the effects of the change on various attributes of accounting* (e.g., Bartov, Goldberg, & Kim, 2005), liquidity and cost of capital (e.g., Daske, Hail, Leuz, & Verdi, 2008) of the affected companies, as well as on analysts' forecasts via *regression analysis*. On the other hand, the adoption of IFRS is analyzed by *survey based studies* and the capital market reactions by *event studies*. Furthermore, empirical studies examine the application of options offered in IFRS. In addition, *descriptive studies* address the impact of the adoption of IFRS in comparison to local GAAPs on equity and net income (e.g., Hung & Subramanyam, 2007).

During the last decade, several studies devoted to value relevance have been conducted on different markets of Eastern and Central Europe: Poland (Dobija & Klimczak, 2010; Gornik-Tomaszewski & Jermakowicz, 2001), the Czech Republic (Hellström, 2006; Jindrichovska, 2001), Romania

(Filip & Raffournier, 2010), and the Baltic states (Pritchard, 2002). This study is the first one that is going to be devoted to the Russian market.

Due to the limited papers on this topic on the emerging markets, there is no much empirical research on the value relevance of accounting information. The relationship of accounting information and market values on the data of Polish listed companies is studied in (Gornik-Tomaszewski & Jermakowicz, 2001) examining the relationship between accounting numbers and market values for a sample of listed companies. The study takes place on the data from 1996 to 1998 when Polish Accounting Standards totally complied with European Union Directives. According to the results of this study both earnings and book value of equity are positively associated with stock prices. During the period 1997–2007 the value relevance of Polish accounting information was increased due to the development of the capital market in the country (Dobija & Klimczak, 2010).

Another study was conducted on the market of Czech Republic (Jindrichovska, 2001). The author studied the relationship between market returns and earnings per share over the period 1993–1998 and the results revealed the relationship between earning-to-price ratios and price relatives. The value relevance of accounting information of Czech versus Swedish companies is studied in (Hellström, 2006). In compliance with the expectations the results showed that even though the value relevance of accounting information in the Czech Republic increases over time, during the period 1994–2001, the accounting information was less value relevant than in Sweden.

The issue of value relevance in Baltic countries (Estonia, Latvia, and Lithuania) is studied in (Pritchard, 2002). According to the results of this research during 1995–2000, Lithuania had the weakest relationship between returns and earnings and Estonia had the highest value relevance. In the research (Jindrichovska, 2001) it is noted that information that is reflected in stock prices is much more valuable than that in earnings shown in accounting statements.

In the study conducted by Filip and Raffournier (2010) the value relevance of earnings is analyzed and the earning changes in Romania are measured. The results show that the relationship between accounting earnings and stock returns is comparable to the levels reported by studies conducted on more advanced markets, and that it is higher for securities issued by small companies.

There has been no research of this sort on the Russian market that can be compared to the studies mentioned above.

Value relevance, as defined in the academic literature, is not a stated criterion of the FASB. Rather, tests of value relevance represent one approach to operationalization of the FASB's stated criteria of relevance. In the extant literature, an accounting amount is defined as value relevant if it has a predicted significant association with equity market values (Barth, Beaver, & Landsman, 2001). So, an accounting amount will be value relevant only if it reflects information relevant to investors in valuing the firm and is measured reliably enough to be reflected in share prices. The first study we are aware of that uses the term "value relevance" to describe this association is (Beaver & Dukes, 1972). The topic of value relevance and the impact of IAS/IFRS voluntary or mandatory adoption on value relevance and accounting quality were widely discussed (Aubert & Grudnitski, 2011; Barth, Landsman, & Lang, 2008; Chen, Tang, Jiang, & Lin, 2010; Cormier, Demaria, Lapointe-Antunes, & Teller, 2009; Devalle, Onali, & Magarini, 2010; Goodwin, Ahmed, & Heaney, 2008). Interestingly, but the RAS value relevance is not discussed, at least not in any official pronouncements.

It is essential to mention that value relevance research needs only assume that share prices reflect investors' consensus beliefs based on publicly available information, by this we mean that further empirical inferences will relate to the extent to which the accounting amounts under study reflect the amounts t implicitly assessed by investors and reflected in equity prices. As a result, value relevance research does not require, assuming market efficiency (Barth et al., 2001) specify that the price model for value relevance research (the model implemented in the current study) does not require an assumption of market efficiency.

It is worthy to note that the value relevance of accounting numbers is related to the confidence that investors place on the accounting standards used to prepare them (which is reflected in the consensus beliefs of investors) together with institutional and corporate environment of the firm (Ball, 2006).

Holthausen and Watts (2001) classify the value-relevance studies into three categories.

(1) *Relative association studies* compare the association between stock market values (or changes in values) and alternative bottom-line measures. For example, a study might examine whether the association of an earnings number, calculated under a proposed standard, is more highly associated with stock market values or returns than earnings calculated under existing GAAP. Other examples compare the associations of foreign GAAP and US GAAP earnings. These studies usually test for differences in the R^2 or adjusted R^2 of regressions using different bottom line accounting numbers.

(2) *Incremental association studies* investigate whether the accounting number is helpful in explaining value or return, or that accounting number is typically deemed to be value relevant if its estimated regression coefficient is significantly different from zero. Some incremental association studies make additional assumptions about the relation between accounting numbers and inputs to a market valuation model in order to predict coefficient values. Differences between the estimated and predicted values are often interpreted as evidence of measurement error in the accounting number.

(3) *Marginal information content studies* investigate whether a particular accounting number adds to the information available to investors. They typically use event studies to determine if the release of an accounting number is associated with value changes. Price reactions are considered to be evidence of value relevance.

The results of this study will contribute to the group of relative association studies. This chapter also contributes to the stream of literature looking at the value relevance of reconciliations between accounting numbers under two different standards. The existing works in that stream cannot evaluate the way value relevance of reconciled items evolves over time. In Horton and Serafeim (2010) it was revealed that IFRS appears to reveal timely value-relevant information. That is why with regards to the results of the present study we believe that the market reacts to the IFRS reconciliations and incorporates this information into stock prices subsequently. This assumption is consistent with the mandatory disclosures revealing news and with the overall advantage of increasing transparency throughout the market (Horton & Serafeim, 2010).

IFRS ADOPTION: THE CASE OF RUSSIA

"The accounting system in any society is directly related to the level of political, economic and legal development of that country...and is always a result of the environment in which it exists" (McGee & Preobragenskaya, 2004). Against this backdrop, in order to understand the roots and character of the current accounting system in Russia, it is essential to look at how it has been developing during the last few decades.

During the period 1917 1985, the Russian accounting system was adapted to structures of a centrally planned economy, which meant that the main emphasis was put on control and measurement function of accounting. During that time a set of accounting standards (RAS – Russian Accounting Standards), more or less corresponding with IFRS, was developed and put into force.

As the original plan by the Russian Finance Ministry to fully adopt all IAS by 2000 failed, a new accounting reform plan was issued in July 2004 by the Ministry of Finance for 2004–2010 with the several potential outcomes (Bagaeva, 2008) according to which by 2010, all companies should prepare (in addition to RAS statements) consolidated financial statements in accordance with IFRS.

Several steps outlined by the plan have been delayed and the reform is still ongoing with an approximated new target by the year 2015 for the full adoption of IFRS for consolidated financial statements (Bagaeva, 2008). IFRS in Russia will not replace national financial reporting standards: preparing consolidated financial statements under IFRS will only be required for companies with publicly traded securities, banks, and insurance companies whereas standalone financial statements of these entities will be prepared under statutory rules.

In spite of the accounting reform taking place in Russia for a few years now and RAS partly embracing IFRS, assimilating IFRS in practice still presents a number of challenges because of the fundamental differences between national and international attitudes and practices which arise from diverse historical, cultural, and legal traditions.

As stated by a few scholars (Ostrenko, 2010; Volegova, 2011), there is still quite a discrepancy between the IFRS requirements and the revised RAS, which manifests itself in quite a few technical differences, but more importantly in the application of the principles that lay the basis for IFRS. The other question is cost expenses that arise from publishing the financial statements according to two different standards. Thus, we focus our attention not on the issue of partial legal adoption of IFRS, but we rather address the issue of real adoption of new standards by companies and accounting profession. Therefore, there is a difference between the accounting and reporting practices adopted and stated in legal documents and the practices observed in the business reality. Hence, based on the research done by scholars and auditing companies,[2] we outline the following main impediments to full adoption of IFRS in Russia:

- *Persistence of strong linkages between accounting and taxation coupled with no tradition of using financial reports for purposes of market-oriented decision-making*;

Although the legal separation between tax and financial accounting exists, the majority of people involved in accounting and reporting still consider the tax service to be the main user of the information they prepare. In accounting practice, this attitude becomes apparent when accountants ignore accounting rules aimed at providing useful information that could be used for decision making purposes when the rules do not affect the tax calculation.

- *Differences in fundamental definitions and accounting concepts and practices coupled with complicated nature of some IFRS/IAS*;

Another reason why accounting rules are not always implemented is the difficulty of implementing them both due to conceptual differences and lack of methodological support. Thus, with a started adoption of IFRS, a number of concepts and tools that had never been used in Soviet practices have been introduced into the Russian accounting.

One of them is the "substance over form" concept, which is at the heart of the IFRS implementation problem. IFRS are written in a conceptual way and can be characterized as a "substance over form" approach to accounting. On the contrary, Russian legislation and regulations are very specific and prescriptive which is partly connected with the code nature of the Russian law that is based on quite precise and strict instructions which should be followed according to the situation. Thus, unlike IFRS, transactions in RAS are accounted for in accordance with their legal form. Another new accounting concept concerns the "true and fair view" which is one of the most investor-centered concepts in IFRS. Due to the lack of long-standing market-orientation tradition, the fair value concept is not widely applied under RAS except for investments in market traded securities. Similarly, financial statements are generally prepared on a historical cost basis with only limited use of impairments.

- *Lack of consequently professional judgment*;

Based on the main conceptual discrepancies between IFRS and RAS, a number of technical differences in the implementation of the accounting standards emerged. As the Big 4 companies provide regular and comprehensive updates on the major differences in reporting and accounting practices with regards to local jurisdictions, here, we present just a few examples in order to illustrate the nature of those differences.

- *Consolidation and group accounting*;

Under IFRS, the determination of whether or not entities are consolidated by a reporting enterprise is based on the concept of "de facto" control, with control being the parent's ability to govern the financial and operating policies of an entity to obtain benefits. In RAS, on the contrary, there is presently no such category as "consolidated financial statements" although there is a requirement for the parent company to prepare separate and consolidated financial statements if it has subsidiaries (as legally defined).

- *Intangible assets*;

In general, intangible assets acquired outside a business combination are recognized at fair value under IFRS, and at cost under RAS. Moreover, internal costs related to the phase of research and development are expensed as incurred under IFRS accounting models, whereas RAS allow for internally developed intangibles and research and development costs to be recognized if they will bring future economic benefit. Finally, goodwill is never amortized in accordance with IFRS, whereas in accordance with RAS, goodwill is amortized over 20 years, but not longer than the economic life of the acquiree.

- *Valuation of assets and Impairment*;

Generally, under RAS valuation of assets is still tax-driven, for example, standardized amortization periods and depreciation methods are determined by governmental authorities for taxation purposes, regular impairment reviews which do not have to be undertaken and residual values are not taken into account in determining depreciation. With regards to revaluation, IFRS require goodwill and intangible assets with indefinite lives to be reviewed at least annually for impairment and more frequently if impairment indicators are present. Unlike IFRS, in RAS there is no accounting guidance for assessing the impairment of long-lived assets (except for mentioning the accounting for impairment in RAS 14/2007 Accounting for Intangible Assets).

These are just a few examples of technical differences between IFRS and RAS which illustrate that there is still a wide gap between the two standards with regards to legalized practices, and even more with regards to real day-to-day implementation.

It is important to say that the internationalization of the transitional economy, either through foreign customers and suppliers or through foreign investors entering into the capital markets or foreign companies establishing themselves in the country, changes the informational environment of transitional economies (Hellström, 2007). Entrance of investors from well functioning markets into the transitional economy encourages domestic enterprises to be more responsive and accountable to a large number of stakeholders that has a positive effect on the change in business environment. That is the reason for the increase in the importance of IFRS standards.

RESEARCH HYPOTHESIS AND SAMPLE

As stated in the introductory section, the research objective of the present study is to answer the following research question: Does the voluntary adoption of IFRS in Russia increase the value relevance of financial reporting?

One way to look at the value relevance relationship between the two reporting standards under study in the present chapter is to assume that IFRS should be more value relevant for emerging economies than their local reporting standards due to differences in institutional environments and financial reporting incentives, that is, the focus of emerging economies' reporting standards on tax authorities or banking institutions as the main users of financial and accounting information rather than shareholders or potential investors. Thus, the local standards are supposed to give less valuable information for the stock market as they do not take it into consideration. There is another argument in favor of IFRS being more value relevant than local standards of developing countries voiced by Hove (1986): "existing accounting practice in almost all developing countries was imposed by developed countries initially through colonialism and then through the operations of transnational corporations … rather than in response to the societal needs of those countries." As a result of this, Hove (1986) sees the local standards being more representative of the differing needs of market actors and more appropriate for the nature of institutional arrangements in emerging economies, on one hand and international standards being more representative (and thus value relevant) of the developed market needs in connivance with the stock market and investment activities on the other hand. Following this argument we can hypothesize that IFRS being developed for the Anglo-Saxon economic model, based on financial markets functioning and independent accounting profession, should be more value relevant for its main institution, that is, the stock market unlike the local standards developed mainly with accordance to the needs of financial (lenders) and governmental (tax authorities) institutions.

On the other hand, the stock market itself is a part of the national institutional framework, meaning that stock prices on the national market might reflect the underlying economic performance of the companies in a way that is different from how this is represented on other national markets within a different institutional setting, which leads to the conclusion that local accounting standards might incorporate more value relevance information with regards to national peculiarities. Another argument for this proposition is grounded in the fact that most of the value relevance studies executed in transition economies (e.g., Lin & Chen, 2005) with institutional framework closer to Russia than to the Anglo-Saxon world have shown that their local accounting standards prove to be more value relevant in comparison to IFRS.

Walter (2008) points out that there is an overall underestimation of the "often large gaps that can persist between formal rules and institutions, on one hand, and actual policy as well as actor behaviour on the other." Thus, Walter (2008) proposes a notion of "mock compliance" (i.e., superficial rather than substantial compliance) which is especially pronounced in developing countries that have gone through major economic crises. In these circumstances, external and domestic pressures have made it difficult for many emerging countries to openly oppose compliance with international standards, as deep crises have the effect of de-legitimizing existing policies and practices. However, because such compliance can be very costly for particular politically influential domestic interests, it takes the form of window dressing without deep substantive compliance with the new norms and standards. Following this argument, we can hypothesize that Russian adoption of IFRS might follow the same way in this situation and there should not be much difference observed in the value relevance of RAS versus IFRS, as effectively as only the old RAS norms might be applied in practice. In support of this statement, there are a few articles discussing the practical implementation of IFRS in Russia, being quite a long way from the full adoption of most standards (Ostrenko, 2010). Apart from unresolved conceptual differences, there are a few institutional drawbacks that inhibit the practical implementation of IFRS in Russia (e.g., lack of appropriate enforcement), which again point out the fact that actual IFRS adoption is still in its first phase with a conclusion that not yet fully implemented and enforced standards cannot lead to a higher value relevance in an institutional setting not designed for them.

The final argument with regards to nonsignificant differences in value relevance between IFRS and RAS concerns the opportunities for managerial discretion and manipulation. In fact there are incentives for earnings management under both standards, for tax reduction purposes under RAS and for investor attraction purposes under IFRS (as these standards are mostly voluntary adopted by companies seeking access to the foreign capital). In this respect one could expect downward earnings manipulation under RAS and upward earning manipulation under IFRS. In addition to that, the natural flexibility of IFRS and a variety of accounting choices provided can lead to an even higher accounting numbers manipulation in the circumstances of a code law country with low investor protection and weak standards enforcement mechanisms.

Overall, in spite of the empirical research results supporting the higher value relevance for local GAAP in emerging economies in comparison to IFRS, from a theoretical point of view, we find the proof of IFRS being more value relevant than local financial reporting standards of the developing countries if adopted in the full version and followed in practice. However, when introducing the "mock compliance" issue and the discrepancies in institutional environments, we find the proof for nonsignificant difference in value relevance between IFRS and local standards due to partial adoption and noncompliance in practice, and the fact that "accounting quality is a function of overall institutional settings" (Soderstrom & Sun, 2007).

Thus, the following *hypothesis* is to be tested in the present study:

> **H1.** There is no significant difference between the value relevance of financial information disclosed by Russian public companies under RAS and the value relevance of financial information disclosed by Russian public companies under IFRS.

We examine this hypothesis in subsequent sections of the chapter.

The sample consists of Russian public and listed companies that voluntarily report under IFRS for at least two years. This condition is introduced in order to avoid significant differences in accounting numbers attributed only to the first adoption of IFRS. In this study we use annual financial data for the following time period 2006–2009.

Overall, there are *233 Russian companies* reporting under IFRS. First, from these we exclude all banking and financial institutions (insurance companies, brokerages, depositaries, stock exchanges, etc.) as their business specifics do not allow us to compare them with other production or service firms. These exclusions account for *89 companies*. Second, to study the value relevance issue, we need only companies traded on Russian stock exchanges. That is the reason why companies that are not open joint stock are excluded. These exclusions account for *39 companies*. Third, there are

Russian open joint stock companies that are actually not traded: their shares are distributed through closed auctions or among cofounders. These exclusions account for 29 *companies*. Finally, there are a number of companies with non-sufficient or absent data: with no annual data presented, with IFRS data reported in non-Russian currency and with a lack of information on the number of shares outstanding or on share prices (due to low liquidity). These exclusions account for 9 *companies*. As a result the sample is comprised of 67 companies (Table 1).

It is absolutely essential to note that all the 67 sample companies adopted IFRS prior to the year 2006, which means that we do not have to take into account the accounting consequences of the first-year IFRS adoption. In all four years, the size of the sample allows us to make statistically valid inferences. The study is based only on the primary information taken from the companies' annual reports.

RESEARCH DESIGN

The study of the influence of IFRS adoption in Russia on the value relevance of financial reporting encompasses examining the impact of IFRS adoption on the difference between the book and market value of companies (the market-to-book ratio). This variable can be operationally determined as the ratio of the market capitalization of the company to its book value. Theoretically, it shows how relevant the financial reporting is (i.e., to which degree the financial reported information shows the real value of the company and its financial situation). This variable is chosen because one of the reasons for the adoption of international standards in Europe was to

Table 1. Sample Distribution by Industry/business Area.

Industry	Number of Sample Companies
Power generation	21 (31.34%)
Manufacturing	19 (28.35%)
Telecommunications	11 (16.42%)
Natural resources	4 (5.97%)
Wholesale and retail	4 (5.97%)
Transport	3 (4.48%)
Real estate	3 (4.48%)
Services	2 (2.97%)

ensure the generation of useful information for the stock market, which would imply narrowing the gap between a company's book and market value.

In this chapter we use price regression model (deflated by book value per share to reduce scale effects (Barth & Kallapur, 1996; Brown, Lo, & Lys, 1999; Easton & Sommers, 2003) to ensure comparability of the future results with already existing ones and to determine to what extent the market value of the firm implied by stock market investors is reflected in accounting numbers (Gjerde, Knivsfle, & Saettem, 2008).

The following model is used in this chapter:

$$\frac{P'_t}{\mathrm{BVPS}'_t} = \theta_0 + \theta_1 \times \frac{1}{\mathrm{BVPS}'_t} + \theta_2 \times \frac{\mathrm{EPS}_t}{\mathrm{BVPS}'_t} + \varepsilon_t \qquad (1)$$

where

- P'_t – inefficiency-adjusted share price quoted in the stock market at the end of year t: $P'_t = P_{t+0.5}/(1+k_r)$, where k_r is the required rate of return in the first half of year $t+1$. Here, we assume that time lag in market reaction to reported financial information averages six months.

Data collection is based on the presumption that share market prices should be the same for two regressions (for RAS and IFRS) in order to preserve consistency and control for differences in external factors over time (thus fixing external factors' effects).

We use the following logic to choose the appropriate time lag. First, comparable studies assume there is a time lag between the publication of financial statements and the stock market reaction on an average that is equal to three months. Thus for RAS, the time lag equals to six months, as the reports are usually available three months after the fiscal year end. Second, most of the Russian companies adopting IFRS publish their IFRS statements by the end of June (six months after the fiscal year end), that is, earlier than required by the stock exchange authorities. Finally, when the second set of accounts is published under a different standard, the reaction should be more or less immediate, as the investors, etc. already possess information from the RAS accounts. Hence, the time lag assumed in this study equals six months.

$P_{t+0.5}$ is the closing share price in a range of one week (seven days) around the end of June (in case no deals were made on June 30).

The adjustment rate used in the study is the refinancing rate of the Russian Central Bank applied for half a year (six months) as a discount rate to make financial figures and market share prices comparable over time. We have chosen this interest rate as it is a good approximation of the deposit rates in the banking market.

- $BVPS'_t = BVPS_t - EPS_t$, where $BVPS_t$ is the reported book value of equity per share at the end of year t and EPS_t is the reported net profit per share in year t. EPS_t is subtracted from $BVPS_t$ to reduce collinearity.

In order to calculate book value of equity per share and earnings per share, we use the weighted yearly average of outstanding ordinary shares adjusted for treasury stock. In most cases this figure already accounts for stock splits and reverse stock splits that happened after the reporting date (companies provide this information in the "Subsequent events" section of their annual financial reports).

In addition to that, one more adjustment is evidently needed in order to calculate earnings per share, that is, we should check for the existence of preference shares, look at their characteristics, and then deduct the income attributable to preference shareholders from the net income (thus obtaining the net income attributable to ordinary shareholders). This adjustment is required because we analyze the value relevance based on the market price of ordinary shares only.

- θ_0; θ_1; and θ_2 – unknown parameters;
- ε_t – random error.

At the first step of the analysis, we study the presence of significant differences in the market-to-book ratios ($P'_t/BVPS'_t$) under IFRS and RAS. The study of these differences is performed by applying parametric and nonparametric tests depending on whether the variables in question follow a normal distribution or not.

If the differences do not prove to be significant, then we will conclude that IFRS adoption does not influence value relevance of financial reporting, at least on the analyzed sample of Russian public companies. If the differences prove to be significant, we can move to the second step of analysis to determine which standard is more value relevant.

As the second step, we analyze the comparative value relevance of book value of equity per share and earnings per share by comparing the *adjusted R^2 from price regressions*. The difference between two sets of accounting standards is analyzed by a two-sample unconditional comparison test focusing on differences in adjusted R^2 (*Cramer test*). The reporting standard with significantly higher adjusted R^2 will be regarded as more value relevant in comparison to the other one.

In the next section of this chapter, we present the results obtained during the empirical study and hypothesis testing.

RESULTS

In this section, we present the results of the empirical study on the comparative value relevance between the financial information presented under the RAS versus the financial information presented under the IFRS with a main focus on testing the developed hypothesis on the sample of Russian public listed companies.

Table 2 presents the descriptive statistics for the three variables (P'/BVPS′, 1/BVPS′, and EPS/BVPS′) for four subsequent years under the two different reporting regimes for 67 companies in the selected sample.

Following the data presented in Table 3, let us observe keenly the differences between the variables reported under RAS versus those reported under IFRS, and also examine if these differences show some sort of tendency over the four years this present study encompasses.

In Table 3, the results of comparing P'/BVPS′ (the adjusted share price to the adjusted book value per share) ratios under RAS and IFRS over the years 2006–2009 are presented.

As can be seen from the table, over the years 2006–2008 there has been a pronounced tendency of convergence between the P'/BVPS′ ratios under the two reporting standards (from 52% to 7% difference, with the P'/BVPS′ ratio under RAS being higher than the P'/BVPS′ ratio under IFRS). However, in 2009, the P'/BVPS′ ratio under RAS proved to be around 27% lower than the same ratio under IFRS. Considering that the prices (P') used in calculating the ratios are the same under the two reporting standards, the differences in the P'/BVPS′ ratio can be attributed only to the differences in the BVPS′ variable (which is computed as BVPS diminished by EPS). Table 4, thus, presents the results of comparing BVPS (i.e., book value per share) variable under RAS and IFRS over the years 2006–2009, which show that BVPS has been consistently lower under RAS compared to IFRS by around 10%.

In addition to that, Table 5 presents the results of comparing EPS (i.e., earnings per share or net income per share) variable under RAS and IFRS over the years 2006–2009, which show a general tendency for EPS under RAS to converge with and even exceed the EPS under IFRS over the examined time frame (from EPS under IFRS being higher than EPS under RAS

Table 2. Descriptive Statistics of Variables for the Years 2006–2009.

Variable Name	Min.	Max.	Mean	Median	Standard Deviation
2006					
P′06/BVPS′06_RAS	0.0344	6.0897	0.4616	0.1671	1.1194
P′06/BVPS′06_IFRS	0.0388	3.5031	0.3037	0.1360	0.6105
1/BVPS′06_RAS	0.0013	8.2340	0.5569	0.0654	1.4007
1/BVPS′06_IFRS	0.0010	4.5973	0.4579	0.0555	0.9491
EPS06/BVPS′06_RAS	−0.1296	2.9982	0.2533	0.1409	0.4869
EPS06/BVPS′06_IFRS	−0.4632	0.8318	0.2148	0.1723	0.2349
2007					
P′07/BVPS′07_RAS	0.0117	2.1427	0.2453	0.1105	0.4386
P′07/BVPS′07_IFRS	0.0329	2.1105	0.2043	0.1085	0.3724
1/BVPS′07_RAS	0.0005	15.4722	0.7111	0.0555	2.4068
1/BVPS′07_IFRS	0.0005	45.2868	1.2586	0.0502	6.4727
EPS07/BVPS′07_RAS	−0.2269	1.5056	0.2017	0.1134	0.2733
EPS07/BVPS′07_IFRS	−0.7092	0.6466	0.2062	0.1524	0.2335
2008					
P′08/BVPS′08_RAS	0.0000	2.1257	0.2233	0.0313	0.4401
P′08/BVPS′08_IFRS	0.0000	2.9357	0.2081	0.0297	0.4719
1/BVPS′08_RAS	0.0002	59.7695	1.9289	0.0696	8.1069
1/BVPS′08_IFRS	0.0002	45.4148	1.8674	0.0419	6.6477
EPS08/BVPS′08_RAS	−0.2420	4.2249	0.1487	0.0423	0.5579
EPS08/BVPS′08_IFRS	−0.5673	1.4300	0.1019	0.0674	0.2856
2009					
P′09/BVPS′09_RAS	0.0000	3.6514	0.2884	0.0396	0.6352
P′09/BVPS′09_IFRS	0.0000	10.3728	0.3942	0.0354	1.5216
1/BVPS′09_RAS	0.0005	4.3746	0.5243	0.0643	1.0009
1/BVPS′09_IFRS	0.0005	8.9955	0.6533	0.0396	1.5811
EPS09/BVPS′09_RAS	−0.4100	1.0834	0.1095	0.0549	0.2294
EPS09/BVPS′09_IFRS	−0.7404	0.5856	0.0557	0.0781	0.2106

Table 3. RAS versus IFRS – Differences in *P*′/BVPS′.

Variable Name	Min.	Max.	Mean	Mean_RAS/Mean_IFRS
P′06/BVPS′06_RAS	0.0344	6.0897	0.4616	1.5199
P′06/BVPS′06_IFRS	0.0388	3.5031	0.3037	
P′07/BVPS′07_RAS	0.0117	3.1427	0.2453	1.2007
P′07/BVPS′07_IFRS	0.0329	2.1105	0.2043	
P′08/BVPS′08_RAS	0.0071	3.1257	0.2233	1.0730
P′08/BVPS′08_IFRS	0.0049	2.9357	0.2081	
P′09/BVPS′09_RAS	0.0099	3.6514	0.2884	0.7316
P′09/BVPS′09_IFRS	0.0057	10.3728	0.3942	

by 32% in 2006 to the difference of 21% in the inverse direction in 2009). The results for 2006–2008 are consistent with the notion that under RAS earnings (i.e., net income) should be lower than those reported under IFRS due to the still persisting tax link in the RAS. The result obtained for 2009 does not contradict that notion because it is based on the net income attributable to ordinary shareholders only rather than on overall net income. In fact, the overall net income (attributable to all shareholders, both ordinary and preference) in the year 2009 on the sample under examination is lower under RAS as compared to IFRS by approximately 10%.

Consequently, Table 6 presents the results of comparing BVPS′ (i.e., book value per share adjusted by earnings per share) variable under RAS and IFRS over the years 2006–2009, which show the consistently increasing difference between RAS and IFRS with regards to BVPS′ being lower under IFRS. Considering the fact that we have found no consistent change for BVPS, this tendency should be mostly attributed to the increasing differences in the EPS variable under the two reporting standards.

Finally, Table 7 presents the results of comparing EPS/BVPS′ (i.e., earnings per share to adjusted book value per share) variable under RAS and

Table 4. RAS versus IFRS – Differences in BVPS.

Interim Variable Name	Min.	Max.	Mean	Mean_RAS/Mean_IFRS
BVPS06_RAS	0.1215	780.99	137.5105	0.8927
BVPS06_IFRS	0.2175	1000.24	154.0377	
BVPS07_RAS	0.0646	1893.22	180.6478	0.9304
BVPS07_IFRS	0.0221	2204.75	194.1681	
BVPS08_RAS	0.01673	4451.63	218.8787	0.8914
BVPS08_IFRS	0.0220	5342.76	245.5551	
BVPS09_RAS	0.2286	1828.79	194.1543	0.9062
BVPS09_IFRS	0.1111	2090.91	214.2556	

Table 5. RAS versus IFRS – Differences in EPS.

Interim Variable Name	Min.	Max.	Mean	Mean_RAS/Mean_IFRS
EPS06_RAS	−0.1405	641.925	25.9795	0.6841
EPS06_IFRS	−9.8038	832.022	21.4899	
EPS07_RAS	−0.3969	933.50	3.3746	0.9034
EPS07_IFRS	−0.9826	732.83	4.5565	
EPS08_RAS	−462.387	109.605	40.1109	0.7406
EPS08_IFRS	−114.118	210.807	44.4022	
EPS09_RAS	−151.386	562.2650	30.8422	1.2089
EPS09_IFRS	−148.348	447.939	45.0867	

Table 6. RAS versus IFRS – Differences in BVPS′.

Interim Variable Name	Min.	Max.	Mean	Mean_RAS/Mean_IFRS
BVPS′06_RAS	−28.485	363.572	88.6584	0.9186
BVPS′06_IFRS	0.222	345.38	96.5110	
BVPS′07_RAS	−104.78	1674.098	140.5369	0.9384
BVPS′07_IFRS	0.01095	1471.92	149.7659	
BVPS′08_RAS	−10.715	4342.02	215.5041	0.8942
BVPS′08_IFRS	−2.9170	5456.87	240.9986	
BVPS′09_RAS	−9.4729	1701.26	168.1748	0.8724
BVPS′09_IFRS	0.1039	1642.97	192.7657	

Table 7. RAS versus IFRS – Differences in EPS/BVPS′.

Variable Name	Min.	Max.	Mean	Mean_RAS/Mean_IFRS
EPS06/BVPS′06_RAS	−0.1296	2.9982	0.2533	1.1792
EPS06/BVPS′06_IFRS	−0.4632	0.8318	0.2148	
EPS07/BVPS′07_RAS	−0.2269	1.5056	0.2017	0.9782
EPS07/BVPS′07_IFRS	−0.7092	0.6466	0.2062	
EPS08/BVPS′08_RAS	−0.2420	4.2249	0.1487	1.4593
EPS08/BVPS′08_IFRS	−0.5673	1.4312	0.1019	
EPS09/BVPS′09_RAS	−0.4100	1.0834	0.1095	1.9659
EPS09/BVPS′09_IFRS	−0.7404	0.5856	0.0557	

IFRS over the years 2006–2009, which shows the overall tendency of increasing difference between the two standards with EPS/BVPS′ being higher under RAS compared to IFRS by 18% in 2006 and by 97% in 2009 consistent with the observations as shown above.

Before studying the value relevance levels differences between the financial information reported under IFRS and RAS, we should first check for the presence of any statistically significant differences in the adjusted market-to-book ratios (i.e., *P*′/BVPS′) between the statements prepared under IFRS and RAS for four consequent years (i.e., 2006–2009) on the selected sample of Russian public listed companies.

Table 8 presents the results of distribution normality check for the dependent variables (*P*′/BVPS′) both for IFRS and RAS data.

One-sample; Kolmogorov-Smirnov test has shown that in all cases the data is not distributed normally (two-tailed significance levels in all cases do not exceed 0.05). As a result, in further steps of the study only nonparametric tests should be applied.

Table 8. Distribution Normality Test Results (One-Sample Kolmogorov–Smirnov Test).

	RAS				IFRS			
	P'09/ BVPS'09	*P*'08/ BVPS'08	*P*'07/ BVPS'07	*P*'06/ BVPS'06	*P*'09/ BVPS'09	*P*'08/ BVPS'08	*P*'07/ BVPS'07	*P*'06/ BVPS'06
Normal parameters								
Mean	0.2884	0.2233	0.2453	0.4616	0.3942	0.2081	0.2042	0.3037
Standard deviation	0.6352	0.4401	0.4386	1.1194	1.5216	0.4719	0.3724	0.6105
Most extreme differences								
Absolute	0.329	0.334	0.352	0.414	0.398	0.336	0.323	0.342
Positive	0.329	0.334	0.352	0.414	0.360	0.336	0.342	0.342
Negative	−0.325	−0.306	−0.287	−0.351	−0.398	−0.330	−0.332	−0.332
Kolmogorov–Smirnov *Z*	2.252	2.584	2.462	2.654	2.727	2.606	2.259	2.191
Asymp. Sig. (two tailed)	0.000	0.000	0.000	0.000	0.000	0.000	0.000	0.000

The results of a nonparametric two related samples test with regards to differences between P'/BVPS' under RAS P'/BVPS' under IFRS are presented in Table 9.

According to the test results, there is no statistically significant correlation between compared samples (two-tailed significance levels in most cases exceed 0.05), which means that there is a statistically significant difference between the adjusted market-to-book ratios (i.e., P'/BVPS') calculated on the basis of IFRS and RAS data in all studied time periods except for the year 2007. Thus, the study of differences in value relevance between the two sets of financial information reported under different standards makes sense with this as an only exception. However, in the further research we would still keep the year 2007 observations for comparison and consistency reasons.

Next, (before directly comparing the level of value relevance between IFRS and RAS applied by a sample of Russian companies) we run eight separate OLS regressions according to price regression model (in which the accounting-based variables specified according to the two reporting regimes enter simultaneously to explain the corresponding market-based variable) to see if the price regression model and coefficients (i.e., the estimates of the unknown parameters) are statistically significant. Results of the regressions are presented in Table 10.

To increase the power of the test we also carried out pooled regressions (all years, all RAS vs. all years, all IFRS) as shown in Table 11.

The overall results obtained in this chapter are as follows:

- On the base of the sample, for RAS regressions in 2008–2009 the price regression model applied in this study is statistically nonsignificant (two-tailed significance levels in all cases exceed 0.05) with the R^2 being equal to 19.8% and 0.9% respectively with nonsignificant coefficients (two-tailed significance levels in all cases exceed 0.05).
- On the base of the sample, for RAS regressions in 2006–2007, the price regression model applied in this study is statistically significant (two-tailed significance levels in all cases do not exceed 0.05) with the R^2 being 44.6% and 32% respectively, but with only one statistically significant positive coefficient (two-tailed significance level does not exceed 0.05). This coefficient corresponds to the following independent variable EPS/BVPS′, and equals 1.028 in 2006 and 0.479 in 2007.
- On the base of the sample, for IFRS regressions in 2006 and 2008, the price regression model applied in this study is statistically nonsignificant (two-tailed significance levels in all cases exceed 0.05) with the R^2 being

Table 9. Wilcoxon Signed Ranks Test Results.

		Ranks		
		N	Mean rank	Sum of ranks
P′09/BVPS′09_IFRS – *P*′09/BVPS′09_RAS	Negative Ranks	39	24.89	697.00
	Positive Ranks	26	21.33	384.00
	Ties	2		
	Total	67		
P′08/BVPS′08_IFRS – *P*′08/BVPS′08_RAS	Negative Ranks	39	29.10	1018.50
	Positive Ranks	25	634.5	634.50
	Ties	3		
	Total	67		
P′07/BVPS′07_IFRS – *P*′07/BVPS′07_RAS	Negative Ranks	45	24.97	824.00
	Positive Ranks	22	25.06	401.00
	Ties	0		
	Total	67		
P′06/BVPS′06_IFRS – *P*′06/BVPS′06_RAS	Negative Ranks	39	23.17	556.00
	Positive Ranks	28	17.94	305.00
	Ties	0		
	Total	67		

	Test statistics			
	P′09/BVPS′09_IFRS – *P*′09/BVPS′09_RAS	*P*′08/BVPS′08_IFRS – *P*′08/BVPS′08_RAS	*P*′07/BVPS′07_IFRS – *P*′07/BVPS′07_RAS	*P*′06/BVPS′06_IFRS – *P*′06/BVPS′06_RAS
Z	−1.710	−1.526	−2.104	−1.626
Asymp. Sig. (two tailed)	0.087	0.127	0.035	0.104

Table 10. OLS Price Regression Results.

RAS: 2006			IFRS: 2006		
Variables	Coefficients	Sig. level	Variables	Coefficients	Sig. level
1/BVPS'06_RAS	0.005	0.965	1/BVPS'06_IFRS	−0.048	0.653
EPS06/BVPS'06_RAS	1.028	0.004*	EPS06/BVPS'06_IFRS	−0.052	0.905
Constant	0.198	0.326	Constant	0.337	0.029
R^2	0.446		R^2	0.074	
Standard error	1.0278		Standard error	0.6247	
R^2 adj.	0.157		R^2 adj.	−0.047**	
Model significance level	0.015*		Model significance level	0.902	
RAS: 2007			IFRS: 2007		
1/BVPS'07_RAS	0.014	0.584	1/BVPS'07_IFRS	−0.007	0.431
EPS07/BVPS'07_RAS	0.479	0.040*	EPS07/BVPS'07_IFRS	0.364	0.021*
Constant	0.159	0.053	Constant	0.138	0.058
R^2	0.320		R^2	0.240	
Standard error	0.4244		Standard error	0.3693	
R^2 adj.	0.063		R^2 adj.	0.017	
Model significance level	0.043*		Model significance level	0.049*	
RAS: 2008			IFRS: 2008		
1/BVPS'08_RAS	−0.004	0.606	1/BVPS'08_IFRS	−0.002	0.814
EPS08/BVPS'08_RAS	0.144	0.165	EPS08/BVPS'08_IFRS	−0.015	0.947
Constant	0.209	0.001	Constant	0.214	0.003
R^2	0.198		R^2	0.032	
Standard error	0.4389		Standard error	0.4799	
R^2 adj.	0.005		R^2 adj.	−0.034**	
Model significance level	0.231		Model significance level	0.971	
RAS: 2009			IFRS: 2009		
1/BVPS'09_RAS	−0.03	0.979	1/BVPS'09_IFRS	0.015	0.904
EPS09/BVPS'09_RAS	0.021	0.960	EPS09/BVPS'09_IFRS	−3.847	0.000*
Constant	0.287	0.21	Constant	0.599	0.008
R^2	0.009		R^2	0.533	
Standard error	0.6494		Standard error	1.3168	
R^2 adj.	−0.045**		R^2 adj.	0.251	
Model significance level	0.998		Model significance level	0.001*	

*Significant at the 0.05 level (two tailed).

**An adjusted R^2 tries to allow for the fact that an independent variable that is really completely unrelated to the dependent variable will probably have some relationship to the dependent variable in a data set just by luck. The adjusted R^2 reduces the R^2 by how much fit would probably happen just by luck. Sometimes this reduction is more than the calculated R^2, so a negative adjusted R^2 appears.

Table 11. Regression Analysis for RAS and IFRS, 2006–2009.

RAS: 2006–2009			IFRS: 2006–2009		
Variables	Coefficients	Significance level	Variables	Coefficients	Significance level
1/BVPS′06_RAS	0.009	0.874	1/BVPS′06_IFRS	0.001	0.883
EPS06/BVPS′06_RAS	0.728	0.004*	EPS06/BVPS′06_IFRS	−0.252	0.035*
Constant	0.258	0.226	Constant	0.398	0.035
R^2	0.357		R^2	0.294	
Standard error	0.5781		Standard error	0.5968	
R^2 adj.	0.294		R^2 adj.	0.205	
Model significance level	0.025*		Model significance level	0.048	

* Significant at the 0.05 level (two tailed).

equal to 7.4% and 3.2% respectively; and all coefficients are nonsignificant (two-tailed significance levels in all cases exceed 0.05).

- On the base of the sample, for IFRS regressions in 2007 and 2009, the price regression model applied in this study is statistically significant (two-tailed significance levels in all cases do not exceed 0.05) with the R^2 being 24% and 53.3% respectively, but with only one statistically significant coefficient (two-tailed significance level does not exceed 0.05). This coefficient corresponds to the following independent variable EPS/BVPS′, and equals 0.364 in 2007 and −3.847 in 2009.
- The results on pooled sample (all years, all RAS vs. all years, all IFRS) show that both models are significant (with significance level equal to 0.05). The explanatory power of RAS model is slightly higher than the one with IFRS data (R^2 of 35.7% vs. R^2 of 29.4%). Again only one coefficient out of two is significant (EPS/BVPS′).

Let us now summarize the empirical results obtained after running price regressions both for RAS and IFRS samples.

First, it is interesting to note that in the year 2008, the price regression model applied in the current study proved to be statistically nonsignificant both for RAS and IFRS samples with no statistically significant coefficients as well, while in the year 2007, the price regression model applied proved to be statistically significant both for RAS and IFRS samples with a single statistically significant positive coefficient (being the one for the EPS/BVPS′ independent variable). Thus, 2007–2008 are the ones when the price regression analysis results for RAS and IFRS samples correspond with each other.

On the contrary, year 2006 and 2009 present an inversely different case such that in 2006 the price regression model is statistically significant for the RAS sample, while in 2009 the price regression model is statistically significant for the IFRS sample with a single statistically significant coefficient (being the one for EPS/BVPS′ independent variable) in both cases. However, the coefficient for the EPS/BVPS′ independent variable was positive for the RAS 2006 sample, and negative for the IFRS 2009 sample.

Consequent upon this, we can see from the sample of Russian companies over the years 2006–2009, income statement accounting components are more value relevant than the balance sheet accounting components.

Even though for some years during the analyzed time period, the price regression model did not prove to be statistically significant, we are still interested in the incremental difference between the value relevance of financial information presented under the RAS versus the value relevance of financial information presented under the IFRS.

To test if there is any statistically significant difference between RAS and IFRS with regards to the value relevance, we apply the two sample unconditional test focusing on the differences in the R^2. Initially, we intended to test the differences between adjusted R^2 as they have a lesser upward bias in small samples compared to R^2. However, in three regression pairs out of four, the adjusted R^2 is negative (see Table 10), which does not allow for proper comparison. Thus, in further tests we focus on R^2. We estimate significance levels for all comparisons of R^2 using the procedure outlined in Cramer (1987). Statistical comparisons are based on the expectations and variance of R^2 where Z-statistic is computed as $(R_1^2 - R_2^2)/\sqrt{(\sigma_1^2 R_1^2 + \sigma_2^2 R_2^2)}$, and has an approximated normal distribution under the null hypothesis of no difference in R^2. The t-value of the differences in R^2 is based on the assumption of two independent samples.

Table 12 presents the results of the Cramer test.

We observe that in all the four observation years and the overall observation period the differences in the R^2 of the price regressions between RAS and IFRS are quite substantial. They are: 37.2% in 2006, 8.0% in 2007, 16.6% in 2008 (all the higher values of the R^2 attributed to RAS), and 52.4% in 2009 (with the higher value of the R^2 attributed to IFRS). These computed differences could intuitively suggest that the statistically significant difference in the R^2 should be present. However, as can be seen from the table above in all observed cases, the H_0 hypothesis was accepted meaning that no statistically significant differences have been found between the R^2 reported for price regressions under RAS and IFRS. The explanation to this phenomenon is the fact that even in cases when the

Table 12. Cramer Test Results.

		R^2 RAS – R^2 IFRS	Z-statistic	t-statistic*
2006				
R^2 RAS	0.4460	0.3720	0.5261	1.9977
R^2 IFRS	0.0740		$\|Z\|<t$: H_0 accepted	
σ^2 RAS	1.0564			
σ^2 IFRS	0.3903			
2007				
R^2 RAS	0.3200	0.0800	0.2661	1.9977
R^2 IFRS	0.2400		$\|Z\|<t$: H_0 accepted	
σ^2 RAS	0.1801			
σ^2 IFRS	0.1364			
2008				
R^2 RAS	0.1980	0.1660	0.7781	1.9977
R^2 IFRS	0.0320		$\|Z\|<t$: H_0 accepted	
σ^2 RAS	0.1926			
σ^2 IFRS	0.2303			
2009				
R^2 RAS	0.0090	−0.5240	−0.5439	1.9977
R^2 IFRS	0.5330		$\|Z\|<t$: H_0 accepted	
σ^2 RAS	0.4217			
σ^2 IFRS	1.7340			
For pooled regression (2006–2009)				
R^2 RAS	0.357	0.063	0.1331	1.9690
R^2 IFRS	0.294		$\|Z\|<t$: H_0 accepted	
σ^2 RAS	0.3342			
σ^2 IFRS	0.3562			

*Two-tailed test at the significance level of 0.05.

absolute differences between the R^2 were quite substantial, they were leveled out by substantial standard errors of the R^2 estimation (e.g., σ^2 RAS in 2006 equals 1.056, and σ^2 IFRS in 2009 equals 1.734).

Therefore, we state that from the examined sample of Russian public listed companies applying both RAS and IFRS during the time period 2006–2009, there is no statistically significant difference between the value relevance of the financial information reported under the RAS and the value relevance of the financial information reported under the IFRS. This implies that the performed empirical study has proved the hypothesis stated earlier in this chapter with regards to no comparative value relevance difference between the two sets of financial reporting standards under examination in the Russian financial accounting settings.

CONCLUSION AND FURTHER RESEARCH

The present research chapter is devoted to the issue of IFRS adoption in Russia (by public listed companies) with the main focus on how it affects the value relevance of financial reporting on the Russian market. Due to the wide presence of private information channels for financial and accounting data in the Russian "insider" economy, the current study focuses on the needs of external users of financial reporting information, that is, non-majority shareholders and potential investors who do not have an access to the privileged sources of information.

Overall, empirical studies on the value relevance of accounting information under IFRS found mixed results, with some studies showing that the change to IFRS improves value relevance (Barth et al., 2008; Bartov et al., 2005; Horton & Serafeim, 2006), and others that it worsens value relevance (Lin & Chen, 2005), while others find no conclusive evidence either way (Niskanen, Kinnunen, & Kasanen, 2000). Based on an extensive review of theoretical and empirical literature on the issue of IFRS formation, adoption and practical implementation of both developed and emerging economies, we formulated the following research hypothesis: "There is no significant difference between the value relevance of financial information disclosed by Russian public companies under Russian Accounting Standards and the value relevance of financial information disclosed by Russian public companies under International Financial Reporting Standards." Next we tested the comparative value relevance between IFRS and RAS by the means of OLS price regression (on book values of equity and net income figures) adjusted for scale effects on a sample of 67 Russian public listed companies that voluntary report under IFRS during the period of four consecutive years (2006–2009).

Tests applied in the study showed that in all the observed cases, no statistically significant differences have been found between the R^2 reported for price regressions under RAS and the R^2 reported for price regressions under IFRS, meaning that on the examined sample of Russian public listed companies applying both RAS and IFRS during the time period 2006–2009, there was no statistically significant difference found between the value relevance of the financial information reported under the RAS and the value relevance of the financial information reported under the IFRS. Thus, the empirical study has proved the formulated research hypothesis. It is interesting to note here that the results obtained in the present study are in accordance with the results obtained in the empirical studies of developing economies' accounting practices, which in most cases found that the local standards are no worse than IFRS or even outperform IFRS on the reported financial information value relevance criterion (Callao, Jarne, & Lainez, 2007; Hellström, 2006; Niskanen et al., 2000).

One of the explanations could be that the costs associated with IFRS disclosure are quite highly relative to the benefits. In this case, disclosure is less desirable, since it leads to a reduction in firm value (Cuijpers, & Buijink, 2005; Verrechia, 1983).

Conclusively, we should go back and answer the main research question of the present study: Does the voluntary adoption of IFRS in Russia increase the value relevance of financial reporting? According to the empirical results there is no statistically significant difference in the value relevance between RAS and IFRS, which implies that for external users of financial information (predominantly potential investors and non-majority shareholders), there should be no reason to prefer one over another with regards to making inferences for future investment decisions.

In order to prepare this study to be further used for obtaining theoretical and empirical insights, we should first outline a number of limitations of the present research.

First, potential criticism refers to only 67 observations that might give little statistical power or backing to reject the null hypothesis of IFRS and RAS being equally value relevant. This criticism is correct if we were analyzing a sample and could expand the sample size. In our case, we have all observations available (i.e., there are no more companies that report under IFRS and have enough accounting and trading information to perform the price regressions). The sample could be expanded by including other countries, but this approach will change the selected benchmark for testing the value relevance of adopting IFRS.

Second, the self-selection bias is present in the sampling technique as the IFRS adoption is still voluntary in Russia even for public listed companies. Even though the nonrandom sampling might bias the obtained empirical results, so far this is the only sampling technique available on the Russian market.

It is essential to note that the results obtained in this study are difficult to be generalized to other countries, as the RAS institutional specifics are quite unique for the Russian environment.

There are several directions for further research. First, is to go on with the analysis and to replicate it from 2009 to subsequent years. This will help us to make the comparison with the results we got. Another possible direction is to work with the model and to adapt it to the specifics of emerging markets (e.g., adjust data for inflation, see Filip & Raffournier, 2010) or to test another model (e.g., see Horton & Serafeim, 2010). The results may then be more specified for the highly inflated Russian market. One more valuable research would be to compare the value relevance of the accounting information presented according to different standards before and after the implementation of the new accounting regulations that will require IFRSs for all Russian companies (since 2015).

According to accounting theory, more transparency and better corporate governance increases firm value as a result of managers' decisions improvement. As IFRS increases transparency, disclosure has a positive effect on firm value that will increase the benefits for investors over time and the global competitiveness of Russian stock market.

With regards to the results obtained, we see that there is a high demand for IFRS adoption in Russia, especially from users of accounting information, leading Russian companies and a lot of international companies working in Russia.

In addition, we also believe that further research in this area is needed in order to track the changes in financial reporting value relevance over time with regards to change in the Russian institutional environment and economic development.

NOTES

1. Data taken from AICPA IFRS Resources: http://www.ifrs.com
2. See IAS Plus: http://www.iasplus.com

REFERENCES

Albu, N., Albu, C. N., Bunea, S., Calu, D. A., & Gîrbină, M. M. (2011). A story about IAS/IFRS implementation in Romania: An institutional and structuration theory perspective. *Journal of Accounting in Emerging Economies*, *1*(1), 76–100.

Ali, M. J., Ahmed, K., & Eddie, I. A. (2009). The adoption of IFRS in emerging economies: The case of South Asia. *Journal of Accounting in Emerging Economies*, *9*, 1–30.

Aubert, F., & Grudnitski, G. (2011). The impact and importance of mandatory adoption of international financial reporting standards in Europe. *Journal of International Financial Management and Accounting*, *22*(1), 1–26.

Bagaeva, A. (2008). An examination of the effect of international investors on accounting information quality in Russia. *Advances in Accounting*, *24*, 157–161.

Ball, R. (2006). International financial reporting standards (IFRS): Pros and cons for investors. *Accounting and Business Research, International Accounting Policy Forum*, 5–27.

Barth, M. E., Beaver, W. H., & Landsman, W. R. (2001). The relevance of the value relevance literature for financial accounting standard setting: Another view. *Journal of Accounting and Economics*, *31*, 77–104.

Barth, M., & Kallapur, S. (1996). The effects of cross-sectional scale differences on regression results in empirical accounting research. *Contemporary Accounting Research*, *13*, 527–567.

Barth, M. E., Landsman, W. R., & Lang, M. H. (2008). International accounting standards and accounting quality. *Journal of Accounting Research*, *46*(3), 467–498.

Bartov, E., Goldberg, S. R., & Kim, M. (2005). Comparative value relevance among German, US, and international accounting standards: A German stock market perspective. *Journal of Accounting Auditing and Finance*, *20*(2), 95–119.

Beaver, W., & Dukes, R. (1972). Interperiod tax allocation, earnings expectations, and the behavior of security prices. *The Accounting Review*, *47*, 624–652.

Brown, S., Lo, K., & Lys, T. (1999). Use of R-squared in accounting research: Measuring changes in value relevance in the last four decades. *Journal of Accounting and Economics*, *28*, 83–115.

Callao, S., Jarne, J., & Lainez, J. (2007). Adoption of IFRS in Spain: Effect on the comparability and relevance of financial reporting. *Journal of International Accounting, Auditing and Taxation*, *16*, 148–178.

Chen, H., Tang, Q., Jiang, Y., & Lin, Z. (2010). The role of international financial reporting standards in accounting quality: Evidence from the European Union. *Journal of International Financial Management and Accounting*, *21*(3), 220–278.

Cormier, D., Demaria, S., Lapointe-Antunes, P., & Teller, R. (2009). First-time adoption of IFRS, managerial incentives, and value-relevance: Some French evidence. *Journal of International Accounting Research*, *8*(2), 1–22.

Cramer, J. S. (1987). Mean and variance of R2 in small and moderate samples. *Journal of Econometrics*, *35*, 253–266.

Cuijpers, R., & Buijink, W. (2005). Voluntary adoption of non-local GAAP in the European Union: A study of determinants and consequences. *European Accounting Review*, *14*, 487–524.

Daske, H., Hail, L., Leuz, C., & Verdi, R. (2008). Mandatory IFRS reporting around the world: Early evidence on the economic consequences. *Journal of Accounting Research*, *46*(5), 1085–1142.

Devalle, A., Onali, E., & Magarini, R. (2010). Assessing the value relevance of accounting data after the introduction of IFRS in Europe. *Journal of International Financial Management and Accounting*, *21*(2), 85–119.

Dobija, D., & Klimczak, K. M. (2010). Development of accounting in Poland: Market efficiency and the value relevance of reported earnings. *The International Journal of Accounting*, *45*(3), 356–374.

Easton, P., & Sommers, G. (2003). Scale and scale effects in market-based accounting research. *Journal of Business Finance and Accounting*, *3*(1–2), 25–56.

Filip, A., & Raffournier, B. (2010). The value relevance of earnings in a transition economy: The case of Romania. *The International Journal of Accounting*, *45*, 77–103.

Gjerde, O., Knivsfle, K. H., & Saettem, F. (2008). The value-relevance of adopting IFRS: Evidence from 145 NGAAP restatements. *Journal of International Accounting, Auditing and Taxation*, *17*, 92–112.

Goodwin, J., Ahmed, K., & Heaney, R. (2008). The effects of International financial reporting standards on the accounts and accounting quality of Australian firms: A retrospective study. *Journal of Contemporary Accounting and Economics*, *4*(2), 89–119.

Gornik-Tomaszewski, S., & Jermakowicz, E. (2001). Accounting-based valuation of Polish listed companies. *Journal of International Financial Management and Accounting*, *12*, 50–74.

Hellström, K. (2006). The value relevance of financial accounting information in a transition economy: The case of the Czech Republic. *The European Accounting Review*, *15*, 325–349.

Hellstrom, T. (2007). Dimensions of environmentally sustainable innovation: The structure of eco-innovation concepts. *Sustainable Development*, *15*, 148–159.

Holthausen, R. W., & Watts, R. L. (2001). The relevance of the value-relevance literature for financial accounting standard setting. *Journal of Accounting and Economics*, *31*, 3–75.

Horton, J., & Serafeim, G. (2006). *Market response to and the value relevance of reconciliation adjustments from UK GAAP to IFRS GAAP: First evidence from the UK*. Working Papers Series. Retrieved from http://ssrn.com/abstract=923582

Horton, J., & Serafeim, G. (2010). Market reaction to and valuation of IFRS reconciliation adjustments: First evidence from the UK. *Review of Accounting Studies*, *15*, 725–751.

Hove, M. R. (1986). Accounting practices in developing countries – Colonialism's legacy of inappropriate technologies. *International Journal of Accounting*, *22*, 81–100.

Hung, M., & Subramanyam, K. R. (2007). Financial statement effects of adopting international accounting standards: the case of Germany. *Review of Accounting Studies*, *12*(4), 623–657.

Jindrichovska, I. (2001). The relationship between accounting numbers and returns: Some empirical evidence from the emerging market of the Czech Republic. *The European Accounting Review*, *10*, 107–131.

Lin, Z. J., & Chen, F. (2005). Value relevance of international accounting standards harmonization: Evidence from A-share and B-share markets in China. *Journal of International Accounting, Auditing and Taxation*, *14*(2), 79–103.

McGee, R., & Preobragenskaya, G. (2004). Problems of implementing International Accounting Standards in transition economy: A case study of Russia. Florida: Working Paper #9780387238470. Barry University, FL.

Niskanen, J., Kinnunen, J., & Kasanen, E. (2000). The value relevance of IAS reconciliation: Empirical evidence from Finland. *Journal of Accounting and Public Policy*, *19*(2), 119–137.

Ostrenko, E. V. (2010). Main issues of IFRS adoption by companies. *Managerial Accounting and Finance*, *3*(23), 54–71.

Pritchard, J. N. (2002). The relationship between accounting numbers and returns in the Baltic stock markets. Working Paper #0206. CERT, Heriot-Watt University, Edinburgh. Retrieve from http://www.sml.hw.ac.uk/downloads/cert/wpa/2002/dp0206.pdf

Soderstrom, N. S., & Sun, K. J. (2007). IFRS adoption and accounting quality: A review. *European Accounting Review*, *16*(4), 675–702.

Verrechia, R. (1983). Discretionary disclosure. *Journal of Accounting and Economics*, *5*, 179–194.

Volegova, N. V. (2011). IFRS and RAS: Main differences. *Managerial Accounting and Finance*, *1*(25), 49–68.

Walter, A. (2008). *Governing finance: East Asia's adoption of international standards*. Ithaca, NY: Cornell University Press.

THE TRUE AND FAIR VIEW CONCEPT IN ROMANIA: A CASE STUDY OF CONCEPT TRANSFERABILITY

Cătălin Nicolae Albu, Nadia Albu and David Alexander

ABSTRACT

Purpose – *The purpose of this chapter is to examine the transfer of a concept issued in one culture to a different setting, featuring different characteristics from the one in which the concept appeared.*

Methodology/approach – *Secondary data have been collected by analysing accounting regulations issued after the fall of communism with respect to true and fair view (TFV). Primary data have been collected by conducting eleven semi-structured interviews with representatives of major actors involved in the process of financial reporting. We have further developed and tested two research propositions.*

Findings – *We find that the perception of TFV in Romania depends firstly on the category of actors. Second, we find that merely including a rule or a concept in the regulations of a certain setting does not*

Accounting in Central and Eastern Europe
Research in Accounting in Emerging Economies, Volume 13, 61–90

ISSN: 1479-3563/doi:10.1108/S1479-3563(2013)0000013008

automatically mean that they will be applied de facto consistently with their original meaning, issued from a different setting.

Implications – *We conclude that concept intertranslatability cannot be assumed under the circumstances investigated in our chapter, with immediate implications for other cases presupposing that concept transfer works, such as International Financial Reporting Standards (IFRS).*

Research limitations – *The small number of interviews we have conducted may be viewed as a limitation of our study; however, special care was exercised when choosing interviewees, and they are key persons within their organizations, or representative of all the interested parties in the process of financial reporting in Romania.*

Originality/value – *We contribute to an increasing literature on accounting harmonization and applicability of global standards and concepts in local contexts.*

Keywords: True and fair view; TFV override; Romania; concept transferability; accounting harmonization; accounting regulations

> … it will be seen that it is easier to knock down a dictator than to push away a dictatorship.
> – Paler, 1995, p. 43

> … se va vedea că e mult mai uşor să dobori un dictator decât să înlături o dictatură.
> – Paler, 1995, p. 43

INTRODUCTION

The purpose of this chapter is to examine the transfer of a concept issued in one culture to a different setting, featuring different characteristics from the one in which the concept appeared. Specifically, in the context of various (and sometimes contradictory) influences suffered by the Romanian financial reporting model after the fall of communism, we explore within the Romanian setting a possible gap between how the true and fair view (TFV) concept is included in the official Romanian legislation, and how it is actually perceived by various actors involved in accounting practice, with immediate implications for other very topical issues involving concept transferability, such as the adoption of IFRS, and more generally, accounting harmonization. In order for accounting harmonization to achieve its objectives (involving the application of accounting concepts created for one environment in a different setting), we have to assume concept transferability works.

In this chapter we broadly accept the ideas developed in a number of recent papers (e.g., Alexander & Archer, 2003; Mouck, 2004; Shapiro, 1997, 1998), not always quite consistently with each other, applying to the accounting domain the concept of institutional and inter-subjective reality developed by Searle (1995, 2006a, 2006b). Searle (1995, Chap. 3, 2006b, p. 19) argues for an unavoidable relationship between institutional facts through collective representation and language. Over and above the intuitively obvious similarities regarding shared beliefs (institutional facts) and shared meanings (language) is the more fundamental point that the move from object (e.g., metal) to status function by means of collective representation (e.g., money) is only possible if there is a mechanism for creating, and communicating, this collective representation.

We contribute to literature on accounting harmonization and applicability of global standards and concepts via the case of TFV. Global harmonization of accounting is arguably the most challenging and controversial issue currently confronting accounting standard setters and market regulators (Collett, Godfrey, & Hrasky, 2001, p. 171). Accounting harmonization has been placed within the "inherent and inevitable subjectivity of the financial reporting function in every aspect" (Alexander, 2010) and researchers investigated various national perspectives on international accounting harmonization (see, e.g., Alexander & Albu, 2011, and the respective special issue). Results are mixed, in that some papers argue for an increased degree of harmonization in certain circumstances (e.g., Bradshaw & Miller, 2008), while others testify for a reduced degree of harmonization and even a high degree of non-compliance within the same (Mechelli, 2009) or different (Herrmann & Thomas, 1995) geographical setting, to only offer but a few examples. Studies are needed to bring more detailed perspectives on this process.

We illustrate these issues through the case of the UK-originated concept of TFV. TFV is imposed in the European Union (EU) through the European Fourth Directive, becoming "a European accounting principle" (Ordelheide, 1993). Unlike previous literature, we focus particularly on studying how the concept is actually perceived by various actors in an emerging economy which has only recently joined the EU (i.e., Romania) and whether there is a gap between the official (as reflected in the official accounting documents) and the practitioners' perspectives. We investigate such "paradoxical situations where accounting suited to an advanced market economy is introduced by fiat into a nascent market economy" (Bailey, 1995, p. 603). This is a "*higher order* (italics in original, N.A.) reflection on the terms that are being used by practitioners" (Lyas, 1993, p. 156).

The Romanian case is a particularly interesting one to use in this context. Romania is one of the newest EU members (since January 2007), and a country whose accounting model has suffered influences from various other internationally relevant accounting models. Romania followed the chart of accounts tradition of continental European inspiration through to the 1940s when the communists took control. From 1947 until 1989, Romania had an accounting system of Russian origins.

After the fall of communism in 1989 there were several accounting reforms, under different foreign influences, but the accounting regulation remained a public one. Romania has had an Accounting Law since 1991, and various Orders issued by the Minister of Public Finances (ro. Ordinul Ministrului Finanţelor Publice-OMFP) in the guise of implementation guidelines. The first stage of reform was based on the French code law accounting; the second stage was an Anglo-Saxon-International Accounting Standards (IAS)-oriented one, with the third stage representing the implementation (enactment) of European Directives. The orientation toward the Anglo-Saxon-IAS model was considered a "cultural intrusion" (Delesalle & Delesalle, 2000; Roberts, 2000).

Based on the signifier-signified distinction used within the concept transferability literature, we are investigating both (1) how TFV is included in the national regulations and (2) how Romanian accountants perceive the matters associated with TFV in practice. We set out to explore the perceptions of representative key players: regulators, preparers, auditors, professional bodies, and users in relation to TFV by means of 11 in-depth semi-structured interviews. We find that the perception of TFV in Romania depends on the category of actors: for auditors, professional bodies, and users, TFV is a guide or a vital concept, closely related to substance over form, relevance and usefulness for users, while for regulators and preparers, it is primarily compliance with rules. The European Directive provisions regarding the TFV are consistently included in the Romanian regulations, but if for regulators and preparers these provisions are a form of compliance, for the other actors TFV is an overarching principle requiring more than formal compliance. For us, this means concept transferability cannot be assumed in an internationalized world. The practical application of concepts issued from other settings, even though the words may be there, will be influenced by the local traditions (or their lack). Given the recent debate on accounting harmonization/convergence and the need for a single set of accounting standards applicable in a comparable manner around the world (i.e., IFRS), we contribute to this literature by discussing the meaning of accounting concepts in different accounting cultures and the debatable assumption that they are easily transferable from one culture to another.

The chapter proceeds as follows. The second section presents the chapter's theoretical foundation, including the theoretical framework, that is, concept transferability, the development of propositions, and the method. The third section gives an outline of legal/regulatory requirements in Romania after the fall of communism, and explores the perceptions of TFV in the same setting. The fourth section discusses our findings in depth and concludes, outlining the significant general messages to be drawn from our in-depth case study.

THEORETICAL FRAMEWORK, PROPOSITIONS DEVELOPMENT AND METHOD

Theoretical Framework

For the purpose of this chapter, we broadly accept the ideas developed in a number of recent papers (e.g., Alexander & Archer, 2003; Mouck, 2004; Shapiro, 1997, 1998), not always quite consistently with each other, applying to the accounting domain the concept of institutional and intersubjective reality developed by Searle (1995, 2006a, 2006b).

Many "objects" exist only through generally agreed social construction. Metal in its natural state exists without human thought (equals social construction), money does not, being, by definition, a generally accepted medium of exchange, between members of society who choose to accept the notion and operate within its applications.

Searle's (1995) theoretic starts by making an ontological commitment to physical objects (brute facts), and then, based on the concept of "intentionality" explains how social objects come into being. According to Searle (1995) people have the *ability to share beliefs or desires* – termed *collective intentionality* – that in certain conditions can give rise to a specific type of social facts, namely, *institutional facts*. More exactly, *institutional facts* come into being by ascribing a *status function* to a physical object (*brute fact*) by means of *collective intentionality*. This rationale is used in accounting to describe how accounting concepts are socially constructed:

> By virtue of collective intentionality, ownership claims, income, and other conceptual objects of accounting can, under appropriate conditions, be *institutional facts*. (Alexander & Archer, 2003, p. 5, emphasis original, N.A.)

This chapter is written, and needs to be read, in the context, of the principles of Saussurean linguistics. In essence this can be expressed succinctly:

- The use of a particular word as signifier (ro. semnificat) is arbitrary. There is no rationale for, or significance from, cat being cat and not rumplestiltskin;
- The use of a particularly conceived concept as signified (ro. semnificant) is arbitrary. The famous example, from Saussure himself, is that French conceives of two types of river, one that flows directly into the sea and one which does not. Two concepts require two words (un fleuve and une rivière respectively). English thinking never made this conceptual distinction, and therefore only has one word for the one concept: river. Not surprisingly (since it is also a language of Latin origins), Romanian follows the French conceptualization, the two words being un fluviu and un râu respectively;
- The relationship between a word and a concept is itself arbitrary. "Cat" could just as well signify a small nocturnal flying mammal instead of a furry four-legged, one tailed, friendly, independent and potentially vicious mammal, and "bat" the reverse.

All three "arbitrarinesses" are created and understood by collective acceptance, not by intrinsic rationale or fact.

Searle (1995, p. Chap. 3; 2006b, p. 19) argues for an unavoidable relationship between institutional facts through collective representation and language. Over and above the intuitively obvious similarities regarding shared beliefs (institutional facts) and shared meanings (language) is the more fundamental point that the move from object (e.g., metal) to status function by means of collective representation (e.g., money) is only possible if there is a mechanism for creating, and communicating, this collective representation. "The essential thing about human beings is that language gives them the capacity to *represent*" (2006b, p. 19, emphasis original). We are now in a position to consider the intertranslation issue raised by McKernan (2007, p. 164).

McKernan (2007, p. 164) quotes Davidson (1974, p. 189), apparently favorably, as arguing that intertranslatability[1] has to be possible as "we cannot make good sense" of the alternative, because the alternative implies the existence of "different conceptual schemes or conceptual relativism." The logical link is immediately accepted. Languages are conceptual schemes, as the arguments from Saussure and Searle in the immediately preceding paragraphs show. Conceptual schemes are collectively accepted across a community. Different conceptual schemes would suggest different communities, and therefore a lack of intertranslatability.

One issue concerns the argument that if a clear logical reconciliation is possible, however long and convoluted, then there is no lack of intertranslatability. Arguably the issue of intertranslatability can be solved by means of equivalent expressions: fr. un fleuve = a river flowing into the sea; fr. une rivière = a river flowing into another river. But on the other hand the fact still remains that English and French are constructed with two different conceptual frameworks regarding large volumes of water flowing downhill.

Various papers have previously treated the issues of translation and transferability in accounting. For example, some authors (Colasse, 1997; Kosmala, 2005; Sucher, Seal, & Zelenka, 1996; Walton, 1993) distinguish between *signifier* and *signified* in the context of Saussurean linguistics when discussing TFV, but without a clear argument on this issue. Archer and McLeay (1991), Belkaoui (1978, 1989), Doupnik and Richter (2002), and Kelly (1994) discuss translations. Evans (2004) uses TFV as one of her case studies, but from a linguistics-based perspective, arguing that "(t)his suggests that speakers of different languages also perceive and interpret accounting concepts in different ways" (p. 239). More recently, Evans, Baskerville, and Nara (2010) advance the study in accounting translation issues by incorporating lessons from other domains. Haried (1972, 1973) is preoccupied by the semantic problems in communication and seeks to adapt some techniques in order to test and analyze the meaning associated with accounting concepts.

Development of Research Propositions

The notion of harmonization is much referred to, but less often explained or defined. Definition is in fact surprisingly difficult, and the idea is frequently contrasted with, and at the same time confused with, that of standardization. Feleagă, Feleagă, & Dragomir (2009) suggest a rather vague definition which is in fact probably fully as far as it is safe to go:

> Both harmonization and standardization involve a reduction in accounting diversity. But whereas harmonization seems to imply consensus and coordination in the context

> of a more flexible approach, standardization, on the other hand, implies a stricter path to a state of uniformity. (pp. 16–17)

In essence, therefore, the suggestion is that standardization is nearer to uniformity than harmonization is. Alexander and Nobes (2010, p. 80) make effectively the same suggested distinction. There are linguistic difficulties here, in that Accounting Standards, especially more principle-based standards, do not actually seek uniformity. In this sense, therefore, accounting standards do not seek to "standardize."

It is also worth emphasizing that the Feleagă et al. (2009) quote above refers to consensus, which implies (eventual) agreement, and not to compromise, which would imply disagreement, or more precisely an agreement to disagree and carry on, ignoring the still existing differences. It is surely reasonable to suggest that sometimes so-called harmonization never gets beyond an uneasy compromise, rather than a true "consensus in the context of a more flexible approach."

This notion of harmonization links directly to issues of transferability or intertranslatability. Whilst fully recognizing that we are dealing with relatives rather than absolutes, a reasonable degree of "consensus and coordination" within and between entity financial reports, or indeed between any two conceptually based comparators, is surely a necessary condition for a meaningful cross-understanding sufficient to enable a valid comparison; in other words to provide intertranslatability, or conceptual transferability.

Global harmonization of accounting is arguably the most challenging and controversial issue currently confronting accounting standard setters and market regulators (Collett et al., 2001, p. 171). Literature on accounting harmonization has been reviewed elsewhere (see, e.g., Baker & Barbu, 2007; Guggiola, 2010; Mustaţă & Matiş, 2010 among others). Literature provides an increasing number of contributions in recent years, and demonstrates the difficulties in investigating the issues associated. Accounting harmonization has been placed within the "inherent and inevitable subjectivity of the financial reporting function in every aspect" (Alexander, 2010) and researchers investigated various national perspectives on international accounting harmonization (see Alexander & Albu, 2011, and the respective special issue). Results are mixed, in that some papers argue for an increased degree of harmonization in certain circumstances (e.g., Bradshaw & Miller, 2008), while others testify for a reduced degree of harmonization and even high degree of non-compliance within the same (Mechelli, 2009) or different (Herrmann & Thomas, 1995) geographical setting to only offer but a few examples. Studies are needed to bring more detailed perspectives on this process.

To try to summarize a little, we can suggest that harmonization, and the capacity for transferability of understanding, really go hand in hand, and each is a necessary condition for the other. They both stem from the fundamental existence of "collective intentionality," as explained and discussed above, and such collective intentionality may or may not exist in any particular postulated or investigated circumstance. We can hypothesize that, if transferability of understanding is in fact possible, then a degree of harmonization is pre-supposed, in the sense of consensus and coordination. But it is important to note that we are absolutely not saying that standardization/uniformity, let alone harmonization, are *sufficient* conditions for effective transferability. This is because there is always the additional dimension of different conceptual frameworks, cultures, language influences and indeed the whole gamut of human-influenced socially constructed perceptions and interpretations of words, objects, ideas, etc., which create distortion, blockage, and "noise" in the transfer process.

We contribute directly to this literature, and illustrate its practical implications, by bringing insights on the sometimes assumed transferability of accounting concepts in contexts very different from the one that originated the concept. We contend that such intertranslatability is not easy to assume, and we use the Romanian case on TFV to advance the extant understanding. We investigate a dangerous case whereby simply translating words expressing concepts proper to a certain community into another community's language leads to an *assumption* of intertranslatability of those concepts.

Even though TFV was extensively addressed in literature, recent papers addressing this issue (Kosmala, 2005; Nobes, 2009) call for further investigation, especially in different jurisdictions, to get a complete picture of the "new Europe." We analyse therefore how the meaning of an accounting concept is constructed (and construed) within a certain environment, by different actors within their particular environment. Also, we respond to a recent call to study accounting practices in their institutional setting (Nobes, 2009). Because so little is known in the international literature about Romanian accounting (except for a few papers, e.g., Matiş, Strouhal, & Bonaci, 2009), we also contribute to literature with an investigation of the Romanian situation by exploring such a paradoxical situation "where accounting suited to an advanced market economy is introduced by fiat into a nascent market economy" (Bailey, 1995, p. 603).

It is relevant to note that the importance of the production of economically meaningful information, flexible and focused on the situation of the particular entity concerned, which the TFV concept permits and encourages, increases as entities become larger and their sources of finance become more disparate. The different industrial and financing structures between Romania and, for example, the United Kingdom are likely to be one explanatory factor relating to differences of perception and operationalization regarding financial reporting.

TFV is an icon of British self-regulation (Hamilton & Ó hÓgartaigh, 2009, p. 915). Cook (1997, p. 695) describes the UK perspective on TFV as a means of describing the underlying commercial reality, a means of escape when the existing rules do not fit, a strength of the reporting obligation, and "a brake of the proliferation of detailed rules." Romania joined the EU on January 1, 2007. This resulted in the full enactment of the provisions of the European Directives (including accounting) in the Romanian legislation, just like for any other member state of the EU. TFV is imposed in the EU through the European Fourth Directive. Many papers discussed historically the inclusion of TFV in the European Directives and its implications (Alexander, 1993; Ordelheide, 1993, 1996; Walton, 1991, 1997), as well as its meaning and operationalization in different countries (Burlaud, 1993; Colasse, 1997; Kosmala, 2005; Kosmala-MacLullich, 2003; Sucher et al., 1996; Walton, 1991). Chastney (1975) has discussed its origins and investigated its meaning in the United Kingdom (hereafter UK). Some authors consider that each jurisdiction constructed its own meaning of TFV, based on their culture and pre-existing national GAAP (Alexander, 1993, 1996; Kosmala, 2005; Sucher et al., 1996 etc.), thus the inclusion of TFV in the European legislation would be "a waste of time" (Walton, 1993, p. 53) (of course, in the sense of the desired harmonization). Others regard TFV as an opportunity for Europe, meaning a "subtle instrument of change" (Cook, 1997, p. 703). In France, TFV was made compatible with the existent notions of *régularité* and *sincérité* (Burlaud, 1993; Colasse, 1997). In former communist countries such as Poland (Kosmala, 2005) and the Czech Republic (Sucher et al., 1996) TFV generally is associated with the emphasis on the legal framework, in a generally tax-oriented accounting system. Considering all these, we propose that:

> Pr1) The inclusion of a certain concept issued from a particular context in the regulations of another setting will not ensure de facto application of the concept in the original sense. TFV is included de jure in the Romanian legislation consistently with the provisions of the European Directives, but its application de facto is not consistent with the original UK-originated concept.

The accounting model of most European continental countries is reported to be linked with taxation (Larson & Street, 2004; Nobes & Parker, 2008).

Romania is no exception. When in doubt, Romanian accountants prefer a fiscal rule to an accounting one. This is consistent with the important role of the State in Central and Eastern European emerging economies reported in literature (Kosmala-MacLullich, 2003; Sucher et al., 1996; Vellam, 2004). Additionally, the Romanian accounting profession, just like in any other emerging economy, is characterized by a lower stage of development, with a reduced emphasis on applying professional judgment. So we propose that:

> Pr2) Romanian accountants will likely have difficulty with properly integrating TFV in their work (consistently with the original UK perspective).

Research Method

We started first by investigating the provisions regarding TFV in Romanian regulations after the fall of communism (1989), that is, the Accounting Law (no. 82/1991 with subsequent revisions), and the OMFP no. 1752/2005 containing details regarding the financial statements and accounting treatments among others (secondary data). Second, and as an important input into our investigation, we have carried out 11 in-depth semi-structured interviews of significant Romanian actors involved in the financial reporting process, to complement our understanding of TFV as resulted from the review of accounting regulations (primary data). Details, the various categories, and the way we refer to each interviewee in the chapter, are given in the appendix. It is important to stress that, whilst our interviewee set is neither random nor large enough for any statistical analysis, they are in most cases leading influences, and key decision-makers, in relation to their respective roles.

CASE STUDY

The TFV in Romanian Regulations after the Fall of Communism

In Romania, accounting issues are dealt with by the Accounting Law (no. 82/1991, with subsequent revisions), accompanied by Ministerial Orders (in guise of implementation guidelines). The Accounting law deals with general aspects regarding the organization of the accounting system by entities, with company's records, general terms regarding the preparation of financial statements, with the accounting system of public entities, and with contraventions and infringements to the Accounting Law. Practical details are given afterwards through means of Ministerial Orders (to explain, e.g., accounting principles or the layout and composition of the financial statements). These are, of course, lower-level acts, being issued by a Minister (of Public Finances), not by the Parliament.

Regarding TFV, the 2008 revision of the Accounting law stipulates that:

> Par 9 (1): The official documents accounting for the economic-financial position of persons in par. 1 are the annual financial statements, established according to the law, and which should give a TFV of the financial position, financial performance and other information pertaining to the company's activity.
>
> Par 30: The financial statements will be accompanied by a statement of the persons set in par. 10 (1) by which they assume responsibility for the preparation of the financial statements and confirm that:
>
> (a) the accounting policies used when preparing the financial statements comply with applicable accounting regulations;
> (b) the financial statements give a TFV of the financial position, financial performance and other information pertaining to the company's activity;
> (c) the juridical person is a going concern.

We note that "TFV" (ro. imagine fidelă; fr. image fidèle) obviously translates the Romanian directly from the French. Para 30 is interesting, as the three requirements, (a), (b) and (c), *all* have to be confirmed. The TFV requirement is not here, even in 2008, superior to recognized compliance with applicable accounting regulations.

In its turn, the lower level regulation, that is, the OMFP 1752/2005[2] (ensuring conformity with European Directives), stipulates that:

> Section 1 General provisions regarding annual financial statements
>
> Par 9. Financial statements give a TFV of the entity's assets, liabilities, financial position, profit or loss.
>
> Par 10. If the observance of the present regulations is not sufficient to give a TFV within the meaning of Par 9, additional information must be presented.
>
> Par 11. Where, in exceptional cases, the application of a provision of this present regulation is against the obligation explained in par. 9, that provision must be departed from in order to give a TFV within the meaning of par. 9. Any such departure must be disclosed in the notes, together with the reasons for such a departure and its impact on the assets, liabilities, financial position and profit or loss.

Thus, a relevant provision "must be departed from" as far as is necessary to give a TFV. We note that the TFV override is only referred to in the lower-level regulation, which at least from a perception point of view may raise some inconsistency issues with the provisions of the accounting law, where no such reference is made. However, since the 4th European

Directive is enacted in Romania as a member state of the EU, the override should automatically be applicable to the extent it is required, with no immediate legal consequences for the preparers and the entities applying it. We will see later that this is not the case in the Romanian environment.

After 1989, the route took Romanian regulations, at times unevenly and with deviations, from the mechanical attitudes of communist form-filling, combined with a formulaic, and arguably meaningless, incorporation of the words TFV, through to the de jure unequivocal inclusion of the requirements of Article 2 of the Fourth Directive. The concept (signified) represented in Romanian thinking by the words (signifier) can be expected to have changed. This does not for a moment imply, however, that former associations will have disappeared. We now turn to our empirical investigations which seek to explore and analyze current attitudes and perceptions by actors actually involved in regulation and practice in Romania.

Perception of TFV in Romania

Translation Issues

As alluded to above, TFV was included in the Romanian legislation using a translation via French: "imagine fidelă" (fr. image fidèle; en. faithful image[3]). Given the discussions generally raised by the translation issues (see Alexander, 1993; Kosmala, 2005; Sucher et al., 1996) and particularly by the French translation (Alexander, 1993; Burlaud, 1993), we investigated whether a translation by two words (en. *true and fair*) instead of one (fr. fidèle; ro. fidelă) would not be more closely related to the original meaning of TFV. Two of the preparers had no opinion regarding translation, but P3 linked the translation to the meaning of TFV:

> Personally, I hope I understood what TFV means ... I do not think that the wording (translation) is to blame, it's the explanation. "Fidelă" means not only obeying the rules. The problem is that it is a concept that we totally ignore, therefore I personally believe that a different wording would not have had different meaning.

A1 supports the same opinion; a Romanian specific wording would not have changed the concept, its application or perception. A2 also considers the meaning more important than the wording:

> The Ministry of Public Finances took the French approach because our legal system is closer to the French one. But the majority of practitioners do not care that it is taken from French at all, they apply OMFP 1752 and that's it. For large companies where TFV actually matters, they are already influenced by the British accounting culture.

Concluding, the interviewees agree that the translation of TFV in Romanian is adequate and is not the primary factor that affects its perception in practice. More, it is not a debatable topic, because all were more interested in discussing the meaning of this concept, not the wording. This is quite an interesting difference from other countries where translation issues appeared. For example, Kosmala (2005) shows that in Poland there is a multiplicity of translations and grammatical constructions for TFV, and differences exist between different actors regarding the preference for one or two-word translation.

Perceptions of TFV

R2 considers TFV as "mainly a theoretical concept, which is not very well defined in the literature," and PB2 states that "the concept of TFV has no definition." Yet, A1 sees TFV as "the Pater noster prayer" for auditors, A2 considers TFV "as a guiding principle," and PB1 indicates TFV as "a vital concept for the auditors." Quite interestingly, A2 added that "it still is something too theoretical to many, but they will come round."

Interestingly and of course, not arbitrarily, the two users we have interviewed perceive TFV through the lens of accounting principles and the quality of information produced, which seems to be quite dissimilar to the way Romanian preparers seem to think. The auditors' point of view reconnects with the point of view of the users we interviewed, as they perceive TFV through the needs of the users of financial statements. For A1, "giving a TFV means that the financial information gives to users an image of the reality of transactions for decision making" and "for the auditor, TFV means 'significant' for the client [...] My actual clients are the users and the shareholders." For PB1 and PB2, the professional judgment is fundamentally linked to TFV. One of the users (U1) also agrees with this:

> I believe that they (N.A. accountants) strictly follow the provisions of the law, and do not apply professional judgment to obey the spirit of the law; yet, they strongly believe that the financial statements they prepare do give a TFV. I do think that for a lot of entities and accountants, this is more of a formal statement rather than an actual concept.

As regards synonyms or equivalent terms, R2 hesitated to give one, but considered TFV different from "correct" (ro. corectă; fr. correcte) and "true" (ro. reală; fr. réelle). He underlined that TFV does not mean "correct presentation" (ro. prezentare corectă; fr. présentation correcte) because it is difficult to use the word "correct" when dealing with a lot of estimates. Also, he argues that the concept is not similar to "true" (as in "*true* financial statements") (ro. situaţii financiare *reale*; fr. états financiers *réels*) as "we suppose that they are true since they are prepared and signed."

A2 perceives the TFV concept as being closely related to substance over form and considers that privileging form over substance is the "greatest threat to TFV in Romania," considering the orientation of Romanian accounting thinking toward compliance with the regulations. The regulator's opinion was that "regularity (compliance) is necessary, but it may not be enough." Despite this assertion, the general line of the discussion with the regulator's representatives shows their expectations regarding the compliance with the regulations.

In France, TFV is closely related to regularity (conformity) and sincerity[4] (fr. régularité et sincérité; ro. conformitate cu regulile şi sinceritate) (Alexander, 1993; Burlaud, 1993) and even in some Anglo-Saxon[5] accounting systems compliance may be considered a fundamental element of TFV (see Alexander & Jermakowicz, 2006; Kirk, 2006). Quite consistently, for PB2, TFV "is strictly related to two qualities of accounting: regularity (conformity) and sincerity. You may most definitely say of accounting which is regular in form and fair in substance, that it is faithful or that it faithfully represents reality." Regarding the regularity issue, the opinions were contrasting even among the same category of actors. P1 and P3 consider that TFV does not mean only compliance with the rules, while P2 and U1 underlined that in Romania TFV means exactly that. PB1 distinguishes the perception of TFV based on two types of audit companies: Big 4 and other multinational network firms and Romanian audit companies. He considers that the two segments are quite different in Romania, and that for Big 4 and other multinational network firms TFV is "clearly something else than regularity (conformity) and sincerity, because they are focused on the needs of their clients ... They conceive TFV related to the materiality concept."

Concluding, for auditors, professional bodies, and users, TFV is closely related to professional judgment, to the economic substance and to the relevance and usefulness for users. Generally, the preparers and the regulators consider that compliance with the law is the most important consideration for giving a TFV. These issues will be developed by an analysis regarding the operationalization of TFV and the TFV override.

TFV Operationalization

The context of TFV is given by the accounting framework (principles, rules) and the role of different actors in this process. We ask ourselves whether the application of OMFP 1752/2005 generates financial statements that give a TFV. The views are contrasting ones. Not surprisingly, R2 thinks that to the extent that companies obey *all* the provisions of the Order, the financial statements prepared give a TFV. Yet, P3 says that companies that do not apply IASs and only prepare financial statements according to Romanian legislation, do not give a TFV, because "there are a number of loopholes, the companies only want to obey the provisions of the law and do not interpret the law, do not apply the law in its spirit." A2 gives some examples of issues to support his opinion that financial statements established according to OMFP 1752/2005 do not give a TFV: lease contracts classification, financial instruments, the accounting treatment for investment properties, employees' benefits, and deferred tax. PB1 adds some more: the use of LIFO and the accounting treatment for buildings bought for resale.

PB2 also considers that financial statements established according to OMFP 1752/2005 do not give a TFV:

> They are false and we cannot talk about accounting in the best interest of the national economy, due to the regulations. We do not have standards, we have regulations. Who issues regulations? It is the State, in its double capacity: regulator and user of its own regulations. It cannot be "clean." The State is only interested in the fiscal duties. [...] We cannot speak therefore about faithfulness. It is only the fiscal image of the company.

Aware of all these issues, A1 considers that financial statements prepared in Romania give a TFV "in respect to the framework used to prepare them" R1 says that many companies actually do not apply the regulations entirely, giving two examples: small companies that do not have the resources to correctly apply the Order to the full, and large but not competitive companies, State-owned, which would have to be declared bankrupt if they applied the Order to the full, yet the State supports them. P3 admits that "it is very difficult to discuss TFV especially for small companies."

As regards the usefulness of financial statements prepared in accordance with OMFP 1752, one of the users we interviewed (U2) thinks that

> Financial statements as prepared under Romanian requirements are of medium use for the needs of a potential investor. Not only is the format difficult to read, but they do not allow for the flexibility of changing it, should there exist a significant change in the nature of the entity's operations that would require it. Also, due to their format and a strict allocation of accounts, these financial statements do not allow for separate presentation in case of material items that would require such a thing.

The restriction U2 posits seems to be correct. Para. 17 of OMFP 1752/2005 states as follows:

> The layout, the sequence and the terminology of items of the balance sheet and of the income statement, preceded by Arab numbers[6] must be adapted if the nature of

> the business' activities so requires. These changes must be made only when required by special regulations issued by regulation authorities.

Two points in particular follow from this. First, flexibility is explicitly not delegated to the level of the individual entity. Second, however, this restriction could be removed, by definition, by application of the "true and fair over-ride" made explicit in paragraphs 10 and 11 as quoted in the third section. U2 seems to discount this possibility. Attitudes toward the TFV override in Romania begin thus to be ascertained, in the light of previous remarks. U2 does not seem to think that TFV can be applied as an override to changing the format (layout) of financial statements prepared in accordance with OMFP 1752/2005. We will refer again to these issues at more length in Subsection "TFV Override."

Regarding the role of different actors in giving a TFV, we consider that the size of the firm and the users it has do matter. The auditors offered the "big picture" of this mechanism:

> Basically, financial statements exist to offer information. Of course, the question is: who is the primary user of this information in Romania? In the Ministry's (of Public Finances, N.A.) opinion, it is the Ministry. Honestly, as they are now conceived, the financial statements in Romania are primarily intended for the use of fiscal authorities. (A2)

> The users' needs are important. If the users are diversified and ask for qualitative information, this quality becomes important; if the company has only one user – the shareholder, he will not be interested in TFV but in the cash it generates. (A1)

We will analyze these statements through the specific context of the three preparers interviewed. P3 works in a company for which "the only users are the owners and the State. They (the owners, N.A.) told us to have this amount of profit, this income tax, and we have to manage with the rest…" As regards the accounting professionals, he says that "they are not very concerned about giving a TFV. It does not matter that what we prepare is irrelevant, because it is actually irrelevant…" P2 works in a large firm, but still fiscal issues and the owner's requirements are very important. Regarding taxation, they consider that fiscal controllers come only to penalize them, and that it is an illegal competition in their sector because small companies do not pay all their taxes or do not record all the wages, thus "stealing" customers and employees away from companies paying taxes. As regards this matter, P3 put it very clearly: "There must be something wrong with the fiscal system if we (accountants, N.A.) are so preoccupied with the fiscal matters, and do not have the time to do anything else."

PB1 considers that the role of auditors matches the role of preparers in providing a TFV, because if accountants and managers may have an incentive of being "biased," the auditor is called to increase the credibility of financial statements. P1 considers that "the role of the auditor is extremely important especially when it's about one of the Big 4. They do not depart from their principles, while Romanian audit companies are more willing to do so." R1 also acknowledged the role of the Big 4, arguing that "banks are audited by one of the Big 4, therefore they prepare more reliable financial statements."

U2 is more moderate as regards the role of auditors, especially in the light of recent scandals:

> It is always the responsibility of the preparer that the financial statements give a TFV. This is more easily achieved where a proper corporate governance structure is in place. The auditor only represents a "second pair of eyes" although recent events worldwide have raised doubts about how "assuring" is this assurance ...

TFV Override

As argued above, TFV override is included in Romanian legislation as it is prescribed in the 4th European Directive. R2 admits that "I know it (the override, N.A.) exists in the Directive, therefore we also took it. We cannot remove it, but probably a very limited number of companies will make use of it; it is to be applied only in extremely exceptional circumstances." Except for A2, all the interviewed people were unaware of examples of TFV override, and each actor has his opinion:

> Preparers: It is very difficult to make the case for an override; therefore I think people stand aside from engaging in a conflict with the fiscal controllers. (P3)
>
> Users: I think that this degree of freedom should be allowed so that judgment can be applied when preparing financial statements. (U2)
>
> Professional bodies: The Ministry of Public Finances still sees the OMFP 1752 as a means to obtain a TFV, as a correct view from the viewpoint of the observance of the provisions of the law. Accordingly, such cases of override are probably seen as inappropriate in respect of their goal. (PB1)

A2 provides some examples of TFV override, because he considers that financial statements prepared in accordance with the regulations (OMFP 1752) do not give a TFV, and the auditors demand adjustments. One example of TFV override is mark-to-market valuation for the shares held by Financial investment entities (ro. Societăţi de Investiţii Imobiliare – SIF). In Romania, only the banks are supposed to apply mark-to-market, but the auditors force such financial investment companies to apply this principle in order not to distort the income statement.

Some interviewees make a distinction as regards the size of the entities. As U1 puts it:

> I have never heard of any such a case. We cannot eliminate this from the regulation, but I think this is only a literal translation of an article from the Directive. I don't think SMEs would ever dare to make use of these provisions. It's a different issue with large entities; they could afford it more easily, as they are large contributors to the State's budget.

Again, it seems to be a difference between companies from the point of view of the auditor when it comes to the override. A2, P3, R1, and PB1 all distinguished between companies audited by Big 4 and the other companies, and to a different extent, they consider that the auditor may influence the accounting policies used, and even impose a TFV override. A2 argued that "Romanian audit companies do not have the authority/force to impose such treatments to the same extent as the Big 4 (they have financial power, prestige)."

Future of TFV

In this context of different perceptions of TFV, we also thought of the future of TFV in Romania. R1 and R2 both confirmed that the concept would be kept in the Romanian legislation, but we asked ourselves if its perception would change and what the potential drivers of this change might be.

PB2 noticed that "We can talk more about TFV now that we have joined the EU." However, A1 insisted that "We have to understand that Romania comes from a period of time (the communist one) when all that was of interest was to "report the over-fulfillment of the plan," not to publish financial information. As long as this way of thinking still exists, TFV will be of little interest." In the same line, PB1 considers that the change will be slow, because "the concept is embedded into the minds of people"; also, when asked during training courses what TFV means, professionals immediately answer "obeying the law" (PB1).

When referring to the change process, A1 considers that it is "pushed by the market." A1, A2, R1, and PB2 agree that "The needs of the users are important," while P1 believes that the "Anglo-Saxon spirit becomes more and more important due to multinational companies" and that "the perception of TFV evolves because of the intent of the preparer." P3 suggests that "If the accountant had more time, he/she would think more about TFV (at least this is what I hope)." However, PB2 thinks that "As long as we have regulations and not standards, we will not have TFV."

Some of the interviewees refer also to a learning process. PB1 considers that the concept should be explained better. Also, as a professional body, Association of Chartered Certified Accountants (ACCA) is considered by the auditors (A2) as having an important role in constraining professionals to think about "the original meaning of the concept." PB2 also insisted on the role of the education in developing competencies related to TFV.

A1 thinks that "A problem is still the fact that users have not protested yet about TFV matters, as there has not been any lawsuit on TFV yet in Romania." PB2 shares the same opinion: "the business environment should make a fuss, the shareholders, as they are mostly affected." A1 believes that "it is a continuous learning process which needs both theory and practice," and it involves shareholders, administrators, auditors, and the regulator. The auditors (especially Big 4) and multinational companies are considered important in this change process by R1, citing the examples of the banking sector and of some big companies where "financial statements are more relevant." Probably, the lack of a powerful enforcement mechanism (in whatever sense this enforcement might be conceived, but certainly not in a "formal" manner) might explain this lack of interest of companies in preparing financial statements which give a TFV. Coercive enforcements bodies exist across Europe (Nobes & Parker, 2008, p. 190) and in countries of Anglo-Saxon culture, yet an efficient enforcement process does not exist in Romania.

DISCUSSION AND CONCLUSION

We aimed in this chapter to examine the transfer of a concept issued in one culture to a different setting, featuring different characteristics from the one in which the concept appeared. In the second section we developed the chapter's theoretical framework, based on the concept of intersubjective construction through collective intentionality. The argument is that most "facts" are socially constructed by general agreement across an epistemic community and, whilst they are indeed generally accepted as "facts" within that community, this acceptance is not universal either across space (different communities) or across time (the same community over different periods). We illustrated this idea by reference to language, to the notion of intertranslatability, and to harmonization. In the third section we reported in detail on perceptions regarding the "case study" of the introduction of "TFV" in Romania. We now draw the strands together and discuss implications.

Romania has a code law system with an obvious preference for the legal form; all the interviewees tentatively agreed that this is the current situation in Romania. This way of thinking may even alter the implementation (use) of IFRSs, an auditor mentioning that these standards are applied in Romania in a "rule-based" not in a "principle-based" approach.

The translation of TFV (signifier) apparently does not influence the perception of different actors (signifieds). This perception depends firstly on the category (auditor, preparer etc.), while other factors such as personal education[7] also impact. For auditors, professional bodies and users, TFV is a guide or a vital concept, closely related to substance over form, relevance and usefulness for users. For regulators and preparers, TFV is primarily compliance with the rules. If a company has other users than the State, some more attention will be paid to the image given by the financial statements (as regards the selection of accounting policies, the additional information disclosed). In this context, even though TFV override is allowed by the Romanian legislation, interviewed preparers argue they have never used it because (mainly) of the fiscal controllers. Also, TFV override is for regulators something exceptional; and since in their opinion the law encapsulates all the possible circumstances, it is somehow inconceivable for them to find justification for this situation. Only an auditor for one of the Big 4 indicated some examples of TFV override, where the auditor demanded some adjustments because he considered that the provisions of the law did not result in the giving of a TFV.[8]

It was a general idea (except for the regulator) that financial statements prepared according to the provisions of OMFP 1752 give a fiscal image, and that they are conceived for a single user – the State, thus not giving a TFV. Two sets of rules contribute to this situation: rules that impede the giving of a TFV (usually the preparers and auditors consider that the IFRS treatment is more appropriate – such as for financial instruments, investment property, provisions), and rules which are applied in a fiscal manner (examples given by the interviewees were lease contracts, methods used for the assets' depreciation, adjustments for inventories or customers, revaluation of assets). Some blame the regulators, others blame the accountants because they do not use their professional judgment, while a third group blamed was the users (and their lack of pressures). Accordingly, it is hoped that users would become a significant driver of the change in the perception of TFV in Romania, followed by education, in order to develop the abilities to make estimates or to use professional judgment. Given the changes in the economic environment, it is expected that the perceptions (signified) will change.

In the second section we argued, with supporting references, that "intertranslatability" cannot be assumed to work successfully. We suggest that the detailed investigations reported on, in the third section, provide a practical example in the accounting sphere of these general propositions. A concept (TFV) conceived in a broadly Anglo-Saxon common law environment where the major purpose of financial reporting is the capitalist investor, and adopted and adapted in a variety of international contexts, has been taken over, de jure, in a rather piecemeal and unclear way as described in detail above. Various players have grappled with the task of coming to terms with its inclusion in national requirements (or of rationalizing why it can be ignored). By interviewing key players from a number of different fields relating to the accounting function, we provide evidence that, within their own functional communities, nested within the complexities of Romania as a country in a time of continuous change, there is difference of view and disagreement in a number of important respects. We do not find this surprising. Players who have different purposes for accounting information will perceive an imposed new concept in different ways.

The concept is not well "intertranslatable" from its external origins. The successive waves of reforms with French, British-IASs, and finally European Directives influences had, in our opinion, a small influence on the perception of TFV in Romania. The signifier was included in Romanian legislation in 1991 and did not change, while the code law accounting system marked TFV as being compliance with the rules (signified). However, the actors and their power (users and Big 4 auditors) involved in the accounting process may influence (and in time, change) this perception. For the time being, the accountant is not perceived (not even by himself/herself) as a driver of change regarding the image given by the financial statements.

Given the complexity of the accounting reform, however, there is no wonder in this context that Romanian accountants do not seem enthusiastic about departing from an accounting provision in order to give a TFV! Auditors (especially one of the Big 4) are more likely to demand such a departure as they would feel it necessary in order to give a TFV by Romanian companies. All this discussion may raise serious questions as to the success of the full transfer of the TFV concept to Romania. In the terminology used in the second section, we find considerable support for the proposition that TFV and the Romanian reporting practice relate to different socially constructed conceptual schemes, and that "intertranslatability" between these schemes is problematic.

We also show very clearly here that speakers of *the same* language, when faced with TFV as a new concept, interpret this accounting concept in different ways which appear to be influenced by their role in relation to the overall accounting function. As we show, our interviewees are largely uninterested in the translation issue, but very involved in the meaning and implications of the concept. This seems to justify our emphasis on concept rather than verbalism in our theoretical exposition. Intertranslatability is therefore suggested here as arising from "conceptual relativism, with language connections" rather than from any "predisposition to particular ways of thinking" *caused* by language differences. Both our theoretical exposition and our empirical findings are consistent with this proposition. In this context, our empirical analysis also provides support for concerns expressed by Zeff (2007) that

> ... if one takes a concept embedded in the accounting traditions in one country but that has never been known or applied in another, even if it is translated as accurately as practicable into the language of the second country, the concept may not be understood. The words may be understood, but the concept may not be understood. (p. 296)

The above discussion is very consistent with the two propositions developed in Subsection "Development of research propositions." Regarding Pr1, in order that accounting harmonization can work, we have to assume the successful transfer of a concept issued in another culture to a different setting, featuring other characteristics than the one in which the concept appeared. If there are different cultural settings, and given that harmonization requires a reduction in differences of interpretation, application and operation, all three of which are strongly culturally influenced, then harmonization can only be achieved by a successful transfer across those cultural settings. To put the point the other way round, if transfer from one cultural setting to a different one "featuring other characteristics" cannot be achieved, then effective operational harmonization will not occur. Through our Romanian-based research we have shown that the historical cultural context for TFV (the UK and related countries) is very significantly different from that of Romania, and that harmonization regarding TFV is generally rejected, that is, the transfer has not "worked."[9] The inclusion of TFV in the "Romanian legislation" is clearly shown. The override inclusion is, strictly, not so clear and absolute as it should be, being explicit in the (inferior) Order, but not in the (superior) Law. But we have argued nevertheless that its de jure requirement is definitive. However, the de facto position is another matter.

The "translation" of the original UK-based TFV concept in the Romanian setting, via the European Directives, has resulted in the inclusion of all TFV provisions present in the European legislation (de jure), but the practical application of these provisions is remote from the original approach (de facto). The regulators interviewed, who of course represent, or are themselves, the creators of all OMFPs (including 1752 and its successor), see no problems or inconsistencies between its detailed requirements and their operationalization, and TFV. But the general picture given by the other interviewees points very much in the opposite direction. A whole series of quotations and summarized responses in the Section "TFV operationalization" suggest that the overall content of the Order produces financial statements which are aimed at the achievement of purposes which are not consistent with a TFV. Indeed, in some cases, the comments explicitly suggest that the Order was designed and created, by the Ministry of Public Finances, in full knowledge that it would NOT give a TFV in the investor-relevant sense of its origins, or of the philosophy of IASB and the Fourth Directive. This evidence supports the de facto proposition of Pr1.

There is an important difference between Pr2 and Pr1, in that the latter is conceived in the present tense, while the former is oriented toward the future. The issue with Pr2, given the conclusions to Pr1, is whether or not relevant actors can change their perception of, and operationalization of, the various regulations. Such change would require motivation, opportunity and competence. Motivation could come from the regulator (which seems unlikely here) or from users (also apparently not, according to several comments in the third section). Opportunity is again crucially dependent on regulators and tax authorities (i.e., on the Ministry of Public Finances in one form or another), and also perhaps on owners/management being willing to pay the costs of a properly achieved subjective preparation and appraisal of market-relevant information. Competence is harder to evaluate, but one can "read between the lines," and suggest that an international qualification, such as ACCA, or international experience such as would be acquired by an extended period of work with a "Big 4" firm, is likely to be a necessary input in the general case. Overall, the implications are that Pr2 be accepted as a valid summary of the situation.

The above analysis suggests important policy-related conclusions. To summarize, using phrases developed in the second section of the chapter:

- significant moves toward harmonization require effective concept transferability;

- the existence of significantly different socially constructed conceptual schemes, in different cultural contexts, is a significant barrier to concept transferability;
- our empirical interviews in the Romanian case study provide strong evidence of a failure of concept transferability regarding TFV;
- further, and going beyond the Evans (2004, p. 239) conclusion quoted in the second section, there is some evidence of a local *assumption* of successful concept transfer, especially by the (very powerful) regulators. This is doubly dangerous: ignorance of failure is much worse than recognized failure.

The implications of our findings are of general significance, well beyond the country-based scenario of our in-depth research. First, similar issues and difficulties are likely to arise in other similar (emerging) countries.

Second, Romania is a transitional economy more influenced than many by a legalistic code-law tradition common in many European (and perhaps South American) countries. An assumption of a more-or-less automatic supremacy of detailed regulations and an expectation of detailed instructions (found also, e.g., in the Chinese standards "adopting" IFRS) is a wide-spread phenomenon. Again, there are likely, and researchable, implications for the adoption of an IFRS way of thinking (whether or not linked also with EU Directives).

Our conclusion on the intertranslatability question is clearcut. This is that intertranslatability cannot be assumed. This is not just true in itself as a language issue, despite the significant implications (problems?) for conceptual relativism and the existence of different conceptual schemes. It is true *because of* conceptual relativism and the existence of different schemes. Our in-depth analysis is seen to present potentially generalizable important issues, worthy of extension and development elsewhere.

NOTES

1. The word is surely tautological. "Inter" means between (two things) and "trans" means across (between two things). We continue to use it for consistency.
2. Romania's latest accounting regulation is OMFP 3055/2009, applicable starting January 1, 2010. No significant changes were noted in this regulation with regard to TFV. More, since the new regulation is still in its first years of use, the perceptions based on the provisions of OMFP 1752/2005 are still valid.

3. This is in line with Alexander (1993) and Burlaud (1993), translating "image fidèle" by "faithful image."

4. For a detailed explanation regarding these concepts, see Alexander (1993) and Burlaud (1993). For the purpose of this chapter, we mention two ideas of these studies: (1) In France, "régularité et sincérité" existed in the national regulations before the 4th European Directive enactment, which simply added a third concept, "image fidèle"; (2) for some, régularité et sincérité means TFV, but the authors agree that there are cases in which régularité et sincérité are not sufficient to give a TFV, so régularité et sincérité do not automatically result in giving a TFV. It should be emphasised that our English words, regularity and sincerity, as used here, are literal translations of concepts only understandable in their native context.

5. There are significant differences between United States, UK, Australia, New Zealand, etc., although these countries are generally considered as Anglo-Saxon accounting culture.

6. Such articles are, for example, types of current or noncurrent assets etc.

7. Some of the interviewees mentioned an international-based education (ACCA etc.), while others were not even familiar with the English origin version of the concept (i.e., "true and fair view").

8. These findings are in line with those of Sucher et al. (1996), in that they also document in the Czech Republic differences in the significance of TFV between initiators, users and preparers of financial statements.

9. This situation is very clearly illustrated by the motto opening the chapter: although Romania (or any other country) has removed its dictator at the fall of communism, the mentality would take much more time to change. Implications for the accounting setting are obvious.

ACKNOWLEDGMENTS

The authors wish to thank the anonymous reviewers, participants and discussants of the 30th congress of the Francophone Accounting Association in Strasbourg (May 27–29, 2009), the 11th IAAER World Congress of Accounting Educators and Researchers (November 4–6, 2010), the 32nd congress of the Francophone Accounting Association in Montpellier (May 9–11, 2011), the American Accounting Association's International Accounting Section 17th Annual Mid-Year Conference, Tampa, January 26–28, 2011, and Lisa Evans, George Georgiou, Marek Schreuder, Mădălina Gîrbină, Stere Mihai, and Lavinia Olimid for their useful suggestions and comments. Also, we wish to thank Cornelia Lefter for her in-depth suggestions and advice regarding legal matters in Romania. We thank James Mullen for his thorough review of linguistic matters. All remaining infelicities are the sole responsibility of the authors. The authors acknowledge the financial support from research project CNCSIS-UEFISCSU, project number PNII-RU TE_341/2010.

REFERENCES

Alexander, D. (1993). A European true and fair view? *European Accounting Review*, *2*(1), 59–80.

Alexander, D. (1996). Truer and fairer: Uninvited comments on invited comments. *European Accounting Review*, *5*(3), 483–493.

Alexander, D. (2010). Some personal thoughts on financial reporting. *Accounting and Management Information Systems*, *9*(2), 200–209.

Alexander, D., & Albu, C. N. (2011). Introduction to the special issue on "National Perspectives on International Accounting Harmonization." *Accounting and Management Information Systems*, *10*(2), 102–105.

Alexander, D., & Archer, S. (2003). On economic reality, representational faithfulness and the true and fair override. *Accounting and Business Research*, *33*(1), 3–17.

Alexander, D., & Jermakowicz, E. (2006). A true and fair view of the principles/rules debate. *Abacus*, *42*(2), 132–164.

Alexander, D., & Nobes, C. (2010). *Financial accounting: An international introduction* (4th ed.). Harlow: Prentice Hall.

Archer, S., & McLeay, S. (1991). Issues in transnational financial reporting: A linguistic analysis. *Journal of Multi-Lingual and Multicultural Development*, *12*(5), 347–361.

Bailey, D. (1995). Accounting in transition in the transitional economy. *European Accounting Review*, *4*(4), 595–623.

Baker, C. R., & Barbu, E. M. (2007). Trends in research on international accounting harmonization. *The International Journal of Accounting*, *42*, 272–304.

Belkaoui, A. (1978). Linguistic relativity in accounting. *Accounting, Organizations and Society*, *3*(2), 97–104.

Belkaoui, A. (1989). Accounting and language. *Journal of Accounting Literature*, *8*, 281–292.

Bradshaw, M. T., & Miller, G. S. (2008). Will harmonizing accounting standards really harmonize accounting? Evidence from Non-U.S. firms adopting U.S. GAAP. *Journal of Accounting, Auditing & Finance*, *23*(2), 233–263.

Burlaud, A. (1993). Commentary on the article by David Alexander 'A European true and fair view'. *European Accounting Review*, *2*(1), 95–98.

Chastney, J. (1975). *True and fair view – History, meaning and the impact of the fourth directive*. Research Committee Occasional Paper No. 6. Institute of Chartered Accountants in England and Wales, London.

Colasse, B. (1997). The French notion of the image fidèle: The power of words. *European Accounting Review*, *6*(4), 681–691.

Collett, P. H., Godfrey, J. M., & Hrasky, S. L. (2001). International harmonization: Cautions from the Australian experience. *Accounting Horizons*, *15*(2), 171–182.

Cook, A. (1997). Requirement for a true and fair view – A UK standard-setter's perspective. *European Accounting Review*, *6*(4), 693–704.

Davidson, D. (1974). On the very idea of a conceptual scheme. *Proceedings and addresses of the American Philosophical Association, 47, 5–20.* Reprinted in Inquiries into truth and interpretation (1984, pp. 183–198); OUP, Oxford.

Delesalle, F. E., & Delesalle, E. (2000). *La comptabilité et les dix commandements.* Paris: Fid édition.

Doupnik, T. S., & Richter, M. (2002). Interpretation of uncertainty expressions: A cross-national study. *Accounting, Organizations and Society*, *28*(1), 15–35.

Evans, L. (2004). Language, translation and the problem of international accounting communication. *Accounting, Auditing & Accountability Journal*, *17*(2), 210–248.

Evans, L., Baskerville, R., & Nara, K. (2010). *Translation and its problems: An interprofessional perspective and lessons for accounting*. Working paper submitted to APIRA, Sydney.

Feleagă, L., Feleagă, N., & Dragomir, V. D. (2009). National standards and European accounting harmonization: Twenty years of scientific literature in review. *European Journal of Management*, *9*(2), 10–21.

Guggiola, G. (2010). IFRS adoption in the E.U., Accounting harmonization and markets efficiency: A review. *International Business & Economics Research Journal*, *9*(12), 99–112.

Hamiton, G., & ÓhÓgartaigh, C. (2009). The third policeman: 'The true and fair view', language and the habitus of accounting. *Critical Perspectives on Accounting*, *20*, 910–920.

Haried, A. A. (1972). The semantic dimension of financial statements. *Journal of Accounting Research*, *10*(2), 376–391.

Haried, A. A. (1973). Measurement of meaning in financial reports. *Journal of Accounting Research*, *11*(1), 117–145.

Herrmann, D., & Thomas, W. (1995). Harmonization of accounting measurement practices in the European community. *Accounting and Business Research*, *25*(100), 253–265.

Kelly, L. G. (1994). Translatability: Limits. In R. E. Asher & J. M. Y. Simpson (Eds.), *The encyclopedia of language and linguistics* (Vol. 9), Oxford: Pergamon Press.

Kirk, N. (2006). Perceptions of the true and fair view concept: An empirical investigation. *Abacus*, *42*(2), 205–235.

Kosmala-MacLullich, K. (2003). The true and fair view in the context of the Polish transition economy: Some local insights. *European Accounting Review*, *12*(3), 465–487.

Kosmala, K. (2005). True and fair view or rzetelny i jasny obraz? A survey of Polish Practitioners. *European Accounting Review*, *14*(3), 579–602.

Larson, R. K., & Street, D. L. (2004). Convergence with IFRS in an expanding Europe: Progress and obstacles identified by large accounting firms' survey. *Journal of Accounting, Auditing and Taxation*, *13*, 89–119.

Lyas, C. (1993). Accounting and language. In M. J. Mumford & K. V. Peasnell (Eds.), *Philosophical perspectives on accounting. Essays in honour of Edward Stamp*. London: Routledge.

Matiş, D., Strouhal, J. & Bonaci, C. G. (2009). Regulators and regulations for financial instruments in the context of financial crisis – Two emergent countries' point of view. *Accounting in Emerging Economies, Volume 9 of the book series: Research in Accounting in Emerging Economies*, pp. 345–378.

McKernan, J. F. (2007). Objectivity in accounting. *Accounting Organizations and Society*, *32*(1–2), 155–180.

Mechelli, A. (2009). Accounting harmonization and compliance in applying IASB standards: An empirical survey about the first time adoption of IAS 7 by Italian listed groups. *Accounting in Europe*, *6*(2), 231–270.

Mouck, T. (2004). Institutional reality, financial reporting and the rules of the game. *Accounting Organizations and Society*, *29*(5–6), 525–541.

Mustaţă, R., & Matiş, D. (2010). Systems for material harmonization measurement within the changing global accounting environment: A review. *Journal of Organisational Transformation and Social Change*, *7*(1), 47–87.

Nobes, C. W. (2009). The importance of being fair: An analysis of IFRS regulation and practice. *Accounting and Business Research*, *39*(4), 415–427.

Nobes, C., & Parker, R. (2008). *Comparative international accounting* (10th ed.). Harlow: Prentice Hall.
Ordelheide, D. (1993). True and fair view – A European and a German perspective. *European Accounting Review*, *2*(1), 81–90.
Ordelheide, D. (1996). True and fair view – A European and a German perspective II. *European Accounting Review*, *5*(3), 495–506.
Paler, O. (1995). *Vremea întrebărilor (A time to question)*. Ed. Albatros, Ed. Universal Dalsi.
Roberts, A. (2000). The recent Romanian accounting reforms: another case of cultural intrusion? In Y. Kalyuzhnova & M. Taylor (Eds.), *Transitional economies: Banking, finance, institutions* (pp. 146–166). Basingstoke: Palgrave.
Searle, J. R. (1995). *The construction of social reality*. London: Penguin Group.
Searle, J. R. (2006a). *What is language: Some preliminary remarks*. Retrieved from http://socrates.berkeley.edu/~jsearle/whatislanguage.pdf
Searle, J. R. (2006b). Social ontology. *Anthropological Theory*, *6*(1), 12–29.
Shapiro, B. P. (1997). Objectivity, relativism, and truth in external financial reporting: What's really at stake in the disputes? *Accounting Organizations and Society*, *22*(2), 165–185.
Shapiro, B. P. (1998). Toward a normative model of rational argumentation for critical accounting discussions. *Accounting, Organizations and Society*, *23*(7), 641–663.
Sucher, P., Seal, W., & Zelenka, I. (1996). True and fair view in the Czech Republic: A note on local perceptions. *European Accounting Review*, *5*(3), 545–557.
Vellam, I. (2004). Implementation of international accounting standards in Poland: Can true convergence be achieved in practice? *Accounting in Europe*, *1*, 143-167.
Walton, P. (1991). The true and fair view: A shifting concept. ACCA Occasional Paper No. 7, Chartered Association of Certified Accountants, London.
Walton, P. (1993). Introduction: the true and fair view in British accounting. *European Accounting Review*, *1*, 49–58.
Walton, P. (1997). The true and fair view and the drafting of the Fourth Directive. *European Accounting Review*, *6*(4), 721–730.
Zeff, S. (2007). Some obstacles to global financial reporting comparability and convergence at a high level of quality. *The British Accounting Review*, *39*, 290–302.

FURTHER READING

Fourth Council Directive of 25 July 1978, on the annual accounts of certain types of companies (78/660/CEE), as published on January 1, 2007 as a result of Romania and Bulgaria adhering to the European Union, European Union Official Journal, L 222, 14.8.1978, p. 11.
Accounting Law no. 82/1991, Official Journal of Romania no. 265/27.12.1991, revised, Official Journal no. 454/18.06.2008.
Order of the Minister of Public Finances no. 1752/2005 for the approval of accounting regulations in accordance with the European Directives, Official Journal of Romania, no. 1080 bis/30.11.2005.
Order of the Minister of Public Finances no. 3055/2009 for the approval of accounting regulations in accordance with the European Directives, Official Journal of Romania, no. 766 bis/10.XI.2009.

APPENDIX – LIST AND DETAILS OF INTERVIEWS

	Category	Abbreviation	Duration	Date
1.	Preparer	P1	50 min.	November 28, 2008
2.	Preparer	P2	70 min.	December 1, 2008
3.	Preparer	P3	45 min.	December 12, 2008
4.	Auditor	A1	60 min.	December 3, 2008
5.	Auditor	A2	60 min.	December 16, 2008
6.	Regulator	R1	60 min.	November 26, 2008
7.	Regulator	R2	45 min.	December 10, 2008
8.	Representative of the Chamber of Financial Auditors of Romania (Camera Auditorilor din România)	PB1	75 min.	November 26, 2008
9.	Representative of the Body of Expert and Licensed Accountants of Romania (Corpul Experţilor Contabili şi Contabililor Autorizaţi din România)	PB2	50 min.	December 22, 2008
10.	User	U1	50 min.	August 10, 2009
11.	User	U2	60 min.	August 20, 2009

INSTITUTIONAL PRESSURES AND THE ROLE OF THE STATE IN DESIGNING THE FINANCIAL ACCOUNTING AND REPORTING MODEL IN ESTONIA

Lehte Alver, Jaan Alver and Liis Talpas

ABSTRACT

Purpose – *The chapter shows how globalization and the IFRSs have affected the development of financial accounting and reporting in Estonia. This is interpreted through institutional theory.*

Design/methodology/approach – *The theoretical framework takes into account the prior papers published using institutional theory for defining pressures affecting the development of financial reporting model. The discussion part is presented in three sub-sections. Coercive institutional pressure is analyzed using Estonian accounting legislation from 1990–2012 and normative pressure by focusing on the impact of Big 4 audit companies in the Estonian context. The authors also give an overview of mimetic institutional pressures. As a methodological technique literature review and document analysis are used.*

Accounting in Central and Eastern Europe
Research in Accounting in Emerging Economies, Volume 13, 91–120

ISSN: 1479-3563/doi:10.1108/S1479-3563(2013)0000013009

Findings – *In the context of coercive institutional pressure the development of accounting legislation in Estonia has been mostly influenced by the IFRSs and European Union. In the light of recent events it seems that Estonia has the opportunity to follow its own way deciding which accounting principles should be applied to SMEs. Mimetic institutional pressure affecting Estonian accounting system is International Accounting Standards Board (IASB), which practices Estonian Accounting Standards Board (EASB) copies. Normative institutional pressures influencing the development of the Estonian accounting system are the Big 4 audit firms.*

Originality/value – *Although using institutional theory to interpret the development of financial reporting framework is not new its application is underexplored in the context of post-Soviet countries such as Estonia. The chapter potentially contributes to the accounting reforms evidence in emerging economies.*

Keywords: Estonian accounting system; reporting system; institutional theory; coercive, normative and mimetic institutional pressures

INTRODUCTION

Estonia is a country in the Baltic Region of Northern Europe. It covers an area of 45,200 km^2. The population is about 1.3 million. Estonia has an impressively transparent governance system, where government decisions are almost instantly made available on the Internet. Estonia has a modern market-based economy since the end of 1990s and one of the highest per capita income levels in Eastern Europe. Proximity to the Scandinavian markets, location between the East and West, competitive cost structure and skilled labour force has been the major Estonian comparative advantages in the beginning of the 2000s. Tallinn as the largest city has emerged as a financial centre and the Tallinn Stock Exchange joined recently with the OMX system. The current government has pursued relatively sound fiscal policies, resulting in balanced budgets and low public debt. Nowadays the most important branches of Estonia's economy are food, construction, and electronic industries. The predecessor of Tallinn Stock Exchange was established in 1920 and liquidated in 1941. In 1995 the Tallinn Stock Exchange was established again and the first transactions started on May 31, 1996. From 2008 Tallinn Stock Exchange is a member of NASDAQ

OMX. Estonia is a member of WTO since November 13, 1999. Estonia became a NATO member state on March 29, 2004 and a European Union (EU) member state on May 1, 2004. From January 1, 2011 euro is the official currency in Estonia.

In the context of accounting Estonia is one of the less-known states in Europe. Until the beginning of the 20th century, there is very little information about accounting in Estonia. This is quite apparent considering that there is practically no accounting-related academic literature even in the local level in the Estonian language. Few authors publishing about Estonian accounting issues include Alver, Alver, Mackevičius, Paupa, and Bailey (1998), Alver, Alver, Mackevičius, and Paupa (2001), Alver and Alver (2009), Haldma (2001, 2003, 2006), Tikk (2010), and Bailey (1995).

The Estonian accounting regulation has only a relatively brief history compared to those of some other European countries. One reason was the constant changing of conquerors, all of whom exerted influence on Estonian history in every respect, including accounting. The Russian Revolution of 1917 gave Estonia the opportunity for freedom and the Republic of Estonia was proclaimed on February 24, 1918. The first period of independence lasted 22 years. Estonia underwent a number of economic, social, and political reforms necessary to come to terms with its new status as a sovereign state. During 1918–1940 the czarist *Russian Commercial Code* regulated all areas of business activities in the independent Republic of Estonia, including accounting and taxation. This law was in force since 1834. The Code established the classification of enterprises, the books of accounting records, which each enterprise had to keep and the general accounting requirements. According to the Code all enterprises were classified as big, medium, and small. The number of obligatory books were established and named by the Code. The Code also described how to document and record business transactions, how to make corrections, and retain the books. Correct keeping of accounting records (books) was very important. The main shortcomings of the Russian Commercial Code were as following. Due to its longevity the Code was outdated. The bookkeeping requirements were set up for trading companies, but not for industrial enterprises. Many of the obligatory accounting books mentioned in the Code were not used in the real life. The most important law from this period (in force from January 1, 1926) was indisputable the Law of Golden Balances establishing the valuation principles for securities, inventories and tangible fixed assets. The second law in force from 1935 was the Law of Language for Business Enterprises. From 1935 it became obligatory to keep books in Estonian language only. Unfortunately the prepared

Bill of the Law of Accounting was not enacted during the first Republic of Estonia.

The independence was lost after incorporating Estonia into Soviet Union (USSR) in 1940, and in fact after the World War II, the Soviet system of bookkeeping was in use. From 1945 until 1990 the Soviet influence on accounting development was obvious, because Estonia was a part of the USSR and accounting in Estonia was a part of the Soviet accounting system.

Estonia regained independence in 1991 after the collapse of the USSR. The transition from command economy to market economy had a huge impact on a great number of aspects in business society, and thus also on accounting. The old bookkeeping system with detailed rules serving the primary task of controlling that the national economic plans were fulfilled was replaced by an accounting system with the primary task of preparing financial reports to the market, but also to give information to management for decision making.

Nations all around the world are following the fast pace convergence of national Generally Accepted Accounting Principles (GAAP) with that of the International Financial Reporting Standards (IFRSs). This convergence is mostly influenced by globalization as countries worldwide have been striving for the same purposes – to increase their economic growth and to improve the welfare of their residents. These aims are mainly pursued by developing countries, including Estonia. To achieve these aims, Estonia has opened its market to multinational corporations, has joined the international economic associations and developed a more transparent approach in its accounting principles to adapt to the demands of international financial markets. To accomplish this Estonia has adjusted its GAAP to IFRSs. Some authors, for example, Fontes, Rodrigues, and Craig (2005) in Portugal, Al-Omari (2010) in Jordan and Irvine (2008) in the United Arab Emirates (the UAE), have also noted that countries around the world are converging their national standards with that of the IFRSs. But the post-IFRS experience of emerging economies has been diverse. According to Albu and Albu (2012), some implementations have reportedly been relatively successful (see, e.g., Peng & van der Laan Smith, 2010 in the case of China; Boolaky, 2010 for Mauritius; and Chamisa, 2000, for Zimbabwe) but others have been less so because of noncompliance with the standards, or have even ended in failure (see, e.g., Mir & Rahaman, 2005 with regard to Kuwait and Pakistan).

One can argue that globalization is one of the lead factors affecting countries worldwide to adopt IFRSs, especially developing countries.

Globalization has been defined by Granell (2000) as "a worldwide pressure to change," by Stiglitz (2001) as the "closer integration of the countries and peoples of the world" and is also interpreted by Irvine (2008) as "a universal process of institutionalization that both relies on and results in greater interdependence between economies, political systems, culture and societies." As globalization has been considered one of the many factors that have had a considerable influence on many countries worldwide to adopt IFRSs, then according to prior studies, (Barbu & Baker, 2010; Al-Omari, 2010), some can perceive the convergence of IFRSs as the development of new worldwide institution, which has achieved great legitimacy among developing countries and also in international level.

The purpose of this chapter is to show how the globalization and IFRSs have affected the development of financial accounting and reporting in Estonia. This is interpreted through institutional theory. Although using institutional theory to interpret factors affecting the development of financial reporting framework is not new, its application is underexplored in the context of post-Soviet countries such as Estonia. Therefore, in the literature review the authors give an overview of the theoretical framework taking into account the prior papers published that have used institutional theory in their research for defining pressures affecting the development of financial reporting model. The discussion part is presented in three sub-sections, divided between coercive, normative, and mimetic institutional pressures. This is followed by the concluding remarks. The chapter potentially contributes to the accounting reforms evidence in emerging economies, its progresses and obstacles. This analysis is important to understand pressures affecting the development if financial reporting system in emerging countries such as Estonia and take the possible influences into account when developing new accounting legislation in the future. Therefore, the possible future directions regarding accounting in Estonia are discussed briefly using also institutional theory.

METHODOLOGY AND THEORETICAL FRAMEWORK

The authors have analyzed the coercive institutional pressure based on the Estonian accounting legislation from 1990 till 2012 and have divided the integration of Estonian financial accounting and reporting system into the international framework into three stages: (1) introductory stage that (1990–1994), (2) system building stage (1995–2002), and (3) system improving stage (since 2003). Following, the authors have focused to the analysis of normative institutional pressure taking into account the impact Big 4 auditing companies have in the Estonian context. Finally, the authors give an overview of mimetic institutional pressures affecting accounting and reporting system in Estonia. As a methodological technique literature review and document analysis are used in all the three subsections. For collecting examples and reactions to the changes in Estonia in light of the three institutional pressures, among other things the doctoral thesis and papers written by the Estonian researchers have been used.

LITERATURE REVIEW

The integrity and usefulness of an institutional approach to explain and interpret accounting activities in an international level has been acknowledged by many authors (Albu, Albu, Bunea, Calu, & Gîrbină, 2011; Al-Omari, 2010; Baker & Rennie, 2006; Barbu & Baker, 2010; Barbu, Farcane, & Popa, 2012; Irvine, 2008; Judge, Li, & Pinsker, 2010; Kury, 2007; Mezias & Scarselletta, 1994). For example, American neoinstitutional theorist Richard Scott defined institutionalization as "the process by which actions are repeated and given similar meaning by self and others." Sometimes actions are repeated because explicit rules or laws exist to ensure their repetition (*legal and political influences*), sometimes activity patterns are supported by norms, values, and expectations (*cultural influences*), sometimes by desire and to be or look like another institution (*social influences*) (Hatch, 1997). The institutional approach emphasizes the importance of institutions, as well as such related phenomena as rules, habits, routines, norms, and culture. This theoretical framework is useful to understand accounting change because it "pays attention to history, to the evolution of institutions and to the causal factors of social change" (Albu et al., 2011). Therefore, the institutional theory represents a valuable framework to explain the country-specific factors affecting the development of financial accounting and reporting in Estonia, as an interplay between practices, routines, and institutions.

American sociologists Powell and DiMaggio (1983) distinguish between three different institutional pressures and give them distinctive labels. They argue that when the pressure to conform comes from governmental regulations or laws, then *coercive institutional pressures* are at work. Coercive institutional pressures in this concept involve the capacity to establish rules, inspect others to conformity to them, and, as necessary, manipulate sanctions – rewards or punishments – in attempt to influence future behavior (Scott, 2001).

When an economy is relatively small and poor, for example, developing, it is more dependent on international norms and standards than when the economy is relatively large and wealthy. Arguably, the mechanism most used by international nongovernmental organizations to coercively bring about change within a national economy is foreign aid. There is some previous accounting literature to support the impact of coercive institutions on the adoption of international standards. For example, Touron (2005) argued that coercive isomorphism was predictive of adoption of the US GAAP by French firms in the 1970s due to domination of the global economy by the United States at the time. Furthermore, Hassan (2008) found that external coercive pressures from foreign aid provided by the IMF were influential in Egypt's moving toward the adoption of the IFRSs. (Judge et al., 2010)

Irvine (2008) and Barbu and Baker (2010) observe the International Accounting Standards Board (IASB) as one of the coercive pressures encouraging the countries around the world to adopt the IFRSs. Others believe that implementation of IFRSs in developing economies may help to increase the trust in the accounting information, to attract new investors and resources. Ruder, Canfield, and Hollister (2005) state that the fact that various economic systems are converging around IFRS, although there are considerable variations between countries in their accounting standards and practices. This convergence around a worldwide set of standards has important implications for national corporate governance practices, including Estonian. Judge et al. (2010) seek to identify what might be the institutional predictors of adoption of international accounting standards. Using archival data from 132 nations, they find relatively robust support for the institutional perspective on the adoption of the IFRSs. Notably, the comparison of institutional variables (i.e., level of foreign aid, import penetration, the relative education level within a nation) with the cultural and legal variables identified by the previous literature (Ding, Jeanjean, & Stolowy, 2005; Hope, Jin, & Kang, 2006) shows the institutional variables are more robust in predicting IFRS adoption. (Judge et al., 2010)

Powell and DiMaggio (1983) take a narrower approach to coercive institutional pressure and observe that as conglomerate corporations increase in size and scope, it is common for subsidiaries to be subject to standardized reporting mechanisms. Subsidiaries most adopt accounting practices, performance evaluations, and budgetary plans that are compatible with the policies of the parent corporation. For example, what accounts receivable should be discounted for in the balance sheet or what accounting principles should be used when accounting for inventories. This leads to a pressure on companies in two ways – first, the prepared financial statements have to meet the demands of the parent company, who perhaps prepares the financial statements according to IFRS, and second, the subsidiary has to prepare the financial statements according to local GAAP.

When the pressure comes from cultural expectations, for instance via the professional training of organizational members, then according to Powell and DiMaggio (1983) *normative institutional pressures* are at work. Normative systems are typically viewed as imposing constraints (Scott, 2001). For example, the World Bank requirement that projects financed by the bank be "certified by internationally reputable firms of accountants" has aided in the proliferation of the international operations of the Big 4 international accounting firms (Irvine, 2008). Al-Omari (2010) also views the Big 4 accounting firms under normative institutional pressure as these companies play a profound role in the globalization of accounting and represent the normative pressures that effect organizations and the choices they make in accordance to their reporting and practices implemented. Other authors have also researched the influences of the Big 4 accounting firms on the preparation of the financial statements. Although this analysis has not been made in the context of institutional theory, they can still be used to assess the influences of Big 4 accounting companies to the development of accounting practices. Therefore, one can argue that the Big 4 accounting firms play a profound role in the globalization of accounting and represent the normative pressures that effect organizations and the choices they make in accordance to their reporting and practices implemented (Al-Omari, 2010). In Estonia, where the Big 4 auditing firms make up to 88% of the total revenue produced by 10 largest auditing firms (Vetevoog, 2009), one can certainly apprehend the pressure from Big 4 auditing firms to prepare the annual reports according to their standards. Chand (2005) believes that the Big 4 companies are endowed with an effective presence in the world capital market, and are considered to be one of the many international forces behind the process and advancement of harmonization of accounting standards.

Most analyses conducted in respect of Big 4 auditing companies compare the audit quality of Big 4 auditing firms and other auditing firms. For example, in the United States, the investigation showed that the quality of audits conducted by Big 4 auditing firms depends on the size of the operations of client. Because the bigger client gets more public attention, the risk of getting sued increases for the auditing firm. Lawrence, Minutti, and Zhang (2007) state that when Big 4 and non-Big 4 companies audit a client with similar size, the differences in audit quality disappear. Consistent with prior research is also the analysis of Reynolds and Francis (2000) which outlays the fact that the Big 4 companies report more conservatively when it comes to bigger clients. They explain this phenomenon with the fact that with this kind of behavior, the Big 4 companies try to protect their reputation.

Simunic (1980) argues that the accounting services provided by different accounting firms are perceived by investors to be different in quality, with brand name auditors (currently Big 4 auditors) perceived as being more credible than others. In line with this argument, Becker, DeFond, Jiambalvo, and Subramanyam (1998) and Francis, Maydew, and Sparks (1999) have noticed that owing to their superior knowledge and reputation capital, brand name auditors conduct higher-quality audits. This is supported by a study issued by the General Accounting Office (GAO) of the United States that corroborates the essential aspects in terms of Big 4 audit outcome. The Big 4 audit opinion serves as an effective quality label, whereas most of the second-tier firms are not able to bid successfully for large because of a lack of industry knowledge, geographic pressure and reputation. According to Gray and Ratzinger (2010), the GAO argues that a Big 4 audit report is characterized by a distinctive quality label, and therefore contains credible and high quality information.

Gray and Ratzinger (2010) further researched whether there are differences between the Big 4 firms in particularly, how their national offices might interpret some specific accounting (GAAP) or auditing (GAAS) question. In a later focus group, an auditor pointed out that there are frequent conversations between representatives of the different Big 4 firms that results in a convergence of their interpretations. For example, when some new accounting or auditing issue arises, that will prompt discussions between the firms. She went on to say that the firms are fairly open in discussing their audit methodologies, so that the methodologies used by the firms are constantly evolving over time. However, the auditors agreed that the differences in interpretations become wider when Big 4 and non-Big 4 firms are compared (Gray & Ratzinger, 2010). The authors are in the opinion of that the cooperation of Big 4 companies indicates that the financial statements audited by them may therefore be drafted even more according to their regulations. Sawers (2007) believes that this is why British Financial Reporting Council has actively reacted against the dominance of Big 4 auditing firms and has orientated itself in the international level toward increasing the likelihood of major "public interest entities" selecting non-Big 4 auditors.

Mezias and Scarselletta (1994) and Barbu and Baker (2010) think that in the United States, professional accountants constitute examples of normative isomorphism "with a common culture, in the sense of shared definitions of problems and common repertoires for managing those problems." Therefore, participants in accounting policymaking might exhibit high levels of shared knowledge and beliefs, and this professionalization may contribute to a more orderly, consensual process when making decisions. To conclude, theorists embracing a normative conception of institutions emphasize the stabilizing influence of social beliefs and norms, which are internalized an imposed by others (Scott, 2001).

Powell and DiMaggio (1983) call desires to look like other organizations *mimetic institutional pressure* and explain them as responses to uncertainty that involve copying others organizational structures, practices and outputs. More generally, the wider the population of personnel employed by, or customers served by, an organization, the stronger the pressure felt by the organization to provide the programs and services offered by other organizations. Thus, either a skilled labour force or a broad customer base may encourage mimetic isomorphism (Powell & DiMaggio, 1983). Mimetic institutional pressure is viewed differently by many authors. Powell and DiMaggio (1983) see not-for-profit organizations as an example of mimetic institutional pressure. These organizations may change their organizational structure to be more similar to the for-profit firms and carry a powerful message to potential partners in joint ventures that "the sleepy nonprofit organization is becoming more business minded."

Barbu and Baker (2010) consider different local accounting standards-setting bodies in various countries to be an evidence of mimetic isomorphism as they have adopted structures and procedures similar to those of the IASB and Financial Accounting Standards Board (FASB). In the opinion of Al-Omari (2010), mimetic institutional pressures refer to the copying and duplicating of successful organizational behavior by other organizations. Successful multinational corporations have contributed to increasing the desirability of expanding and accepting the global harmonization of financial reporting. Therefore, the sophisticated and developed systems within those corporations portray desirable practices and behaviors which are seen essential and imperative to organizations within the developing economies (Al-Omari, 2010). Irvine (2008) argues that the UAE openness to its globalized environment and its increasing reliance on international trade having been established, it is inevitable that these relationships bring a pressure on the UAE to adopt westernized forms of accountability and financial reporting, particularly those of its "influential trading partner(s)."

Further, organizations require more than material resources and technical information if they are to survive and thrive in their social environment. They also need social acceptability and credibility (Scott, 2001). Zucker (1987) believes that the difference between institutionalized and noninstitutionalized environments often appears to be simply a matter of rationality. In this view, the economic success factor is viewed as the product of rational decision making. Conforming to the institutional demands wins social support and ensures survival to an organization, not because it makes more money or better products, but because it goes along with accepted conventions. Therefore, it is understandable how under different institutional pressures not only organizations and firms, but also countries adapt to the demands of the World Bank, IASB, Big 4 companies and trade partners to achieve social legitimacy. This kind of behavior further supports the harmonization of international accounting standards and the rise of a new international institution. As coercive, normative and mimetic pressures are viewed differently by many authors it is vital to determine which pressures are influencing the development of the Estonian accounting system taking into consideration the accounting history of Estonia, the openness to global processes and participation in the international capital market.

DISCUSSION

Coercive Institutional Pressure

During half of century accounting in Estonia was a part of the Soviet accounting system. The Soviet accounting system applied in Estonia was an integral part of the centralized administrative institutional structures for the direction and control of the command economic system. The collapse of centrally planned economies in the late 1980s and early 1990s changed the accounting environment in the former socialist countries, including Estonia, dramatically. Estonia's economic system was transformed from a centrally planned to a market-based economy, which involved significant legal and institutional changes in regulations and especially accounting regulations and gave rise to the development of a new accounting environment.

After declaring the restoration of the independence of the Republic of Estonia in 1990, it became possible to begin reform of accounting and join the system of accounting of developed market orientated countries. The first step on the way to change the situation was made in 1990, while Estonia remained, albeit reluctantly, a constituent republic of the USSR. On July 6, 1990, the Regulation of Accounting was adopted by the National Government and came into force on January 1, 1991. It is of special interest because it was the first measure adopted in any of the constituent republics of the USSR to mark a departure from the path of the Soviet accounting evolution. As pointed out by Alver, Alver, Mackevicius, Paupa, and Bailey (1998), this event marked the beginning of the spread of accounting disharmony within the territories comprising the USSR. It was really an "accounting step" on the transition from command economy to market economy. Although, legally, the measure was a regulation and not statute (i.e., not approved by a legislative assembly but adopted by the executive action of the government) it was comparable to a fundamental, or basic, accounting law. Paradoxically, in some sense, as pointed out by Bailey (1995), the Estonian Regulation on Accounting, adopted prior to the recovery of independence in 1991, was more considered measure and wider in scope than the legislation introduced subsequently in Latvia and Lithuania. Because of lack of local accounting sophistication there was some inability to distinguish between the suitable and unsuitable aspects of accounting procedures and practices transferred. Therefore, foreign advice appeared to be of great support in designing local accounting legislations. It is worth notice that three of the seven members of the Estonian Accounting Board during the period of preparation of the new Accounting Act in 1993–1994 had international working experience.

In 1991 the Estonian Accounting Board (later named the Estonian Accounting Standards Board – the EASB) took on the responsibility for the development of accounting in Estonia. The main tasks of the Board were declared to issue mandatory accounting guidelines and to make recommendations concerning the methods which were to come into force. All the developments of accounting were expected to be initiated and prepared for legislation and implementation by the Board. At that time the EASB was an independent governmental unit, established by the government of Estonia and operating within the administrative jurisdiction of the Ministry of Finance as defined in the paragraph 32(1) of the Estonian Accounting Act (the EAA). The Board had to arrange accounting guidelines related to the EAA.

The first step toward the formation of auditing environment in Estonia was made by the Estonian Regulation on Auditing in 1990 (the Estonian Auditing Act was enforced in 1999). During the following years, 1992–1995, all the Big 6 audit firms started to operate in Estonia. In 1994 the first set of auditing guidelines was enacted in Estonia. These steps made an essential contribution to and helped create a favorable environment for the preparation and enforcement of the EAA. However, it is evident, that both accounting as a whole and financial as well as management accounting in Estonia and the other transition economies underwent evolutionary changes in the first half of the 1990s. The main problem was following: how to build a forward-looking and flexible accounting regulation system, which would enable to overtake and to integrate into the European accounting framework. The traditional system basing on the accounting law would be too inflexible to reflect the rapid changes in transition circumstances. Although the Principal Administrator and Head of Accounting at the EU Commission Van Hulle (1993) expressed an idea that the use of the law as a means of standard setting can also be an interesting mechanism against too frequent (and sometimes unnecessary) changes. But this was not the case for transition countries, because of missing stable and effective accounting regulation system.

The Regulation was in force until 1995. This document introduced a number of new accounting concepts and principles, new terms and a new set of annual financial statements (including the balance sheet, the income statement and the statement of changes in the financial position and notes). The main characteristic of that period is that it was mixed from past (some elements of the former Soviet accounting system remained in force), present (real usage of new methods, principles and financial statements), and future (usage of many new terms of market economy which really were not represented in the Estonian economy).

More substantial and complex step of the accounting reform in Estonia was related to the first EAA which came into effect on January 1, 1995 (EAA, 2013). Chapter 1 of the EAA specified the objective of the EAA, which was to create the legal bases and establish general requirements for organizing accounting and reporting in the Republic of Estonia based on internationally accepted accounting principles. In paragraph 3 of the EAA internationally accepted accounting and reporting principles were defined as the accounting directives of the European Community and the principles, standards and recommendations developed and approved by the International Accounting Standards Committee (the IASC, predecessor body of the IASB). The annual financial statements included the balance sheet, the income statement and notes. The statement of cash flows was compulsory part of notes. (EASB, 2000).

Estonia was the first nation in Europe to align national GAAP with international accounting standards by law. According to Alver and Alver

(2009), the Accounting Act of 1995 stated that the Estonian *good accounting practice* (the Estonian GAAP) is based on the standards, interpretations and guidelines promulgated by the IASC. The true and fair view was declared to be the most important reporting principle but still the Accounting Act did not contain a detailed set of rules and can best be characterized as constituting legal framework. The legal framework was general and applied to all legal entities and physical persons registered as businesses in Estonia (Alver & Alver, 2009).

The Estonian good accounting practice was declared to be based on internationally recognized principles, which were established with the Accounting Act and the Estonian accounting guidelines. In some sense, this concept was a unique combination of Anglo-American approach and Continental (European) approach. According to Haldma (2003), in the Estonian accounting regulation the Accounting Act represents the European approach and the Estonian GAAP – Anglo-American approach. Such combination had a number of advantages, especially in the first period of creation of accounting regulation (transition period) and enabled the flexible manner of the transition process. The analysis of the accounting regulations in the Eastern and Central European countries revealed that, besides Estonia, only Slovenia has introduced the mentioned double set accounting regulation. In the second half of the 1990s this approach was implemented in several market economy countries – for example, in Germany, Norway, Sweden (Haldma, 2003).

From 1995 till 2000 the EASB issued 16 guidelines to improve particular aspects of accounting in Estonia including accounting principles, preparation of financial statements, revenue recognition etc. The only problem was that the guidelines were not obligatory. They were only recommendations and in the case of contradictions with the Accounting Act, requirements of the Accounting Act had to be followed.

The first Accounting Act was in force from 1995–2002 and was changed several times. Unfortunately, these changes were mostly cosmetic (Alver & Alver, 2009). The first Accounting Act of Estonia had considered the valid international accounting requirements, as well as the majority of the requirements of the 4th Directive of EU. On November 28, 1995 Estonia submitted an official application accession to the EU (Estonia – 5 Years, 2013). As the Government of Estonia had expressed Estonia's desire to enter the EU, the EASB merged the requirements of the European directives with IASC's conceptual framework and treatments by carefully choosing the alternatives in the directives that result in convergence.

The accounting reform continued by the implementation of the new version of the EAA and a new set of guidelines. Both of them came into effect on January 1, 2003. The goal of the EAA was declared to create the legal basis and establish general requirements for organizing accounting and financial reporting pursuant to internationally recognized principles. The new Accounting Act modified also the status of the EASB, which became an independent commission. Instead of the former two basic statements (the balance sheet and the income statement) the annual report now included four statements: the balance sheet, the income statement, the cash flow statement, and the statement of changes in owner's equity (Alver & Alver, 2009). The new Accounting Act brought the Estonian accounting legislation closer to the International standards and also contributed to a better organization of the economic environment. The financial reports by business entities became more informative and enabled different interest groups to have a better overview about the reporting company's financial position, assets and liabilities (Tikk, 2010).

The main characteristic of the new EAA and guidelines is clear orientation to the IFRSs and the possibility to base the accounting methods and presentation of the information in financial statements according to the Estonian GAAP or the IFRSs. The Estonian GAAP is basically a simplified summary of IFRSs, primarily meant for small and medium-size entities. The recognition and measurement rules are based on IFRSs, but the disclosure requirements are less demanding (EASB webpage, 2013).

To further understand the coercive pressures, including organizations and events that affected the development of Estonian accounting system, the authors have focused to the system improving stage starting from 2003.

In May 2004 the Republic of Estonia joined the EU. From this day forward, Estonia has the obligation to follow in its activities the legislation of the EU. The main sources of primary law are the Treaties establishing the EU. Secondary sources include regulations and directives which are based on the Treaties. Regulations, directives and decisions are mandatory to follow for member states (European Union Information Centre). Although directives set sometimes quite specific objectives, they leave the implementation to the EU's member states. Regulations are directly applicable to member states and take effect without the need for implementing measures (European Union Information Centre).

In 2004 the financial reporting in the EU was regulated by the Fourth Council Directive 78/660/EEC (in force since July 25, 1978), which treated the preparation of annual financial statements of certain types of companies (The Council of the European Communities, 1978), and the Seventh

Directive 83/349/EEC (in force since June 13, 1983), which defined the preparation of consolidated statements (The Council of the European Communities, 1983). The above-mentioned directives were incorporated to the EAA when joining the EU. Because the Fourth and Seventh Directive were not based on IFRSs, differences between the Estonian guidelines and the EU legislation existed in 2004.

However, there was no need to improve the Estonian GAAP, because according to the regulation accepted by the European Parliament and European Council in 2002 (1606/2002), all EU listed companies were required to prepare their consolidated statements in accordance with the IFRSs. This requirement entered into effect from 2005 and represented a preliminary peak in the internationalization process of financial accounting in Europe. For other companies the implementation of the IFRSs is recommended. Although the Estonian GAAP was already oriented to the IFRSs, all guidelines were amended again (Tikk, 2010), because differences between the international accounting standards adopted by the EU and accepted by the IASB existed. The main reason behind the differences is that the IFRSs adopted by the IASB do not take effect in the EU automatically.

On December 1, 2005 several changes were introduced in the EAA. With the updated Accounting Act the necessity of providing the users of financial statements with adequate information was emphasized. Besides, the EAA required more information in the management report, such as the description of the main fields of activity as well as products and services and also the main financial ratios. Guidelines, which were oriented to the IFRSs, already required this kind of information to be disclosed in the notes of the annual report. With the updated version of the EAA, this requirement was also introduced to the law. Thus, the demand for change in the law was determined by the IFRSs.

In 2007 the EAA was amended again. According to Loot (2007), the reason of the amendments was necessity to follow the disclosure principle in all business transactions or events, where a business entity issuing securities is one of the parties. The change was intended to harmonize the European Parliament and Council Directive 2004/39/EC (the Markets in Financial Instruments Directive) and implement Directive 2006/73/EC and 2004/109/EC (the Transparency Directive). Thus, the demand for change in the EAA was determined by the EU legislation.

The amendments in the EAA which came into force in 2008 required that the annual report should disclose the entity's main field of activity according to the Classification of Economic Activities used in Estonia. According to the explanatory memorandum, such amendment provides for quick identification and processing of registers maintained by the court. The EASB and the Estonian Board of Auditors (the EBA) saw the change in the context of the annual report inappropriate and suggested that such information should be collected outside the annual report. As a result, such information shall be published after the notes and annexes of the annual report (Loot, 2008). Thus, the change in the law was rather administrative in nature, which was designed to help users (registration departments of courts) to better process the data.

In 2009, several changes were introduced to the EAA. The main change worth noting was the development of uniform financial reporting taxonomy, which was directly related to the action plan for e-filing of the annual reports. Firstly, the taxonomy of the annual report that meets the Estonian GAAP was developed (except the taxonomy on consolidation or liquidation and final report) (Loot, 2009). Taxonomy was introduced in 2010. As the electronic submission of annual reports is not widespread throughout the world, the authors think that it can be seen as an independent project of Estonia, which can be qualified as exceptional in the world. Therefore, in this case, compelling institutional pressure is the Republic of Estonia, who has been able to set rules and has the ability to see that others follow these rules.

In 2010 the EAA was amended again influenced by the changes in the Auditing Act (it was updated because of the requirements of International Standards on Auditing (ISA)). To draw a parallel here, to merge with the demands of international legislation other Estonian laws besides the EAA has been influenced by international standards and organizations.

In 2011 the changes in the EAA were the result of Estonia's accession to the euro area and the substitution of national currency from Estonian kroon to euro. The functional currency changed to euro instead of kroon as well.

In conclusion, it may be noted that due to the membership in the EU, the coercive institutional pressure affecting the development of the Estonian accounting environment is the previously mentioned EU. The legislation of the EU (regulations and directives) directly influences the EAA. As the EU has based its accounting regulations mainly on the IFRSs, then in the international perspective one can rather see the IASB as the main coercive institutional pressure affecting the development of the EAA and the Estonian GAAP.

At societal level there have been many discussions, how the Estonian GAAP should look like in the future. The chairman of the EASB Ago Vilu sees the Estonian guidelines remaining closely tied with the IFRSs. This view is supported by the adoption of IFRS for SMEs by the IASB in 2009

(Oja, 2011). In the EU the use of IFRS for SMEs has not been approved, because according to the European Commission, IFRS for SMEs is not suitable to use for micro-enterprises (Hirvoja-Tamm, 2010) and it is not in line with the Fourth and Seventh Directive of the EU (Hirvoja-Tamm, 2010). Therefore, in October 2011, the European Commission decided not to adopt the IFRS for SMEs into the European legislation. Furthermore, the Commission proposed to simplify accounting rules for SMEs by amending the Accounting Directives (78/660/EEC and 83/349/EEC). With that the Commission aims to reduce the administrative burden for small companies. Simplifying the preparation of financial statements would also make these more comparable, clearer and easier to understand. It would also allow users of financial statements such as shareholders, banks and suppliers to gain a better understanding of companies' performance and financial position. Furthermore, under the proposed revision of the Transparency Directive (2004/109/EC), listed companies (including small and medium-sized issuers) would no longer be obliged to publish quarterly financial information. This would contribute to further cost savings and should help to discourage short-termism on financial markets (European Commission, 2011, October 25). In December, 2011 the proposals to revise the accounting Directives and the Transparency Directive were approved by the European Parliament. After formal approval by the Council, the Directive will enter into force following publication in the Official Journal (European Commission, 2011, December 14). Member States should take into account the specific conditions and needs of their own markets when making decisions about how or whether to implement a micro-entity regime within the context of Council Directive 78/660/EEC (The European Parliament and the Council, 2012). The Commission hopes that most Member States will see this as an opportunity to reduce the burden on the smallest companies within their jurisdiction. By aligning the micro entities' financial reporting requirements with other reporting requirements (such as tax reporting) they can create a one-stop-shop and substantially reduce the reporting burden (European Commission, 2011, December 14).

According to the new Directive, a micro-entity is a company which does not exceed at least two of the following three criteria: total assets of up to € 350,000; net turnover of up to € 700,000; and a maximum of 10 employees and typically have limited liability toward third parties. Approximately 75% of EU companies meet these criteria. According to the Estonian Statistical Office 58,347 companies were operating in Estonia in 2010. From these companies 51,854 entities had less than 10 employees, which is 89% of all the companies (Statistics Estonia, 2012). Therefore, one can argue that the Estonian micro-entities may be interested in adopting the new regulation in Estonia as well.

So far, the majority of the Estonian enterprises prepare their annual financial statements according to the Estonian GAAP, which copies the accounting principles of the "big" IFRS. In 2011, several changes were introduced to the guidelines which will be effective from January 1, 2013. The new guidelines follow mainly the IFRS for SMEs, although some differences exist between two sets of accounting rules.

Estonia is among of the first countries in Europe aligning its local accounting standards with IFRS for SMEs. The same process has been started by many other countries in Europe, for example, Great Britain, Netherlands and Denmark (EASB webpage, 2013).

In the light of the recent events (from one side Estonia aligning its accounting guidelines with the IFRS for SMEs and from the other side – the EU banning the IFRS for SMEs and creating simplified rules for micro-enterprises) it is hard to predict, what will happen in the future and whether Estonia will follow the guidelines set by the EU or the IASB or both. Still, the recent and the future developments further support the fact that the EU and the IASB are the main two coercive institutional pressures affecting the development of financial accounting framework in Estonia.

Normative Institutional Pressure

One can argue that the development of accounting legislation in Estonia is also under pressure of Big 4. This can be proved by the fact that from 2001 members of EASB have been included 3–4 auditors and the chair of the EASB has been from Big 4.

According to § 158 of the Auditing Act (2013)[1] in force in Estonia, the auditing firm, who is in a contractual relationship with a public interest entity, must compose and report to the EBA the transparency report. Therefore, the transparency reports of the Big 4 and other Estonian companies are analyzed to determine the normative pressure of Big 4 auditing firms in Estonia.

For the purposes of Auditing Act (2013), a public interest entity is:

(1) a company whose securities are admitted to trading on a regulated securities market within the meaning of the Securities Market Act;
(2) a company which is a credit institution within the meaning of the Credit Institutions Act;

(3) a company which is an insurer within the meaning of the Insurance Activities Act;
(4) a local government in the administrative territory in which more than 10,000 people live as at the balance sheet date or the total assets of which indicated in the annual financial statements or in the annual financial statements of the consolidation group as at the balance sheet date exceed 20,000,000 euros;
(5) a ministry as a state accounting entity within the meaning of the Accounting Act.

Furthermore, public interest entity is a legal person in whose financial statements or in the annual financial statements of whose consolidation group at least two of the indicators of the financial year exceed the following conditions:

(1) sales revenue or income 66,000,000 euros;
(2) assets as of the balance sheet date 33,000,000 euros;
(3) average number of employees 1,000 persons.

According to the Auditing Act (2013) a public interest entity is a company, foundation, nonprofit association or other legal person, in which the public sector entity has a majority holding or which is under the dominant influence of the public sector entity, in whose annual financial statements or in annual financial statements of whose consolidation group at least three of the indicators of the financial year exceed the following conditions:

(1) sales revenue or income 14,000,000 euros;
(2) assets as of the balance sheet date 7,000,000 euros;
(3) average number of employees 200 persons;
(4) number of members of the supervisory board 8 persons.

Besides the number of public interest entities audited during the financial year, the auditing firm is also obliged to present in the transparency report the amount of revenues gained from the assurance services. This includes revenues gained from performing audits, reviews and other assurance services.

Therefore, the authors have analyzed more thoroughly, how many public interest entities in Estonia are audited by Big 4 companies and how the revenues from the assurance services are divided between Big 4 and non-Big 4 companies. Based on this analysis it is possible to draw some initial conclusions, how Big 4 companies exercise their normative pressure to

Estonian companies, to the development of Estonian accounting framework and audit quality.

According to the EBA webpage (2012), 16 auditing firms have presented the transparency report for the period July 1, 2010 to June 30, 2011. Based on the data reported by the auditing firms, 143 public interest entities have been audited (in 2009 128 entities) during that period from which the Big 4 companies have audited 68% (in 2009 69%).[2] Based on these results it can be argued that as most of the "important" annual reports are being audited by Big 4 companies then due to reputation risk they perform the audits more conservatively than other auditors and therefore influence the preparation and presentation of the annual reports they audit.

When we look how the sales revenue is distributed during the same period between Big 4 and non-Big 4 companies, we can see that in total the auditing firms earned revenues of 13.2 million euros, which is the same as in 2009. The revenues of Big 4 companies made up to 10.4 million euros, which is 79% of the total revenues earned during that period[3] (the same as in 2009). When we look public limited companies, who are also public interest entities, in more detail, we can see that the annual reports of 13 public limited companies out of 14 listed in the Tallinn Stock Exchange in 2010 have been audited by Big 4 companies.

To conclude, we can say that based on the analysis of sales revenue the impact of Big 4 companies on preparation and presentation of annual reports extends beyond public interest entities as the revenues earned also include auditing of nonpublic interest entities. Although no law requires that the audit or the review of the annual reports have to be conducted by Big 4 auditing firms most of the public interest entities have chosen the Big 4 companies to do the job.

If we look at the substance of the annual reports then the research conducted in Estonia show that there are considerable differences between the audit quality of Big 4 and non-Big 4 companies. Kannistu (2008) studied the annual reports of 15 Estonian companies from which 8 annual reports were audited by Big 4 companies and 7 from non-Big 4 companies. Important substantive errors, which include recognition of business transactions, appeared according to Kannistu (2008) only in those annual reports, which were audited by non-Big 4 companies.

Errors in disclosure, which means that the information required by the law to be disclosed was not disclosed or was disclosed partially, appeared in the annual reports audited both by Big 4 and non-Big 4 companies. Furthermore, there were more errors in the annual reports audited by non-Big 4 companies (Kannistu, 2008). The most common mistake was the insufficient description of the accounting principles in the notes of the financial statements and the nondisclosure of the information for individually significant financial objects and transactions (Kannistu, 2008).

Raigla (2007) studied the information disclosed in the notes of the financial statements. Her sample consisted of 20 non-audited financial statements. With her research Raigla (2007) wanted to show that the non-audited financial statements contain more errors and deficiencies than audited financial statements. The investigation revealed that the sampled annual reports did not use cross-references, the numerical values of notes and financial statements differed, the terminology used was insufficient, disclosed information was often inadequate or even wrong (Raigla, 2007). Detected errors on non-audited annual reports were therefore even more extensive than those identified by Kannistu on audited annual reports.

The work performed by Raigla (2007) is supported by a study conducted by the authorized public accountant Villems (2008), who also investigated the most common errors on the annual reports. According to Villems (2008) the annual financial statements commonly do not include detailed notes for income statement and statement of cash flows. The review of accounting principles used is superficial and there are problems in how to reflect capital and operating leases.

According to the research conducted by the World Bank in 2004, the differences in technical proficiency of Estonian auditors result in significant differences in audit quality. High-quality audit delivery can be expected from select audit firms representing approximately 25 percent of profession. Furthermore, the research points out that although there is a significant improvement in the quality of public interest entities audit, the audit quality in SMEs lags behind. The reason behind it is that most sole practitioners and auditors employed in small audit firms do not have access to an audit practice manual. Lacking knowledge about how to apply ISAs many Estonian auditors only use Estonian auditing guidelines, albeit not properly. The authors are in the opinion of that in 2011, the situation has improved compared to the situation in 2004 as in 2010 the new Auditing Act was adopted. The new Auditing Act (2013) was developed based on the ISA. To retain their status as authorized public accountant all authorized public accountants have to retake the auditor's exam, which is based on the new auditing law and ISA's.

According to the investigation conducted by the World Bank and other researchers, one can expect higher quality of annual reports audited by international auditing firms. This suggests that in Estonia the impact of Big 4 companies to the financial statements presentation is significant, as they audit the most of the Estonian public interest entities and therefore directly influence the preparation and presentation of the financial statements and the development of the Estonian financial accounting and reporting framework.

Mimetic Institutional Pressure

Mimetic institutional pressures refer to the copying and duplicating of successful organizational behavior by other organizations (Powell & DiMaggio, 1983). This is mostly used in situations and conditions of uncertainty, when "institutional rules" are replaced by "technical rules" in this case the organization will decide to mimic similar, larger, or more successful organizations. Organizations, as humans, want to be seen as socially acceptable, and not as outsiders. So, the more organizations behave in a certain manner and practice certain procedures, the more pressure there will be on other organizations to copy these behaviors and follow in the same path (Al-Omari, 2010).

The mimetic view therefore stresses conformity with orthodox structures and identity, particularly in times of uncertainty. As successful multinational corporations have expanded their "global reach," they have instituted sophisticated systems of "financial coordination" of their subsidiaries and have modelled to other organizations the desirability of the global harmonization of financial reporting. Intimately connected with the regulatory regimes of the dominant nation states, they have reinforced the desirability, for developing and emerging economies, of conformity with the practices both of multinational corporations and of nations' trading partners (Irvine, 2008).

The collapse of Soviet Union in the early 1990s marked the breakdown of centrally planned economy and the need for a new business model in Central and Eastern Europe, including Estonia. In the transformation process, Estonia directed its course from centrally planned economy to the market economy. This required significant changes in the legislation (including accounting guidelines) as well as in the structures and working principles of different organizations and entities. Because the rest of the world already had had "an experience" in the market economy, it was easier to copy the traditions and practices of entities already operating in the environment of market economy than to come up with something new. This was supported by the formation of branches of international corporations in Estonia immediately after becoming independent.

Nowadays, the trend to copy the structures, customs and outputs of the international companies, has not disappeared in Estonia. This is supported by the tax policy. To increase the amount of direct investments made to Estonia, the Estonian parliament passed the Income Tax Act which came into force on January 1, 2000. With the amended law, the entities operating in Estonia must pay the income tax on profit only when it is distributed, not earned.

The changed tax environment promoted the growth of foreign investments in Estonia. The "immigration" of organizations increased even more after Estonia joined with the EU. This gave more confidence about the business environment in Estonia to the international corporations, which was from that moment forward subject to the common practices and regulations of the EU. Nowadays, when the key to the financial success and a way out of the economic recession seems to be export, it is inevitable and essential to conform to the requirements of international trading partners.

Barbu and Baker (2010) consider different local accounting standards-setting bodies in various countries to be an evidence of mimetic isomorphism as they have adopted structures and procedures similar to those of the IASB and/or the FASB. A good example is Estonia. Similarly to the FASB the EASB has seven members who represent different professional bodies. So the aim of creation of the EASB shows the appearance of mimetic pressure. The authors believe that it is possible to draw some parallels between the standard setting processes of the EASB and the IASB also.

The purpose of the IASB is to develop a single set of high quality, understandable, enforceable, and globally accepted IFRSs, to promote the use and rigorous application of those standards and to bring about convergence of national accounting standards and IFRSs to high quality solutions (IASB webpage, 2013). The EASB operates on a similar basis. The function of the EASB is to issue financial accounting and reporting guidelines explaining and specifying the EAA and to direct activities in the field of accounting (EASB webpage, 2013) The standard development process is also similar for the two organizations – the EASB announces the drafts of the new guidelines and the guidelines already accepted at its web-page.

To conclude, the development of the Estonian GAAP is from one side influenced by the coercive institutional pressure – the EASB follows the IFRSs when drafting the guidelines. On the other hand, this kind of behavior is directly influenced by mimetic institutional pressure because the EASB copies the practices of the IASB.

CONCLUDING REMARKS

As coercive, normative, and mimetic institutional pressures are viewed differently by many authors it is vital to determine which pressures are influencing the development of the Estonian accounting system taking into consideration the accounting history of Estonia, the openness to the global processes and participation in the international capital market.

The results of the authors' research showed that in the context of coercive institutional pressure the development of the accounting legislation in Estonia has been mostly influenced by the IFRSs. These standards have been incorporated to the legislation of the EU, although some differences between the IFRSs issued by the IASB and the IFRSs adopted by the EU exist. As Estonia is the member country of the EU, the effect of the EU legislation to the Estonian standard setting process and the EAA seems to be quite clear. However, in the light of the recent events, it seems that Estonia has the opportunity to follow its own way when deciding which accounting principles should be applied to micro-enterprises as well as small- and medium-size entities. Therefore, it will be interesting to follow, whether the coercive pressures from the IASB and/or the EU will determine the future financial accounting and reporting legislation for most of the Estonian entities.

The authors agree with Al-Omari (2010) that in respect of normative institutional pressure the Big 4 firms play a profound role in the globalization of accounting and represent the normative pressures that effect organizations and the choices they make in accordance to their reporting and practices implemented. In Estonia the Big 4 firms audit most of the public interest entities and can therefore influence the preparation and presentation of their financial statements. So it could be supposed that normative institutional pressures, affecting the development of the Estonian financial accounting and reporting system, are the Big 4 audit firms. Further research in this area is needed to confirm or exclude the normative institutional pressure. This can be done by comparing the annual reports audited by Big 4 and Non-Big 4 firms. The analysis should be conducted in a way that does not only point out the variations from the existing law, but also points out the aspects that are disclosed "voluntarily" and that are common to all Big 4 firms.

International corporations, which structures and practices were copied by the Estonian entities after the collapse of the centrally planned economy in 1990s, can be viewed in the context of mimetic institutional pressure. The trading partners of the Estonian companies, whose requirements have to be met in order to increase the export, can also be viewed as a mimetic institutional pressure. Mimetic institutional pressure does not appear in the context of business only, where entities copy the practices of successful multinational corporations. This copying of the structures and practices may also happen, when the EASB follows the same working principles and processes as the IASB.

The aim of this chapter was to discuss and to analyze the evolution of financial reporting model in Estonia with emphasis on issues within the context of different institutional pressures. The example of Estonia shows that countries, who want to be successful in the international capital markets, have to be compatible with different institutional pressures.

NOTES

1. In accordance with the European Union Directive 2006/43/EU which treats the audit of consolidated and nonconsolidated annual reports.
2. The analysis is conducted by the authors based on the transparency reports.
3. The analysis is conducted by the authors based on the transparency reports.

REFERENCES

Albu, N., & Albu, C. N. (2012). International financial reporting standards in an emerging economy: Lessons from Romania. *Australian Accounting Review*, *22*(4), 341–352. doi:/10.1111/j.1835-2561.2012.00196.x

Albu, N., Albu, C. N., Bunea, S., Calu, D. A., & Gîrbină, M. M. (2011). A story about IAS/IFRS implementation in Romania: An institutional and structuration theory perspective. *Journal of Accounting in Emerging Economies*, *1*(1), 76–100. doi:10.1108/20421161111107868

Al-Omari, A. (2010). The institutional framework of financial reporting in Jordan. *European Journal of Economics, Finance and Administrative Sciences*, *22*, 32–50.

Alver, J., & Alver, L. (2009). Development of accounting and implementation of international financial reporting standards in Estonia. In R. W. McGee (Ed.), *Accounting reform in transition and developing economies*. New York, NY: Springer.

Alver, J., Alver, L., Mackevicius, J., Paupa, V., & Bailey, D. (1998). Baltic States. In D. Alexander & S. Archer (Eds.), *European accounting guide* (3rd ed., pp. 1464–1475), Harcourt Brace Professional Publishing.

Alver, J., Alver, L., Mackevičius, J., & Paupa, V. (2001). Baltic States. In D. Alexander & S. Archer (Eds.), *European accounting guide* (4th ed., pp. 1481–1504). New York, NY: Aspen Law & Business.

Auditing Act. (2013). Retrieved from https://www.riigiteataja.ee/akt/13275292

Bailey, D. (1995). Accounting in transition in the transitional economy. *The European Accounting Review*, *4*(4), 595–623. doi:10.1080/09638189500000042

Baker, R., & Rennie, M. D. (2006). Forces leading to the adoption of accrual accounting by the Canadian Federal Government: An institutional perspective. *Canadian Accounting Perspectives*, *5*(1), 83–112. doi:10.1506/206K-RV7L-2JMN-W3D3

Barbu, E. M., & Baker, C. R. (2010). An historical and neo-institutional analysis of institutions involved in international accounting convergence. *Accounting and Management Information Systems*, *9*(2), 218–241.

Barbu, E. M., Farcane, N., & Popa, A. (2012). Critical analysis of developments in Romanian accounting during the 20th century: A neo-institutional approach. *International Journal of Critical Accounting*, *4*(2), 175–193. doi:10.1504/IJCA.2012.046380

Becker, C., DeFond, M. L., Jiambalvo, J., & Subramanyam, K. R. (1998). The effect of audit quality on earnings management. *Contemporary Accounting Research*, *15*(1), 1–24. doi: 10.1111/j.1911-3846.1998.tb00547.x

Boolaky, P. K. (2010). *IFRS in small island economies: Problems and challenges to the private and public-sector enterprises: Using data from Mauritius*. Retrieved from http://papers.ssrn.com/sol3/papers.cfm?abstract_id=1578075

Chamisa, E. E. (2000). The relevance and observance of the IASC standards in developing countries and the particular case of Zimbabwe. *The International Journal of Accounting*, *35*(2), 267–286. doi:10.1016/S0020-7063(00)00049-2

Chand, P. (2005). Impetus to the success of harmonization: The case of South Pacific Island nations. *Critical Perspectives on Accounting*, *16*(3), 209–226. doi:10.1016/j.cpa.2003.06.002

Ding, Y., Jeanjean, T., & Stolowy, H. (2005). Why do national GAAP differ from IAS? The role of culture. *The International Journal of Accounting*, *40*, 325–350.

Estonia – 5 Years in the European Union. (2013). Retrieved from http://www.vm.ee/?q=en/node/8479

Estonian Accounting Act (EAA). (2013). Retrieved from https://www.riigiteataja.ee/akt/958541

Estonian Accounting Standards Board (EASB). (2000). *Eesti hea raamatupidamistava* [*Estonian Generally Accepted Accounting Principles*]. Retrieved from http://www.easb.ee/index.php?id=685

Estonian Accounting Standards Board (EASB). (2013). *EASB webpage*. Retrieved from http://www.easb.ee/?lang=en

Estonian Board of Auditors (EBA). (2012). *EBA webpage*. Retrieved from http://www.audiitorkogu.ee/?p=201&sd=bc510d5714a8eabfe3e3c76e245ac2c4

European Commission. (2011, December 14). *Financial reporting: Burden reduction for micro-entities – Frequently asked questions*. Retrieved from http://europa.eu/rapid/press-release_MEMO-11-911_en.htm#PR_metaPressRelease_bottom

European Commission. (2011, October 25). *More responsible businesses can foster more growth in Europe*. Retrieved from http://europa.eu/rapid/press-release_IP-11-1238_en.htm

European Union Information Centre. Retrieved from http://elik.nlib.ee/?id=21

Fontes, A., Rodrigues, L. L., & Craig, R. (2005). Measuring convergence of national accounting standards with international financial reporting standards. *Accounting Forum*, *29*(4), 415–436. doi:10.1016/j.accfor.2005.05.001

Francis, J. R., Maydew, E. L., & Sparks, H. C. (1999). The role of Big 6 auditors in the credible reporting of accruals. *Auditing: A Journal of Practice and Theory*, *18*(2), 17–34. doi:10.2308/aud.1999.18.2.17

Granell, E. (2000). Culture and globalization: A Latin American challenge. *Industrial and Commercial Training*, *32*(3), 89–94. doi:10.1108/00197850010371666

Gray, G., & Ratzinger, N. (2010). Perceptions of preparers, users and auditors regarding financial statement audits conducted by Big 4 accounting firms. *International Journal of Disclosure and Governance*, *7*(4), 344–363. doi: 10.1057/jdg.2010.15

Haldma, T. (2001, December). *Accounting and auditing in Estonia*. Article presented at the meeting of 4th international conference on "Audit & Accounting," Riga Managers School, Riga, Latvia.

Haldma, T. (2003). Harmonization of Estonian accounting system with European framework. In O. Ü. Mattimar (Ed.), *Estonian economic policy on the way towards the European Union* (pp. 503–512). Tallinn, Estonia: Berliner Wissenschafts-Verlag GmbH.

Haldma, T. (2006). The factors affecting accounting development in the harmonization process with the international framework: The case of Estonia. In G. N. Gregoriou & M. Gaber (Eds.), *International accounting: Standards, regulations and financial reporting* (pp. 457–482). Oxford, Burlington: Elsevier.

Hassan, M. K. (2008). The development of accounting regulations in Egypt: Legitimating the international accounting standards. *Managerial Auditing Journal*, *23*(5), 467–484. doi:10.1108/02686900810875299

Hatch, M. J. (1997). *Organization theory*. New York, NY: Oxford University Press.

Hirvoja-Tamm, M. (2010). *Eesti väikeste ja keskmise suurusega ettevõtete finantsaruandluse regulatsiooni täiustamise võimalused* [*Possibilities for the improvement of Estonian SME's financial reporting system*]. Master's thesis, Tartu University, Tartu, Estonia. Retrieved from http://dspace.utlib.ee/dspace/bitstream/handle/10062/15151/Hirvoja-Tamm_Merit.pdf;jsessionid = 6F9440571F37304536E9E7AEC944CC3A?sequence = 1

Hope, O.-K., Jin, J., & Kang, T. (2006). Empirical evidence on jurisdictions that adopt IFRS. *Journal of International Accounting Research*, *5*(2), 1–20. doi:10.2308/jiar.2006.5.2.1

International Accounting Standards Board (IASB). (2013). *IASB webpage*. Retrieved from http://www.ifrs.org

Irvine, H. (2008). The global institutionalization of financial reporting: The case of the United Arab Emirates. *Accounting Forum*, *32*(2), 125–142. doi:10.1016/j.accfor.2007.12.003

Judge, W., Li, S., & Pinsker, R. (2010). National adoption of international accounting standards: an institutional perspective. *Corporate Governance: An International Review*, *18*(3), 161–174. doi:10.1111/j.1467-8683.2010.00798.x

Kannistu, S. (2008). *Auditeeritud majandusaasta aruannete avalikustamise nõuete täitmine vastavalt Eesti heale raamatupidamistavale*. [*The fulfilment of the disclosure requirements of Estonian GAAP in the audited financial statements*]. Bachelor's thesis, Tallinn University of Technology, Tallinn, Estonia.

Kury, K. W. (2007). Decoupled earnings: An institutional perspective of the consequences of maximizing shareholder value. *Accounting Forum*, *31*(4), 370–383. doi:10.1016/j.accfor.2007.09.003

Lawrence, A., Minutti, M., & Zhang, P. (2007). *A Study on the adequacy of non-Big 4 audits*. Unpublished manuscript, Laurier Centre for the Advancement of Accounting Research and Education, Ontario, Canada. Retrieved from http://www.rotman.utoronto.ca/accounting/zhang.doc

Loot, H. (2007). *Explanatory notes to the Amendment Bill of the Securities Market Act and Associated Acts*. Parliament of Estonia. Retrieved from http://www.riigikogu.ee/index.php?page = en_vaade&op = ems&enr = 108SE&koosseis = 11

Loot, H. (2008). *Explanatory notes to the Amendment Bill of the Commercial Law, the law for the Non-Profit Organizations and Associated Acts*. Parliament of Estonia. Retrieved from http://www.riigikogu.ee/?page=en_vaade&op=ems&eid=248053

Loot, H. (2009). *Explanatory notes to the Amendment of Accounting Act and Associated Acts*. Parliament of Estonia. Retrieved from http://www.riigikogu.ee/?page=en_vaade&op=ems&eid=653863

Mezias, S. J., & Scarselletta, M. (1994). Resolving financial reporting problems: an institutional analysis of the process. *Administrative Science Quarterly*, *39*(4), 654–678. Retrieved from http://www.jstor.org/stable/2393775

Mir, M., & Rahaman, A. (2005). The adoption of international accounting standards in Bangladesh: An exploration of rationale and process. *Accounting, Auditing and Accountability Journal*, *18*(6), 816–841.

Oja, A. (2011, May 19). *PwC: raamatupidamise reeglite üle käib pidev kaklus*. [*PwC: there is a constant fight over accounting rules*], Äripäev. Retrieved from http://raamatupidaja.ee

Peng, S., & van der Laan Smith, J. (2010). The convergence of Chinese GAAP with IFRS: A process analysis. *Journal of International Accounting Auditing and Taxation*, *19*(1), 16–34. Retrieved from http://www.sciencedirect.com/science/journal/10619518

Powell, W. W., & DiMaggio, P. J. (1983). The iron cage revisited: Institutional isomorphism and collective rationality in organizational fields. *American Sociological Review*, *48*(2), 147–160. Retrieved from http://www.ics.uci.edu/~corps/phaseii/DiMaggioPowell-IronCage Revisited-ASR.pdf

Raigla, A. (2007). *Nõuded majandusaasta aruande lisadele – Koostamine ja vastavus Eestis* [*Requirements to the notes of the financial satements – The formation and compliance in Estonia*]. Bachelor's thesis, Tallinn University of Technology, Tallinn, Estonia.

Reynolds, J., & Francis, J. (2000). Does size matter? The influence of large clients on office-level auditor reporting decisions. *Journal of Accounting and Economics*, *30*(3), 375–400. doi:10.1016/S0165-4101(01)00010-6

Ruder, D., Canfield, C., & Hollister, H. (2005). Creation of worldwide accounting standards: Convergence and independence. *Northwestern Journal of International Law and Business*, *25*(3), 513–588. Retrieved from http://scholarlycommons.law.northwestern.edu/njilb/vol25/iss3/24/

Sawers, A. (2007, June 15). Tackling Big 4 dominance. *The Financial Director*. Retrieved from http://www.financialdirector.co.uk/

Scott, W. R. (2001). *Institutions and organizations* (2nd ed.), London: Sage.

Simunic, D. (1980). The pricing of audit services: Theory and evidence. *Journal of Accounting Research*, *18*(1), 161–190. Retrieved from http://www.jstor.org/stable/2490397

Statistics Estonia. (2012). *Eesti statistika aastaraamat* [*Statistical Yearbook of Estonia*]. Retrieved from http://www.stat.ee/57659?highlight=Statistical,Yearbook,of,Estonia,2012

Stiglitz, J. (2001). *Globalization and its discontents*. New Delhi: Penguin Books.

Sumberg, K. (2004, June 7). *Euroopa Liidu rahvusvahelised raamatupidamise standardid*. [*International financial reporting standards of the European Union*]. [Web log post]. Retrieved from http://www.nasdaqomxbaltic.com/files/tallinn/bors/koolitus/Infohommik070604_FI.pdf

The Council of the European Communities. (1978). Fourth Council Directive 78/660/EEC of 25 July 1978 based on Article 54(3)(g) of the Treaty on the annual accounts of certain types of companies. Retrieved from http://eur-lex.europa.eu/LexUriServ/LexUriServ.do?uri=CONSLEG:1978L0660:19950101:EN:PDF

The Council of the European Communities. (1983). Seventh Council Directive 83/349/EEC of 13 June 1983 based on the Article 54(3)(g) of the Treaty on consolidated accounts. Retrieved from http://eur-lex.europa.eu/LexUriServ/LexUriServ.do?uri=CELEX:31983L0349:en:HTML

The European Parliament and the Council. (2012). Directive 2012/6/EU of the European Parliament and of the Council of 14 March 2012 amending Council Directive 78/660/EEC on the annual accounts of certain types of companies as regards micro-entities. Retrieved from http://eur-lex.europa.eu/LexUriServ/LexUriServ.do?uri=OJ:L:2012:081:0003:0006:EN:PDF

Tikk, J. (2010). The internationalization of the Estonian accounting system. *Annals of the University of Petroşani, Economics, 10*(2), 341–352. Retrieved from http://www.upet.ro/anale/economie/pdf/20100233.pdf

Touron, P. (2005). The adoption of US GAAP by French firms before the creation of the international accounting standards committee: An institutional explanation. *Critical Perspectives on Accounting, 16*, 851–873.

Van Hulle, K. (1993). Harmonization of accounting standards in the EC: Is it the beginning or is it the end? *The European Accounting Review, 2*(2), 387–396. doi:10.1080/09638189300000035

Vetevoog, K. (2009, December 12). *Ülevaade audiitortegevuse turul toimuvast.* [*Overview of the auditing market*]. [Web log post]. Retrieved from http://www.btb.ee/blogi/ulevaade-audiitor-tegevuse-turul-toimuvast

Villems, T. (2008). *Preparation of the annual report* (2nd ed.), Tallinn, Estonia: Pandekt OÜ.

World Bank. (2004). Report on the observance of standards and codes (ROSC). Republic of Estonia. *Accounting and Auditing*. Retrieved from http://www.worldbank.org/ifa/rosc_aa_est.pdf

Zucker, L. (1987). Institutional theories of organization. *Annual Review of Sociology, 13*, 443–464. doi:10.1146/annurev.so.13.080187.002303

EVOLUTION OF ACCOUNTING IN MOLDOVA: SOME REFLECTIONS ABOUT THE IMPORTANCE OF HISTORICAL AND CULTURAL FACTORS

David Alexander and Olesea Ghedrovici

ABSTRACT

Purpose – *The Republic of Moldova is a small country between Romania and Ukraine, which for more than 20 years since its independence, is still experiencing a painful process of economic and institutional reforms. The chapter provides, against a review of literature and national regulations, an analysis and possible perspectives of accounting harmonization processes in relation to historical and cultural preconditions.*

Approach/methodology – *Based on content analysis of national regulations and economic conditions in the Republic of Moldova, with the support of a literature review.*

Findings – *Our findings demonstrate that some features related to mentality, which have been formed as a result of long term political and*

Accounting in Central and Eastern Europe
Research in Accounting in Emerging Economies, Volume 13, 121–142

ISSN: 1479-3563/doi:10.1108/S1479-3563(2013)0000013010

cultural closeness and negation of individualistic and independent thinking values, are determining many contemporaneous changes in all spheres, including accounting.

Originality/scientific value – *There are very few publications about accounting processes in the Republic of Moldova. It is important to analyze the case of the Republic of Moldova in the context of accounting transformation in post-Soviet countries, as almost all of them have similar historical and cultural implications. The research results may be useful for further studies about accounting evolution in post-communist states and also in the Republic of Moldova itself.*

Keywords: Accounting; harmonization; reforms; post-Soviet country

INTRODUCTION

Many recent scientific papers and empirical studies were dedicated to accounting transformations in emerging economies (Borker, 2012; He, Wong, & Young, 2009; Pasekova, 2011), but there are, nevertheless, very few publications about accounting reforms in former Soviet Union countries (McGee & Preobragenskaya, 2006; Mehtiyeva, 2009; Tyler & Vanderhoof, 2001). This can be explained by a traditional closeness of economies and research, its predominantly national orientation and a specific lack of necessity and, even, possibilities (from the local researchers' side) to disseminate information at an international level. Although each of these markets possesses its own historical background and cultural dimensions, many of the former Soviet Union republics share common experiences in economic and social development. That is why analysis of the situation in one country and its extrapolation contributes to the understanding of the situation in other countries, as well.

During a long period of time the Republic of Moldova, a small country in Eastern Europe nestled between Romania and Ukraine, was under Soviet control. This period played a crucial role for future economic and development processes, cultural and social perceptions of democratic and free market values. Moldovan post-Soviet destiny is similar to other former Soviet republics, characterized by long-lasting reforms and attempts to build and maintain a viable economy. The Soviet system of accounting left a significant imprint on the future evolution of bookkeeping and mode of response to harmonization challenges. This is related primarily to difficulties in perception and understanding of less explicit IFRS in comparison with old detailed accounting standards, and the traditional orientation on tax authorities as the major audience. Analysis of publications about other post-soviet countries reveals similar problems for the majority of former Soviet republics after becoming independent and moving towards economic liberalization. Accounting reforms in Ukraine were largely influenced by a variety of transitional and institutional problems, and by a lack of experience in efficient governmental coordination (Solodchenko & Sucher, 2005). Russian business entities also faced many problems when reporting to tax authorities and other supervisory bodies because of the insufficient amount of official accessible explanatory guidance which would interpret disputable or unclear positions in regulations. Their experience has shown that many problems arise when introducing terms borrowed from International Accounting Standards IAS which have not been previously used in the Russian accounting system (Djatej, Sarikas, & Senteney, 2008).

Other non-Soviet (but former socialist) emerging countries on their harmonization path also "struggled" with tax and legally based orientation of accounting and local traditions influence. Organizational and perceptional difficulties in IFRS adoption process were observable, for example, in Czech accounting practices (Strouhal, Bonaci, & Sklenar, 2011). Romanian accounting has faced a series of serious challenges when shifting from centralized to independent accounting and has suffered multiple radical changes in trying to match the level of the European accounting system (Nistor & Filip, 2008). However, in its case the implications of international organizations were crucial, and seemingly more important than the presence of other factors (Albu, Albu, Bunea, Calu, & Girbina, 2011). In other emerging countries, for example Nigeria, this role of tertiary organizations was not sufficient to support the transition (Okaro & Tauringana, 2012).

At the same time, the situation of the Republic of Moldova is distinctly unique, as this is the closest Eastern neighbor of the EU with strong European aspiration, being called the EU "success story" (Schubel, 2011) due to significant progress in implementation of European principles in governance and economic policies. However, a part of its territory (the Pridnestrovian region) is still under Russian administrative and political control.

The purpose of this chapter is to investigate in the case of Moldova the role of historical preconditions and cultural perceptions in development of one of the most important business facilities – its language, called

Accounting. We observe a great importance of various indirect factors in the ability to accept and assimilate positive international experience and satisfy the demand for qualitative reporting and information management. Therefore, the major question of the research is: how have historical and cultural conditions influenced accounting evolution and attitudes towards harmonization in Moldova, and, as result, the level and success of IFRS[1] implementation.

There are some notable publications about the determinants which explain accounting solutions. Nobes (1984) has listed seven factors that may reshape the evolution of accounting systems:

- Legal systems of the country (common law or roman law)
- Providers of finance (private, banks or other)
- Taxation (if there is or is not a link between taxation and commercial accounting)
- Inflation (if it influences accounting thinking)
- Theory
- The profession, its size and development
- Accidents that may denaturize the accounting information.

So, accounting developed in different countries differently because of differences in these institutional and organizational patterns.

Hofstede (1980, 1983) indicated four cultural factors, which could affect accounting:

- Individualism versus collectivism
- Large versus small distance
- Strong versus weak uncertainty avoidance
- Masculinity versus femininity.

According to Hofstede, all the Western capitalistic countries are individualistic societies, where rules should be valid for all groups and individual interest is more important than collective interest. In societies with large power distance, accountants are not consulted but are only instructed. High uncertainty avoidance presumes the existence of exact rules and professional judgment is less important. In masculine societies, achievement is the most important objective, while in feminine societies work is necessary to live, rather than an end in itself.

Analyzing Hofstede's classification, in 1988, Gray developed a hypothesis that the higher a country ranks in terms of individualism, and the lower in terms of uncertainty avoidance and power distance, then the more likely it is to rank highly in terms of professionalism.

Recent publications about the accounting system of Moldova do not cover these significant aspects and are mostly related to the educational or legal part of accounting evolution (Armitage, Neider, & Shelaru, 2003; Frecauteanu, 2008). Although it is a small country with a relatively small market, Moldova's geo-political position is extremely attractive from many strategic points of view. Evolution of accounting, one of the most important infrastructural elements of business, is a hidden area of potential breaking or growing point of future economic and social development.

This chapter is intended to cover the gap in existing literature about accounting transformation issues in Moldova, to provide an analysis of national circumstances, framework and obstacles in regard to accounting harmonization and to open horizons for further research and discussion about particular cases of harmonization in post-Soviet countries.

The structure of the chapter includes analysis of historical and cultural preconditions with special emphasis on the Soviet time's influences in the second section, which the authors found important for future development of Moldovan accounting. This analysis is followed by a multisided presentation of modern economic conditions in the Republic of Moldova, in the third section. The fourth section is dedicated to accounting transformations and culture, as a part and consequence of the circumstances described in the previous sections. Finally, the authors propose a brief reflection about the current harmonization process in accounting in the context of historical and cultural preconditions and their impact (the fifth section), and offer some brief conclusions.

HISTORICAL AND CULTURAL PRECONDITIONS IMPORTANT FOR ACCOUNTING DEVELOPMENT

Moldova has passed through a long history of foreign domination or influence – Ottoman Empire, Kingdom of Romania, Russian Empire in the XIX century, Soviet Union, Romania in the XX century. A small territory in the heart of Europe was always in the area of interests for "big powers." After the declaration of independence, these processes have gained extreme intensity. With extensive support from the Russian Federation, the eastern part of Moldova has separated from central Government and proclaimed its independent Pridnestrovian Moldavian Republic. The military conflict which took place in 1992 is frozen today, but the Pridnestrovian region is still a cradle of many political and economic problems for the country.

These conditions will explain many future processes and tendencies, including those that refer to accounting transformations.

Despite long term foreign domination during many centuries, other relatively recent historical facts have also directly or indirectly influenced the development of the economy and its component parts.

In 1929 (Moldova was Moldavian Autonomous Soviet Socialist Republic at that time), Joseph Stalin published "Year of the Great Turn." This was a starting point for the radical changes in the economic policy of the Soviet Union, which presumed acceleration of collectivization and elimination of so-called "New Economic Policy" (NEP). In its essence this "great turn" or "great break" was similar to the Chinese "big jump" in 1958–1960, when leaders wanted to skip the intermediary stages of economic and social development, portraying a miracle in a beautiful future, based on exploitation of human enthusiasm and a free work force. In one of the results, however, the grain stocks contracted with western partners were withdrawn from the people in Soviet republics. This caused massive hunger in many regions, including Moldova.

At the same time, Stalin and his associates considered it vitally important to subordinate the Soviet republics, so those who promoted national ideas were considered enemies, and Soviet repressions became the main mechanism to transform this belief into life. Deportations of people to Siberia, Northern Urals took place even in 1941, the year the Second World War began, and in 1944–1953, after the war. The most talented, educated, and creative persons were deported or executed. The rest of the population became small screws in Stalin's machine. In addition, the Soviet Government promoted migration of Russian elites to Moldova in order to support the regime. Soviet policy was based on "moldovenism" – the idea that Moldovans are absolutely different from Romanians in their language, culture and history. The drastic consequences of these measures will be visible even many years later.

In a time when democratic countries developed competition and promoted new ideas and individualism values, the Soviet Union and its republics wallowed in their fears, "herd" behavior and total lack of independent thinking. Additionally, the mentality grown up in those conditions has contaminated two generations of people. Institutional control was an indispensable element of life.

Therefore, the economic conditions created in 1980 ("perestroika") came like a thunderbolt, causing desperation and tragedies in many families. People were like blind puppies, thrown out on to the open street. These memories of uncertainty and sensations also explain why the Communist

Party of Moldova returned to power in 2001, using the peoples' association of communism with stability and welfare. Mentality is an exclusive force.

The above mentioned and other multiple historical circumstances have contributed to the development of specific cultural behavior, which, in turn, has influenced various organizational and social arrangements. Particularly, massive corruption that deeply took root in the public consciousness has interfered with the Moldovan economic and political system initially through the perception of collectivism. If everything is common and belongs to everybody, than perhaps corruption is not a crime. The state hypocrisy and wish to make people believe in ephemeral values was a bomb with a slowed-down mechanism.

The artificially created Moldovan state (Ernu, 2012), based on invented language, mixing of cultures, sticking together two historically different territories (the left and right banks of the river Dniestr) has drugged its citizens with the idea of a non-existing nation. People get confused with the identification of "our" and "another's" history. The Soviet Union has conceptualized these directions and for a certain period of time, Soviet generations were forced to believe that their big country is the best, and it does not matter that you forget your mother's tongue; you speak Russian, and that is enough. This critical lack of respect towards fundamental values became a serious barrier for economic (and accounting) transformations in the modern Moldovan state. This "as granted" respect toward foreign visions still predominates in political and social decisions.

MOLDOVAN ECONOMIC HISTORY AT A GLANCE

Moldova is a country of controversy – it is the poorest country in Europe, but the first in the world to use HD voice for mobile telephones; it is famous for the biggest wine collection in the world (Milestii Mici), but, not surprisingly, Moldova attests the highest amount of alcohol consumption per capita.

During the Soviet times, the Moldovan economy was identical to the economy of other Soviet republics – production and distribution were controlled by Government, no private ownership, no competition, no financial markets. This period played a crucial role for future economic and development processes, cultural and social perceptions of democratic and free market values. Moldovan post-Soviet destiny is similar to other former Soviet republics, characterized by long lasting reforms and attempts to build and maintain a viable economy. However, Moldova has the biggest European aspirations among other post-Soviet countries (not taking into consideration the Baltic Tigers), it keeps the course of European integration and makes huge efforts to reach this aim, although this process in hard and tiresome.

The collapse of the Soviet Union has had a major impact on modern economic development of Moldova and movement towards a market economy. Immediately after declaring its independence, Moldova announced liberalization of prices and created conditions for privatization. But Moldovan extreme dependence on Russian energy supplies and a vast range of other noneconomic, social factors, including underdeveloped institutional and social infrastructure, and corruption have further slowed down Moldova's transition to a developed economy.

The process of reform was painful in all spheres. Financial liberalization in the country, similar to most of the Eastern Bloc countries, was a response to the former highly regulated markets. It became clear that the old-style Keynesian policies were incapable of dealing with contemporary challenges; the assumptions of this type of nation-state became outdated. The pressure to liberalize was gradually increased from the outside and by domestic regional elites. Like many other newly opened emerging markets, Moldova became a target for international flows of capital, due to the fact that consumer credit and housing finance in developed countries ran out. Foreign direct investments net value reached the maximal value of $711,460,000 in 2008. This growth is significant, comparing to $11,568,000 in 1994 (PWC Investing Guide, 2012). The Netherlands, Cyprus, Italy, and Russia are the most important investors in Moldova, according to IMF. The "fresh" and unexploited economy with its high potential returns justified the perceived risk.

Unfortunately, the first results of free markets experiences and liberalization were sad for the majority of the population. Price liberalization induced inflation of 2,600% in 1992. The GDP decreased 30.9% as compared to 1993 (Hensel & Gudim, 2001). Lack of competitive national products, rash opening of internal markets and reforms dictated by international financial institutions, but unadjusted for domestic conditions, have destroyed Moldovan internal production. In essence, Moldovan liberalization reduced to "wild" privatization, enrichment of some segments of population and oligarchization of society. According to some unofficial estimations, in the poorest country in Europe some people have properties worth hundreds of millions of dollars.

Unfortunately, but not wholly unexpectedly, after a decade of euphoria caused by national consciousness satisfaction and economic efforts to liberalize, such as unrestricted flow of capital, stock market development, massive privatization, Moldova, like also many other countries, faced severe economic crises. A large range of social and economic problems rose like mushrooms after the rain. These undesired processes reflected the existing institutional imbalances and weaknesses, and likewise showed the double-faced character of financial liberalization, which has been discredited, and that a new era of regulatory reform, based on aggressive state interventionism to restrain market forces, was dawning (Altvater, 2009; Stiglitz, 2008; Wallerstein, 2008). On a wave of these moods, the Moldovan Communist Party won the elections in 2001 and 2005, coming to power on an antireform platform and with a long-standing antipathy towards western values. They tried initially to use their control of both executive and legislative branches to undo in part the break-up of collective farms, reassert state control over the allocation of agricultural inputs and outputs, and reinstate a range of price controls. However, lately the policies of the Communist government became relatively softer and more liberal, in essence. They introduced a zero income tax rate for reinvested earnings, provided good conditions for free economic zones (Valkanes, Taraclia, International Free Port of Giurgiulesti, Free International Airport of Marculesti, and others) and the economic growth steadied. Surprisingly, the Liberal and Liberal-Democratic government, which came to power in 2010, have eliminated the income tax facility, organized severe controls of business entities and totally disappointed people who still believed in liberal values. Therefore, the attitude to liberalization and liberal principles is very controversial in the Republic of Moldova.

The Moldovan domestic economy depended largely on the centralized distribution of goods within the markets during the Soviet times. The region, as with all other Soviet republics, developed the economy with strong emphasis on one particular sector. Due to lack of natural resources and relatively good climate condition, agriculture became the leading sector in Moldova. Moldova has a big agricultural potential, which has not been fully exploited due to lack of modernization of this sector. Some industrial objectives (metallurgical factory, cement production plant and other) were situated on the left bank of the river Dniestr, which, as it was mentioned before, is controlled by Russia since 1992. When the Moldovan economic machine became independent and centrally controlled chains of distribution disappeared, all key sectors, including agriculture, experienced great difficulties in these new circumstances. Moldova did not possess any administrative, human or institutional capacities to face new economic challenges. Despite the fact that the Moldovan economy has registered a permanent growth after 2001, these rates are insufficient to reach at least the pre-"perestroika" levels.

During the past decades there were a number of cross-country studies in regard to economic growth in transition (Abdelal, 2001; Campos & Coricelli, 2003; Havrylyshyn, 2008). They have demonstrated a significant correlation between the structural reforms, liberalization, and institutional development. The need for structural economic reforms is still a crucial factor for ensuring sustainable development in Moldova. Historical conditions have played a negative role in this case, also. There is no doubt, that in order to be relevant and successful, structural reforms have to be planned and well-coordinated. The Moldovan post-Soviet government (like many post-Soviet governments in former republics of USSR) has interpreted their independence from Russia in the extreme radical form. National identity became maximally distanced from Russian traditions, and, thus, western values were accepted as undisputable and perfect (Skvortsova, 2002). The first Moldovan prime-minister Mircea Druc was an active pro-Romanian politician. At the same time, pro-Russian supporters from the eastern region of Moldova have contested this point of view. As a result, the Government's inability to consolidate these different approaches caused Moldovan failure to formulate and implement pragmatic economic reforms, and contributed to further problems with the Pridnestrovian region.

The political chaos caused the "wild privatization" process, so the main state-owned companies began to belong to private individuals, who discovered institutional and control gaps during that period. The fight for national values and nationalism problems (language, national identity) which appeared in post-soviet space, were used, practically, as a veil to cover massive larceny of everything. Privatization of the 1990s made Moldova an oligarchic country where business elites with enormous wealth have transformed their power into political influence. Many people were forced to emigrate to Russia, Italy, Spain, looking for at least illegal work. Moldova has registered a stable GDP growth since 2000, but, alas, from 38% to 50% of the GDP (according to different estimations) belongs to remittances.

National issues still remain painful for Moldovan society, part of it being pro-European and another part looking to the East and Russia. These artificially created problems are still used to manipulate peoples' choices. Maslow's hierarchy of needs looks in many cases of political and economic decisions for Moldova as an inverted pyramid where spiritual and cultural values (esteem, independency) which cover a small part of people's needs, are put on the foundation. As a result, the Moldovan economy today can be described as a "parasite" phenomenon, which is based on economic rules and principles in conditions of a non-existing economy.

ACCOUNTING CULTURE: REFORMS AND STUMBLES

The case of Moldova shows very clearly that our applied inductive discipline is highly influenced by political and economic conjuncture. Not only the accounting per se and its regulatory framework, but also its technical nature and development perspectives, are affected by multiple conditions. It is not a new idea and, particularly in the 1970s, there was a growing awareness of accounting becoming a "political phenomenon with economic consequences" (Artsberg, 2001).

Following the Hofstede's and Nobes's classification of factors, we have developed a comparative analysis of factors and their influence on accounting culture and procedures. Mostly Soviet period circumstances were taken into account, as that period had major impact on future evolutions. Comments are provided below (Tables 1 and 2).

For Moldova and other post-Soviet countries historical circumstances, which refers to the extermination of elites (Werth et al., 1999) and independent thinking for decades, have annihilated the essence of many professions, including the accounting profession. The role of an accountant was very clerical and all information served for control purposes exclusively. The creative feature, professional judgment, decision making, point of view were all useless. A "dissident" analysis was the biggest danger on both macro and micro levels.

The echo of this attitude is observed today, in the 21st century. The concept of accounting transparency is new in Moldova. Very few business managers and accountants have become accustomed to the idea that the main users of accounting information are those who provide capital. The old-fashioned mentality from both business and authorities' perspectives still keeps the consideration that tax authorities are their main audience. This fact causes massive corruption, and, vice versa, the existence of corruption determines the need to satisfy authorities in order to reduce the necessity to pay bribes. As a result, again, tax authorities become a point of main interest and managers and owners (and other external stakeholders) are not taken into consideration.

These old traditions and perceptions represent major obstacles for the development, but also a source of significant accounting mistakes and misunderstandings. For example, one of the largely disputed problems is related to accruals, which in essence do not require documental support, but accountants still refuse to make entries without documents. This creates problems with proper revenue recognition, measurement and disclosure. In

Table 1. Nobes's Factors and Analysis for Moldova.

Factors	Description	Consequence
Legal system	Roman law	Dominance of legal code, high dependence on regulation and norms
Providers of finance	Until "perestroika" reforms (1986) bank financing for private needs did not exist	Lack of experience and demand for qualitative reporting in order to obtain financing, misunderstanding of reform's necessity
Taxation	Strong relationship between accounting information and taxation	Accounting is oriented to state control bodies as the main audience, lack of perception of accounting as analytical tool
Inflation	No relationship observed	–
Theory	Role of accounting has been reduced to simple data gathering	Lack of demand for qualitative and judgmental reporting, which is able to provide analytical data
Profession	Clerical profession	Inability to understand fully the advantages of IFRS and professional judgment
Other denaturizing accidents	"As granted" acceptance of liberal and other western values as a response to high regulation during Soviet Russian dominance	Lack of enough critical view towards standards and principles suggested by international organizations

Table 2. Hofstede's Factors and Analysis for Moldova.

Factors	Description	Consequence
Individualism/collectivism	Long-term dominance of collectivism values	Independent thinking and innovation is viewed skeptically
Distance	Long distance power	Hierarchy domination in all spheres, lack of initiative, lack of high expectations in terms of professionalism
Uncertainty avoidance	High avoidance	Documental support is important
Masculinity/feminity	Feminine society	Lack of respect toward material values, hypocritical attitude to money

a time when the accounting profession was prestigious and well paid in the Occident for a long time, Moldovan enterprises have recognized only recently that it is important to properly create and interpret the accounting information.

The actual accounting system in the Republic of Moldova is conceptually and practically outdated and should be modernized. This was proposed in the Development Plan on Accounting and Audit in the Corporate Sector 2009–2014 and the new Accounting Law (nr. 113-XVI from April 27, 2007). Many of Moldova's accounting approaches and methods should be revised in order to cope with economic tendencies and changes. Unfortunately, 12 of the currently applied national standards were developed before 1998, or before the adoption of the current Chart of Accounts, 7 were approved in 1998–2000, 7 in 2001–2005 and only two after 2006. Only 13 of the national standards have commentaries, a fact which causes many questions, difficulties and disputes in interpretation of other standards.

Accounting reforms in modern Moldova took place twice, starting in 1998 and 2007. The reform of 1998 was related to Moldovan transition from planned Soviet to market economy. The old accounting system did not satisfy business and macroeconomic needs, being primarily designed for fiscal and governmental authorities. Accounting was not divided into financial and managerial, therefore the application of accounting methods in order to provide information for internal users was limited. The accounting reform was vital for foreign capital attraction. The Moldovan Association of Professional Accountants and Auditors, which was created in 1996 and was the first in the former Soviet Union becoming a member of the International Federation of Accountants, has also played its important role in promotion and support of the necessary reforms. Macroeconomic conditions, professional community and external factor (pressure from international organizations) have all determined choosing the way of reforms.

According to the Government Decree (nr. 1187 from December 24, 1997), the first accounting reform had the following objectives:

1. Creation of the basis for financial information which will correspond to market requirements.
2. Division of accounting from the fiscal system.
3. Introduction of fundamental accounting principles.
4. Creation of conditions for the existence of financial and managerial accounting.
5. Introduction of a new Chart of Accounts.

National Accounting Standards (NAS) were developed on the basis of International Accounting Standards and became valid starting from January, 1998. There were 23 NAS adopted by 2001.

The 1998 reform was relatively successful taking into consideration its scale and importance for the national economy and its transition to market principles. However, after a decade of new standards' exploitation, it became clear that the existing accounting system in the Republic of Moldova was conceptually and practically outdated and should be modernized. The Development Plan on Accounting and Audit in the Corporate Sector 2009–2014 and the new Accounting Law (nr. 113-XVI from April 27, 2007) were the starting points for new transformations. According to the Plan there are two stages of modernization and adjustments:

The first stage (2009–2012) included elaboration of a mechanism of acceptance and adoption of IFRS for the Republic of Moldova.

In the second stage (2012–2014) new standards with practical examples and commentaries should be developed. Also, a new Chart of Accounts, which will appear as a recommendation (in contrast to the compulsory existing Chart), should be proposed.

The reform beginning was dynamic and very decisive, therefore public interest entities those with a "significant importance to the public due to the area (type) of activity, size or number of employees, clients such as financial institutions, investment funds, insurance companies, non-state pension funds, commercial companies listed on the stock exchange in the Republic of Moldova, as well as other legal entities which have a dominant position in the market exceeding two of the following three criteria for the last two consecutive reporting periods:

- Total revenue – 120 million lei,[2]
- Total balance sheet – 60 million lei,
- Average number of staff members – 500 people" (according to the Accounting Law in its first edition).

were required by the Law of Accounting to apply IFRS 1 starting from January 1, 2009, and other entities IFRS from January 1, 2010. However, some obstacles did not permit to reach this objective.

First of all, IFRS adoption preconditions were inefficient from the state authorities' side in implementation of the proper decree nr. 238 of February 29, 2008 about the application IFRS in public entities. The government published an online version of IFRS, however those IFRS were incomplete. The Conceptual Framework for Presentation of Financial Statements also was not developed. The latter, however, could be relevant for identification of essential concepts for elaboration and presentation of financial reports, users' assistance in IFRS interpretation and delivery of some principles, taking into consideration that not all aspects are covered by IFRS.

Another obstacle to IFRS implementation in the Republic of Moldova is related to the fact that entities and accounting firms are facing a phenomenal challenge while implementing IFRS, which is not always easy to overcome. Proper sources are insufficient, and usually massive implication of educational institutions, professional organizations, state authorities and international organizations is required. Assistance from the latter was strong for strategy development (REPARIS program) and relatively weak in terms of concrete support of those who should apply IFRS. There were no workshops or seminars organized for potential users of IFRS or those who want to understand the essence and advantages of IFRS. Entities were left to themselves in implementation of IFRS. As a result, not getting enough support from the state or internal organizations, entities of public interest were not ready to apply IFRS on January 1, 2009 and a new version of the Law of Accounting moved this date to January 1, 2011.

Despite these obstacles, the Moldovan accounting community accepted the idea of IFRS implementation with its traditional Moldovan great love for everything from the West. Actually, introduction of IFRS in Moldova is part of the strategy of partnership of Moldova with the EU. Legal harmonization with the "acquis communautaire" is the essential point of European collaboration with third countries. So, there were almost no discussions about the idea of IFRS implementation, but rather some fears about the mechanisms and technical possibilities of how to do this. At the same time, it is a well-known fact that most successful countries are more skeptical about IASC activities, while developing countries with no own traditions of accounting standards, accept IFRS easily (Artsberg, 2001). This "blind" acceptance of foreign experiences is a source of lack of necessary skepticism. January 1, 2014 is a date when the renewed NAS should become valid and implemented. Usually it is necessary to have at least nine months for comments and at least six months between publication and application. Drafts of the new Accounting Standards were published in April, and as of June 2013 these drafts are still open for comments. However, there are still many critical discussions and negative reflections and nobody knows whether or not they will be applied in 2014. Despite formal problems, there are still many discussions about how to apply IFRS. The Accounting Law of Moldova stipulates that both IFRS and NAS are accepted. According to it "IFRS are standards and interpretations ... which become valid after their approval by the Government of the Republic of Moldova" and "NAS are standards and interpretations ... based on EU directives and IFRS, elaborated and approved by the Ministry of Finance." Many experts consider it unnecessary to develop new national standards, but only to apply the full version of IFRS. However, Moldovan national accounting traditions and, not less important, mentality would rather ask for national standards and will not accept their cancellation. NAS should take into consideration the level of economic development and also specifics of financial reporting in some sectors (NGO, agriculture, etc.). In addition, experience of other European countries indicates a lack of visible prevalence of effects on efforts in the case of IFRS application by SMEs with no perspectives for foreign investments. National standards represent a more viable alternative for entities without global aspirations.

IFRS successful implementation is a long and hard process. Many additional national strategies should be adapted to support IFRS in the country. For example, in 2012 Borker has proposed the following steps:

- Establish culturally sensitive educational and professional training programs
- Establish culturally focused upgrade programs for existing accounting professionals
- Set realistic deadlines for the transition to IFRS
- Integrate values of professionalism, flexibility, transparence through NAS setting bodies
- Establish a change management program for government, accounting professionals

These measures, of course, should be supported by the creation of infrastructure for IFRS implementation. And, all these are not simple or cheap.

SOME APPARENT HARMONIZATION PROS AND CONS

Accounting standardization which brought IFRS into the Moldovan national accounting system is a form of triggering the potentially positive consequences in this direction. Implication of IFRS could be double-fold. First, NAS are often less demanding that IFRS in the part of disclosure, recognition and measurement. In particular, the application of IFRS in the real-estate sector is extremely important as construction constitutes a significant part of the Moldovan economy. For example, NAS 11 "Construction contracts" does not require recognizing losses on completion as they are identified. This method distorts the original state of information. Generally speaking, IFRS are more accurate in this role.

Second, the application of IFRS would change the nature of provisions or deposit insurance as well. For example, the evaluation performed by the World Bank for ROSC Moldova (ROSC, 2004) shows significant differences in the amount of provisions under IAS 39 and for statutory purposes. This difference demonstrates that under the IAS provisions are 20% lower than those for statutory purposes. Accounting techniques and rules are far from being absolutely objective and neutral. A similar case was observed in 1993 when the German Daimler-Benz company, after listing on the NYSE, presented their annual report for 1992 according to US GAAP and according to German principles. GAAP's variant reported a loss of 586 million US dollars and the German variant showed a 168 million Deutsche marks gain (Financial Times, 1993).

Again, application of IAS and IFRS causes discrepancies in some data and interpretations. IFRS-based financial statements have a high potential to influence banking stability in conditions of free capital movement and overall liberalization, acting from both entity's and bank's sides. It is obvious from both theoretical and practical points of view that there is a link between microeconomic restructuring, qualitative financial reporting and the health of financial institutions. Unclear or imprecise information provided by the client may cause problems for banks. IFRS would change the situation ensuring high compliance with the bank's requirements and entities' needs.

However, the implementation of IFRS can also bring some unexpected effects related to potential new crises. The biggest trap can be associated with an introduction of "fair value" measurement instead of "historical cost". Therefore, during a boom market accounting artificially boosts financial institutions' capital and encourages them to invest or lend. In case of economic decline the market price of assets will go down and banks will intensify efforts in selling assets. This will provoke a more significant fall of an assets' value. Eventually, the owner's equity will also decrease. As a result of liquidity insufficiency a deeper crisis would arise. Provisions for bad and doubtful debts will have the same effect. In a period of optimism, bankers and other lenders are prepared to lend and are confident they will be repaid. At a time of depression they will focus on the probability of default and the measure to which their exposure is not covered. For the small Moldovan economy and market, these processes can be fatal.

The above paragraph however requires emphasis on another factor, also rather missing from developments in Moldova. This is the importance of educating the users regarding the underlying meaning, and the underlying assumptions, of financial reporting under IFRS requirements. To take again the example of fair value, the whole point of this is that it purports to give an indication of the value in the market of the item concerned at the date of the balance sheet. This is certainly not irrelevant, and is likely to be more informative than historical cost would be. But it is not necessarily an indication of the eventual cash or profits/losses which are likely to arise in the future. Bankers, lenders, investors, and government planners all need to intelligently and knowledgably interpret the financial information they receive. Here too, major educational developments may be required.

From the other side, intensification of harmonization processes in accounting, including IFRS implementation in Moldova, has the hidden potential of eliminating Moldovan specialists from the accounting services market, at least for a certain period of time. The growing competition in this sector will be determined by elimination of national features of accounting and application of universal accounting rules. If a country is relatively less efficient in these services (due to mentality and education), the law of competition suggests allocating them to others. Of course, physical presence is still extremely important for accounting procedures, but information and technologies development will definitely eliminate this problem in the near future. In fact, accounting professionalism is a result of globalization, as in the context of the individual accountants with more focus on professional development, learning, and practice, which would achieve more successes in an extremely competitive atmosphere. The reduction of national barriers, dictated by globalization, will force these tendencies to improve. Growing international business activities and the influence of foreign operations are additional factors that will contribute to fundamental modifications in accounting professions and understanding the role of accounting services.

Recent changes and accounting standardization are inevitable for Moldova. It is necessary to accept the rules of globalization and internationalization of business. At the same time, there is no doubt that not all global tendencies and various concrete application of them should be taken as granted. There is a strong necessity to analyze and measure the impact of each modern innovation for the conditions of a certain country, taking into consideration its mentality, level of development and economic culture.

CONCLUDING REMARKS

Accounting is a sphere that is very sensitive to various political and cultural transformations. Accounting reforms in Moldova have been executed with significant support of international organizations and huge resources were attracted for this process. The biggest problem today is lack of interest and demand for qualitative information due to the specific mentality existing for decades. Moldova is in the process of implementation of IFRS now. Although all entities are not obliged to use IFRS, enterprises of public interest are required to do this. There is a serious possibility that other businesses will not prefer IFRS, because the process of transition to IFRS is expensive, but the need for it is not obvious. Many practitioners do not have much knowledge about the IFRS, and many do not consider them necessary. Foreign investments represent a weak perspective for the majority of Moldovan enterprises, thus, IFRS will be properly applied only when companies perceive and understand the benefits in using them.

The analysis and investigation developed in the chapter have demonstrated that historical and cultural preconditions are of great importance in determining the successful implementation of IFRS and further accounting development. Different factors, starting from pre-war Stalinist policies and ending with more recent Soviet times, ennoble the attitude towards fiscal bodies, and determine nowadays the mode of perception and acceptance of IFRS and accounting harmonization in general. Based on Nobes's and Hofstede's classification of factors that may change the accounting development, our findings demonstrate the importance and influence of almost all of them in the case of Moldova. Ignoring these influences and their implications is likely to lead to a lack of success in seeking to change future directions. Historical and cultural factors do matter.

Therefore, the aspiration to attain EU membership is a good motivation for the Moldovan government today, but not sufficient for local entities without any global potential. In addition, a wide range of other indirect factors have an impact on the implementation process, and these influences are likely to continue. Country-specific considerations are required. In this regard, the extended analysis of multidisciplinary historical and cultural factors for successful or unsuccessful IFRS implementation may become an important direction for further research. This proposition is surely generalizable, even if Moldova provides a particularly strong example.

NOTES

1. For the purpose of this paper we refer to IFRS solely, as it is stipulated in the Law of Accounting nr. 113-XVI. Internationally, IFRS are standards issued by International Accounting Standards Board (IASB) from 2001 onward, and IAS were issued by IASC in the period 1973–2001.
2. 1 Moldovan Leu is equal to about 0.06 Euro, according to the National bank of Moldova as on June 27, 2013.

REFERENCES

Abdelal, R. (2001). *National purpose in the world economy: Post-Soviet states in comparative perspective*. Ithaca, NY: Cornell University Press.

Accounting Law. (2007). Accounting Law nr. 113-XVI from April 27, 2007. Retrieved from http://lex.justice.md/index.php? action = view&view = doc&lang = 1&id = 324098 (in Romanian language).

Albu, N., Albu, C. N., Bunea, S., Calu, D. A., & Girbina, M. M. (2011). A story about IAS/IFRS implementation in Romania. *Journal of Accounting in Emerging Economies*, *1*(1), 76–100.

Altvater, E. (2009). *Was Marx right after all? A critical analysis of the global financial crisis*. Retrieved from http://www.periodicos.ufpa.br/index.php/ncn/article/viewfile/279/514

Armitage, J., Neider, M., & Shelaru, M. (2003). Accounting reform in the Republic of Moldova. *International Business and Economics Research Journal*, *2*(4), 29–36.

Artsberg, K. (2001). *International Accounting standardization vis-a-vis European accounting harmonization*. Retrieved from http://www.snee.org/filer/papers/23.pdf

Borker, D. (2012). Accounting, culture and emerging economies: IFRS in Central and Eastern Europe. *Interantional Business and Economics Research Journal*, *11*(9), 1003–1018.

Borker, D. R. (2012). Accounting, culture and emerging economies: IFRS in the BRIC countries. *Journal of Business and Economic Research*, *5*, 313–324.

Campos, N., & Coricelli, F. (2003). Growth in transition: What we know, what we don't and what we should. *Journal of Economic Literature, XL* (3), 793–836.

Djatej A., Sarikas R., & Senteney D. (2008). In R. McGee (Ed.), *Accounting reforms in transition and developing economies* (Chapter 9, pp. 139–155). UK: Springer.

Ernu, V. (2012). *De ce România şi Republica Moldova sînt state artificiale şi cînd va exploda bomba socială în Europa? – Interviu cu Vasile Ernu (Why Romania and the Republic of Moldova are artificial states and when the social bomb will blow up – Interview wilth Vasile Ernu)*. Retrieved from http://www.criticatac.ro/19843/de-ce-romania-republica-moldova-sint-state-artificiale-cint-va-exploda-bomba-social-europa-interviu-cu-vasile-ernu/

Financial Times. (1993). Daimler-Benz pierces accounting mystique. *Financial Times*, September 23.

Frecauteanu, A. (2008). Sistemul contabil din Republica Moldova: Realizari, problem si perspective de dezvoltare. *Stiinta Agricola, 2*(2008), 92–95.

General Documents of the Working Party on Domestic Regulation on the Disciplines for the Accountancy Sector (set of documents, adopted in various years). Retrieved from http://www.wto.org/english/tratop_e/serv_e/accountancy_e/accountancy_e.htm

Government Decree. (1997). Government decree nr. 1187 from December 24, 1997. Retrieved from http://lex.justice.md/document_rom.php?id = CD70267F:3CBF191C

Gray, S. J. (1988). *Towards a theory of cultural influence on the development of accounting systems internationally*. Retrieved from http://www.acis.pamplin.vt.edu/faculty/%20tegarden/5034/handouts/Gray-Abacus-1988.pdf

Havrylyshyn, O. (2008). Growth recovery in CIS countries: The sufficient minimum threshold of reforms. *Comparative Economic Studies, 50*(1), 53–78.

He, X., Wong, T. J., & Young, D. (2009). Challenges for implementation of fair value accounting in emerging markets: Evidence from IFRS adoption in China. INTACCT *Research Workshop materials*, Spain.

Hensel, S., & Gudim, A. (2001). *Moldova's economic transition: slow and contradictory*. Retrieved from http://pdc.ceu.hu/archive/00002399/01/Moldova-s_Economic_Transition.pdf

Hofstede, G. (1980). *Culture's consequences: International differences in work-related values*. Thousand Oaks, CA: Sage.

Hofstede, G. (1983). Dimensions of national cultures in fifty countries and three regions. In *Explications in cross-cultural psychology* (pp. 335–355). Lisse, Netherlands: Swets & Zeitlinger.

Ministry of Finance of the Republic of Moldova. (2009–2014). *Development plan on accounting and audit in the corporate sector*. Retrieved from http://www.mf.gov.md/ro/actnorm/contabil/plan/. (In Romanian language).

Mehtiyeva, N. (2009). *Accounting and audit reforms in transition economies: The case of Azerbaijan*. Master thesis, Lunds Universitet. Retrieved from http://lup.lub.lu.se/luur/%20download?func = downloadFile&recordOId = 1474576&fileOId = 2435463

National Accounting Standards of the Republic of Moldova. (1998/2001). Retrieved from http://www.mf.gov.md/ro/actnorm/contabil/standarts/ (all in Romanian language).

Nistor, C. S., & Filip, C. (2008). *The evolution of public accounting in Romania in the post-communist period*. Retrieved from http://papers.ssrn.com/sol3/%20papers.cfm?abstract_id = 1107774

Nobes, C. (1984). *International classification of financial reporting*. London: Croom Helm.

Okaro, S., & Tauringana, V. (2012), From SAS to IFRS: An investigation of nigeria transition road map implementation problems. In V. Tauringana & M. Mangena (Eds.), *Accounting in Africa* (Vol. 12, pp. 155–176). Research in Accounting in Emerging Economies. Bingley, UK: Emerald Group Publishing Limited.

Pasekova, M. (2011). Financial reporting in Slovakia. In *Harmonization of SMEs financial reporting in CEE countries* (pp. 263–306). Czech Republic: WSEAS press.

PWC Investing Guide. (2012). Retrieved from http://www.pwc.com/en_MD/md/assets/document/investing_guide_moldova_2012.pdf

ROSC. (2004, June). *Report on the observance of standards and codes, accounting and auditing.* Retrieved from http://documents.worldbank.org/curated/en/2013/06/18310007/moldova-reports-observance-standards-codes-rosc-accounting-auditing-update

Schubel, D. (2011). *Interview.* Retrieved from http://www.allmoldova.com/en/int/interview/dirk-schubel-131211.html

Skvortsova, A. (2002). The cultural and social makeup of Moldova: A bipolar or dispersed society. In P. Kolsto (Ed.), *National integration and violent conflict in post-Soviet societies: The cases of Estonia and Moldova.* US, Maryland: Rowman & Littlefield.

Solodchenko, I., & Sucher, P. (2005). Accounting in Ukraine since independence: Real politic, problems and prospects. *European Accounting Review*, *14*(3), 603–633.

Stalin, J. (1929). *The year of great turn (Год великого перелома).* Retrieved from http://www.petrograd.biz/stalin/12-1.php

Stiglitz, J. (2008). The fruit if hypocrizy. *The Guardian*, September 16. Retrieved from http://www.theguardian.com/commentisfree/2008/sep/16/economics.wallstreet

Strouhal, J., Bonaci, C., & Sklenar, R. (2011). Impact of international harmonization on Czech accounting legislature (focused on mergers). *International Journal of Mathematical Models and Methods in Applied Sciences.* Retrieved from http://www.naun.org/multimedia/NAUN/m3as/17-772.pdf

Tyler, R., & Vanderhoof, G. (2001). Georgia enterprise accounting reform. *Sibley International Report for USAID.* Retrieved from http://pdf.usaid.gov/%20pdf_docs/PDABU715.pdf

Wallerstein, I. (2008). *the demise of neoliberal globalization.* Retrieved from http://mrzine.monthlyreview.org/2008/wallerstein010208.html

Werth, N., Bartosek, K., Panne, J. L., Margolin, J. L., Paczkowski, A., & Courtois, S. (1999). *The black book of communism: Crimes, terror, repression.* Cambridge, MA: Harvard University Press.

FURTHER READING

Campos, N., & Coricelli, F. (2002). Growth in transition: What we know, what we don't and what we should. *Journal of Economic Literature*, *XL*(3), 793–836.

General Documents. (n.d.). *General documents of the working party on domestic regulation on the disciplines for the accountancy sector.* Retrieved from http://www.wto.org/english/tratop_e/%20serv_e/accountancy_e/accountancy_e.htm

Government Decree. (2008). Government decree nr. 238 from February 29, 2008. Retrieved from www.mf.gov.md

MsGee, R., & Preobragenskaya, G. (2006). *Accounting and financial system reform in Eastern Europe and Asia.* USA: Springer.

INTELLECTUAL CAPITAL DISCLOSURE OF ROMANIAN LISTED COMPANIES

Nicoleta Maria Ienciu and Dumitru Matiș

ABSTRACT

Purpose – *This chapter expands the existing literature by examining voluntary intellectual capital disclosure provided by listed Romanian companies in 2010 annual reports.*

Design/methodology/approach – *The chapter aims to determine the extent of intellectual capital disclosure within Romanian listed companies. Within this chapter we have conducted a content analysis using the annual reports of 71 companies listed on Bucharest Stock Exchange (BSE), main market (Bursa de Valori Bucure_ti – BVB). The intellectual capital framework developed by Sveiby in 1997 was used in our analysis and the frequency of disclosure was used as the measure of disclosure.*

Findings – *The results show that the key components of intellectual capital are relatively poorly reported by Romanian listed companies. The main areas of intellectual capital disclosure focus firstly on structural capital, then on relational capital and at the end on human capital.*

Accounting in Central and Eastern Europe
Research in Accounting in Emerging Economies, Volume 13, 143–162

ISSN: 1479-3563/doi:10.1108/S1479-3563(2013)0000013011

Research limitations/implications – *The existence of information related to intellectual capital is used as the measure of the level of intellectual capital disclosure. Also, our exploratory investigation concerns only one fiscal year.*

Originality/value – *According to the authors' knowledge the present chapter is a pioneering study developed at national level which highlights the intellectual capital disclosure practices of Romanian listed companies by examining their 2010 annual reports. The chapter highlights new insights of the level of intellectual capital disclosure within companies which operates in small capital market.*

Keywords: Intellectual capital; disclosure; annual reports; Romania; listed companies; content analysis

INTRODUCTION

The emerging of "new economy," mainly driven by information and knowledge, has been identified by the Organization for Economic Cooperation and Development as the explanation lying at the base of the development of intellectual capital, which is a fundamental topic in business (Hornery, 1999). One way or another, intellectual capital plays a significant role in the economic, administrative, technological and social development of contemporary times, being difficult to quantify. More exactly, the importance of intellectual capital is highlighted, more accurately, by means of (Petty & Guthrie, 2000, p. 157):

- information technology revolution and the informational society;
- increase in volume of knowledge and knowledge based economy;
- models for change in terms of interpersonal and society activities; and
- innovation emerged as main determining factor for competition.

Although such evolutions are regarded from the point of view of knowledge based economy there are many arguments supporting the idea that intellectual capital holds an instrumental role in determining the value of an entity and the performance of national economies (Burton-Jones, 1999; Mouritsen, 1998).

In the last period, specialists from different fields of expertise (Campbell & Rahman, 2010; Choong, 2008; Khan & Ali, 2010; Sharafi, Moghadam, & Sharafi, 2012; Vafaei, Taylor, & Ahmed, 2011) have shown a particular interest for intellectual capital researches which are focused on the importance given to knowledge and investment in immaterial elements of the entity and to "cognitive fields" in which the ideas matter and create value for entity.

A large number of researchers avoid defining intellectual capital, but consider it as the basic value of a company (Edvinsson & Malone, 1997; Stewart, 1997). They support the idea that intellectual capital aids companies in the process of creating value and offering competitive advantages. As a result, intellectual capital can be regarded as one of the most valuable "assets" and the most powerful competitive weapon in business. Hiroyuki Itami, a well-known researcher in the field of intellectual capital, defines the term as an intangible asset, including elements of technology, information about clients, trademarks, reputation, and corporate culture, which are priceless items for a competitive company (1987). While for Stewart (1997) intellectual capital is a set of knowledge, information, intellectual property, and expertise that can be used in order to create wealth, for Bontis (2001), intellectual capital represents the individual knowledge of employees and organizational knowledge contributing to obtaining competitive advantage.

The reporting of intellectual capital within financial statements and other complementary financial reporting documents is voluntary. The components of intellectual capital fail to meet the criteria required for inclusion or acknowledgement within financial statements and are not measured in monetary terms (Van der Meer-Kooistra & Zijlstra, 2001).

The literature presents an abundance of studies, conducted in various parts of the world related to intellectual capital reporting within annual reports (April, Bosma, & Deglon, 2003; Bontis, 2003; Brennan, 2001; Guthrie & Petty, 2000; Olsson, 2001), as part of the initial public offering prospectus (Bukh, Nielsen, Gormsen, & Mouritsen, 2005) and included in presentations[1] for various stakeholders (Garcia-Meca, Parra, Larran, & Martinez, 2005).

When analyzing the information included in the annual reports, most studies start from the classification model[2] of intellectual capital supplied by Sveiby in 1997 (April et al., 2003; Bozzolan, Favotto, & Ricceri, 2003; Brennan, 2001; Bruggen, Vergauwen & Dao, 2009; Guthrie & Petty, 2000; Olsson, 2001). The results of these studies are relatively similar, most of them concluding that most reported intellectual capital related information are those referring to external/relational capital, the internal/structural capital holds the second position, while certain studies state that human capital is either as equally reported as the internal/structural capital

(Brennan, 2001; Guthrie, Petty, Ferrier, & Wells, 1999), or to a larger extent (Abeysekera & Guthrie, 2005; Oliveira, Rodrigues, & Craig, 2006) or smaller extent (Bozzolan et al., 2003; Goh & Lim, 2004) than it.

The chapter expands the existing intellectual capital disclosure literature by providing an analysis of voluntary disclosure information within Romanian entities for the 2010 fiscal year. In order to achieve such objective we have undergone an applicative, quantitative research, using as method of research the content analysis of the annual reports of Romanian companies listed on Bucharest Stock Exchange (BSE).

The structure of the chapter is as follows. In the next section we briefly outline the prior work existing in the field, drawing attention to international studies considering that at national level the intellectual capital disclosure literature is very poor. The second section details the research methodology developed within the chapter followed by the third section which assesses the content analysis of annual reports of Romanian companies and summarize the main results of the performed analysis. The chapter ends by presenting the main conclusions and the future perspectives of research.

LITERATURE REVIEW

Research in the field shows that over time significant efforts have been made to understand the level of intellectual capital information reporting and its use by stakeholders. The literature presents a plethora of studies conducted in various parts of the world regarding the reporting of intellectual capital within annual reports (Brennan, 2001; Guthrie & Petty, 2000; Ienciu & Ienciu, 2012; Olsson, 2001; Sonnier, 2008; Vafaei et al., 2011).

The annual reports prepared and published by companies listed on capital markets have been used to investigate the practice of disclosure information on intellectual capital (Brennan, 2001; Guthrie, Petty, & Ricceri, 2006). Empirical studies show that annual reports are deemed as the most useful sources of information used by management to report the company's most significant aspects, and at the same time, as communication means allowing the company to connect with various stakeholders (Guthrie & Petty, 2000). They also present the advantage of being supplied regularly, offering the possibility for comparative analysis of management policies and attitudes throughout the reporting period (Guthrie, Petty,

Yongvanich, & Ricceri, 2004). In many jurisdictions, annual reports are imposed by law in accordance with a standard base, for all entities. Nevertheless, the risk remains for annual reports to fail reflecting the objective reality of the entity, in the event the entity uses them as "advertising documents" and not in accordance with accounting standards and corporate law (Abeysekera, 2008, p. 19).

The content analysis of the annual reports having been used by various researchers, because it represents a good instrument for a comparative assessment of positions and trends used in preparing the statements. Australian researchers have been amongst the first to adopt the content analysis as a means to examine the practices used by companies to manage and prepare the statements on intellectual capital. Guthrie and Petty (2000), by referring to the Australian annual disclosure practices, focus on intellectual capital disclosure within 19 annual reports. They use the method of content analysis and a modified version of Sveiby's model in order to classify information on intellectual capital. The three dimensions of the intellectual capital conceptual framework (internal capital, external capital, and human capital) together with the related subcategories (nine for the internal capital framework, nine for the external capital, and six for the human capital) are encoded with the value zero when the variable is not included in the annual statement, one if the value is presented in a discursive fashion, two when the information is approached from a quantitative point of view, and three when the information is assessed monetarily. The results from Australian researches are far from being systematic, despite the attention and significance granted to intellectual capital. Australian companies do not have an agreed framework for preparing reports concerning the intellectual capital, moreover, it appears the "notion of assessing and reporting intellectual capital is enclosed into a rhetorical framework lacking in content" (Guthrie & Petty, 2000, p. 246).

Brennan (2001) conducted a similar study with relation to Irish companies, analyzing annual reports from 21 companies listed on the stocks market. The author used an identical scheme as Guthrie and Petty (2000) in order to encode data in the content analysis of annual reports and has identified similar results to the Australian study. The results indicated that the Irish context was similar to the Australian one because there is no disclosure framework for intellectual capital; hence the companies assess their intellectual capital by using the qualitative method and less the quantitative one. Just as Guthrie and Petty (2000) have noticed, these results emphasize the difficulties encountered by companies in the administrative process for assessment and disclosure of intellectual capital.

A study conducted by Olsson (2001) examined the annual reports of the 18 most important companies listed at the Swedish Stock Exchange, selected based on their turnover, drafting a list of five elements in order to evaluate the level of human capital disclosure. The study pointed out that neither company granted more than 7% space, as part of their annual reports, for presenting information on human resources, as the information found in the statements had both quantitative and qualitative deficiencies.

The international comparative study conducted by Subbarao and Zeghal (1997) on the content analysis of annual reports in countries such as United States, Canada, Germany, United Kingdom, Japan, and South Korea, show a clear difference between these countries in terms of quantity of information presented in the annual reports. The results of the analysis state that the European entities report more information connected to human resources than Asian or Nord American entities, and there are also some clear distinctions in terms of activity sectors (Vithana, Riham, & Amir, 2011).

At national level, the existing studies are very few (Bogdan, Platon, & Popa, 2011; Feleagă, Feleagă, Dragomir, & Râbu, 2011; Ienciu & Ienciu, 2012; Ienciu & Matiș, 2011; Morariu, 2011) and for this reason we consider that the Romanian intellectual capital disclosure literature is underdeveloped. In their research, Bogdan et al. (2011) aim to measure the extent of intellectual capital disclosure using 2005–2009 annual reports of Romanian listed manufacturing companies on BSE as the source of their documentation. They conclude that 50% of Romanian manufacturing companies disclose intellectual capital information, most of them referring to relational capital. This result is similar with those obtained by Ienciu and Matiș (2011) whose research aims to examine voluntary intellectual capital disclosure provided by listed Romanian entities in annual reports from the year 2009. They conclude that the relational capital is the most disclosed element (38%) of intellectual capital, followed by human capital (27%) and structural capital (21%).

Not the same idea is supported by Morariu (2011) which has conducted a similar study regarding the intellectual capital disclosure within Romanian listed companies. By analyzing the 2009 annual reports of 98 Romanian companies the results of the study indicate that the structural capital is the most disclosed element of intellectual capital in a proportion of 47.3%, followed by relational capital (27.48%) and at the end by human capital (25.22%). These findings are also supported by Feleagă et al. (2011) which examined the degree to which different categories of intellectual capital are disclosed in the annual reports of a sample of large European companies. By referring to 18 companies included in the STOXX® Europe TMI Software & Computer Services Index, from six countries they evidence that the structural capital has the largest reporting rate of 42% of the IC attributes disclosed, the relational capital are the second most reported elements, in the proportion of 34% while human capital comprise the most neglected elements, with 24% of the total disclosures.

In a recent research, Ienciu and Ienciu (2012) examine the determinants that can influence the level of intellectual capital disclosure. Using data collected from 2010 annual reports of 68 Romanian listed companies they analyzed if the level of intellectual capital disclosure is influence by a series of elements such as firm size expressed by turnover, equity, number of employees, industry sector and financial situation (recorded profit or loss). According to their results, only the financial situation of a company has a significant influence level of intellectual capital disclosure.

Considering that the intellectual capital disclosure literature in Romania is somewhat in its early stage of development within the present paper we intend to expand the low intellectual capital disclosure literature existing at national level. In this regard we have conducted a study using the content analysis method with regards to the annual reports of companies listed on the Romanian capital market, intending to analyze the relevance of the ideas that have been studied until now by transferring them into the chosen sample of companies.

RESEARCH DESIGN

The current chapter contains a study performed on 71 companies listed on the BSE, main market (starting on December 31, 2010). The participant companies are from industries such as: manufacturing, mining, and quarrying, constructions, financial services, transport, wholesale and retail trade, tourism (see the appendix). In the study we took into account all the companies listed on the BSE market. Thus, from a total of 104 companies, we analyzed 71 companies (considered the most traded), 8 of them being suspended and 25 non-listed. The sample was chosen based on the fact that listed companies are obligated to publish their annual reports, for public interest. The sources used for collecting data on intellectual capital were the annual reports for the fiscal year 2010, because we consider them the most important sources of information made available by the companies to the external users and in particular to the shareholders.

Hence, we have performed a content analysis of the annual reports of companies listed on BSEs, wherein we have monitored the three dimensions of the intellectual capital conceptual framework (structural capital, relational capital, and human capital) together with the related subcategories (for the purpose of classifying information, we have used a modified version of Sveiby's model presented by Bozzolan et al., 2003) which we have grouped as follows: two subcategories for the framework of structural capital (*the intellectual property* – patents, copyrights, registered trademark; *the infrastructure assets* – corporate culture, management of processes, IT system, networks systems, research projects, financial relations), five for relational capital (*the customers* – company's customers, the loyalty of customers, customer relations, customer involvement, attracting new customers; *the reputation/image of the company*; *the supply and distribution channels* – relations with suppliers and competitors; *the cooperation* – in business, research, concluded contracts; *concluded agreements* – franchises, licenses) and four for the human capital (education; employees; work-related knowledge, and work-related competencies) (Table 1).

Table 1. The Analyzed Key Components of Intellectual Capital.

Structural Capital	Relational Capital	Human Capital
Intellectual property	*Customers*	*Education*
Patents	Customers	*Employees*
Copyrights	Customer loyalty	*Work-related knowledge*
Trade-marks	Business collaboration	*Work-related competence*
Infrastructure assets	Customer involvement	
Corporate culture	Attracting new customers	
Management processes	*Company reputation*	
Information systems	*Supply and distribution channels*	
Networking systems	Relationships with suppliers	
Research projects	Relationships with competitors	
Financial contacts	*Collaborations*	
	Business collaboration	
	Research collaborations	
	Contracts	
	Agreements	
	Franchising agreements	
	Licensing agreements	

Source: Bozzolan et al. (2003, p. 549).

The content analysis was performed throughout information appearance approach and the variables have been encoded with the score (value) zero when the companies do not provide any information, one when the information is presented in a discursive fashion (text and/or numeric) and with two when the information is assessed in monetary terms. At the end, we have calculated an average of scores based on following formulas:

$$\text{Scoring SC} = \frac{\sum_{i=1}^{n}\left(\sum_{j=1}^{m1} \text{SCD}j/m1\right)}{n} \tag{1}$$

$$\text{Scoring RC} = \frac{\sum_{i=1}^{n}\left(\sum_{j=1}^{m2} RCDj/m2\right)}{n} \tag{2}$$

$$\text{Scoring HC} = \frac{\sum_{i=1}^{n}\left(\sum_{j=1}^{m3} \text{HCD}j/m3\right)}{n} \tag{3}$$

where

SCDj/RCDj/HCDj = Structural capital/relational capital/human capital dimensions (components considered for our research)
$m1$ = Structural capital dimension (2 analyzed components)
$m2$ = Relational capital dimension (5 analyzed components)
$m3$ = Human capital dimension (4 analyzed components)
n = The analyzed population (71 analyzed companies)
i = The values of structural capital/relational capital/human capital dimensions for each company in part

Our main concern when using the content analysis as research method is its reliability. In this sense, the study presents several methods meant to increase the objectivity of data collection and analysis. First of all, the analysis of documented information was performed by two people (two coders), one of them studying the documents and giving codes to every information found, and the other person, confirming independently, the encoding of each element (inter-coder reliability). Second of all, we have predefined the elements before conducting the documents' content analysis, and after a certain period of time, we have reexamined the documented information in order to confirm the proper encoding of their content (intra-coder reliability).

Table 2. The Scoring System of Information Regarding

	Aerostar	Alro	Altur	Alumil Rom Industry	Amonil	Antibiotice	Armatura	Artego	Azomures	Banca Comerciala Carpatica
Structural Capital	1	1	1	1	1	2	1	1	1	1
Intellectual property	0	0	0	0	0	2	0	1	0	0
Infrastructure assets	2	1	2	1	1	2	1	1	1	2
Relational Capital	1	0	0	0	0	1	1	1	1	1
Customers	1	0	1	1	0	1	1	1	1	2
Company reputation	0	0	0	0	0	0	0	0	0	1
Supply and distribution channels	1	1	1	1	1	1	1	1	1	1
Collaborations	1	0	0	0	1	1	1	1	1	1
Agreements	0	0	0	0	0	1	0	0	0	0
Human Capital	1	1	1	0	0	1	1	0	1	1
Education	0	1	1	0	0	1	1	0	1	1
Employees	2	1	1	1	1	1	1	0	2	1
Work-related knowledge	0	0	0	0	0	0	1	1	0	1
Work-related competencies	1	0	1	0	0	1	0	0	0	1

	Dafora	Electroaparataj	Electroarges	Electromagnetica	Electroputere	Farmaceutica Remedia	Grupul Industrial Electrocontact	Impact Developer Constructor	Mecanica Ceahlau	Mechel Targoviste
Structural Capital	1	1	1	1	1	1	1	1	2	1
Intellectual property	0	0	0	0	0	0	0	0	1	0
Infrastructure assets	1	1	1	1	1	1	1	1	2	1
Relational Capital	1	1	1	0	0	1	0	1	0	1
Customers	1	1	1	1	1	1	1	1	0	1
Company reputation	0	0	0	0	0	0	0	0	0	0
Supply and distribution channels	1	2	1	1	1	1	1	1	0	1
Collaborations	1	0	1	0	0	1	0	1	1	1
Agreements	0	0	0	0	0	0	0	0	0	0
Human Capital	1	0	1	1	0	1	0	1	1	1
Education	1	0	1	0	0	1	0	1	1	1
Employees	1	1	1	2	1	1	0	1	1	1
Work-related knowledge	1	0	0	0	0	0	0	1	0	0
Work-related competencies	1	0	0	0	0	0	0	1	0	0

	SSIF Broker	Santierul Naval	SC Fondul Proprietatea	Transilvania Constructii	SIF Banat Crisana	SIF Moldova	SIF Muntenia	SIF Transilvania	SIF Oltenia	Sinteza
Structural Capital	1	1	1	1	1	1	0	1	1	1
Intellectual property	0	0	0	0	0	0	0	0	0	0
Infrastructure assets	1	1	1	1	1	1	0	1	1	1
Relational Capital	0	1	1	1	0	0	0	0	0	0
Customers	0	1	1	2	0	0	0	0	0	0
Company reputation	0	0	0	0	0	0	0	0	0	0
Supply and distribution channels	0	1	1	1	0	0	0	0	0	1
Collaborations	0	1	0	0	1	1	1	1	1	1
Agreements	0	0	1	0	0	0	0	0	0	0
Human Capital	1	1	1	1	1	1	1	1	1	1
Education	1	1	1	0	1	1	1	1	1	1
Employees	1	1	1	2	1	1	1	1	1	1
Work-related knowledge	0	0	0	0	0	0	0	0	0	0
Work-related skills	0	0	1	0	0	0	0	1	1	0

Intellectual Capital within Romanian Listed Companies in 2010.

Banca Transilvania	Bermas	Biofarm	Boromir Prod	BRD	CNTEE Electrica	Carbochim	Casa de Bucovina	Cemacon	Comelf	Compa	Compania Energopetrol	Concefa	Condmag
1	1	2	1	1	2	1	1	0	1	1	0	1	1
0	0	2	0	0	2	0	0	0	0	0	0	0	0
1	1	1	1	1	2	1	1	0	1	2	0	2	1
1	1	1	1	1	1	1	0	1	1	1	0	1	1
1	1	1	1	1	1	1	1	1	1	1	0	1	1
1	0	0	0	0	1	0	0	0	0	0	0	0	0
1	1	1	1	1	1	1	0	1	1	2	0	1	1
1	1	1	1	2	1	1	0	1	1	1	0	1	1
0	0	0	0	0	0	0	0	0	0	0	0	0	0
0	1	1	0	1	1	0	1	1	0	1	0	0	1
0	1	1	0	1	1	0	0	0	0	1	0	0	1
1	1	1	1	1	1	1	2	2	1	1	1	1	1
0	0	1	0	1	0	0	0	0	0	1	0	0	0
0	0	0	0	1	1	0	0	0	0	1	0	0	0

Mefin	Mj Maillis Romania	Oil Terminal	Oltchim	OMV Petrom	Petrolexportimport	Prefab	Prodplast	Retrasib	Romcarbon	Rompetrol Rafinare	Rompetrol Well Services	Ropharma	SNTGN Transgaz
1	1	1	1	0	0	1	0	1	1	1	1	0	1
0	0	0	0	0	0	0	0	0	0	0	0	0	0
1	1	1	2	0	0	1	0	1	1	1	1	0	1
1	0	1	0	1	1	0	0	1	1	1	0	0	1
1	1	2	1	1	2	1	1	1	1	1	1	0	1
0	0	0	0	1	0	0	0	0	0	0	0	0	1
1	1	1	1	1	2	1	1	1	1	1	1	0	1
1	0	1	0	1	1	0	0	1	1	1	0	0	1
0	0	0	0	1	0	0	0	0	0	1	0	0	0
0	1	1	1	1	1	1	1	0	1	1	1	1	1
0	1	1	1	1	1	0	1	0	1	1	1	1	1
1	1	1	1	1	1	1	1	1	1	1	1	1	1
0	0	0	0	0	0	0	0	0	0	0	0	0	1
0	0	0	0	1	0	1	0	0	0	0	0	0	0

Siretul Pascani	SOCEP	TMK Artrom	Teraplast	Titan	Turbomecanica	Turism Felix	Turism Hoteluri Marea Neagra	UAMT	Vae Apcarom	Ves	Vrancart	Zentiva	TOTAL
1	1	0	1	1	1	1	1	1	1	1	1	1	**0.59**
0	0	0	0	1	0	1	0	0	0	1	0	0	
1	1	0	1	1	1	1	1	2	1	1	1	1	
1	0	1	1	1	1	0	1	1	1	1	1	0	**0.53**
1	1	1	1	1	1	1	1	2	1	1	1	0	
0	0	0	1	1	0	0	0	0	1	0	1	0	
1	0	1	1	0	1	1	1	1	1	1	1	1	
1	0	1	1	1	1	0	0	0	1	0	1	0	
0	0	0	0	0	0	0	1	0	0	1	0	0	
0	0	0	1	1	0	1	1	0	1	1	1	1	**0.52**
0	0	0	1	1	0	1	0	0	1	1	1	0	
1	1	0	1	1	1	1	2	1	1	1	1	2	
0	0	0	0	0	0	0	0	0	0	0	0	0	
0	0	1	1	1	0	0	0	0	0	0	1	1	

ANALYSIS AND RESULTS

Starting from the classification of the intellectual capital elements by means of the modified version of the Sveiby's model presented above (Bozzolan et al., 2003), we have performed a content analysis of the annual reports of the companies listed on the Bucharest Stock Exchange and we have obtained the following results (see Table 2):

We can observe from the scores obtained and presented above that the information regarding structural capital, relational capital, and human capital provided by the Romanian listed companies are qualitative information (presented in a discursive fashion).

According to the above table we can notice the interest manifested by Romanian companies for the intellectual capital disclosure. The obtained scores of each component of intellectual capital was 0.59 (structural capital), 0.53 (relational capital), and 0.52 (human capital). This scores signifies that most companies report information related to intellectual capital, information which are mostly qualitative, nonfinancial, and nonmonetary.

If we were to perform an analysis of information reported for the three groups of components related to intellectual capital, we should mention that aspects reported with regards to the structural capital were part of the field of research projects and information regarding the relational capital referred to four elements in particular: customers, company's reputation, distribution chains, cooperation, and licenses. As far as human capital disclosure is concerned we argue that only one company offered no information whatsoever for this topic. The most frequently reported element and the closest to human resource was the one regarding the number of employees, while the rest of annual reports were divided between the knowledge of human capital, competences thereof and the employees training.

Our results are similar to those existing in literature (Bozzolan et al., 2003; Feleagă et al., 2011; Morariu, 2011) according to which the structural capital records the highest disclosure rate in comparison with the other two elements of intellectual capital. This finding is due to the fact that in Romania the companies accord more importance to infrastructural elements than relational and human ones. For them, the "core" of intellectual system is represented by organizational components (i.e., corporate culture, management of processes, IT system, network systems, intellectual property, and other similar goods) followed by relational components (company's customers, loyalty of customers, customer relations, customer involvement, image of company, relations with suppliers and competitors, partnerships, etc.), and human elements (educational system, employees, work-related knowledge, work-related competencies) without which the system cannot functioning properly.

Based on these results we are asking: *Is there a lack of interest for intellectual capital's components within Romanian listed companies, or more likely a lack for a disclosure and evaluation framework for the intellectual capital which makes this information be considered irrelevant for the company?* The results regarding the level of intellectual capital disclosure in Romania can be explained by the fact that although management would like to provide more relevant and useful information to the public, they cannot act in such a way, because the danger of competitors' "espionage" persists. As underlined by Williams (2001) as well, *such disclosure can catch attention from undesired parts as well.* Therefore, although there are sufficient arguments to convince management that disclosure information on intellectual capital is a necessity, they would not act because such disclosure could affect the company in a negative way, in particular for the case where the intellectual capital groundwork is a poor one. On the other hand, the annual statement can indicate that one priority for the company consists in investing financial resources in the internal "production" or the purchase of new assets. Or, to the contrary, a report from a company disposing of little intellectual capital might have a negative impact on the company's reputation on the stock market, because in this way it can be considered unsuccessful.

CONCLUSION, LIMITATIONS, AND FURTHER RESEARCH DIRECTIONS

Within this chapter, we aimed to expand the existing intellectual capital disclosure literature by providing an analysis of voluntary disclosure information within Romanian entities. In order to achieve the purpose of our study, we have made a content analysis, of 2010 annual reports of companies listed on the BSEs, wherein we have monitored the three dimensions of the intellectual capital conceptual framework (structural capital, relational capital, and human capital) together with the related subcategories, proposed by Karl-Eric Sveiby's (1997) and developed by Bozzolan et al. (2003).

As a result of the study, we draw the conclusion that the treatment of intellectual capital framework in Romania is in an initial stage. Most

Romanian companies handle this matter with indifference, disclosure only certain information in connection to this subject, without creating a general disclosure framework. The obtained results indicate that most information related to intellectual capital is presented in a discursive mode within annual reports and not under monetary terms. These findings lead us to conclude that as long as Romanian listed companies do not have an agreed framework for preparing reports concerning the intellectual capital they present voluntary random information. It seems that the discursive mode for intellectual capital disclosure information is agreed for the most Romanian companies maybe because this is the easy way to present information related to intellectual capital. Similar to prior works (Bozzolan et al., 2003; Feleagă et al., 2011; Goh & Lim, 2004), the structural capital is the most reported element of intellectual capital, followed by relational capital and human capital.

Our results are valuable in at least two ways. First this chapter expands the existing intellectual capital disclosure literature at national level and second it validates the results of other studies representing a basis for comparison with them.

The study presents several limitations. For the time being, the limitation of the study is given by the relatively small population of companies participating to the analysis. During future research, we will consider the analysis of annual reports of more Romanian companies. Also, our exploratory investigation concerns only one fiscal year. In this regard as a research perspective we will analyze the evolution of intellectual capital disclosure within Romanian companies' behaviour for a longer period of time. Another limitation of our study is represented by the use of frequency of information related to intellectual capital as the measure of the level of intellectual capital disclosure. For our future research we intend to use other modalities to codify the information collected through content analysis (e.g., the number of appearance of the words or phrases). In addition we look forward to analyze more elements of intellectual capital in order to increase the relevance of the study.

NOTES

1. Symposiums: presentations on web sites, etc.
2. He divided intellectual capital in employees' skills, internal structure, and external structure.

ACKNOWLEDGMENTS

This work was possible with the financial support of the Sectoral Operational Programme for Human Resources Development 2007–2013, cofinanced by the European Social Fund, under the project number POSDRU/107/1.5/S/76841 with the title "Modern Doctoral Studies: Internationalization and Interdisciplinarity."

REFERENCES

Abeysekera, I. (2008). Motivations behind human capital disclosure in annual reports. *Accounting Forum*, *32*, 16–29.

Abeysekera, I., & Guthrie, J. (2005). An empirical investigation of annual reporting trends of intellectual capital in Sri Lanka. *Critical Perspectives on Accounting*, *1*, 151–163.

April, K. A., Bosma, P., & Deglon, D. A. (2003). IC measurement and reporting: Establishing a practice in SA mining. *Journal of Intellectual Capital*, *4*, 165–180.

Bogdan, V., Platon, J., & Popa, D. N. (2011). Intellectual capital reporting and disclosure in the annual reports of romanian manufacturing listed companies – Methodology and discussion of results. *Annals of Faculty of Economics*, *1*(2), 466–476.

Bontis, N. (2001). Assessing knowledge assets: A review of the models used to measure intellectual capital. *International Journal of Management Reviews*, *3*(1), 41–60.

Bontis, N. (2003). Intellectual capital disclosure in Canadian corporations. *Journal of Human Resource Costing & Accounting*, *7*, 9–20.

Bozzolan, S., Favotto, F., & Ricceri, F. (2003). Italian annual intellectual capital disclosure: An empirical analysis. *Journal of Intellectual Capital*, *4*, 543–558.

Brennan, N. (2001). Reporting intellectual capital in annual reports: Evidence from Ireland. *Accounting, Auditing & Accountability Journal*, *14*, 423–436.

Bruggen, A., Vergauwen, P., & Dao, M. (2009). Determinants of intellectual capital disclosure: Evidence from Australia. *Management Decision*, *47*, 233–245.

Bukh, P. N., Nielsen, C., Gormsen, P., & Mouritsen, J. (2005). Disclosure of information on intellectual capital in Danish IPO prospectuses. *Accounting, Auditing & Accountability Journal*, *18*, 713–732.

Burton-Jones, A. (1999). *Business, work and learning in the new economy: Business economy*. Oxford: Oxford University Press.

Campbell, D., & Rahman, M. R. A. (2010). A longitudinal examination of intellectual capital reporting in Marks & Spencer annual reports, 1978–2008. *The British Accounting Review*, *42*, 56–70.

Choong, K. K. (2008). Intellectual capital: definitions, categorization and reporting models. *Journal of Intellectual Capital*, *9*(4), 609–638.

Edvinsson, L., & Malone, M. S. (1997). *Intellectual capital: Realizing your company's true value by finding its hidden brainpower*. New York, NY: HarperCollins.

Feleagă, L, Feleagă, N., Dragomir, V. D., & Râbu, L. M. (2011, June). *Intellectual capital disclosure: European evidence*. Paper session presented at the 6th International Conference Accounting and Management Information Systems, pp. 369–380. Bucure_ti, Romania. Retrieved from http://cig.ase.ro/amis2011/fisiere/amis%202011.pdf?IDF=_blank

Garcia-Meca, E., Parra, I., Larran, M., & Martinez, I. (2005). The explanatory factors of intellectual capital disclosure to financial analysts. *European Accounting Review*, *14*, 63–94.

Goh, P. C., & Lim, K. P. (2004). Disclosing intellectual capital in company annual reports: Evidence from Malaysia. *Journal of Intellectual Capital*, *5*, 500–510.

Guthrie, J., & Petty, R. (2000). Intellectual capital: Australian annual reporting practices. *Journal of Intellectual Capital*, *1*, 241–251.

Guthrie, J., Petty, R., Ferrier, F., & Wells, R. (1999). *There is no accounting for intellectual capital in Australia: review of annual reporting practices and the internal measurement of intangibles within Australian organizations.* Paper presented at the International Symposium – Measuring and reporting intellectual capital: Experience, issues and prospects, pp. 9–10, Australia.

Guthrie, J., Petty, R., & Ricceri, F. (2006). The voluntary reporting of intellectual capital: Comparing evidence from Hong Kong and Australia. *Journal of Intellectual Capital*, *7*, 254–271.

Guthrie, J., Petty, R., Yongvanich, K., & Ricceri, F. (2004). Using content analysis as a research method to inquire into intellectual capital reporting. *Journal of Human Resource Costing & Accounting*, *5*, 282–293.

Hornery, S. (1999). Speech delivered at the International Symposium Measuring and Reporting Intellectual Capital: Experiences, Issues, and Prospects, OECD: Amsterdam.

Ienciu, N. M., & Ienciu, I. A. (2012). Determinants of intellectual capital reporting: Evidence from the Romanian stock market. *The Romanian Economic Journal*, *15*(43), 145–162.

Ienciu, N. M., & Mati, D. (2011). *Intellectual capital: The annual reporting practices.* Paper session presented at the 6th International Conference Accounting and Management Information Systems, pp. 380–394, Bucure_ti, Romania. Retrieved from http://cig.ase.ro/amis2011/fisiere/amis%202011.pdf?IDF=_blank

Itami, H. (1987). *Mobilizing invisible assets.* London: Harvard University Press.

Khan, M. H.-U.-Z., & Ali, M. M. (2010). An empirical investigation and users' perceptions on intellectual capital reporting in banks. Evidence from Bangladesh. *Journal of Human Resource Costing & Accounting*, *14*(1), 48–69.

Morariu, C. M. (2011). Determinants of Intellectual capital disclosure in the case of Romanian companies. Paper session presented at the 6th International Conference Accounting and Management Information Systems, pp. 395–416, Bucure_ti, Romania. Retrieved from http://cig.ase.ro/amis2011/fisiere/amis%202011.pdf?IDF=_blank

Mouritsen, J. (1998). Driving growth: Economic value versus intellectual capital. *Management Accounting Research*, *9*(4), 461–482.

Oliveira, L., Rodrigues, L., & Craig, R. (2006). Firm-specific determinants of intangibles reporting: Evidence from the Portuguese stock market. *Journal of Human Resource Costing & Accounting*, *10*, 11–33.

Olsson, B. (2001). Annual reporting practices: Information about human resources in corporate annual reports in major Swedish companies. *Journal of Human Resource Costing & Accounting*, *6*, 39–52.

Petty, R., & Guthrie, J. (2000). Intellectual capital literature review. Measurement, reporting and management. *Journal of Intellectual Capital*, *1*(2), 155–176.

Sharafi, M., Moghadam, Y. M., & Sharafi, T. (2012). The relationship between dimensions of intellectual capital and knowledge creation: Case study of the headquarters of national gas corporation of Iran. *Management Science Letters*, *2*, 147–160.

Sonnier, B. (2008). Intellectual capital disclosure: High-tech versus traditional sector companies. *Journal of Intellectual Capital*, *9*(4), 705–722.

Stewart, T. A. (1997). *Intellectual capital*. London: Nicholas Brealey Publishing.

Subbarao, A. V., & Zeghal, D. (1997). Human resources information disclosure in annual reports: an international comparison. *Journal of Human Resource Costing & Accounting, 2*, 53–73.

Sveiby, K. E. (1997). *The new organizational wealth: Managing and measuring knowledge-based assets*. New York, NY: Berrett-Koehler.

Vafaei, A., Taylor, D., & Ahmed, K. (2011). The value relevance of intellectual capital disclosures. *Journal of Intellectual Capital, 12*(3), 407–429.

Van der Meer-Kooistra, J., & Zijlstra, S. M. (2001). Reporting on intellectual capital. *Accounting, Auditing & Accountability Journal, 14*, 456–474.

Vithana, K. G., Riham, R., & Amir, M. (2011). *A multi-stakeholder perspective on the value relevance of human capital; Practice of human capital accounting and human capital discolsure: A review of existing literature*. Paper presented at the 4th European Conference on Intellectual Capital. Retrieved from http://academia.edu/1116998/A_Multi-Stakeholder_Perspective_on_the_Value_Relevance_of_Human_Capital_Practice_of_Human_Capital_Accounting_and_Human_Capital_Disclosure_A_Review_of_Existing_Literature

Williams, S. M. (2001). Are intellectual capital performance and disclosure practices related? *Journal of Intellectual Capital, 2*, 192–203.

APPENDIX: THE ANALYZED COMPANIES

Companies	Industries	Turnover	Equity	Number of employees	Financial status
Aerostar	Manufacturing	152697736	68461773	1,609	Profit
Alro	Manufacturing	1968015548	1547424970	3,908	Profit
Altur	Manufacturing	97363421	101683327	1,025	Profit
Alumil Rom Industry	Wholesale and retail trade	113620804	54395154	283	Profit
Amonil	Manufacturing	216879371	82460992	859	Profit
Antibiotice	Manufacturing	215805947	246904973	1,523	Profit
Armătura	Manufacturing	29960064	16575680	350	Loss
Artego	Manufacturing	151932486	75721210	1,187	Loss
Azomureş	Manufacturing	1144100219	391176847	2,494	Profit
Banca Comercială Carpatica	Financial services	465660000	253729000	2136	Profit
Banca Transilvania	Financial services	8169498000	1656337000	5,923	Profit
Bermas	Manufacturing	23072059	20297808	258	Profit
Biofarm	Manufacturing	65102889	129713542	335	Loss
Boromir Prod	Wholesale and retail trade	162445501	97781873	1,336	Profit
BRD	Financial services	9945297354	4267624000	7,966	Profit
C.N.T.E.E Transelectrica	Manufacturing	2924508220	2367708101	2,188	Profit
Carbochim	Manufacturing	32312149	61645013	323	Profit
Casa de Bucovina	Tourism	4689441	31707753	76	Profit
Cemacon	Manufacturing	48619215	32603390	284	Profit
Comelf	Manufacturing	125959062	30867140	1,096	Profit
Compa	Manufacturing	310818158	264869809	1,840	Profit
Compania Energopetrol	Constructions	23928018	9711186	241	Profit
Concefa	Constructions	111760311	106937898	476	Loss
Condmag	Manufacturing	145313194	78205804	917	Profit
Dafora	Mining and quarrying	269018676	170493978	1,112	Profit
Electroaparataj	Mining and quarrying	67491473	24637135	516	Loss
Electroarges	Manufacturing	104621157	15614013	578	Loss
Electromagnetica	Manufacturing	291780238	117141948	1,638	Loss
Electroputere	Manufacturing	183652042	246464140	2,514	Loss
Farmaceutica Remedia	Wholesale and retail trade	134276445	21269924	375	Loss
Grupul Industrial Electrocontact	Manufacturing	12570834	15870706	178	Loss

Appendix: (*Continued*)

Companies	Industries	Turnover	Equity	Number of employees	Financial status
Impact Developer & Contractor	Constructions	151688180	333718186	160	Profit
Mecanica Ceahlău	Manufacturing	31703491	33672325	336	Loss
Mechel Târgovişte	Manufacturing	1107164182	314049855	3,513	Profit
Mefin	Manufacturing	27405427	31562187	611	Profit
MJ Mailis România	Manufacturing	66228272	14187214	130	Loss
Oil Terminal	Transport	134573360	163786825	1,273	Profit
Oltchim	Manufacturing	1946943238	251266231	4,199	Loss
OMV Petrom	Manufacturing	16750726457	13568598447	29,861	Profit
Petrolexportimport	Whole sale and retail trade	116634015	20821885	26	Loss
Prefab	Manufacturing	71520050	212174792	535	Loss
Prodplast	Mining and quarrying	66132786	39255283	279	Profit
Retrasib	Manufacturing	47507537	21848966	121	Loss
Romcarbon	Manufacturing	93812673	124256170	747	Loss
Rompetrol Rafinare	Manufacturing	8665021543	1562562987	1,127	Loss
Rompetrol Well Services	Mining and quarrying	104860057	102526961	334	Profit
Ropharma	Wholesale and retail trade	351997844	81736819	698	Profit
S.N.T.G.N. Transgaz	Transport	1119389990	2188009344	4,918	Profit
S.S.I.F. Broker	Financial services	8320098	86498877	132	Loss
Şantierul Naval Orşova	Manufacturing	125966956	104088623	778	Profit
SC Fondul Proprietatea	Financial Services	576629495	12139275376	12	Profit
SC Transilvania Constructii	Constructions	58939826	123065693	347	Profit
SIF Banat Crişana	Financial services	124521972	413631925	94	Profit
SIF Moldova	Financial services	143263791	340659625	84	Profit
SIF Muntenia	Financial services	199611642	1243467003	16	Profit
SIF Transilvania	Financial services	145772000	578107896	102	Profit
SIF Oltenia	Financial services	122257591	456464535	93	Profit
Sinteza	Manufacturing	12287236	168800862	108	Profit

Appendix: (*Continued*)

Companies	Industries	Turnover	Equity	Number of employees	Financial status
Siretul Paşcani	Manufacturing	14224366	21596665	373	Profit
Socep	Transport	58818012	87433445	626	Profit
T.M.K. Artrom	Manufacturing	678876133	165452894	1,377	Loss
Teraplast	Manufacturing	194916101	140754190	540	Profit
Titan	Manufacturing	294472572	157601009	964	Profit
Turbomecanica	Manufacturing	63049103	75765775	738	Loss
Turism Felix	Tourism	55448042	169250203	844	Profit
THM Marea Neagră	Tourism	39232579	342184634	589	Profit
UAMT	Manufacturing	46115941	36501243	392	Profit
Vae Apcarom	Manufacturing	87390128	54029578	243	Profit
Ves	Constructions	51002409	22352419	626	Profit
Vrancart	Manufacturing	115072962	78164337	989	Profit
Zentiva	Manufacturing	218505848	285623358	738	Profit

THE DETERMINANTS OF INTELLECTUAL CAPITAL DISCLOSURE: EVIDENCE FROM ROMANIA

Cristina Maria Morariu

ABSTRACT

Purpose – *The main purpose of this chapter is to investigate the association between intellectual capital disclosure (ICD) level and two potential explanatory determinants: industry type and company size.*

Design/methodology/approach – *Twenty-one annual reports of Romanian public companies represented the sample companies. For each company, an ICD index was constructed based on an intellectual capital (IC) framework composed of 33 IC items. The results obtained for ICD Index are then used for statistical testing: descriptive statistics, T test, Pearson correlation, and multiple regression analysis.*

Findings – *Industry type by its own does not seem to influence ICD level and company size by its own does not influence the IC disclosure. However, the combination of the two variables significantly combines together to predict ICD.*

Accounting in Central and Eastern Europe
Research in Accounting in Emerging Economies, Volume 13, 163–186

ISSN: 1479-3563/doi:10.1108/S1479-3563(2013)0000013012

Research limitations/implications – *A specified list of IC items may not provide the whole picture of ICD practices. Future research could consider interviewing managers about their disclosure rationale. A larger sample could help to further improve the extrapolation of the results. Furthermore, this study challenges researchers to extend the area of analysis by considering the relation between ICD and other possible determinants. Last but not least, a longitudinal study could provide more insights.*

Practical implications – *The results obtained represent a basis for comparison with those obtained by other studies carried out in other developing countries. Furthermore, they can be used in meta-analysis.*

Originality/value – *This chapter is one of the first investigating ICD in the case of Romanian companies. Accordingly, our chapter contributes to the ICD literature by providing new empirical evidence on the determinants of ICD in a developing country context.*

Keywords: Intellectual capital; disclosure index; determinants; Romania; company size; industry type

INTRODUCTION

In time, economists such as Walras and Fisher considered human beings, or their acquired abilities and skills (English Classical school), as a component of capital (Kendrick, 1961; Kiker, 1966). Their reasons for inclusion were (1) the cost of rearing and educating human beings is a real cost; (2) the product of their labor adds to the national wealth; (3) an expenditure on a human being that increases this product will, ceteris paribus, increases national wealth (Kiker, 1966, p. 485). In our days, perspective has changed in the way that researchers and practitioners concentrate their attention on the abilities and skills embedded in the human beings. By doing so, in time a new concept has been born, developed, and continues to challenge practitioners and researchers: intellectual capital (IC).

The concept of "intellectual capital" was advanced by Mueller and List (as cited in Kendrick, 1961, p. 105) and referred to technical knowledge, know-how, forms of organization, and tangible capital goods. It is the result of investment in the discovery and the spread of productive knowledge. In 1997, Stewart defines it as "packaged useful knowledge" that includes organization's processes, technologies, patents, employees' skills and information about customers, suppliers and stakeholders (as cited in Luthy, 1998, p. 4). In 1996, Brooking defines IC as combined intangible assets that enable the company to function and comprises market assets, intellectual property assets, human-centered assets, and infrastructure assets (as cited in Luthy, 1998, p. 4–5). In Edvinsson and Malone's view, IC is formed of human capital and structural capital (customer, organizational, innovation, and process capital) and considers it as debt issue (as cited in Lonnqvist, 2002). Organisation for Economic Co-operation and Development (OECD) defines IC as human capital and structural capital, where the former refers to software, distribution, and supply chain, and the latter refers to employee's resources, customers, and suppliers. Lonnqvist defines IC as immaterial sources of value related to employees' capabilities, organization's resources, and the way of operating them and the relationship with its stakeholders (Lonnqvist, 2002, p. 14). Some authors (Roslender & Fincham, 2001, p. 387) are saying that IC is the "new" goodwill, something that the business builds up over time, and which provides the major foundation for its continued competitive advantage. According to Stanciu (2008), IC is an underlying characteristic of the employees, from which future benefits are expected to flow to the company and that encompasses the following: skills, capabilities, experience, knowledge, and last but not the least morality. Ricceri, in 2008, launched the idea according to which IC encompasses both resources that exist at a particular point in time (a stock of IC) and the fluid way these resources are used and interact with other resources to achieve the organization's goal (Striukova, Unerman, & Guthrie, 2008, p. 298). In 1997, Sveiby (as cited in Guthrie & Petty, 2000, p. 242) developed a framework for understanding IC that classifies intangibles into three parts: internal structure (consisting of items such as patents, concepts, models research and development, computer and administrative systems, organizational culture, and spirit), external structure (consisting of items such as relationships with customers, suppliers, brand names, trademarks, and reputation), and employee competence (consisting of items such as education, skills, training, values, and experience).

To facilitate general comparative analysis with the results obtained by other empirical studies, present research is using the same IC classification categories as those developed by Guthrie and Petty (2000).

The review of the literature written in the field of the determinants of intellectual capital disclosure (ICD) helped us to acknowledge the gap existing between the number of the studies carried out in different countries and even different continents (as per Table 1) corroborated with the small number of literature existing so far in the case of Romanian companies

Table 1. Feature of Studies Analyzing the Determinants of ICD.

Authors	Year	Country	Size	Industry type	Info Asymmetry	Leverage	Ownership	Age	Profitability	Nationality	Auditor type	Listing Status	Foreign Activity	Business Complexity	Business Strategy	Techn Adv
P. R. Beaulieu et al.	2002	Sweden	Yes	No	N/A	N/A	N/A	N/A	N/A	N/A	N/A	N/A	N/A	N/A	N/A	N/A
S. Bozzolan et al.	2003	Italy	Yes	Yes	N/A	N/A	N/A	N/A	N/A	N/A	N/A	N/A	N/A	N/A	N/A	N/A
Garcıa-Meca et al.	2005	Spain	Yes	No	N/A	No	N/A	N/A	No	N/A	N/A	Yes	N/A	N/A	N/A	N/A
S. Bozzolan et al.	2006	Italy and United Kingdom	Yes	Yes	N/A	No	No	N/A	No	No	N/A	N/A	N/A	N/A	N/A	N/A
L. Oliveira et al.	2006	Portugal	Yes	Yes	N/A	No	Yes	N/A	No	N/A	Yes	Yes	No	N/A	N/A	N/A
G. Boesso and K. Kumar	2007	Italy and United States	Yes	Yes	N/A	N/A	N/A	N/A	N/A	N/A	N/A	N/A	N/A	Yes	N/A	N/A
G. White et al.	2007	Australia	Yes	N/A	N/A	Yes	Yes	N/A	No	N/A	N/A	N/A	N/A	N/A	N/A	N/A
A. Brüggen et al.	2009	Australia	Yes	Yes	No	N/A	N/A	N/A	N/A	No	N/A	N/A	N/A	N/A	N/A	N/A
R. Orens et al.	2009	Belgium, France, Germany and The Netherlands	Yes	N/A	Yes	Yes	N/A	N/A	N/A	N/A	N/A	N/A	N/A	N/A	N/A	N/A
G. Rimmel et al.	2009	Japan	No	No	N/A	N/A	Yes	Yes	N/A	N/A	N/A	N/A	N/A	N/A	N/A	N/A
G. White et al.	2010	Australia & United Kingdom	Yes	N/A	N/A	No	N/A	N/A	N/A	Yes	N/A	N/A	N/A	N/A	N/A	N/A
C. C. Huang et al.	2010	Malaysia	No	No	N/A	N/A	N/A	N/A	No	N/A	N/A	No	N/A	N/A	Yes	Yes
M. C. Branco et al.	2011	Portugal	Yes	Yes	N/A	N/A	N/A	N/A	N/A	N/A	N/A	N/A	N/A	N/A	N/A	N/A
Total studies where the variable was tested			13	10	2	6	4	1	5	3	2	3	1	1	1	1
Total studies where the variable influences ICD			11	6	1	2	3	1	0	1	2	2	0	1	1	1
% Studies where variable was tested/Total Studies			100%	77%	15%	46%	31%	8%	38%	23%	15%	23%	8%	8%	8%	8%
% Studies where variable influences/Total Studies variable was tested			85%	60%	50%	33%	75%	100%	0%	33%	100%	67%	0%	100%	100%	100%

Yes means that the variable was tested and that it influences ICD.
No means that the variable was tested but that it does not influences ICD.
N/A means that the variable was not tested.

(Feleagă, Feleagă, Dragomir, & Ionescu, 2010; Morariu, 2010, 2011). Additionally, an issue exists as to whether companies in Central and Eastern Europe countries, like Romania, should be expected to act differently than companies in more developed countries do. Romania presents specific features regarding its capital market, companies' financing structure, and corporate governance systems. It provides for a different institutional setting from most developed and capital market-oriented countries, where most of the ICD studies have been made. The concept of IC and hence ICD is not as well developed in Romania as it is in more developed countries. We believe that the acknowledgement of the determinants of ICD is likely to encourage greater debate over IC management and its reporting thereof.

Challenged by all the differences underlined above, we carry out an empirical study having as main objective to investigate if in the case of Romanian public companies there is any association between ICD level and two potential explanatory determinants: industry type and company size.

Twenty-one annual reports as in December 31, 2009, of Romanian companies listed on the Bucharest Stock Exchange (BSE) were collected and represented the sample companies. IC framework used in this study is a combination of that used by Guthrie and Petty (2000) and the framework resulted from the work performed by a panel of researchers from the World Congress on Intellectual Capital (WCIC). The resulted framework is composed of 33 IC items. These 33 IC items are used within our methodology to construct an IC disclosure index (ICD_Index) for each company. Results obtained for ICD_Index are then used when testing (through descriptive statistics, T test, Pearson correlation, and multiple regression analysis) whether certain factors such as company size and industry type influence ICD.

Being a pioneering study in the case of Romanian companies, our chapter contributes to the ICD literature by providing empirical evidence of the status of IC reporting and of determinants of ICD in a developing country context. In addition, the results obtained represent a basis for comparison with those obtained by other studies carried out in other developing countries; the results can be used in meta-analysis, that is, researchers can use statistical tools to contrast and combine the results of our study with other individual studies considered to be "combinable" in the hope of identifying patterns among study results, inconsistency of results across studies, or other interesting relationships that may come to light in the context of multiple studies. This will increase the power of the analysis (as more data are used), improve the precision of estimates, explain heterogeneity between the results of individual studies, and assess whether effects are similar in similar situations. Last but not least, our study challenges researchers to extend the area of analysis by considering the relation between ICD and other possible determinants.

To address our purpose, the chapter is structured as follows: the next section briefly explores the relevant research studies carried out in the area of ICD and the determinants of ICD; additionally we are using the results therein as arguments for our hypotheses development. The following section then explains the research methodology used to conduct the empirical analysis. Independently, another section presents and examines the results of the research. The final section provides a summary of the chapter including conclusions and also discussing the key limitations of the study and future research implications of its findings.

LITERATURE REVIEW AND HYPOTHESES DEVELOPMENT

Literature Review

The central research question addressed by this chapter can be formulated as follows: "What are the key drivers of voluntary disclosure in the case of Romanian public companies?" There are several studies carried out aiming to provide evidence regarding the factors that may have contributed to the disclosure of IC. According to the previous literature, the following factors have been tested so as to confirm whether they influence ICD: company size, industry type, information asymmetry, leverage, ownership, company's age, profitability, nationality, auditor type, listing status, and foreign activity. The empirical evidence has sometimes shown a clear positive relationship (size, capital intensity, foreign listing, internationality, and ownership structure) and sometimes a mixed relationship (leverage, audit firm size, and profitability) in relation to the levels of ICD.

According to our research, the first study to be considered relevant for the purpose of our study was that of Beaulieu, Williams, and Wright (2002). The authors were trying to determine the extent of ICD practices in the case of a sample of 30 Swedish listed companies. In this respect, the chapter considered the effect of three variables: size, profitability, and industry classification. The empirical results indicate that only size is significantly associated with the disclosure of IC items.

One year later, in order to provide some empirical insights to the factors that might explain the type and amount of information disclosed about intangibles, Bozzolan, Favotto, and Ricceri (2003) tested the influence of size and industry on the extent and the content of ICD. They found that size and industry seemed to explain differences in IC reporting behavior among Italian companies. Extending the research in the field of ICD by considering a comparison between Italian and UK firms, Bozzolan, O'Regan, and Ricceri (2006) consider more variables that could possibly influence the level of IC disclosure that are size, industry type, leverage, ownership, profitability, and nationality. The results of the study reveal a modest support for industry type influencing ICD and that firm size influences ICD. Against expectations, the study finds no support for nationality variable on ICD. Italian companies were additionally considered by Boesso and Kumar (2007). The authors examine what factors, in addition to the needs of financial markets, drive the voluntary disclosure practices of companies in Italy and the United States. Their results show that in addition to investors' information needs, factors such as company emphasis on stakeholder management, relevance of intangible asset, and market complexity affect both the volume and the quality of voluntary disclosures.

Garcıa-Meca, Parra, Larran, and Martinez (2005) used univariate analysis and found in the case of Spanish companies a positive relation between a proactive intangibles disclosure strategy (in presentations to sell-side analysts) and size, international listing, market-to-book ratio, and type of meeting. They also used multivariate analysis and found that while leverage, profitability, industry, and an investor relations department have no influence on the extent of disclosure of intangibles, a partial variation was explained by firm size and type of meeting.

In their chapter, Oliveira, Rodriguez, and Craig (2006) study the disclosure practices in the case of 56 Portuguese companies and identify size, industry type, ownership structure, audit type, and listing rules as key variables of interest. Leverage, profitability, and foreign activity do not seem to influence ICD. In line with their results are those obtained by Branco, Delgado, Sousa, and Sá (2011) who find size and industry to be explanatory variables for the extent of ICD in the case of Portuguese companies after investigating ICD both in annual reports and on the Internet.

Using the information from four continental European countries (Belgium, France, Germany, and The Netherlands), Orens, Aerts, and Lybaert (2009) conducted a content analysis of corporate Web sites on the presence of IC information. The data show that IC disclosure is positively associated with firm size, lower information asymmetry, and leverage.

Moving on to another continent, Australia, White, Lee, and Tower (2007) used an ICD index score of voluntary disclosures to test statistically the relationship between voluntary disclosures and traditional agency theory variables in the case of 96 biotechnological Australian listed companies. The key drivers of voluntary ICD were the level of board independence, firm age, level of leverage, and firm size. By extending the research, White, Lee, Yuningsih, Nielsen, and Bukh (2010) compare the nature and extent of voluntary ICD in the case of 156 UK and Australian biotechnology companies. Considering the same continent, Bruggen, Vergauwen, and Dao (2009) examined the determinants of the decision to disclose IC in annual reports in the case of 125 Australian listed companies. The chapter finds that industry type and firm size play a key role as a determinant for the disclosure of intellectual property in annual reports and no relationship between the level of information asymmetry and ICD.

When it comes to Asia, the results seem to contradict somehow those obtained earlier, in other countries. Rimmel, Nielsen, and Yosano (2009) applied a disclosure index regarding IC included in the IPO prospectuses of Japanese companies to test whether industry type, ownership structure prior to the IPO, company age, and company size influenced disclosure. The results show that the first three factors (industry, ownership, and size) are not significant when it comes to explaining voluntary disclosure of information. Nevertheless, company age did, however, have a significant influence on the extent of disclosure for Japanese companies. Similar results are obtained by Huang, Tayles, and Luther (2010) but in the case of availability of internal IC information of Malaysian companies. With the aim to explore several contingency variables (environmental uncertainty, business strategy, technological advancement, market-to-book ratio, size, profitability, and industry type) in the context of management accounting and the availability of internal IC information, the authors developed a questionnaire that was posted to managers of Malaysian companies. It is found that industry and size are not significantly related to the availability of internal IC information in Malaysian companies.

Regarding Romanian stage of research in respect of determinants of ICDs, Morariu (2011) concluded that in the case of Romanian listed companies, there is no association between the level of ICD, company size, and industry type and no combination between company size and industry type.

Ienciu and Ienciu (2012) conducted an empirical study on the entities listed on the BSE. The objective of their study was to develop the determinant factors of IC reporting such as size of entity expressed by turnover, equity, number of employees, industries wherein entities operate and recorded profit or loss. In order to achieve their objective, the authors have used the content analysis of participating entities' financial statements. The conclusion of their study revealed that only the financial situation of entities represents a determinant factor of the reporting level of IC.

Table 1 presents a summary of the features of the studies concerned with the determinants of ICD.

Research Hypotheses

According to the mixed results obtained by previous studies, we can observe that the determinants of ICD are not clearly shown, yet. In addition, Romanian companies were not the subject of a similar study at all. Like studies made by Beaulieu et al. (2002), Bozzolan et al. (2003, 2006), Garcıa-Meca et al. (2005), Oliveira et al. (2006), Boesso and Kumar (2007), Bruggen et al. (2009), Orens et al. (2009), and Branco et al. (2011), we propose that company size is an important factor for IC disclosure in the case of Romanian companies, as larger companies can afford the cost to provide this voluntary information. Additionally, it is generally accepted that large entities belonging to a certain industry have the tendency to conduct more detailed and comprehensive reporting. Finally, size is the most commonly used independent variable, as all 13 studies reviewed (see Table 1) considered it in their analysis and 85% of the studies showed that there is a positive correlation between the size of the company and the level of ICD. All these arguments lead to our first null hypothesis:

Hypothesis 1. There is no relation between company size and IC disclosure.

Prior research has also noted that voluntary disclosures are influenced by industry type. It has been found that voluntary disclosures are more frequent and comprehensive in some industries, such as utility and financial services, than in others, such as publishing industry. Literature provides complementary interpretation keys for explaining the industry effect on corporate disclosure: this is because proprietary costs vary across industries (Meek, Roberts, & Gray, 1995); firms are pressed to disclose industry-related information in their annual reports (Cooke, 1992) by external investors who need information on a company's relative position in an industry in order to assess company value (Dye, 1985); disclosure within an industry may also be shaped by the behavior of a dominant company (Cooke,

1992); the international exposure of a particular industry might affect the extent of disclosure (Raffournier, 1995); IC is in some industries more important than in others and therefore value relevant for investors. The results obtained with respect to the variable industry type are mixed; in the way that the studies reviewed which considered that industry type as a determinant for ICD (Boesso & Kumar, 2007; Bozzolan et al., 2003; Bozzolan et al., 2006; Branco et al., 2011; Bruggen et al., 2009; Oliveira et al., 2006) were almost balanced by the number of studies that concluded that industry type does not have influence on ICD (Beaulieu et al., 2002; Garcıa-Meca et al., 2005; Huang et al., 2010; Rimmel et al., 2009). This, corroborated with the fact that 77% of the studies tested this correlation, brought us to the following null hypothesis:

Hypothesis 2. There is no relation between industry type and IC disclosure.

Last but not least, we test whether there is any combination between company size and industry type that may have influenced the level of ICD and formulate the following hypothesis:

Hypothesis 3. There is no relation between any combination of company size and industry type and IC disclosure.

METHODOLOGY

Sample Selection

Our sample consists of Romanian firms that are listed on BSE, where a total of 98 companies are classified in four segments: tier I (22), tier II (48), tier III (1), and unlisted (27). For the purpose of our study, we consider the analysis of the annual reports as in December 31, 2009, in the case of companies traded within tier I. As our study focuses only on Romanian companies, we have eliminated foreign companies even if traded on BSE. As such from the initial number of 22 companies, we have eliminated one company (Erste Group Bank) because it was not locally run (it is just listed on BSE at international category). As such, our final sample consists of 21 companies. The reason for including the tier I companies is because they are a homogeneous subgroup. The sample companies are furthermore classified according to the classifications and the definitions provided by the Global Industry Classification Standard (GICS) in June 30, 2010. Accordingly, the sectors and industries that the sample companies belong to are as follows: materials sector (metals and mining, chemical industry) with three observations, health-care sector (pharmaceuticals) with two observations, financial sector (commercial banks, real estate management and development, capital markets) with ten observations, utilities sector (electric utilities, gas utilities) with two observations, industrials sector (marine, aerospace and defense) with two observations, energy sector (oil, gas, and consumable fuels) with two observations. Companies' classification into sectors and industries has been revised independently by a second researcher.

Definition of Variables

Dependent Variables

In order to analyze the determinants of ICD, we have considered ICD_Index as dependent variable. Based on the total of the 33 IC items, we are constructing a weighted disclosure index calculated in accordance with the following formula:

$$\text{ICD\_Index} = \left(\frac{\sum_{i=1}^{n} di}{M} \right) \times 100\%$$

where ICD_Index is the IC disclosure index dependent variable; M is the total number of IC items, which is 33; IC items used are a combination of those used by Guthrie and Petty (2000) and those resulted from the work performed by a panel of researchers from the WCIC. The resulted IC framework is composed of 33 IC items as shown in Table 2; *di* expresses the IC item *i*; dichotomous scoring for each of the 33 IC items was used (disclosure = 1, nondisclosure = 0). Hence, the maximum possible score attainable by a company is 33 with a minimum theoretical score of 0 when the IC item's value is 1 if it was disclosed and 0 when there is no disclosure.

Independent Variables

This subsection describes how the independent variables (company size and industry type) are defined and measured.

Size. Researchers have commonly used different measures as proxies for company size. Alternative proxies of firm size include total assets

Table 2. Framework of IC Items.

Internal (Structural) Capital	External (Customer/Relational) Capital	Employee Competence (Human Capital)
Intellectual property	Brand	Know-how (employee know-how)
Patents	Customers (customer knowledge)	Education (employee knowledge)
Copyrights	Customer loyalty (customer capital)	Skills – vocational qualification (employee skills)
Trademarks	Company names (company reputation)	Work-related knowledge (expertise)
Infrastructure asset	Distribution channels	Work-related competencies (productivity)
Management philosophy	Business collaboration	Entrepreneurial spirit
Corporate culture (organizational culture)	Licensing agreements	Human capital
Management processes (management quality)	Favorable contracts	Human assets
Information systems	Franchising agreements	
Networking systems (expert networks)	Relational capital	
Financial relations	Supplier knowledge	
Corporate university/corporate learning		
Cultural diversity		
Structural capital		

(Bruggen et al., 2009; Oliveira et al., 2006); turnover (Bozzolan et al., 2003; Bozzolan et al., 2006; Oliveira et al., 2006); market capitalization (Garcıa-Meca et al., 2005; Oliveira et al., 2006; White et al., 2007; White et al., 2010); and number of employees (Boesso & Kumar, 2007; Huang et al., 2010; Oliveira et al., 2006). While market capitalization is a market-related characteristic, the other three proxies are structure-related characteristics. In a previous study, Morariu (2011) used turnover to capture company size and the results showed that company size (that is turnover) does not influence the level of ICD_Index. Because (1) we consider that total assets are not relevant unless comparison is made within the same industry and (2) the number of employees is less relevant as there are industries that can be more labor intensive than others, we decided for this study to use the value of market capitalization as a proxy for company size. Accordingly, size is measured as the natural logarithm of market capitalization as of December 31, 2009.

Industry Type. For constructing a comparable framework with other studies, we have used the classifications and the definitions provided by GICS in June 30, 2010, for the classification of the Romanian sample companies into sectors of activity and industries. Furthermore, for the purposes of testing our hypotheses, the industries are classified into traditional industries (food, automobiles, chemicals, construction, electronics, manufacturing, oil, utilities, textile/clothing, and tourism/leisure) and knowledge-intensive business services (KIBS) (Internet application provision, biotechnology, entertainment, IT distribution, high-tech manufacturing, media, retail, software, systems integration, telecommunications, and Web services). To capture the influence of industry type on the voluntary disclosure of intangibles information, we use a dichotomous variable (applying 1 for firms belonging to knowledge-intensive industries and 0 otherwise). In general, intangible assets are assumed to play a more important role in nontraditional industries, whereas traditional industries depend more on tangible assets. It is expected that industries with high levels of intangibles will voluntarily provide more information about intangibles, consistent with prior studies. Table 3 provides a picture of the companies classified under both criteria: GICS versus KIBS classification criteria.

RESULTS AND ANALYSIS

Descriptive Statistics

In order to have a first impression of the data introduced and to check for errors or problems, we have computed for the basic descriptive statistics: mean, minimum, and maximum values for each variable. Table 4 presents our first descriptive statistics.

This output shows the number (N) of companies with no missing data on that variable. The valid N (list-wise) is the number (21) which has no missing data on any variable. Table 4 also shows the minimum and the maximum score that any company had on that variable. These values are normal. Please note that "industry type" is a nominal variable (dichotomous variable) and is normal to account a minimum value of "0" and a

Table 3. Companies Classified under the KIBS and GICS Criteria.

KIBS Criteria	Traditional Industry	Knowledge Intensive	Knowledge Intensive	Traditional Industry	Traditional Industry	Traditional Industry
GICS criteria	Materials sector (metals and mining, chemical industry)	Health-care sector (pharmaceuticals)	Financial sector (commercial banks, real estate management and development, capital markets)	Utilities sector (electric utilities, gas utilities)	Industrials sector (marine, aerospace and Defense)	Energy sector (oil, gas, and consumable fuels)
No. of companies	3	2	10	2	2	2
Company names	ALRO S.A.	ANTIBIOTICE S.A.	BANCA COMERCIALA CARPATICA S.A.	C.N.T.E.E. TRANSELECTRICA	SOCEP S.A.	OIL TERMINAL S.A.
	AZOMURES S.A.	BIOFARM S.A.	BANCA TRANSILVANIA	S.N.T.G.N. TRANSGAZ S.A.	TURBOMECANICA	OMV PETROM
	OLTCHIM S.A. RM.		BRD – GROUPE SOCIETE GENERALE			
			IMPACT DEVELOPER & CONTRACTOR S.A.			
			S.S.I.F. BROKER S.A.			
			SIF BANAT CRISANA S.A.			
			SIF MOLDOVA S.A.			
			SIF MUNTENIA S.A.			
			SIF OLTENIA S.A.			
			SIF TRANSILVANIA S.A.			

Table 4. Descriptive Statistics.

		ICD_Index	Ln_Comp_Size_MV	Industry_Type
N	Valid	21	21	21
	Missing	0	0	0
Mean		0.1876	8.6429	0.52
Median		0.1818	8.7582	1.00
Mode		0.18	7.50[a]	1
Standard deviation		0.13161	0.70562	0.512
Skewness		0.966	0.433	−0.103
Standard error of skewness		0.501	0.501	0.501
Minimum		0.03	7.50	0
Maximum		0.45	10.15	1

[a]Multiple modes exist. The smallest value is shown.

maximum of "1." As it can be observed, in the case of scale variables (ICD_Index and Company_size), the mean and the median of each variable are very similar, which supports that ICD_Index and Company_size are approximately normally distributed variables. In addition, the statistic skewness is <1 (0.966 and 0.433) in both cases, which also supports that the variables are normally distributed. In the case of ICD_Index, the value is very close to 1, but as long as it is lower than 1, then we can consider as being approximately normally distributed.

Testing Hypothesis 1

In the case of hypothesis 1, both independent and dependent variables are scale variables, so it is a basic two-variable associational hypothesis. Accordingly, to test the hypothesis, we chose Pearson correlation. Before testing Pearson correlation, we must first check whether the two variables have a linear relationship. For this we are going to generate a scatterplot. We considered both a curve and a linear line.

From Fig. 1, we can observe that there is a positive correlation between the variables, but that the correlation is relatively week (r^2 is only 0.159 or 0.179). In addition, it seems that the linear line fits the point better than the curve, so we can consider that the variables have a linear relationship and we can continue out testing with Pearson correlation. Table 5 presents the results obtained for Pearson correlation (r). It shows that the two variables are not significantly correlated $r\ (21) = 0.399$, $p - 0.073 > 0.05$. Because the p-value of $0.073 > 0.05$, it means that r is not statistically significant and

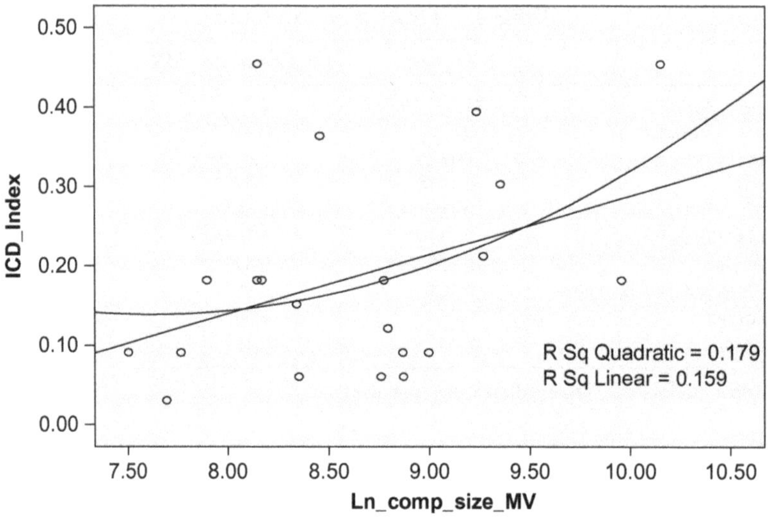

Fig. 1. Correlation between ICD_Index and Company_size.

Table 5. Pearson Correlation Results.

	ICD_Index	Ln_Comp_Size_MV
ICD_index		
Pearson correlation	1	0.399
Sig. (2-tailed)		0.073
N	21	21
Ln_comp_size_MV		
Pearson correlation	0.399	1
Sig. (2-tailed)	0.073	
N	21	21

thus it suggests that hypothesis 1 is not being rejected. Consequently, we can state that in the case of Romanian listed companies, company size does not influence the IC disclosure. Similar results were obtained in the case of Japan (Rimmel et al., 2009) and Malaysia (Huang et al., 2010).

Testing Hypothesis 2

Within hypothesis 2, the independent variable is nominal and the dependent variable is an approximately normally distributed scale variable.

Accordingly, hypothesis 2 is a basic two-variable difference hypothesis and for testing it we chose the *T*-test. The results of the *T*-test are presented in Table 6 (since the independent samples *T*-test procedure compares the two group means, it is useful to know what the mean values are, and consequently we present their values in Table 7). The test compares the means for two groups of cases. We can observe that the significance value for Levene's test is high (0.147 that is greater than 0.05) and because of this, we shall consider the results that assume equal variances for both groups. Regarding the significance value for the T-test, we can observe it is also high (0.195 respective 0.207) and corroborated with the fact that the confidence interval for the mean difference contains zero, and then we cannot conclude that there is a significant difference between the two group means. In conclusion, the results obtained do not reject the null hypothesis 2 and thus in the case of Romanian companies industry type does not seem to influence IC disclosure. Similar results were obtained in the case of Japan (Rimmel et al., 2009), Malaysia (Huang et al., 2010), Sweden (Beaulieu et al., 2002), and Spain (Garcia-Meca et al., 2005).

Table 6. Results of *T*-test: Group Statistics.

Industry_type	*N*	Mean	Standard Deviation	Standard Error Mean
ICD_Index				
Traditional	10	0.2273	0.15402	0.04871
Knowledge_intensive	11	0.1515	0.10141	0.03058

Table 7. Results of *T*-test: Independent Samples Test.

	Levene's Test for Equality of Variances		*T*-test for Equality of Means						
	F	Sig.	t	df	Sig. (2-tailed)	Mean difference	Standard error difference	95% Confidence interval of the difference	
								Lower	Upper
ICD_Index									
Equal variances assumed	2.288	0.147	1.344	19	0.195	0.07576	0.05638	−0.04224	0.19376
Equal variances not assumed			1.317	15.347	0.207	0.07576	0.05751	−0.04658	0.19809

Testing Hypothesis 3

In the case of hypothesis 3, we have one normally distributed scale-dependent variable (ICD_Index) and two independent variables from which one is nominal (Industry_type) and the other is scale (Company_size). Accordingly we are using multiple regression analysis to test the hypothesis 3. Our option for regression analysis is explained by the fact that it is widely used for prediction, it helps to understand which among the independent variables are related to the dependent variable, and to explore the forms of these relationships. We agree that the performance of regression analysis depends on the form of the data-generating process and it often depends to some extent on making assumptions about this process. These assumptions are sometimes testable if many data are available. We are aware that our sample is small, but regression models for prediction are often useful even when the assumptions are moderately violated (which is not our case), although they may not perform optimally. Last but not least, we argue in favor of multivariate regression because it takes into accounts several predictive variables simultaneously, thus modeling the property of interest with more accuracy. The results of multiple regression analysis are presented in Tables 8–10.

Simultaneous multiple regression was conducted to investigate the best predictors of ICD_Index. When the combination of variables to predict IC disclosure included company size and industry type, $F(2,18)=3.745$,

Table 8. Multiple Regression Results: Model Summary.

Model	R	R^2	Adjusted R^2	Standard Error of the Estimate
1	0.542[a]	0.294	0.215	0.11658

[a]Predictors: (constant), Industry_type, Ln_comp_size_MV.

Table 9. Multiple Regression Results: ANOVA.

Model	Sum of Squares	df	Mean Square	F	Sig.
1					
Regression	0.102	2	0.051	3.745	0.044a
Residual	0.245	18	0.014		
Total	0.346	20	0		

[a]Predictors: (constant), Industry_type, Ln_comp_size_MV.

Table 10. Multiple Regression Results: Coefficients.

Model	Unstandardized Coefficients		Standardized Coefficients	t	Sig.
	B	Standard error	Beta		
1					
(Constant)	−0.506	0.321		−1.575	0.133
Ln_comp_size_MV	0.086	0.037	0.462	2.297	0.034
Industry_type	−0.096	0.052	−0.373	−1.855	0.08

$p = 0.044 < 0.05$. This indicates that the combination of the variables significantly combines together to predict ICD. The standardized beta coefficients are presented in Table 10. Note that company size significantly predicts ICD when both two variables are included ($p = 0.034 < 0.5$). It means that for every unit increase in company size, a 0.086 increase in ICD_Index is predicted. Industry type is not an important factor in predicting the level of ICD_Index ($p = 0.08 > 0.05$). The adjusted R^2 is 0.215. This indicates that 21.5% of the variance in ICD_Index was explained by the model. According to Cohen (1988), this is a medium effect.

CONCLUSIONS

The main purpose of our research chapter is to investigate the association between ICD level and two potential explanatory determinants: industry type and company size. In this respect, 21 annual reports as in December 31, 2009, of Romanian companies listed on the BSE were collected and represented the sample companies. For each company, an IC disclosure index was constructed that had a common base containing the 33 IC items. These items represent a combination of those used by Guthrie and Petty (2000) and the framework resulted from the work performed by a panel of researchers from the WCIC. To compute the disclosure index, dichotomous scoring for each of the 33 IC items was used (disclosure = 1, nondisclosure = 0). Further on, we have used ICD index to formulate and to test our hypotheses. As such, the study tested if (1) company size is a determinant of ICD (hypothesis 1) using Pearson correlation analysis; (2) industry type is a determinant of ICD (hypothesis 2) using *T*-test analysis; and last but not least (3) if there is any combination between company size and industry type that can determine the level of ICD (hypothesis 3) using multiple regression analysis. Company size was measured using the natural logarithm of market capitalization and industry type was a dichotomous variable (traditional vs. Knowledge-intensive industry). According to the results obtained, we concluded that in the case of Romanian listed companies there is no association between the level of ICD and company size (r (21) = 0.399, $p = 0.073 > 0.05$), nor between industry type and ICD ($p = 0.195$ respective $p = 0.207$). Romania presents specific features regarding its capital market, companies' financing structure, and corporate governance systems. It provides for a different institutional setting from most developed and capital market-oriented countries, where most of the ICD studies have been made. Accordingly, our results may be explained by the fact that the concept of IC and hence ICD is not as well developed in Romania as it is in more developed countries (in the annual reports of Romanian companies, there is little information about IC) that high costs associated with gathering, interpretation, and reporting information on IC do not make sense in a cost-benefit analysis. Culture may have also an impact on Romanian stakeholders' perception on the importance of IC information, and because of this, Romanian companies may not understand the advantages of having IC information disclosed: increasing the relevance of financial statements because IC is regarded as an additional element to the financial reporting; decreasing the level of information asymmetry; and the reduction of loan costs (Depoers, 2000). Surprisingly though, when we tested the effect of these two variables taken together on the ICD variation we found that they significantly combine together to predict ICD (F (2, 18) = 3.745, $p = 0.044 < 0.05$). This can be explained by the fact that reporting task in the case of large companies from knowledge-intensive industries is not that chaotic. Additionally, for such companies it makes sense to find the necessary financial resources to allocate so to disclose information about their most important asset "intellectual capital." In this respect, our results are similar to those obtained in the case of Japan (Rimmel et al., 2009), Malaysia (Huang et al., 2010), Sweden (Beaulieu et al., 2002), and Spain (Garcia-Meca et al., 2005).

As any research chapter, our study is subject to a number of limitations. Analyzing the annual reports based on the specified list of IC-related terms may not provide the whole picture or ICD practices. Some research on disclosure practice uses the survey method for collecting data. Future research could consider interviewing managers about their disclosure rationale. While we believe that our sample is representative for Romanian listed companies, a larger sample could help to further improve the extrapolation of this study. This study is based on the annual reports for 2009 only; a longitudinal study could provide more insights and could include not only levels of ICD but also an analysis of changes in ICD. In addition, this study challenges researchers to extend the area of analysis by considering the relation between ICD and other possible determinants.

Despite its limitations, in terms of findings, our study confirms some of the previous results obtained in the case of Romanian listed companies; that is, companies' size does not influence the level of IC reporting (Ienciu & Ienciu, 2012; Morariu, 2011). The same result is obtained in the case of Malaysia (Huang et al., 2010), which is an emerging economy too. Additionally, our study provides new evidence regarding the fact that in the case of Romanian companies, company size and industry type significantly combine together to predict ICD.

Considering its implication, we can conclude that our chapter contributes to the ICD literature by providing empirical evidence of the determinants of ICD in a developing country context. In addition, the results obtained represent a basis for comparison with those obtained by other studies carried out in other developing countries and can be used in meta-analysis; that is, researchers can use statistical tools to contrast and combine the results of our study with other individual studies considered to be "combinable" in the hope of identifying patterns among study results, inconsistency of results across studies, or other interesting relationships that may come to light in the context of multiple studies. This will increase the power of the analysis (as more data are used), improve the precision of estimates, explain heterogeneity between the results of individual studies, and assess whether effects are same in similar situations.

ACKNOWLEDGMENTS

This chapter is a revised version of a chapter presented at the 6th International Conference on Accounting and Management Information Systems held at the Bucharest Academy of Economic Studies, Bucharest, Romania, on June 8–9, 2011, and at the 4th European Conference on Intellectual Capital held at Arcada University of Applied Sciences, Helsinki, Finland, on April 23–24, 2012. The author thanks for the constructive feedback received from unknown reviewers, participants to the two conferences, and especially to Prof. Mathew Tsamenyi. Additionally, the author gratefully acknowledges the invaluable suggestions and comments received from the reviewers and guest editors of RAEE Accounting in Central and Eastern Europe. Special thanks go to Prof. Cătălin Nicolae Albu for ad hoc advices and assistance provided during this period.

REFERENCES

Beaulieu, P. R., Williams, S. M., & Wright, M. E. (2002). Intellectual capital disclosures in Swedish Annual Reports. *Proceedings of World Congress on Intellectual Capital* (pp. 135–156), Reading, United Kingdom. Retrieved from: http://books.google.co.uk/books?id=pjMOHnClt9EC&pg=PA135&lpg=PA135&dq=Intellectual+Capital+Disclosures+in+Swedish+Annual+Reports,+World+Congress+on+Intellectual+Capital&source=bl&ots=zzhh1WV_1Y&sig=o7MNJj8aKtG8Blb44oNcbYxGKhM&hl=en&sa=X&ei=BpDZUc-TN6Py0gW1y4DIDg&ved=0CD8Q6AEwAg#v=onepage&q=Intellectual%20Capital%20Disclosures%20in%20Swedish%20Annual%20Reports%2C%20World%20Congress%20on%20Intellectual%20Capital&f=false

Boesso, G., & Kumar, K. (2007). Drivers of corporate voluntary disclosure: A framework and empirical evidence from Italy and the United States. *Accounting, Auditing & Accountability Journal*, *20*(2), 269–296. doi:10.1108/09513570710741028

Bozzolan, S., Favotto, F., & Ricceri, F. (2003). Italian annual intellectual capital disclosure: An empirical analysis. *Journal of Intellectual Capital*, *4*(4), 543–558. doi:10.1108/14691930310504554

Bozzolan, S., O'Regan, P., & Ricceri, F. (2006). Intellectual Capital Disclosure (ICD), a Comparison of Italy and the UK. *Journal of Human Resource Costing & Accounting*, *10*(2), 92–113. doi:10.1108/14013380610703111

Branco, M. C., Delgado, C., Sousa, C., & Sá, M. (2011). Intellectual capital disclosure media in Portugal. *Corporate Communications: An International Journal*, *16*(1), 38–52.

Bruggen, A., Vergauwen, P., & Dao, M. (2009). Determinants of intellectual capital disclosure: Evidence from Australia. *Management Decision*, *47*(2), 233–245. doi:10.1108/00251740910938894

Cohen, J. (1988). *Statistical power and analysis for the behavioural sciences* (2nd ed.). Hillsdale, NJ: Lawrence Erlbaum Associates.

Cooke, T. E. (1992). The impact of size, stock market listing and industry type on disclosure in the annual reports of Japanese listed companies. *Accounting & Business Research*, *22*, 229–237. doi:10.1080/00014788.1992.9729440

Depoers, F. (2000). A cost-benefit study of voluntary disclosure: Some empirical evidence from French listed companies. *The European Accounting Review*, *9*(2), 245–263. doi:10.1080/09638180050129891

Dye, R. A. (1985). Disclosure of non-proprietary information. *Journal of Accounting Research*, *23*, 123–145. Retrieved from http://www.jstor.org/discover/10.2307/2490910?uid=3738032&uid=2129&uid=2&uid=70&uid=4&sid=21102436014171

Feleagă, L., Feleagă, N., Dragomir, V. D., & Ionescu, B. (2010). Intellectual capital and organizational information systems. *Proceedings of the 4th European Conference on Information Management and Evaluation* (pp. 61–67), Lisbon, Portugal.

Garcıa-Meca, E., Parra, I., Larran, M., & Martinez, I. (2005). The explanatory factors of intellectual capital disclosure to financial analysts. *European Accounting Review*, *14*(1), 63–94. doi:10.1080/0963818042000279713

Guthrie, J., & Petty, R. (2000). Intellectual capital: Australian Annual Reporting Practices. *Journal of Intellectual Capital*, *1*(3), 241–251. doi:10.1108/14691930010350800

Huang, C. C., Tayles, M., & Luther, R. (2010). Contingency factors influencing the availability of internal intellectual capital information. *Journal of Financial Reporting and Accounting*, *8*(1), 4–21. doi:10.1108/19852511011055916

Ienciu N. M., & Ienciu I. A. (2012). Determinants of intellectual capital reporting: Evidence from the Romanian stock market. *The Romanian Economic Journal*, *43*, 147–163. Retrieved from http://www.rejournal.eu/Portals/0/JE%2043/Ienciu.pdf

Kendrick, J. W. (1961). Some theoretical aspects of capital measurement. *American Economic Review*, *51*(2), 102–111. Retrieved from http://www.jstor.org/discover/10.2307/1914473?uid=3738032&uid=2129&uid=2&uid=70&uid=4&sid=21102436014171

Kiker, B. F. (1966). The historical roots of the concept of human capital. *Journal of Political Economy*, *74*(5), 481–499. Retrieved from http://www.jstor.org/discover/10.2307/1829595?uid=3738032&uid=2129&uid=2&uid=70&uid=4&sid=21102436014171

Lonnqvist, A. (2002). *Measurement of intangible assets – An analysis of key concepts*. Retrieved from http://www.ebrc.fi/kuvat/275-294.pdf

Luthy, D. H. (1998). *Intellectual capital and its measurement*. Retrieved from http://www3.bus.osaka-cu.ac.jp/apira98/archives/pdfs/25.pdf

Meek, G. K., Roberts, C. B., & Gray, S. J. (1995). Factors influencing voluntary annual report disclosures by U.S., U.K. and Continental European Multinational Corporations. *Journal of International Business Studies*, *26*(3), 555–572. doi:10.1057/palgrave.jibs.8490186

Morariu, M. C. (2011). Determinants of intellectual capital disclosure in the case of Romanian companies. *Proceedings of the 6th International Conference on Accounting and Management Information Systems* (pp. 395–415), Bucharest, Romania.

Morariu, M. C. (2010). Reporting of intellectual capital from the Romanian companies' perspective. *Proceedings of the 7th International Conference on Intellectual Capital Knowledge Management and Organisational Learning* (pp. 302–310), Hong Kong, China.

Oliveira, L., Rodriguez, L. L., & Craig, R. (2006). Firm-specific determinants of intangibles reporting: Evidence from the Portuguese stock market. *Journal of Human Resource Costing & Accounting*, *10*(1), 11–33. doi:10.1108/14013380610672657

Orens, R., Aerts, W., & Lybaert, N. (2009). Intellectual capital disclosure, cost of finance and firm value. *Management Decision*, *47*(10), 1536–1554. doi:10.1108/00251740911004673

Raffournier, B. (1995). The determinants of voluntary financial disclosure by Swiss listed companies. *The European Accounting Review*, *4*(2), 261–280. doi:10.1080/09638189500000016

Rimmel, G., Nielsen, C., & Yosano, T. (2009). Intellectual capital disclosures in Japanese IPO prospectuses. *Journal of Human Resource Costing & Accounting*, *13*(4), 316–337. doi:10.1108/14013381011010150

Roslender, R., & Fincham, R. (2001). Thinking critically about intellectual capital accounting. *Accounting, Auditing & Accountability Journal*, *14*(4), 383–398. doi:10.1108/09513570110403425

Stanciu, M. C. (2008). Intellectual capital, a challenge to get the "true and fair view". *Accounting and Management Information Systems*, *24*, 72–87.

Striukova, L., Unerman, J., & Guthrie, J. (2008). Corporate reporting of intellectual capital: Evidence from UK companies. *British Accounting Review*, *40*, 297–313. doi:10.1016/j.bar.2008.06.001; Received December 11, 2006; Revised June 13, 2008; Accepted June 17, 2008; Available online August 8, 2008.

White, G., Lee, A., & Tower, G. (2007). Drivers of voluntary intellectual capital disclosure in listed biotechnology companies. *Journal of Intellectual Capital*, *8*(3), 517–537. doi:10.1108/14691930710774894

White, G., Lee, A., Yuningsih, Y., Nielsen, C., & Bukh, P. N. (2010). The nature and extent of voluntary intellectual capital disclosures by Australian and UK biotechnology companies. *Journal of Intellectual Capital*, *11*(4), 519–536. doi:10.1108/14691931011085669

INTANGIBLE ASSETS AND THEIR REPORTING PRACTICES: EVIDENCE FROM SLOVENIA

Mateja Jerman

ABSTRACT

Purpose – *The purpose of this chapter is to examine the reporting practices on intangible assets from the perspective of a post-transition economy. The chapter explores the significance of intangibles and the content of the disclosures provided by companies in annual reports.*

Methodology/approach – *The analysis is qualitative in nature. Annual reports of selected Slovene publicly traded companies are analysed. The research is based on the analysis of required disclosures by International Financial Reporting Standards (IFRS) and an analysis of voluntary disclosures provided by companies for the 2007–2011 financial years.*

Findings – *The results indicate that intangibles are less significant in comparison with publicly traded companies from traditionally developed economies. The analysis of disclosures reveals that companies provide almost exclusively the disclosures required by IFRS, while voluntary disclosures are not provided. Furthermore, results indicate deficiencies in financial reporting practices related to required disclosures.*

Accounting in Central and Eastern Europe
Research in Accounting in Emerging Economies, Volume 13, 187–204

ISSN: 1479-3563/doi:10.1108/S1479-3563(2013)0000013013

Research limitations – *The analysis is conducted on a small sample of companies. This is a consequence of the fact that a limited number of companies is trading on Ljubljana Stock Exchange. In the primary and standard quotation of shares, only 25 companies are present.*

Practical implications – *Since a growing stream of research emphasises the importance of intangibles for companies' performance, the findings indicate possibilities for improvement of financial reporting.*

Originality/value – *The research findings contribute to existing research in the field of accounting for intangibles from the perspective of a post-transition economy. More studies of this kind in transition and post-transition economies using IFRS have yet to be performed.*

Keywords: Intangible assets; financial reporting; annual reports; IFRS; disclosure analysis

INTRODUCTION

As stated by Lev and Daum (2004), since the beginning of the 1990s, a significant change regarding the asset composition of business enterprises has become apparent. Tangibles are being substituted by intangible value creators in today's knowledge economy (Boedker, Mouritsen, & Guthrie, 2008; Marr, 2007). Intangible assets are the fundamental source of competitive advantages (Corrado, Hulten, & Sichel, 2009; Guthrie, 2001; Lev, 2001). Despite the fact that intangibles affect the firm's value, many problems related to the existing accounting practice with particular emphasis on external reporting remain (Roslender, 2009).

According to International Financial Reporting Standards (IFRS), a large amount of internally generated intangibles cannot be recognised in financial reports, since they do not meet the criteria for recognition [for instance, International Accounting Standard 38 – Intangible Assets (IAS 38) states that brands, mastheads, publishing titles, customer lists, and items similar in substance that are internally generated should not be recognised as assets in financial accounts]. For the purpose of initial recognition, it must be highly probable that future economic benefits will arise from the asset, and the cost of the asset has to be measured reliably. Most intangibles satisfy the criteria for recognition in financial accounts only when they are acquired separately, or via a merger or acquisition. This is especially the case of goodwill. IAS 38 assumes that fair value of an intangible asset acquired in a business combination can be measured reliably. In cases in which internally generated intangibles do not meet the criteria for recognition, they are immediately expensed in income statement.

Thus in 2004, International Accounting Standards Board (IASB) moved ahead of the U.S. Generally Accepted Accounting Principles (GAAP), with the issuance of IFRS 3 – business combinations and the revised versions of International Accounting Standard 38 – Intangible Assets (IAS 38) and International Accounting Standard 36 – Impairment of Assets (IAS 36). Standards substantially changed the accounting for intangibles. Since that time, intangibles that are recognised in financial statements are allocated into groups of those with finite useful lives and those with indefinite useful lives. Assets with indefinite useful lives are only subject to annual impairment test, while those that do have finite useful lives are subject to impairment and amortisation. The previous standard required all intangibles to be amortised and tested for impairment. Since the introduction of the new accounting approach for intangibles with indefinite useful lives, these are no longer amortised and thus do not lose their value on a systematic basis (usually the straight-line method was in use); however, they do lose their value in cases when they are impaired. For the purpose of impairment process, a recoverable amount of the asset has to be assessed. When active market prices for an asset are not available (which is often the case for intangibles), companies shall determine value in use (most often defined as the present value of future cash flows). Value-in-use estimation is based on assumptions about future expectations derived from the assets. Unless companies are willing to convey private information about the companies' process of impairment, users of financial accounts do not receive reliable information that would enable them to assess accurately future cash flows deriving from these assets. As a consequence, the reporting practice of companies is essential.

The purpose of this chapter is to examine the reporting practices on intangible assets of selected Slovene companies by analysing the significance of intangibles and the content of obligatory and voluntary disclosures provided in annual reports. Our analysis is based on companies from the primary and standard quotations on the Ljubljana stock exchange; it is based on data from 2007 to 2011. Since there is little research being done on samples of companies from transition and post-transition economies, the research findings contribute to existing research in the field of accounting for intangibles from the perspective of a post-transition economy.

The chapter is structured as follows. The introduction is followed by the reporting practices about intangibles in traditionally developed and transition economies. The methodological part consists of the methodological framework, where the data collection and research methodology are explained. The results of the analysis and discussion are presented in the next part. The chapter ends with concluding remarks.

THEORETICAL BACKGROUND

Reporting Practices about Intangibles in Traditionally Developed Economies

Lev (2001) emphasises that the failure to recognise intangibles in financial accounts would lead to systematic undervaluation of companies by investors, especially in cases in which companies operate in knowledge- and technology-intensive industries. Consequently, many authors (Edvinsson & Malone, 1997; Lev, 2001; Sveiby, 1997) advocate a different accounting approach for intangibles; authors often recommend a larger extent of disclosures (Bontis, 2003; Gelb, 2002; Ritter & Wells, 2006). However, Skinner (2008) argues that the claim for reform is rather weak since little evidence supports the claim that current accounting practices have adverse capital market effects, that is misallocation of resources and higher cost of capital for intangible-intensive companies. In continuation, this chapter is focused on reporting practices of intangibles and does not address arguments that would support modifications of the current accounting approach in use.

The analysis of Glaum and Wyrwa (2011) is an in-depth analysis of how European companies dealt with IFRS disclosures in merger and acquisition accounting. The analysis is conducted on a sample of 322 European publicly traded companies that are part of blue chip indices from 12 EU countries; the analysis is based on data from 2009. The data show that goodwill is the most significant intangible asset, representing 43.8% of common equity on average. Holtzman and Sinnett (2009) examined 5951 companies that were included in the capital IQ database. On average, the share of goodwill in 2007 amounted to 15.4% of total assets and in 2008 to 14.1% of total assets (Holtzman & Sinnett, 2009). In 2007, the highest share of goodwill was present in the pharmaceutical industry and the technology industry. In the latter, the share of goodwill amounted to 22.4% of total assets on average, while in the case of the pharmaceutical industry the average share was 21.8%.

The rising share of goodwill on the balance sheet is a consequence of increasing differences between market and book values of the companies (Marr, 2007) and more numerous mergers and acquisitions that were made in such circumstances (Muller, Neamtiu, & Riedl, 2009).

Analyses of disclosures about intangibles provided in annual reports of IFRS users were explored by Carlin, Finch, and Ford (2007); Paananen (2008); Carlin and Finch (2010); and Massoudi, Izan, and Tarca (2011). Users of the U.S. GAAP were analysed by Hayn and Hughes (2006); Sevin, Schroeder, and Bhamornsiri (2007); and Chen and Feng (2010).

The studies that analysed the quality of reporting practices in the field of intangible assets predominately refer to goodwill. This kind of study has been more common since the introduction of IAS 36. Sevin et al. (2007), Carlin and Finch (2010), and Chen and Feng (2010) analysed the reporting practices regarding accounting for goodwill; their findings were similar. Sevin et al. (2007) determined that the deficiencies in financial reporting are related to the disclosures about the CGU (cash-generating unit) recoverable amounts. Companies often did not provide information about the methodology of testing goodwill for impairment. Carlin and Finch (2010) analysed Australian publicly traded companies representing almost half of the Australian stock market capitalisation. They also found a lack of clear disclosures about the discount factors used in the process of recoverable amount calculation and the tendency to use discount factors for the level of the entity instead of a risk-adjusted discount factor for single CGU. Chen and Feng (2010) explored factors that might influence the extent of goodwill disclosures provided by companies. The analysis was performed on the data of 569 American companies, which reported in accordance with Statement of Financial Accounting Standards 142 – Goodwill and Other Intangible Assets (FAS 142) from the period 2003 to 2005. A positive and statistically significant relation between the extent of disclosures and the relative importance of goodwill impairment, the relative importance of goodwill in the balance sheet, and the complexity of business operations (number of business segments) was found. Moreover, the analysis confirms the positive effects of FAS 142, which motivates management to convey more disclosures when goodwill and its impairments are more valuable.

Paananen (2008) analysed the extent of goodwill disclosures in relation with the institutional environment. The sample was based on 100 randomly selected publicly traded companies from the United Kingdom, France, and Germany that report under IFRS. The analysis was conducted on data from the end of the first year of the adoption of IFRS (2005, in most cases). She determined that in the United Kingdom, where investors have greater protection, the extent of disclosures is on average higher than in Germany and France.

Massoudi et al. (2011) explored factors that influence the extent of disclosures about the impairment process required by IAS 36. The analysis was based on all types of impairments required by IAS 36, including those of intangible assets. The sample was based on a total of 174 companies from Australia and the United Kingdom. The analysis was focused on data from 2005. They discovered that the extent of analysed disclosures is higher in cases when companies recorded a higher impairment of assets and when the company was audited by one of the big four auditing firms.

In contrast, research from transition and post-transition countries regarding intangible reporting practices is lacking. Literature review from those economies reveals an intriguing phenomenon: negative goodwill was more frequently recognised than in traditionally developed economies (Epstein, Nach, & Bragg, 2007, p. 510; Henry & Holtzman, 2007). The research of Henry and Holtzman (2007) shows that negative goodwill was recognised in the case of selected American companies only by 0.06% of the sample; this analysis was made on data from 2004. In contrast, the research conducted by Lahovnik (2000) provided evidence that in 39.5% of Slovene acquisitions the acquirer paid the acquiree at least 50% less than its book value of equity capital (recognition of negative goodwill). In the case of Polish companies, it was established even by Schroeder (2007) that the recognition of negative goodwill was particularly frequent. These results suggest that, in countries in transition and post-transition, companies possessed intangible assets that were not recognised in the balance sheet, as the acquirers were not willing to buy companies for more than their book value. Consequently, instead of goodwill, the acquirer often recognised negative goodwill.

In accordance with accounting rules in IAS 22 – business combinations (superseded by IFRS 3) – negative goodwill was recorded in the statement of financial position and afterwards usually amortised within 20 years based on a straight-line method. However, IFRS 3 (currently in use) requires that any gain in a bargain purchase is recognised immediately in profit or loss account.

Despite the fact that research about the value relevance and value reliability of intangibles has become more common since the introduction of the new accounting approach in IFRS, there is still lack of research based on samples of companies from transition and post-transition countries.

RESEARCH FRAMEWORK

Research Question and Methodology

Since studies indicate the growing importance of intangibles in today's knowledge economy, we are interested in reporting practices of Slovene publicly traded companies. Do they meet IFRS requirements and do they provide any voluntary disclosures that might enable users of financial account to better assess future cash flows of a company?

In order to answer the research question, we have focussed our analysis on selected Slovene publicly traded companies that report in accordance with IFRS. Slovenia has undergone significant changes in recent decades. In 2004, it became a Member State of European Union (EU), and in 2007 it successfully implemented the euro. Since Slovenia became a Member State of the EU, the implementation process of IFRS was obligatory for consolidated accounts of publicly traded companies whose securities are traded on the EU capital market. Publicly traded companies that are not obliged to prepare consolidated accounts are allowed to prepare individual accounts in accordance with Slovene Accounting Standards.[1] The use of IFRS is obligatory for banks (since 2006) and insurance companies (since 2007). Other enterprises may use IFRS if so decided by their respective general assemblies, but for the minimum period of five years.

The analysis is performed on data from the five-year period of 2007–2011. Financial institutions were excluded (four companies) from the analysis. The bases for our analysis are 105 annual reports prepared by 21 companies. Annual reports prepared in accordance with Slovene Accounting Standards were excluded from subsequent analysis (13 annual reports). Two reports were excluded because they were not publicly available. Thus, the final number of reports prepared in accordance with IFRS is 90 (the list of companies included in the analysis is presented in Appendix A). This enables us to compare reporting practices of IFRS users among traditionally developed countries and a post-transition economy.

The analysis focuses on companies that are part of the primary and standard quotations on Ljubljana Stock Exchange (21 companies). On December 31, 2011, these companies represented 87.7% of the market capitalisation of shares (Ljubljana Stock Exchange, 2012). The methodology for the selection of companies is in line with previous studies (Carlin & Finch, 2010; Glaum & Wyrwa, 2011), in which only companies that represent a significant part of market capitalisation are included in the sample.

These types of studies assume that larger companies provide a broader extent of disclosures in comparison with smaller companies. Since our sample is smaller in comparison with similar studies based on samples from traditionally developed economies, we attempted to expand the sample to all Slovene publicly traded companies. Publicly traded companies that were not included in the analysis (43 companies) provided smaller extent of disclosures about intangibles in comparison with companies included in primary and standard quotation. Therefore, we did not include them in further analysis.

Data about the carrying amount of total assets, common equity, revenues from sales, and return on equity were gathered from Slovene financial database GVIN (2012). Market-to-book value (MTBV) ratios were gathered from Ljubljana Stock Exchange. The ratio is taken for the end of each financial year. The carrying amount of intangible assets, goodwill, and their disclosures were collected from publicly available consolidated accounts. The data we used are for the financial periods that ended on December 31.

DATA ANALYSIS AND RESULTS

Descriptive Statistics of the Sample

First, the most relevant descriptive statistics are presented (for more details, see Appendix B). The data show that companies had an average value of total assets amounting to €673,731,449 (2011) and average value of total equity €256,406,835 (2011). Standard deviation shows that the size of the companies differs significantly in the primary and standard quotation. This is also evident from data of minimum and maximum values. The MTBV ratio should be emphasised, since there is evidently a serious decrease of the ratio. MTBV ratios from 2008 to 2011 show that market values of common equity are, on average, significantly lower than their book values. It is noteworthy that IFRS require a company to estimate the recoverable amount of an asset when there are circumstances that indicate that an asset might be impaired. An MTBV lower than 1 is also an external indicator that shows that an asset might be impaired.

Secondly, the importance of intangibles in the structure of total assets is analysed (Table 1). It is calculated as the carrying amount of long-term intangible assets (t) divided by the carrying amount of total assets (t). Since studies from developed market economies emphasise the importance of

Table 1. Proportion of Intangible Assets in the Structure of Total Assets – Selected Companies in the 2007–2011 Period (in %).

Year	2007	2008	2009	2010	2011
Number of companies	17	18	18	19	18
Average (%)	4.58	6.08	5.63	3.42	4.51
Standard deviation (%)	6.39	7.17	7.45	3.80	5.00
Minimum (%)	0.10	0.09	0.11	0.11	0.08
Maximum (%)	20.71	20.59	21.93	12.04	15.27

Source: Data from publicly available annual reports.

intangible assets, we expected that the proportion of intangibles would increase over time. Contrary with our expectations, we discovered that in 2011 the average share of intangibles amounted only to 4.51% of total assets value. The highest average share was present in 2008 (6.08%), while the lowest one was present in 2010 (3.42%). Standard deviation shows that companies differ significantly. While the minimum proportion of intangibles in the whole period of analysis does not exceed 1% of total asset value, the highest share exceeded 20% in the 2007–2009 period and decreased to 15.27% in 2011.

Since studies emphasise that goodwill is the most valuable intangible asset, we were interested if this is also true for Slovenia. In Slovenia, acquisitions were substantially less numerous in comparison with developed market economies. Thus, the precondition to recognise goodwill in financial accounts of Slovene companies was often not met.

The importance of goodwill is calculated as the carrying amount of goodwill (t) divided by the carrying amount of long-term intangible assets (t). The data show (Table 2) that the average proportion of goodwill was the highest in 2008, when it amounted to 27%. The lowest value was recorded in 2011, when the value was reduced to 21.47%. Based on our results, we cannot state that goodwill represents the greater part of intangible assets value.

Analysis of Intangible Reporting Practices in Selected Slovene Publicly Traded Companies

First, the analysis of disclosures required by IFRS was done. The findings related to disclosures required by IAS 38 are the following. Companies

Table 2. Proportion of Goodwill in the Structure of Total Value of Intangibles – Selected Companies in the 2007–2011 Period (in %).

Year	2007	2008	2009	2010	2011
Number of companies	17	18	18	19	18
Average (%)	21.63	27.03	23.33	22.80	21.47
Standard deviation (%)	27.41	29.05	26.78	29.04	26.37
Minimum (%)	0.00	0.00	0.00	0.00	0.00
Maximum (%)	94.25	94.58	97.27	97.61	95.72

Source: Data from publicly available annual reports.

often provide general descriptions of accounting policies in use instead of more specific disclosures. In the case of two companies, accounting policies about goodwill were described; however, the companies did not record goodwill. More detailed analysis of disclosures indicates the following:

- For those assets that have finite useful lives, the straight-line method of amortisation is used (one of the companies did not disclose the amortisation method in use in all years of analysis). From the annual reports, it does not result that some other method of amortisation is in use. Most of intangibles apart from goodwill are defined as those with finite useful lives. Only in case of one company was the trademark treated as an intangible asset with an indefinite useful life.
- The division of intangible assets to those with finite and indefinite useful lives is not always clear: 17 (19%) out of 90 reports do not provide this information. Since intangibles (apart from goodwill) are subject to amortisation, and this piece of information has always been provided, it seems logical to assume that these assets have finite useful lives. However, companies shall more clearly state to which group the asset belongs.
- Companies most frequently define the useful lives of intangibles in ranges. In only 13 cases (14.5%), was the exact useful life provided.
- In accordance with IFRS, a company shall choose the cost model or the revaluation model for subsequent measurement (measurement after the initial recognition) of intangibles.[2] All of the analysed companies use the cost model for measuring intangible assets after their initial recognition. As such, intangibles are measured at cost less than any accumulated amortisation and any accumulated impairment. None of the companies use the revaluation method. These findings can be explained by the fact that the revaluation method can be used only if an active

market exists to determine the fair value of an intangible asset. It is uncommon for an active market to exist for an intangible asset. The findings indicate that revaluation increases in selected companies were not present since they are not allowed under the cost model.
- Companies rarely allocate intangibles to reporting segments. In 66 (73%) out of 90 annual reports, intangibles were not reported by business segments.

Based on the qualitative analysis of disclosures, we established that the content of intangible assets other than goodwill is often not clearly described. We encounter difficulties in understanding the specific content of intangibles, especially long-term property rights, since companies usually do not provide their description. Based on available data, we determined that in the structure of intangible assets the most valuable item in the balance sheet is generally long-term property rights. Companies most often do not disclose to what the rights refer. Apart from long-term property rights, companies also recognised intangible assets under development (the proportion is smaller in comparison with goodwill) in their financial accounts. Five of the analysed companies also recorded the value of brand names (in the whole period of analysis with the exception of one company, which recorded the brand name in 2008). Recognition of licenses or patents was the case in three companies. Only one company recorded its list of costumers.

Additionally, we compared the extent of disclosures about intangibles apart from goodwill and those related to goodwill. In contrast to our expectations, we determined that the latter are more numerous.

In accordance with IFRS, goodwill has to be allocated to CGUs. However, companies do not always disclose how goodwill is allocated to CGUs. Those who do most frequently allocate it to a single CGU; the maximum number of CGUs (disclosed in the case of one company) amounts to five. Goodwill was recorded in 70 out of 90 annual reports that are subject to our analysis. The most common deficiencies concern the following:

- It is not always disclosed to which business combination the value of goodwill is aligned. Only 30 out of 70 annual reports (43%) provide this piece of information. The disclosures are usually made only in the year the goodwill was first recognised. However, even in the subsequent years, notes to financial statements shall disclose which business combination lead to the recognition of goodwill.
- There is a lack of clear explanation about the methodology that was used to test goodwill for impairment. In 2007, 36% of the companies

disclosed the method to determine the recoverable amount of CGU, while in 2011 the share grew to 86%. The data show that the number of disclosures in this field is increasing.
- Goodwill has to be tested annually or more frequently for impairment if there are circumstances that indicate that goodwill might be impaired. Only one company emphasised that goodwill is tested for impairment whenever there were circumstances that require the estimation of the CGU recoverable amount. All other companies seem to perform the test at the end of the financial year.

Almost all the companies in the sample use the present value of cash flow projections for the calculation of the recoverable amount of CGUs; in three cases, the adjusted book value method is in use, while in one case the fair value method, less cost to sell, was implemented.

In accordance with the fact that MTBV ratio of most of the companies was significantly lower than 1 on the day of their balance sheet, indicating that the carrying amount of net assets exceeded their market value, companies were supposed to check whether any impairment of assets should be done. If any indication (external of internal) exists that an asset might be impaired, an entity is required to estimate the recoverable amount of the asset. Thus, in such circumstances, companies are required to estimate the recoverable amount. The majority of the analysed companies did not indicate if the intangible assets were tested for impairment.

Based on the analysis of goodwill disclosures, we can deduce that companies most often do not disclose information required by IFRS. The results can be attributed to the non-importance of goodwill in the structure of total assets. Companies are required to disclose information required by IFRS only for material items. However, the reporting practice has improved since the start of the financial crisis. The improvements are most visible in the field of goodwill disclosure. The disclosures about intangibles other than goodwill remained unchanged in major part.

The analysis of reporting practices in the field of intangibles reveals that companies almost exclusively provide required disclosures, while additional (voluntary) disclosures are not the case in Slovenian companies. Voluntary disclosures about intangibles that are recorded in financial statements were most probably not disclosed, since the value of intangibles on average is far less significant in comparison with tangible assets. However, the selected companies even did not manage to identify non-recognised intangibles, at least not for the purposes of external reporting. This might be a consequence of the characteristics of the business environment. Since Slovenian companies are primarily financed by banks, investors on capital markets are not that influential in comparison with Anglo-Saxon countries. Thus, companies are probably not motivated to provide larger amounts of disclosure.

The authors are aware that the study does not provide answers about the reasons that led to such results. The presented results could be a consequence of difficulties in applying IFRS, the non-material importance of intangibles in the balance sheet, or the unwillingness of companies to provide more detailed disclosures. The sample of companies is small, since a limited number of companies are listed on Ljubljana stock exchange. These are the major limits of the presented research.

CONCLUSIONS

Recent studies show that intangible assets are increasingly valuable assets within traditionally developed economies. Most often studies emphasise the relevance of goodwill. However, the presented analysis shows that intangibles and goodwill are not increasingly valuable in the case of selected Slovene publicly traded companies. The results could be a consequence of fewer mergers and acquisitions, which would allow acquirers to record previously non-recognised intangibles (those internally generated that did not meet the criteria for recognition). Furthermore, the reasons could be aligned to acquisition prices that might be not that high in comparison with the value of net assets and as such do not lead to recognition of more numerous and value-relevant intangibles.

Our major findings concern the characteristics of the reporting practices from the perspective of a post-transition economy. The results show that disclosures about intangibles other than goodwill are often too general, with specific descriptions of intangibles usually lacking. The most valuable items among intangibles are generally long-term property rights. Intangible assets apart from goodwill have definite useful lifespans and for their subsequent measurement is used the cost model. None of the companies uses the revaluation model, which is most probably due to the absence of an active market. Voluntary disclosures about intangibles are lacking in the case of selected Slovenian companies. In 2011, goodwill represented about 20% of the total intangible value on average, which does not support the findings of the previous study performed by Glaum and Wyrwa (2011), which suggested that goodwill is generally the most valuable intangible asset in selected EU companies.

The disclosures about intangibles could be improved, especially in cases in which their share in structure of total assets is important. Unless companies provide detailed information about their subsequent measurement, with particular emphasis on goodwill, future economic benefits arising from intangibles cannot be adequately assessed.

Further research should expand the sample by including more transition or post-transition economies, and shall attempt to analyse the significance of intangibles that meet the criteria for recognition in financial accounts. It shall also attempt to provide reporting practice on intangibles by analysing required and voluntary disclosures, identify their quality, as well as the factors upon which the quality of disclosures depends on. Future research should show if our findings are also relevant for other emerging economies; however, it may show that practices between these economies differ. Understanding the quality of disclosures will benefit managers to improve financial reporting and serve as a basis for improving information for users of financial accounts.

NOTES

1. The first Slovene Accounting Standards (SAS) was issued in 1993. To date, changes followed with the issuance of SAS 2001 and SAS 2006.
2. In accordance with the cost model, an asset is carried at cost less than any amortisation and impairment losses (IAS 38.74). The revaluation model requires an asset to be carried at re-valued amount (fair value) less than any amortisation and impairment losses (IAS 38.75).

REFERENCES

Boedker, C., Mouritsen, J., & Guthrie, J. (2008). Enhanced business reporting: international trends and possible policy directions. *Journal of Human Resource Costing & Accounting*, *12*(1), 14–25. doi:10.1108/14013380810872734

Bontis, N. (2003). Intellectual capital disclosure in Canadian corporations. *Journal of Human Resource Costing & Accounting*, *7*(1/2), 9–20. doi:10.1108/eb029076

Carlin, T. M., & Finch, N. (2010). Evidence on IFRS goodwill impairment testing by Australian and New Zealand firms. *Managerial Finance*, *36*(9), 785–798. doi:10.1108/03074351011064654

Carlin, T. M., Finch, N., & Ford, G. (2007). Goodwill impairment: an assessment of disclosure quality and compliance levels by large listed Australian firms. SSRN Working Paper Series. Retrieved from http://papers.ssrn.com/sol3/papers.cfm?abstract_id=963078

Chen, V., & Feng, G. (2010). Disclosure about fair value measurement for goodwill impairment test: an examination of determinants and usefulness. Paper presented at the 2010 AFAANZ Conference, Christchurch, New Zealand. Retrieved from http://www.afaanz.org/openconf/2010/modules/request.php?module = oc_proceedings&action = proceedings.php&a = Accept + as + Paper

Corrado, C., Hulten, C., & Sichel, D. (2009). Intangible capital and U.S. economic growth. *Review of Income and Wealth*, *55*(3), 661–685. doi:10.1111/j.1475-4991.2009.00343.x

Edvinsson, L., & Malone, M. S. (1997). *Intellectual capital: Realizing your company's true value by finding its hidden brainpower*. New York, NY: Harper Business.

Epstein, B. J., Nach, R., & Bragg, S. M. (2007). *GAAP 2008: Interpretation and application of generally accepted accounting principles*. New Jersey: John & Wiley and Sons.

Gelb, D. S. (2002). Intangible assets and firms' disclosures: An empirical investigation. *Journal of Business Finance & Accounting*, *29*(3/4), 457–476. doi:10.1111/1468-5957.00438

Glaum, M., & Wyrwa, S. (2011). *Making acquisition transparent: Goodwill accounting in times of financial crisis*. Frankfurt am Main: Fachverlag Moderne Wirtschaft.

Guthrie, J. (2001). The management, measurement and the reporting of intellectual capital. *Journal of Intellectual Capital*, *2*(1), 27–41. doi:10.1108/14691930110380473

GVIN. (2012). *Financial data and business information [Data file]*. Retrieved from http://www.gvin.com/

Hayn, C., & Hughes, P. J. (2006). Leading indicators of goodwill impairment. *Journal of Accounting Auditing and Finance*, *21*(3), 223–265. doi:10.1177/0148558X0602100303

Henry, T., & Holtzman, M. (2007). Extraordinary items share exclusive company: Only unusual and infrequent events pass muster under FASB 145. *Journal of Accountancy*, *203*(5). Retrieved from http://law-journals-books.vlex.com/source/journal-accountancy-2859

Holtzman, M., & Sinnett, W. (2009). Goodwill impairments. Financial executives research foundations. Retrieved from www.duffandphelps.com/.../articles/09_goodwill_impairments.pdf

Lahovnik, M. (2000). Characteristics of acquisitions in Slovenia. *Economic and Business Review*, *2*, 131–143.

Lev, B. (2001). *Intangibles: Management, measurement and reporting*. Washington, DC: Brookings Institution Press.

Lev, B., & Daum, J. H. (2004). The dominance of intangible assets: consequences for enterprise management and corporate reporting. *Measuring Business Excellence*, *8*(1), 6–17. doi:10.1108/13683040410524694

Ljubljana Stock Exchange. (2012). *Annual statistics – 2011*. Retrieved from http://www.ljse.si/cgi-bin/jve.cgi?doc = 1595&sid = CyOeN4x2B8wKsKnF

Marr, B. (2007). Measuring and managing intangible value drivers. *Business Strategy Series*, *8*(3), 172–178. doi:10.1108/17515630710684169

Massoudi, D., Izan, H. Y., & Tarca, A. (2011). Impair or not to impair? Factors affecting the application of IAS 36 in Australian and The United Kingdom. Paper presented at the 2011 AFAANZ Conference, Darwin, Australia. Retrieved from http://www.afaanz.org/openconf/2011/modules/request.php?module = oc_proceedings&action = proceedings.php&a = Accept + as + Paper

Muller, K. A., Neamtiu, M., & Riedl, E. J. (2009). Information asymmetry surrounding SFAS 142 goodwill impairments. SSRN Working Paper Series. Retrieved from http://papers.ssrn.com/sol3/papers.cfm?abstract_id = 1429615

Paananen, M. (2008, September 30). *Fair value accounting for goodwill under IFRS: An exploratory study of the comparability in France, Germany and the United Kingdom.* Retrieved from http://dx.doi.org/10.2139/ssrn.1275803

Ritter, A., & Wells, P. (2006). Identifiable intangible asset disclosures, stock prices and future earnings. *Accounting & Finance*, *46*(5), 843–863. doi:10.1111/j.1467-629X.2006.00190.x

Roslender, R. (2009). The prospects for satisfactorily measuring and reporting intangibles: Time to embrace a new model of (ac)counting? *Journal of Human Resource Costing & Accounting*, *13*(4), 338–359. doi:10.1108/14013381011010169

Schroeder, M. (2007). Goodwill on consolidation as an indicator of progress in transition economies: Evidence from Polish listed group financial companies. In V. Murinde (Ed.), *Research in accounting in emerging economies: Accounting, banking and corporate financial management in emerging economies* (Vol. 7, pp. 11–27). Amsterdam; Oxford: JAI Press Inc.

Sevin, S., Schroeder, R., & Bhamornsiri, S. (2007). Transparent financial disclosure and SFAS No. 142. *Managerial Auditing Journal*, *22*(7), 674–687. doi:10.1108/02686900710772582

Skinner, D. J. (2008). Accounting for intangibles – A critical review of policy recommendations. *Accounting and Business Research*, *38*(3), 191–204. doi:10.1080/00014788.2008.9663332

Sveiby, K. E. (1997). *The new organizational wealth: Managing & measuring knowledge-based assets*. San Francisco, CA: Berrett-Koehler.

APPENDIX A: THE LIST OF COMPANIES INCLUDED IN THE ANALYSIS

2007 ($n=17$)	2008 ($n=18$)	2009 ($n=18$)	2010 ($n=19$)	2011 ($n=18$)
Krka	Krka	Krka	Krka	Krka
Mercator	Mercator	Mercator	Mercator	Mercator
Petrol	Petrol	Petrol	Petrol	Petrol
Telekom Slovenije	Telekom Slovenije	Telekom Slovenije	Telekom Slovenije	Telekom Slovenije
Gorenje	Gorenje	Gorenje	NKBM	Gorenje
Intereuropa	Intereuropa	Intereuropa	Gorenje	Intereuropa
Luka Koper	Luka Koper	Luka Koper	Luka Koper	Luka Koper
Sava	Sava	Sava	Sava	Sava
Aerodrom Ljubljana	Aerodrom Ljubljana	Aerodrom Ljubljana	Aerodrom Ljubljana	Aerodrom Ljubljana
Žito	Žito	Žito	Žito	Žito
Pivovarna Laško	Pivovarna Laško	Pivovarna Laško	Pozavarovalnica Sava	Pivovarna Laško
Iskra Avtoelektrika	Iskra Avtoelektrika	Iskra Avtoelektrika	Pivovarna Laško	Iskra Avtoelektrika
Terme Čatež	Terme Čatež	Terme Čatež	Terme Čatež	Terme Čatež
Istrabenz	Istrabenz	Istrabenz	Istrabenz	Istrabenz
Mlinotest	Mlinotest	Mlinotest	Mlinotest	Mlinotest
Kompas MTS	Kompas MTS	Kompas MTS	Kompas MTS	Kompas MTS
Etol	Etol	Etol	Etol	
	Delo prodaja	Delo prodaja	Delo prodaja	Delo prodaja
			Unior	Unior

APPENDIX B: DESCRIPTIVE STATISTICS OF THE SAMPLE

		Average	Standard Deviation	Min	Max	*n*
Total assets (in €)	2007	691,973,481	635,386,471	42,488,763	2,070,473,000	17
	2008	712,341,538	714,545,435	47,080,967	2,540,121,000	18
	2009	691,270,012	708,835,652	49,751,929	2,476,348,000	19
	2010	650,678,241	705,900,046	51,861,778	2,608,854,000	19
	2011	673,731,449	730,834,732	52,533,476	2,647,663,000	18
Common equity (in €)	2007	323,790,843	294,541,527	25,510,416	1,062,741,000	17
	2008	292,606,162	313,780,433	23,850,423	1,065,670,000	18
	2009	282,200,591	328,128,002	15,701,509	1,048,025,000	19
	2010	273,625,388	310,112,513	24,038,928	1,053,327,000	18
	2011	256,406,835	322,217,035	13,402,619	1,139,754,000	18
Revenues from sales (in €)	2007	557,210,263	737,559,723	36,160,605	2,445,258,000	17
	2008	618,068,255	886,243,421	38,623,232	2,949,634,054	18
	2009	553,652,146	788,367,549	33,470,541	2,643,315,000	19
	2010	569,623,802	865,451,475	33,399,177	2,802,752,517	18
	2011	598,883,517	961,428,543	33,229,615	3,270,353,441	18
Market-to-book value	2007	2.50	1.97	0.27	7.73	17
	2008	0.90	0.54	0.24	2.50	18
	2009	0.90	0.62	0.10	2.84	19
	2010	0.79	0.54	0.10	2.37	18
	2011	0.52	0.41	0.02	1.73	18
Return on equity (in %)	2007	11.28	8.09	−5.15	27.39	17
	2008	−0.27	22.71	−81.59	26.26	18
	2009	−13.43	36.59	−130.52	20.39	19
	2010	−3.62	12.51	−25.00	17.32	18
	2011	−3.40	18.14	−64.26	14.84	18

Source: GVIN, Ljubljana Stock Exchange, annual reports.

RECONSIDERING FINANCIAL REPORTING FROM THE PERSPECTIVE OF CORPORATE SOCIAL AND ENVIRONMENTAL RESPONSIBILITY. ROMANIAN COMPANIES' APPROACH

Camelia Iuliana Lungu, Chiraţa Caraiani and Cornelia Dascălu

ABSTRACT

Purpose – *This study analyses the scope of social and environmental reporting from the perspective of integrating it in financial reporting and comments on a new approach regarding the presentation of social and environmental information in the annual reports from Romanian companies' perspective.*

Methodology – *A literature review introduces and justifies the second part of the research. The latter is organised as an exploratory study based on interviews. It presents the current state of Romanian companies'*

Accounting in Central and Eastern Europe
Research in Accounting in Emerging Economies, Volume 13, 205–234

ISSN: 1479-3563/doi:10.1108/S1479-3563(2013)0000013014

availability for reconsidering financial reporting from the perspective of corporate social responsibility.

Findings – *While social and environmental involvement of Romanian companies is at an early stage, there is a basis for future development of corporate reporting by addressing social and environmental aspects. We noticed that companies have the tendency of responding rather to a mandatory framework than a voluntary one.*

Research limitations – *The limitations of the research are linked to the study population. The small number of Romanian companies that publicly manifest interest for social responsibility determined the choice of a qualitative instead of a quantitative research.*

Social implications – *The exploratory study based on the case of Romania accompanies the present state of non-financial versus financial reporting in order to highlight measurable and non-measurable, but relevant, information to be considered in a future reporting framework.*

Originality of the chapter – *The study advances new lines in accounting research by confronting the national and international perspectives of social and environmental reporting. Debates and arguments on the research results add value and utility to the research.*

Keywords: Social; environmental; reporting; corporate responsibility; companies' practice; Romania

INTRODUCTION

To respond the new information needs arising from the awareness of companies' responsibility to their business partners (in the broad sense of stakeholders), new reporting models have emerged in the theory and practice of financial reporting. Traditional financial accounting does not respond anymore to the information required by the process of identifying and reporting entity's activity in the context of sustainable development. The concern of integrating social and environmental factors into traditional financial reporting is gaining acceptance nowadays. For more than 40 years, as the attention to the social and environmental dimensions of business activities has increased, considerably research on accounting as a social and institutional practice has developed. Authors adopting such a perspective demonstrate an appreciation for the continuing and permissive characteristics of accounting and an awareness of the importance of specific factors, which enables accounting to respond to sustainability demands.

The development of social and environmental accounting and reporting over the last 40 years has resulted in a wide range of actual and potential accounts of (typically) organisational interactions with society and the natural environment (Gray, 2010). The core idea sustains that the business sector should play a proactive role in society, in addition to its economic purpose of making profits. These issues have led the industry to engage in a sustainability debate and initiate strategies for responding to the challenges of sustainable development, in the spirit of Brundtland Commission Report (United Nations, UN, 1987). Sustainable development, in the current world environment, is a challenging concept as it confronts the basic 'economic model of the world that runs through conventional accounting and finance' (Gray, 2003, p. 372). Consequently, sustainable development has initiated a new era of accounting renaissance and the profession needs to accept and act towards the realities of our changing environment.

This aspect is currently addressed by Gray and Bebbington (2000) in the form of a fundamental conflict between the conventional business agenda and environmental protection – and, especially, the pursuit of sustainability. The International Finance Corporation (IFC) (2009) laments that lack of accounting data on corporate social and environmental activities is a key barrier to sustainable responsible investment. However, there is no alternative to accounting at the moment for communicating corporate sustainability information (Ngwakwe, 2012). Consequently, accounting's role would be more effective when it incorporated the environment, society and economic impacts into corporate accounting and reporting. Gray (2002) conducted a study on the theoretical approaches of social aspects of accounting. His paper provides a review of 25 years of social accounting literature. The main theme of the essay is that social accounting, at its best, is designed to open up a space for new accountings between the *conventional* accounting literature and practice and the *alternative* critiques and theories.

Conventional accounting also takes a very narrow business-orientated view. It sets out to capture and measure business transactions. Anyway, it does not seek to embrace the interactions between society and nature. Indeed, the natural world is redefined in accounting terms. Simply put, our relations with the environment are at best ignored and at worst seen as opportunities for commercial exploitation or generating profits. The environment only becomes visible in accounting terms when it is captured and quantified (Jones, 2010).

In the recent past, some researchers tried to discover the extent of accountants' involvement in sustainable development activities within their corporations. For instance, Bebbington, Gray, Thomson, and Walters (1994) found that UK accountants, at that time, were not involved in their corporate environmental activities; Deegan and Gordon (1996) discovered that accountants in Australia had not started showing appreciable responses to environmental issues at the time of their research. In addition, Gray et al. (1998) found that accountants did not appear to be spurring corporate environmental responsibility.

Having at the basis the legitimacy theory, this study is based on the idea supported by researchers during the time that companies should behave in a socially responsible way (Gray & Bebbington, 2000; Jones, 2010; Solomon & Solomon, 2004). Our chapter draws on the incentives that further pragmatic sustainability initiatives are required of the accounting profession to boost the role of accounting towards sustainable development; such initiatives may include regulated sustainability accounting and reporting standards, integrating sustainability accounting into accountancy education (Ngwakwe, 2012).

The study advances new lines in accounting research by confronting two perspectives: the international one, where practices and instruments of social and environmental reporting can be found in organisational culture on a large scale, and a national one, where companies are still focused on simply using corporate social responsibility campaigns to address corporate reporting. The chapter develops a theoretical framework designed on multiple approaches: institutional and practical, present and future, and possible and impossible for the accounting community's perception level. Debates and arguments on the case of Romanian companies accompany our proposals in order to add value and utility to the research results.

Within the context presented above, our research has as *purpose* to bring into debate the general idea that *debates on an extended framework for financial statements preparation and reporting that underpin the role of society and environment in a sustainable development context will develop a holistic vision of the economic entity*. This image will be perceived on the current requirements for communicating social and environmental responsibilities, and besides the concepts, principles, policies and information required by traditional accounting.

The chapter is structured as follows. After a brief presentation of the research methodology, the first section addresses the current state of social and environmental information presentations in financial reports in terms of efforts and results achieved by researchers, standardisation organisations and reporting entities. An important part of this section refers to synthesising existing researches on the directions of a possible explanation of financial reporting framework with social and environmental information. The second section aims to highlight the Romanian companies' position in relation to possibilities for extending financial reporting requirements in order to include the disclosure of social and environmental impact. Finally, the findings, limitations and directions for future research are presented.

RESEARCH METHODOLOGY

The theoretical framework used to address the aim of the chapter is mixing legitimacy theory with elements of stakeholder theory and signalling theory. It is based on the idea that corporate social responsibility refers to voluntary initiatives taken by the business community to demonstrate their accountability in relation to stakeholders. Elkington (1997, p. 171) claims that many 'companies engaging in corporate social reporting view their reports as public relations vehicles', while Deegan, Rankin, and Voght (2000) argue that this disclosure is used to address concerns about the legitimacy of the organisation. *Legitimacy theory* asserts, 'an organization seeks approval (or avoidance of sanction) from groups in society' (Kaplan & Ruland, 1991, p. 370). Its arguments suggest that companies with worse social and environmental performance also have incentives for disclosure. Deegan (2002, 2007) summarises a large body of research that examines this use of social and environmental disclosure as a legitimating tool for reducing exposures to what Patten (1992) and Walden and Schwartz (1997) refer to those as social and political pressures.

According to the strategic approach of organisational legitimacy, companies use corporate communication media, such as corporate responsibility disclosures and press releases, to manage perceived sustainability legitimacy by signalling to relevant publics that their behaviour is appropriate and desirable (Aerts & Cormier, 2009). *Signalling theory* (adapted from Zahavi, 1975) suggests that profitable companies have the incentive to distinguish themselves from less successful ones to raise capital at the lowest possible cost. Costly signalling theory suggests that people might engage in costly pro-social behaviours such as environmental conservation particularly when they are motivated to attain status (Griskevicius, Tybur, & Van den Bergh, 2010). *Stakeholder theory*, introduced by Edward Freeman in 1984 posits that there are varieties of strategic publics that can influence an organisation. This means that companies should no longer be held accountable only to their shareholders. Rather, other parties influenced by their operations should also be taken into consideration. Such stakeholders may include customers, employees, suppliers, partners and local neighbourhoods, among others. Supporting the theory, Clarkson, Li, Richardson, and Vasvari (2008) discuss sustainability disclosure in terms of informing investors and other stakeholders, which are becoming increasingly concerned about corporate social and environmental policies and the way of transposing them into practice.

This research chapter aims the participation to the professional judgment construction, according to free manifestation of entity's accounting and reporting policies regarding the corporate social responsibility. Therefore, the main objective of the chapter is to debate the way that the projection of an extended framework for financial statements preparation and reporting that underpin the role of the society and of the environment may respond to the sustainable development context and reality.

To achieve this objective, the research overviews the issues of corporate responsibility and social and environmental reporting from two perspectives:

1. providing an overview of existing policies and practices and
2. constructing an image on the concerns of Romanian companies in the field.

Given the objectives, the research is rather a qualitative one. The data coming from accounting literature, accounting settlers' requirements and entities' experience are gathered, analysed and interpreted in order to bring to light an underlying coherence and sense for the new reporting perspective that may be supported by specialised institutions as well as by Romanian companies.

The chapter focuses on fundamental research, based on literature review intended to provide an overview of existing sustainability-oriented policies and practices. This relates to inductive accounting theory and uses scientific methods for identification of corporate reporting theoretical and practical difficulties in European and international economic entities determined by new approaches regarding social and environmental information reporting. Additionally, an exploratory study based on interviews was conducted, constructing an image on the concerns of Romanian companies in the field. Its results are analysed and discussed in terms of formulating recommendations designated to reshape the current Romanian financial reporting framework. This analysis give the possibility to design a new facet for the overall framework of reporting social and environmental information, by combining theoretical requirements with their implementation in the practices of Romanian companies.

IS FINANCIAL REPORTING THE WAY TO RESPOND SUSTAINABLE BUSINESS?

Financial accounting and reporting shall deliver relevant and reliable information of an enterprise or another organisation to external interested parties. The main reporting instruments (as statement of financial position, statement of comprehensive income, notes, etc.) contain reliable data as they report on the past, reducing their forecasting power, whereas actual and potential stakeholders need future-oriented data to be able to prepare their decisions. Even if the conflict between relevance and reliability in accounting may be solved due to the uncertainty of the future (Altenburger & Schaffhauser-Linzatti, 2007), we support the idea that, in areas such as scope, consistency of methodological approaches to recognition and measurement policies, timeliness, users and elements of reporting, improvements regarding social and environmental impact disclosure are required.

Research on social and environmental reporting has moved on from an initial phase of observation and description to a phase aimed at improvement of available techniques and actual practice. Equally significant is the growing movement by the major accounting organisations to become involved in the development of standards for corporate social reporting and auditing.

Existing research on the choice of accounting methods for corporate reports emphasises private interests. Dierkes and Antal (1985) presented a stepwise process for evaluating the usefulness and use of corporate social reporting information. In particular, shareholders' interests predominate in studies of the effects of accounting information on individual users. Van der Laan, Adhikari, and Tondkar (2005) argue that the manner in which the role of a corporation and its stakeholders is defined in a society will affect the extent and quality of corporate social disclosure in annual reports.

Reporting on social and environmental information has matured over the past decades, but there remains a lack of adequate standardisation (MacLean & Gottfrid, 2000). The concept of non-financial reporting and, in particular, the recognition, measurement and disclosure of social and environmental issues in the financial statements and annual reports of companies is not a new one. According to European Commission (EU), companies are recommended to disclose an analysis that includes both financial and, where appropriate, non-financial key performance indicators relevant to the particular business, including information relating to environmental and employee matters (EU, 2003).

An important concern of information on sustainable development interaction with financial reporting is the need to provide conventional data concepts and terms that are known within the financial statements. Lamberton (2005) makes an important step forward in formalising an accounting model for sustainability. Based on various definitions from the literature, five basic components of the financial accounting model have been identified: accounting reports, accounting principles, accounting records, the objectives of the accounting model, and qualitative characteristics.

SOCIAL AND ENVIRONMENTAL REPORTING AT GLOBAL LEVEL: INCENTIVES FOR ROMANIA

Reporting is an important communication tool, which can ensure greater corporate transparency and enable better engagement with stakeholders. Hopwood (2009) argues that even when sustainability reports are prepared, companies may be using them to cover the issues being asked of them, so that, despite the apparent openness of their reporting, even less is known (Guidry & Patten, 2012).

The objective of this paragraph is to provide a theoretical justification based on the international experience, for a possible use of a social and environmental accounting and reporting framework within Romanian companies. At international level, the social aspects have been a subject for research in accounting since the early issue of accounting journals, the environmental aspects started to be debated in 1982 (Lungu, Caraiani, & Dascălu, 2009). In the 1990s, the concern turned more specifically to environmental issues. An increasing recognition of the impact of humans on the environment has led to a radical re-questioning of traditional economic, ethical and accounting assumptions. For the last couple of years, researchers assert that the demands for businesses to act in ways consistent with social and environmental accounting and sustainable development are growing (Milne, Tregida, & Walton, 2009). Jones (2010) shows the reason why organisations should develop a comprehensive system of environmental accounting and why they should report it to their stakeholders. This argument can be taken into account by Romanian companies and the international experience does nothing but to facilitate the view of the big picture for Romania.

Since the beginning of last century, corporate governance has led, without any doubt, the highest level of attention and debate among legislators, regulators, professionals, business organisations, media and community in general (Parker, 2005). From the companies' perspective, most of the first reports were successful in achieving the objective of public relations, but also received criticism, which led to a more active involvement of a number of NGOs, government and industry initiatives to improve reporting requirements.

The Romanian economy is no exception to these trends. Although the Romanian companies' involvement in the sustainable development is in an early stage, there is a basis for future development, affecting the future evolution of the Romanian economy (Lungu, Caraiani, Dascălu, Cimpoeru, & Sahlian, 2012b). Romanian companies committed to sustainability-oriented activities, even if they are centred mainly on the competitive advantages derived from this practice and the community is the main partner in communicating sustainability (Băleanu, Chelcea, & Stancu, 2011). Responding to the demands generated by the economic practice of companies, the Romanian researchers' interest developed, in order to integrate sustainability into corporate accounting policies (Albu, Albu, Gîrbină, & Sandu, 2011; Caraiani et al., 2006; Dascălu, Caraiani, Lungu, Colceag, & Guşe, 2010; Ienciu, Muller, & Matiş, 2011; Ionaşcu, 2006; Lungu et al., 2012a).

Social and environmental information projected as layers of sustainable development generated at the corporate level is intended mainly to reduce information asymmetry between managers and external stakeholders. Sustainability reporting initiatives as United Nations Global Compact (UNGC), World Business Council on Sustainable Development (WBCSD), Prince of Wales International Business Leaders Forum, Global Reporting Initiative (GRI), Sustainability Accounting Standards Board (SASB) or CSR Europe, as voluntary ones, developed a strategy of bringing companies together for meetings, conferences and seminars. Their aim is to involve companies in disseminating information through public and popular communication channels as web pages, newsletters, scientific papers and best practice studies, and contributing to the diffusion of technologies and sustainability reporting practices.

Supporting the idea that mandatory regulation is likely to be more effective than voluntary regulation, Cho, Chen, and Roberts (2008, p. 451) argue: 'affected firms were already striving to reduce or mitigate environmental disclosure regulations, using political avenues, despite global environmental rises'. According to UNEP, GRI, KPMG Global Sustainability Services, and Stellenbosch University Business School (2010, p. 4), 'a review of mandatory and voluntary sustainability reporting standards and legislation in 30 countries has revealed that both international and national standards, codes and guidelines as well as legislation for sustainability reporting have been strongly evolving'.

The current trend, especially in International Financial Reporting Standards (IFRS), highlights the increasing need to include present- and future-oriented information, required by corporate reporting requirements. Therefore, International Accounting Standard Board (IASB) is urged to improve upon their interest in sustainable development by expediting action on social and environmental considerations in their standard setting and regulatory function. In order to respond these tendencies, IASB has been involved in collaborations with other bodies such as GRI, WBCSD and United Nations Commission on Sustainable Development (UNCSD) on environmental sustainability. This includes meetings, guidelines and environmental standards.

Some positive responses are noticeable from IASB, in terms of social and environmental approach. Standards such as IAS 20 *Accounting for Government Grants and Disclosure of Government Assistance*; IAS 37 *Provisions, Contingent Liabilities and Contingent Assets*; and IAS 38 *Intangible Assets* or IFRIC 5 *Rights to Interests Arising from Decommissioning, Restoration and Environmental Funds* prove IASB interest in social and environmental issues. In addition to existing standards regarding accounting and reporting of social and environmental aspects, the IASB has published a proposed non-mandatory framework to help entities prepare and present a narrative report. The publication is referred to as the Management Commentary (IASB, 2010). It helps users of the annual reports, among others, to understand how non-financial factors have influenced the information presented in the financial statements. The current debates on IASB's framework leave open the future possibility of achieving specific standards addressing social and environmental issues, by replacing the term financial statements with financial reports (IASB, 2006–2010). Future trend is not clear, given the changes of tone expressed in successive projects of IASB's framework.

At the European level, Directive 2003/51 (the 'Modernisation Directive') amended the accounting directives and added that European companies are required to also include non-financial information in their annual and consolidated reports if it is necessary for an understanding of the company's development, performance or position (EU, 2003). Another amendment of the accounting directives (EU, 2006) introduced an obligation for listed companies to include a corporate governance statement in their annual report. By November 2009, all Member States have transposed the Modernisation Directive and most of the Member States have transposed Directive 2006/46 in their national laws. In EU countries, there are government initiatives and requirements to enlarge the scope of conventional reporting to include non-financial information. Some actions are motivated by national environmental and social policy goals, others by external users' pressures to obtain a reliable view on companies' actions. All indications point to continuing expansion of governmental reporting initiatives to new countries and regions over the next few years (Lungu, Caraiani, Dascălu, & Guşe, 2011).

Surveys of social and environmental reporting practice tend to show that both the quantity and the overall quality of reporting are increasing (Gray & Milne, 2002; Holland & Foo, 2003; WBCSD, 2003). This is because there are genuinely complex and difficult issues to be confronted in reporting on corporate actions concerning the society and the environment (Hopwood, 2009). A study by Mammatt, Marx, and van Dyk (2010) shows that as of 2008, there has been an increase in the quality and effectiveness of the social and environmental information reported. More and more companies provide concise and focused sustainability information in their annual report, as proof of reliable disclosure, accompanied by full sustainability reports on their websites, reflecting a growing maturity on CSR disclosures (Lungu, Caraiani, Dascălu, & Colceag, 2010). However, debates continue on the quality of information presented, because some companies report large volumes of data that is difficult for the reader to digest. Even more so, other companies report so little that it merely raises questions regarding their commitment to sustainability and stakeholder reporting overall.

In Western Europe, corporate social responsibility has become a popular concept that no major company can afford to ignore. Between Western and Central Eastern, European countries still remain important differences regarding the social responsibility concept (Steurer & Konrad, 2009). While in the Western Europe both governments and companies are active in this field in Eastern Europe, countries, most of them emerging economies, corporate responsibility and sustainable development are concepts entered in governmental, non-profit organisations and major companies just for a couple of years. The Romanian Government shows interest for the problem of social responsibility and the legislation in the field of environment, employment, restructuring of local authorities was permanently improved (Popa, Blidisel, & Farcane, 2009).

Since 2008, Romania has a new National Strategy for Sustainable Development, characterised by a new philosophy of development of the European Union and worldwide shared. However, there is, so far, no legislation in this area, requiring companies in Romania, listed or not at the capital market to provide stakeholders separate reports or specific information relating to the social and environmental impact (Ienciu, Muller, & Matiş, 2011). According to Braun and Partners Network composite index CSR 24/7 2010 (see www.braunpartnersnw.com), a CSR rating product developed on companies over four countries in Central and Eastern Europe (Hungary, Poland, Bulgaria and Romania), Romanian companies had lowest scores in the areas of economic responsibility, human resources and companies relation with stakeholders. Same report has found that Romanian companies have websites well developed commercially which do not though include information on programs for stakeholders, relations with suppliers or only partial information related to human resources and social reporting under GRI international standards is not common practice.

The low quality of social and environmental reporting in the case of Romanian companies shows that the information provided by the Romanian companies is incomplete and irrelevant, social and environmental accounting and reporting remaining a challenge for the accounting profession and for researchers from Romania.

INTEGRATING SOCIAL AND ENVIRONMENTAL INFORMATION IN FINANCIAL REPORTING – ROMANIAN COMPANIES' APPROACH

Based on the literature review, on practical studies of various researchers and specialised organisations or associations, and on our previous studies, this study makes another step in social and environmental accounting research by developing an interview-based study on the Romanian companies' interest in reporting information on their social and environmental responsibility. Thus, the purpose was to introduce a series of research propositions that opened debates regarding the principles, concepts and forms of social and environmental reporting from Romanian companies' point of view.

This exploratory study aims at presenting an image on the position of Romanian companies already involved in aspects of corporate social responsibility (especially in the marketing and communication), to provide social and environmental information through financial statements. Therefore, interviews based on a given questionnaire were conducted for a group of Romanian companies that self-expressed their interest in corporate social responsibility. Based on their responses, the chapter further introduces reference points for discussions on a *Framework for presenting social and environmental information through annual financial reports.*

The Sample and the Research Method

In choosing the research sample, we sought to identify companies interested in social and environmental aspects. Part of the study subject population was identified in 40 Romanian companies that have publicly declared their support for the actions of corporate involvement in social and environmental responsibility. These companies have voluntarily signed up on the first CSR portal in Romania, www.responsabilitatesociala.ro. The objective of the portal is to convince and then to help companies in Romania to invest in the development of the society and of the communities they activate in. The 40 companies registered on the portal have volunteered information about their practices on social responsibility, thus confirming their interest in reporting a possible environmental and social impact.

Designed as a qualitative research, seeking to interview the key persons with experience in corporate CSR communication, the study aims at presenting the opinions of Romanian companies activating in various industries. A quantitative research, with a statistical and forecasting purpose, will be the subject of a future study that will continue the present research. The qualitative research aim is to bring arguments and scientific support for the constructive debate we proposed that of extending the financial reporting framework towards an integrated one (economic, social and environmental), applicable to Romanian companies. To give a higher credibility to the received responses, the companies included in the study were chosen from the 40 companies voluntarily entered the portal www.responsabilitatesociala.ro.

Then, we applied the constraint of being listed on the Bucharest Stock Exchange (BSE). The companies' listing on BSE provides a high significance to the results of the study because their reporting is subject to the Code of Corporate Governance, which requires listed companies to announce their involvement in corporate social responsibility. The Code requires the listed companies to prepare and disseminate periodic and continuous relevant information, according to the highest standards of financial reporting – IFRS and other reporting standards, namely environmental, social and leadership (environment, social and governance).

Companies fill up a statement called the *Statement Explain or Apply* that has to contain the reference to the economic, social and environmental concerns affecting their operational activities. This includes their interaction with interested third parties – *stakeholders,* and the increasing degree of involvement of their employees, of their representatives and trade unions, and of interested persons outside the company; creditors, consumers and investors – to develop and implement corporate social responsibility practices.

General Statistics for Companies Included in the Study

Based on the interviews conducted, we analysed the results for seven companies, from different industries, and of different size, but representative for the majority of Romanian companies. These seven companies are described in Table 1. The limit of the small number of studied companies is compensated by the fact that the respondents are of various industries, different sizes and different forms of organisation (both limited liability and stock companies). All companies, however, are concerned on social and environmental responsibility policies. Therefore, the diversity of their characteristics provides to our study a higher coverage of opinions on social and environmental reporting.

The interviews based on a questionnaire addressed to the sampled population is relevant in terms of shaping the debate on issues addressed mainly to the regulatory and professional bodies, but not the least to academics and companies.

Questionnaire Design and Research Questions

The design of the questionnaire used in interviews had taken into consideration the main objective of the present survey, to discuss *an extended framework for financial statements preparation and reporting that underpin the role of the society and of the environment in a sustainable development context.*

Through a number of 10 closed questions, with unique, multiple and mixed answers (possibly multiple correlated with the significance of values on a scale from 1, very low importance, to 5, very high importance), we formulated benchmarks to debate elements of a framework for presenting social and environmental impact through annual financial reports. This exploratory study underlines the relationship between informing upon the social and environmental impact with conventional financial reporting of the companies. This is the starting point of a discussion upon whether to

Table 1. General Description of Studied Companies.

Company	Industry	Respondent's Position in the Company	Total Assets	Total Revenues	Share Capital	Results after Tax	No. of Employees
			Million Euro				
C1	Financial	Shareholders' department manager	722	46	74	−11	1377
C2	Soft drinks production	Programmes for the community specialist	281	467	58	41	2026
C3	Pharmaceuticals	Chef executive officer	93	62	10	13	585
C4	Electricity	Capital market and economic analysis branch manager	1048	608	173	2	2185
C5	Cosmetics	CSR specialist	51	119	0.5	17	308
C6	Pharmaceuticals	Chef executive officer	96	210	13	5	1657
C7	Client-oriented software	Communication specialist	30	52	0.03	16	649

adapt and extend the requirements regarding the preparation and presentation of financial statements that refer to social and environmental sustainability reporting.

Four research propositions were identified and tested in the study:

RQ1: Are Romanian companies interested in adopting the presentation of social and environmental impact?

RQ2: Is there a balance between supporting and limitation of a social and environmental impact?

RQ3: From shareholders to stakeholders: Prioritising stakeholders for social and environmental reporting – Are Romanian companies interested?

RQ4: What is the importance of basic elements for social and environmental reporting for integrating into financial reporting framework in Romanian companies view?

In our opinion, the standardisation of reporting social and environmental impact can be achieved only in the context in which companies are both open to accepting replacement of primary user (the shareholder) with a diversified group of users (stakeholders), and interested in providing information for custom categories of stakeholders. Designing a framework of social and environmental reporting should be based on basic concepts, principles and qualitative characteristics of information disclosed, similar to those in traditional accounting. Information provided to users may be quantitative and qualitative, and may comply with a set of quality characteristics and restrictions currently meet within the financial reporting.

Results and Debates

Further, the research results are analysed and debates addressing the potential improvement of social and environmental impact reporting for Romanian companies are introduced.

Companies' Concerns for Adopting the Presentation of Social and Environmental Impact

The first part of this exploratory study is aimed to establish the degree to which companies' management is involved in the pursuit of social and environmental aspects of the company's activity and in reporting social and environmental impact generated by the businesses. In addition, we intended to find the opinion of Romanian companies regarding a possible standardisation of policies and formats for reporting social and environmental impact.

The affirmative answers received from all the companies for the question 'Is the corporate management in your company concerned with social and environmental issues?' assure us that the sample, although small, is appropriate to our goal, to support a redesign of a framework for reporting social and environmental information.

Companies' concern for reporting social and environmental impact is tested by the question 'How does your company report social and environmental impact?' The responses presented in Table 2, column 3, show current involvement of the management in the reporting process. At the same time, they show a lack of comparability of social and environmental information submitted by each company. Companies choose different types of reporting, lacking the comparability, therefore difficult to analyse by stakeholders. The management (referred by us to answer these questions) is aware of the business' impact on society and the environment and that it is concerned with identifying this impact. This assures the quality and the utility of the responses to the questionnaire that will help us outline appropriate conclusions and debates useful equally to Romanian regulators and companies.

The responses (Table 2, columns 4 and 5) to other two questions – *What should be the basis of social and environmental reporting?* and *How should be the content of social and environmental presentations?* – confirm that Romanian companies, which are already involved in corporate responsibility actions or are considering engaging in such actions, will rather accept a standardised reporting for social and environmental impact, whether a nationally developed reporting framework. From companies' perspective, such framework should include minimum mandatory requirements, standardised, based on clear principles and on minimum mandatory formats (four companies). Elements of voluntary reports are supported by the other three companies.

Debates. Starting from the conclusions offered by previous studies conducted by researchers in social and environmental reporting, the idea of describing social and environmental aspects in the financial statements, with an impact on company's performance, is widely accepted. National and international literature review and the analysis of international, European, and especially Romanian companies lead us to the conclusion that Romanian companies need a redesign of extended, social and environmental information disclosure on the facet of mandatory financial reports. Thus, national regulatory bodies of accounting should reconsider methods

Table 2. Companies' Concerns for Implication, Identification and Reporting of Social and Environmental Impact.

Industry	Concerns for Social and Environmental Impact	Presentation of Social and Environmental Impact	Standardised Reporting on Social and Environmental Impact	Formats for Social and Environmental Reporting
0	1	2	3	4
Electricity	Yes	Annual report	Mandatory national policies	Mandatory, industry customised
Cosmetics	Yes	Annual report	Own policies	Minimum, mandatory
Pharmaceuticals	Yes	Annual report/social and environmental media campaigns	Mandatory national policies/ voluntary international policies	Minimum, mandatory/ voluntary, company customised
Soft drinks production	Yes	CSR report	Mandatory national policies	Minimum, mandatory
Client-oriented software	Yes	CSR report	Voluntary international policies	Voluntary, company customised
Financial	Yes	CSR report	Voluntary international policies	Voluntary, company customised

for identifying and regulating a *social and environmental reporting model based on principles, concepts and elements. Such a model may include preset minimum formats and requirements for assuring qualitative information, and may be integrated in the accounting reporting model.*

The Balance between Supporting and Limitation of a Social and Environmental Impact

For an exhaustive approach to testing the success with which specialised national organisms could implement our studies, debates and conclusions within annual reporting of Romanian companies, we identified the issues that limit or support the reporting of social and environmental issues. The results presented in Fig. 1 show that the main issue, according to Romanian managers, limiting social and environmental reporting is human resource shortages.

The second most important issue in limiting the social and environmental reporting are both the lack of national regulations and the difficulty of collecting data and measuring the indicators (Fig. 1).

Regarding the elements supporting the social and environmental reporting, all the answering choices depicted within the questionnaire were selected by at least two of the seven companies included in the study testing (Fig. 2). It is noted that most companies are driven by a possible awareness increase ensured by the issuing of standardised reports on social and environmental information.

Investors' requirements, those of the other stakeholders and the long-term benefits are seen as aspects that contribute to supporting of social

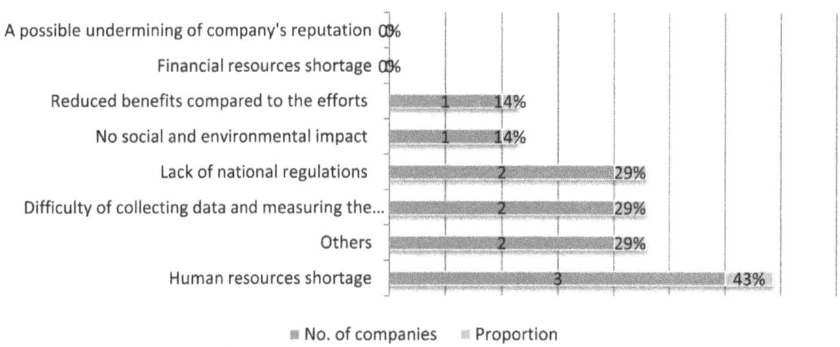

Fig. 1. Aspects That Limit the Reporting of Social and Environmental Impact in Romanian Companies' View.

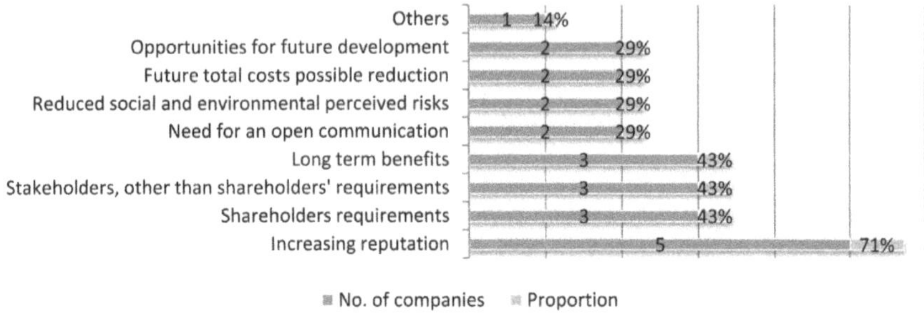

Fig. 2. Aspects That Support the Reporting of Social and Environmental Impact in Romanian Companies' View.

and environmental reporting, by 50% of companies surveyed within our study. The open communication, reducing risks and future costs or opportunities for further development are credited as supporting social and environmental reporting by two of the seven companies included in our study.

Debates. Questionnaire-based testing on the Romanian companies for those aspects that limit social and environmental impact reporting helps us formulate some basic elements. These are *useful for national accounting bodies in achieving a nationally regulated framework of reporting social and environmental information in annual reports or in financial statements.* The specialists and academics should give a higher importance to the identification of companies' position regarding the aspects that support social and environmental reporting. This should be exploited in favour of depicting specific national requirements.

From Shareholders to Stakeholders: Prioritising Stakeholders for Social and Environmental Reporting

To test whether the Romanian companies are interested in the stakeholders' recognition and in prioritising them when preparing the social and environmental disclosures, we have formulated a series of questions measuring the importance given by the companies to potential different users interested in social and environmental published information.

From the results presented (Table 3), we observed that although the shareholders have a high score, of 4.53 out of 5 points, they do not represent the category to which companies offer their utmost importance. The companies offered the highest importance to providing social and environmental information to the community, with a score of 4.86 out of 5 points.

Table 3. Stakeholders Interest in Social and Environmental Information.

Aspects for a Framework Design	
Aspects on interested stakeholders	Importance given by the companies (on a 1 to 5 scale)
Community	4.86
Shareholders	4.53
Customers	4.53
Employees	4.43
Non-governmental bodies	4
Government and government agencies	3.55
Financial creditors	3.44
Suppliers	3.43
Researchers	2.55
Others	2.55
Stakeholders' identification	4.43
Collecting and analysing shareholders' feedbacks	4.53

For the companies included in this study, the importance of providing information to customers is as high as that of informing shareholders. Next in top is the importance conferred to employees, with a score of 4.43 out of 5 points; non-governmental bodies, with a score of 4 out of 5; the state and government agencies; and then financial creditors and suppliers, with a score of 3.55 points.

Debates. To argue the proposition of our research regarding increasing the importance that companies offer to stakeholders and to their prioritisation, we bring into debate *expanding the group of users of financial statements*, as they are listed in the Framework on Preparation and Presentation of Financial Statements (IASB, 2006–2010) *and the explanations regarding their information needs*. Thus, we consider that the importance of social and environmental information disclosure could be addressed by using the requirements of the present financial reporting framework by adapting the needs of each category of users: investors, employees, financial creditors, suppliers, clients, government and government agencies.

At the same time, it would be useful *replacing the generic user – the public – with three distinct categories*: community, non-governmental organisations and other users, to whom the appropriate requirements on financial, social and environmental information should be assigned. Additional requirements for presenting users in relation to the company's targeted priority in preparing social and environmental reports, and for a summary presentation of stakeholders' feedback, are needed. These will permit an easy and unbiased communication between a company and its many different stakeholders, and will provide transparency in communication (and thus debate) between stakeholders.

The gap between companies' concerns and the concerns of researchers in social and environmental reporting was tested by including researchers in a list of possible stakeholders of the company. Indeed, companies do not consider that it is important to provide social and environmental information through specific reports for researchers' use. For future studies, it is interesting to develop these ideas in order to increase companies' confidence in the accounting research.

Identifying Basic Elements for Social and Environmental Reporting for Integrating into Financial Reporting Framework

To answer this research proposition, we tested the Romanian companies' opinion on the standardisation process of reporting social and environmental information. We also tested companies' concern in disclosing general social and environmental aspects in notes to financial statements.

A mixed question, based on a scale of 1 to 5, was designed to test the degree to which companies consider that for a relevant reporting on social and environmental impact, a general reporting framework should present objectives, strategies and principles. We targeted companies' opinion on the reporting of social and environmental impact in financial statements, on the components of financial statements that would better address social and environmental disclosures and on taking into consideration the need for quality of the social and environmental information disclosed.

Debates. The results, presented in Table 4, have led us to a series of *debates directed towards the reformulation of financial reporting objective by including a new dimension: that of the social and environmental impact* along with the financial position, the performance and changes in financial position. Thus, it may be considered to extend the general objective of financial reporting in order to provide information about the reporting entity, as it is useful to shareholders, and to other stakeholders (community, non-governmental organisations, employees, financial creditors, suppliers, clients, government, etc.).

As a way of responding to this objective, companies may prepare the financial statements set, required by the current national accounting regulations, that complies to European Directives, and expanding it with a *statement on social and environmental impact* of company's activity. This statement may synthesise the information presented in the CSR Report and

Table 4. Practical Importance of Social and Environmental Disclosure for Integrating into Financial Reporting Framework.

General Aspects for Social and Environmental Reporting	Importance Given By the Companies (on a 1 to 5 Scale)
Objective of social and environmental reporting	4.86
Strategy for social and environmental impact	4.43
Principles of social and environmental reporting	4.71
Reporting social and environmental impact in annual report (using qualitative as well as quantitative information)	4.42
Disclosure of social and environmental elements in a note to financial statements	4.18
Assurance statement for social and environmental disclosures	4.53

briefly describe the social and environmental strategy of the company. To minimise the costs of compiling such a statement, we tested if Romanian companies would be interested in it. Questions that test the inclusion of a synthesis of social and environmental aspects required by a Social and Environmental Information Reporting Framework (*relying, e.g., on the GRI content index*, that is already synthesised by the companies within their CSR reports) were addressed. By a cross-referenced matrix, companies show where in annual, CSR or other report or web link, the company addresses this kind of requirements.

On a practical level, such a situation may contain qualitative information on

- the company profile;
- the reporting period;
- information on the stakeholders: the priority categories, involvement, feedback information;
- social and environmental strategy;
- principles of presenting the information;
- measurement principles of social and environmental performance elements;
- presentation of social and environmental risks; and
- assurance statement of reported social and environmental information.

At regulatory bodies' level, for a redesign of an extended (economic, social and environmental) reporting framework, it should be taken into discussion *the possibility of principles adaptation by extending the going concern assumption*. Thus, future information based on social and environmental risks must be taken in consideration by the company when it prepares and presents financial statements based on the going concern concept.

To ensure the usefulness of the information provided by companies in the financial statements, we emphasise the revised classification of IASB regarding qualitative characteristics (IASB, 2010). Reporting only on trends in the financial efficiency of the organisation will fail to respond to a wide concept of faithful representation. In the future, Romanian regulatory accounting bodies must have the possibility to adapt the newer international requirements along with *the development of faithful representation concept* within the sustainability context. This will involve presenting the information in the context of the limits and demands placed on environmental or social resources at the sector, local, regional or global level.

At the same time, we consider useful *adding a third constraint*, along with materiality and cost, that is the balance between positive and negative aspects. The presented information should reflect positive and negative aspects of the reporting entity's activity. The entity should disclose both favourable and unfavourable quantitative and qualitative aspects as well as positive and negative trends that can influence the decisions of stakeholders in proportion to their materiality. These developments of the qualitative characteristics requirements may be disclosed, in our opinion, within a note on the risks, the impact and the opportunities generated by a sustainable development. In such note, the companies may present

- a description of the significant impacts the company has on sustainability and associated challenges and opportunities;
- a description of the most important risks and opportunities for the company arising from sustainability trends;
- concise description of governance mechanisms in place to specifically manage these risks and opportunities, and identification of other related risks and opportunities; and
- targets and performance against targets for present period and targets for future periods.

Regarding the elements of financial statements, Romanian companies found useful to present qualitative information using the traditional elements: assets, liabilities, equity, as elements of financial position and income and expenses as elements of performance. In order to extend the financial reporting requirements by including social and environmental impact, accounting professional or regulatory organisations could detail the definitions. The need of presenting social and environmental information, along with the financial ones, also raises concern regarding the assessment and recognition of the items. Given the social and environmental reporting limits drawn both from specialised literature and from this research, we debate that the *presentation of the categories of social and environment assets, liabilities, expenses and income to be made in a note to the financial statements.*

The evaluation and recognition of these elements should be addressed within the constraints of information presentation. The specificity of the activity of each company that generates differential impact suggests that, based on professional reasoning, each company should *adapt their evaluation methods and explain in the accounting policies section the equivalents in monetary units made by the company for environmental and social data.* To complete the *Framework for reporting of social and environmental information*, we propose the alternative of integrating certification of social and environmental information in an audit report. Both the limits of environmental and social reporting, and the fact that external certifications, included in the environmental reports, are made by auditing corporations should be considered. Thus, a change in *the audit report in order to include an observation paragraph on the certification of social and environmental information presented within the financial reports* may respond to external certification requirements.

CONCLUSION

Entities are facing increasing external pressures to decide how, when and if to address the challenges being posed. Organisations re-positioned themselves regarding reporting social and environmental information; they moved from being spectators at an external phenomenon to managers of increasingly inherent corporate resources. Consumers and shareholders are increasingly demanding environmentally friendly products and services that are delivered by socially responsible companies. It is becoming increasingly important for organisations to demonstrate that not only their philosophies but also their investment strategies and day-to-day operations are sustainable. More companies are recognising the competitive advantage in going beyond simple regulatory compliance to sustainability. Organisations adopt business strategies that maintain environmental quality and at the same time enhance competitive advantage and increase profitability.

Current CSR programs of Romanian companies are addressed almost exclusively from the perspective of a communicator. Most companies engage in social responsibility to promote a cause, a cause-related marketing or social marketing, philanthropy, volunteering in the community or socially responsible business practices. The analysis of the Romanian companies' opinion leads us to conclude that while social and environmental involvement of companies is at an early stage, there is a basis for future development. A solution for such an evolution is, in our opinion, the development and implementation of a general framework and of a set of policies regarding environmental and social impact reporting made by companies involved in social responsibility campaigns.

Solutions arise from the *involvement of the civil society* by making the companies to accept, at a certain level, social and environmental disclosure and to learn to see not only the risks but also the benefits of this kind of reporting. It is a feasible and credible solution, given the civil society interest in businesses activating in sensitive areas such as petroleum industry, chemical industry, mining, food and beverage, etc. *The involvement of accounting profession and regulatory bodies* through an extensive approach of financial reporting requirements and the *extensive involvement of academic researchers* should be also considered. In this respect, we support the idea that *academics should be more involved in promoting the ideas of social and environmental corporate responsibility reporting*, both by expanding the research and by including practical disciplines regarding application of voluntary reporting requirements on social and environmental impact by the companies.

Further research will be related to designing the main elements of an extended conceptual framework for Romanian companies that integrate reporting of social and environmental information within their mandatory reporting.

ACKNOWLEDGEMENTS

This work was supported by CNCSIS-UEFISCDI, project number PNII-IDEI ID 1819/2008, Research regarding reassessment of financial reporting in the light of risks and uncertainties generated by contingent social and environmental factors. We appreciate helpful comments and recommendation of the reviewers and editors of the book series Research in Accounting in Emerging Economies, for their constructive suggestions for improvement. We are also grateful for all the comments and recommendation given by the reviewers and participants of 23rd International Congress on Social and Environmental Accounting Research, St. Andrews, United Kingdom, September 2011, on the first draft of this chapter presented at the conference.

REFERENCES

Aerts, W., & Cormier, D. (2009). Media legitimacy and corporate environmental communication. *Accounting, Organizations and Society*, *34*, 1–27.

Albu, N., Albu, C., Gîrbină, M. M., & Sandu, M. I. (2011). Implicaţiile responsabilităţii sociale a organizaţiilor asupra profesiei contabile: cazul României [Implications of organizations' social responsibility on the accounting profession: The case of Romania]. *Amfiteatru Economic*, *29*, 223–236.

Altenburger, O. A., & Schaffhauser-Linzatti, M. M. (2007). About scope and focus of notes – A new approach to highlight intangibles. *30th Annual Congress of European Accounting Association*, 25–27 April 2007, Lisbon.

Băleanu, T. E., Chelcea, L., & Stancu, A. (2011). Responsabilitatea socială corporatistă a primelor 100 de companii din România. O analiză a website-urilor corporatiste (Corporate Social Responsibility of the top 100 companies in Romania. An analysis of corporations' websites). *Amfiteatru Economic*, *29*, 237–250.

Bebbington, K. J., Gray, R., Thomson, I., & Walters, D. (1994). Accountants attitudes and environmentally sensitive accounting. *Accounting and Business Research*, *94*, 51–75.

Caraiani, C., Dumitrana, M., Dumitru, C., Ristea, M., Dascălu, C., Guşe, R., ... Colceag, F. (2006). Green accounting in Romania – A vision to European integration. *46th Congress of the European Regional Science Association (ERSA)*, no. 476, 20p. Retrieved from http://www-sre.wu-wien.ac.at/ersa/ersaconfs/ersa06/papers/476.pdf

Cho, C., Chen, J., & Roberts, R. (2008). The politics of environmental disclosure regulation in the chemical and petroleum industries: Evidence from the Emergency Planning and Community Right-to-Know Act of 1986. *Critical Perspectives on Accounting*, *19*, 450–465.

Clarkson, P. M., Li, Y., Richardson, G. D., & Vasvari, F. P. (2008). Revisiting the relation between environmental performance and environmental disclosure: An empirical analysis. *Accounting, Organizations and Society*, *33*, 303–327.

Dascălu, C., Caraiani, C., Lungu, C. I., Colceag, F., & Guşe, R. G. (2010). The externalities in social environmental accounting. *International Journal of Accounting and Information Management*, *18*(1), 19–30.

Deegan, C. (2002). The legitimising effect of social and environmental disclosures – A theoretical foundation. *Accounting, Auditing and Accountability Journal*, *15*(3), 282–311.

Deegan, C., & Gordon, B. (1996). A study of the environmental disclosure practices of Australian corporations. *Accounting and Business Research*, *26*(3), 187–199.

Deegan, C., Rankin, M., & Voght, P. (2000). Firms' disclosure reactions to major social incidents: Australian evidence. *Accounting Forum*, *24*(1), 101–130.

Dierkes, M., & Antal, A. B. (1985). The usefulness and use of social reporting information. *Accounting, Organizations and Society*, *10*(1), 29–34.

Elkington, J. (1997). *Cannibals with forks: The triple bottom line of 21st century business.* Oxford: Capstone.

EU. (2003). Directive 2003/51/EC. Official Journal of the European Union. Retrieved from http://eur-lex.europa.eu/LexUriServ/LexUriServ.do?uri=OJ:L:2003:178:0016:0022:en:PDF

EU. (2006). Directive 2006/46. Official Journal of the European Union. Retrieved from http://eur-lex.europa.eu/LexUriServ/LexUriServ.do?uri=OJ:L:2006:224:0001:01:EN:HTML

Freeman, R. E. (1984). *Strategic management: A stakeholder approach.* Boston, MA: Pitman.

Gray, R. (2002). The social accounting project and accounting organizations and society privileging engagement, imaginings, new accountings and pragmatism over critique? *Accounting, Organizations and Society*, *27*(7), 687–708.

Gray, R. (2003). Of messiness, systems and sustainability: Towards a more social and environmental finance and accounting. *British Accounting Review*, *34*(4), 357–386.

Gray, R. (2010). Is accounting for sustainability actually accounting for sustainability … and how would we know? An exploration of narratives of organisations and the planet. *Accounting, Organizations and Society*, *35*(1), 47–62.

Gray, R., & Bebbington, J. (2000). Environmental accounting, managerialism and sustainability: Is the planet safe in the hands of business and accounting? *Advances in Environmental Accounting and Management*, *1*, 1–44. Retrieved from http://www.st-andrews.ac.uk/csear/research/discussion/sustainability/

Gray, R., Bebbington, J., Collison, D. J., Kouhy, R., Lyon, B., Reid, C., … Stevenson, L. (1998). *The valuation of assets and liabilities: Environmental law and the impact of the environmental agenda for business.* Edinburgh: ICAS.

Gray, R., & Milne, M. J. (2002). *Sustainability reporting: Who's kidding whom? ACCA Newsletter.* Retrieved from http://www.accanet.com/pdfs/environment/newsletter/gray_milne.pdf

Griskevicius, V., Tybur, J. M., & Van den Bergh, B. (2010). Going green to be seen: Status, reputation, and conspicuous conservation. *Journal of Personality and Social Psychology*, *98*(3), 392–404.

Guidry, R. P., & Patten, D. M. (2012). Voluntary disclosure theory and financial control variables: An assessment of recent environmental disclosure research. *Accounting Forum*, *36*, 81–90.

Holland, L., & Foo, Y. B. (2003). Differences in environmental reporting practices in the UK and the US: The legal and regulatory context. *The British Accounting Review*, *35*(1), 1–18.

Hopwood, A. G. (2009). Accounting and the environment. *Accounting, Organizations and Society*, *34*(3–4), 433–439.

IASB. (2006–2010). *Conceptual framework for financial reporting – Project summary and feedback statement.* Retrieved from http://www.ifrs.org/NR/rdonlyres/6A6ABF86-D554-4A77-9A4A-E415E09726B6/0/CFFeedbackStmt.pdf

IASB. (2010). *IFRS practice statement management commentary.* Retrieved from http://www.ifrs.org/NR/rdonlyres/9EA9F29A-3F34-4E39-9388-989B07563D4E/0/Managementcommentarypracticestatement8December.pdf

Ienciu, A., Muller, V., & Matiș, D. (2011). Environmental reporting within the Romanian companies. *International Journal of Energy and Environment*, *5*(1), 123–131.

International Finance Corporation (IFC). (2009). *Brazil's Stock Exchange promotes sustainability.* Retrieved from http://www.ifc.org/ifcext/sustainability.nsf/Content/SustainableInvesting

Ionaşcu, I. (2006). Mutaţii în exercitarea profesiei contabile în lumea contemporană (Shifts in accounting profession in the world today). *Proceeding of XVI Congress of accounting profession*, CECCAR, Bucharest (pp. 534–541).
Jones, M. J. (2010). Accounting for the environment: Towards a theoretical perspective for environmental accounting and reporting. *Accounting Forum*, *34*, 123–138.
Kaplan, S. E., & Ruland, R. G. (1991). Positive theory, rationality and accounting regulation. *Critical Perspectives on Accounting*, *2*(4), 361–374.
Lamberton, G. (2005). Sustainability accounting – A brief history and conceptual framework. *Accounting Forum*, *29*(1), 7–29.
Lungu, C. I., Caraiani, C., & Dascălu, C. (2009). Reporting green information from environmental management perspective. *Journal of Environmental Protection and Ecology*, *10*(2), 524–539.
Lungu, C. I., Caraiani, C., Dascălu, C., & Colceag, F. (2010). Social and environmental performance disclosure and the correlations to company's characteristics. *Proceedings of the 5th International Conference, Accounting and Management Information Systems* (pp. 678–692).
Lungu, C. I., Caraiani, C., & Dascălu, C. (2012a). Integrating sustainability into the accounting education: a fashionable or a necessary change? *7th International Conference Accounting and Management Information Systems: AMIS 2012* (pp. 234–251).
Lungu, C. I., Caraiani, C., Dascălu, C., Cimpoeru, V. M., & Sahlian, D. N. (2012b). *Repoziţionarea raportării financiare. Studii şi cercetări* [Repositioning financial reporting. Studies and research]. Bucharest: ASE.
Lungu, C. I., Caraiani, C., Dascălu, C., & Guşe, G. R. (2011). Exploratory study on social and environmental reporting of European companies during the crisis period. *AMIS 2011 – Proceedings of the 6th International Conference, Accounting and Management Information Systems* (pp. 989–1005).
MacLean, R., & Gottfrid, R. (2000). Corporate environmental reports: Stuck management processes hold back real progress. *Corporate Environmental Strategy*, *7*, 244–255.
Mammatt, J., Marx, B., & van Dyk, V. (2010). Sustainability reporting and assurance: The way of the future. *ASA Accountancy Journal, December 2009/January 2010*, 22–25.
Milne, M. J., Tregida, H. M., & Walton, S. (2009). Words not actions! The ideological role of sustainable development reporting. *Accounting, Auditing and Accountability Journal*, *22*(8), 1211–1257.
Ngwakwe, C. C. (2012). Rethinking the accounting stance on sustainable development. *Sustainable Development*, *20*(1), 28–41.
Parker, L. D. (2005). Social and environmental accountability research: A view from the commentary box. *Accounting, Auditing & Accountability Journal*, *18*(6), 842–860.
Patten, D. M. (1992). Intra-industry environmental disclosures in response to the Alaskan oil spill: A note on legitimacy theory. *Accounting, Organizations and Society*, *17*(5), 471–475.
Popa, A., Blidisel, R., & Farcane, N. (2009). An evolutionary approach of corporate social responsibility reporting. *Annals of Economics Science Series, Timisoara*, *18*, 1118–1124.
Solomon, J., & Solomon, A. (2004). *Corporate governance and accountability*. Chichester: John Wiley and Sons Ltd.
Steurer, R., & Konrad, A. (2009). Business—Society relations in Central-Eastern and Western Europe: How those who lead in sustainability reporting bridge the gap in corporate (social) responsibility. *Scandinavian Journal of Management*, *25*, 23–36.
UN. (1987). *Report of the world commission on environment and development: Our common future*. Retrieved from http://www.un-documents.net/wced-ocf.htm

UNEP, GRI, KPMG Global Sustainability Services, & Stellenbosch University Business School. (2010). *Carrots and sticks – promoting transparency and sustainability*. Retrieved from http://www.globalreporting.org/NR/rdonlyres/649A345D-8BD7-413D-A696-7E12F6EA37C5/4198/Carrrots2010final.pdf

Van der Laan, S. J., Adhikari, A., & Tondkar, R. H. (2005). Exploring differences in social disclosures internationally: A stakeholder perspective. *Journal of Accounting and Public Policy*, *24*(2), 123–151.

Walden, W. D., & Schwartz, B. N. (1997). Environmental disclosures and public policy pressures. *Journal of Accounting and Public Policy*, *16*, 125–154.

WBCSD. (2003). *Sustainable development reporting: Striking the balance*. Retrieved from http://www.wbcsd.org/DocRoot/fBBNXf7oYVJuJAG77hUt/20030106_sdreport.pdf

Zahavi, A. (1975). Mate selection – Selection for a handicap. *Journal of Theoretical Biology*, *53*, 205–214.

ENVIRONMENTAL DISCLOSURE OF ROMANIAN LISTED ENTITIES

Ionel-Alin Ienciu

ABSTRACT

Purpose – *The purpose of this chapter is to contribute to the understanding of environmental reporting differences in the case of Romanian entities. In order to achieve this purpose, we analyze environmental reporting differences for Romanian listed companies using legitimacy theory as a theoretical background.*

Design/methodology/approach – *We conduct a quantitative research on the Romanian entities listed on the Bucharest Stock Exchange (BSE).*

Findings – *The quality and quantity of environmental information reported by Romanian company still suffer from irrelevancy and incompleteness. The factors explaining the variation of environmental reporting in the case of Romanian listed companies are the export sales percentage, the BSE category, and size of the company, which demonstrate that larger companies tend to disclose more environmental information to respond to the pressure and to maintain their legitimacy.*

Research limitations/implications – *The present study uses the content analysis as a research technique of 64 annual reports of Romania listed entities on the BSE. In this regard, a limitation of the study can be the*

Accounting in Central and Eastern Europe
Research in Accounting in Emerging Economies, Volume 13, 235–254

ISSN: 1479-3563/doi:10.1108/S1479-3563(2013)0000013015

sample size that can be extended and also the content analysis that can be considered subjective.

Practical and social implications – *The chapter is of interest to anyone involved in the process of environmental disclosure, either as entity or other stakeholders.*

Originality/value – *The chapter supplements previous studies regarding environmental disclosure and the theories or factors that can explain environmental reporting differences.*

Keywords: Environmental reporting; Romanian entities; legitimacy theory; public exposure; entity's size

ENVIRONMENTAL DISCLOSURE OF ROMANIAN LISTED ENTITIES

Since the environmental reporting is voluntary at international level, there are major differences in terms of the quality and quantity of the environmental information reported by entities in different sectors and countries. Many studies have investigated various determinants of companies' voluntary disclose practices, but most of all have been inducted in developed counties such as Germany (Cormier, Magnan, & Van Velthnoven, 2005), United Kingdom, and United States (Holland & Foo, 2003), Australia (Frost, 2007), Spain (Larrinaga-Gonzalez, Carrasco-Fenech, Caro-Gonzalez, Correa-Ruiz, & Paez-Sandubete, 2002), Canada (Buhr & Freedman, 2001), and Nordic Counties (Nyquist, 2003). Only a few studies have analyzed environmental reporting within developing countries: Sumiani, Haslinda, and Lehman (2007) (Malaysia); Chatterjee and Mir (2008) (India); Dulacha Barako, Hancock, and Izan (2006) (Kenya) and Owusu-Ansah (1998) (Zimbabwe).

The study expands the existing literature by identifying the determinants of environmental disclosure of a developing country such as Romania. As many other countries from Central and Eastern Europe, Romania inherited heavy environmental problems from the communist period. These problems were caused by the industrial policy based on high productivity that did not take into account the impact on environment and public health. The biggest issues concern sectors like water quality, waste disposal, and air and soil pollution. In Romania the environmental policies were born during the 1990s once with the former Ministry of the Environment. The national objectives regarding the environmental field were elaborated in 1992, "The National Strategy for Environmental Protection" being revised in 1996 and 2002. Starting from 1999, Romania has adopted a *National Strategy for Sustainable Development*, in accordance with the area regulations in Europe and worldwide. Since 2000, the national environmental policies try to assess the European standards and objectives, the environmental aspects becoming an important component for Romania's general policy. The year 2007 marks the integration of Romania into the European Union, the implementation of European environmental policies and the introduction of new European funding programs for environmental protection activities (structural funds). Since 2008, Romania has a new National Strategy for Sustainable Development, characterized by a new philosophy of development of the European Union and worldwide shared. The strategy sets actual targets for the transition to a generating value added development model, aimed at a continuous improvement of the quality of people's life and their relations in harmony with the natural environment.

However, there is, so far, no legislation in this area, requiring organizations from Romania, listed or not on the capital market to provide stakeholders separate reports or specific information relating to the environmental impact. Providing such information would be useful, especially for listed companies and for those operating in industries considered highly polluting. In other words, the entity's commitment regarding the environmental impact or environmental issues remains voluntary in the case of Romanian companies. In the absence of a regulatory framework regarding environmental reporting, we raise the research question: *What can determine the Romanian companies listed on the capital market to report specific information relating to the environment?*

The findings reveal that legitimacy theory can explain environmental reporting differences by Romanian listed companies. Because public exposure and size of the companies determine the variation of environmental reporting in the case of these companies, we state that legitimacy theory is the main argumentation for providing environmental disclosure for this sample.

The chapter is organized as follows. The next section provides a theoretical background, followed by an overview of the literature in the field of environmental reporting. The following section highlights the research methodology, the study findings, and results and the final section provides conclusions, limitations of the study, and directions for future research.

THEORETICAL BACKGROUND – LEGITIMACY THEORY

The study of Hooper and Xu (2012) highlights an overview of legitimacy and the perception of this concept. It stated from the definition of Suchman (1995, p. 574) that defines legitimacy as a generalized perception that the actions of an entity are desirable and proper within a social group in which it operates so are appropriate with the socially constructed system of norms, values, beliefs, and definitions. Thanking into consideration, pragmatic, moral, or cognitive aspect that explains why an entity may be expected to change social values, Suchman (1995) divides academic studies into strategic studies that emphasize a management perspective that manipulates and uses effective symbols to gain societal support (examples given are studies of Ashforth & Gibbs, 1990; Dowling & Pfeffer, 1975) and institutional studies emphasizing cultural pressures that transcend any organization's control (examples given are studies of DiMaggio & Powell, 1983; Meyer & Rowan, 1991).

According to Suchman (1995), we have moral pragmatic legitimacy, moral legitimacy, and cognitive legitimacy. Hooper and Xu (2012, p. 756) make an overview of these three forms of legitimacy. Pragmatic legitimacy or image advertising is driven strategically or institutionally to build and maintain a reputation and is a result of advertising good disposition and good image to the most immediate audiences. Moral legitimacy means to accumulate technical performance and success, while cognitive legitimacy implies unspoken assumptions as to professional legitimacy. Pragmatic and moral legitimacy can be arrived at by cost-benefit approach or ethical judgments by way of public discussion. Pragmatic legitimacy relies on audience's self-interest that it is the right organization for the job, whereas moral and cognitive legitimacy do not (Hooper & Xu, 2012).

Because shareholders can be defined as dominant stakeholders for many companies' especially listed companies, we consider that companies reflect a self-interested egoism and tend to advertise and report as much as it needed to maintain the social contract and to gain capital and image. We are taking about the pragmatic legitimacy, which can be considered an important factor for providing environmental information for many entities. Legitimacy theory is the most common augmentation theory used to explain environmental reporting, to whom was dedicated an entire edition to the famous international journal – *Accounting, Auditing and Accountability Journal* (AAAJ, volume 15, number 3, 2002) – under

Professor Craig Deegan and Professor O'Dwyer (Deegan, 2002; O'Dwyer, 2002). Legitimacy theory, like other theories such as theory of political economy and theory of users, offers insights into the role of information and reports in relations between organizations, the state, individuals, and groups of individuals (Gray, Owen, & Adams, 1996). "Legitimacy" can be directly linked to the concept of "social contract" between the entity and the society to which it belongs (Deegan, 2002).

This theory, according to Lindblom, argues that an organization is legal when the system of values is consistent with the social system to which it belongs, and when there is a mismatch, the legitimacy of the organization is threatened. Entities provide strategies to maintain and restore the line, consist in informing and educating the public, trying to change perceptions, expectations, and reporting of environmental information and are considered part of these strategies (Gray, Kouhy, & Lavers, 1995). In other words, legitimacy theory (Deegan, 2002), or the "social contract" between the entity and society (O'Donovan, 1999), explains the reporting practices of environmental information.

So, within this study we analyze if legitimacy theory can explain environmental reporting in the case of Romanian companies listed on the stock market. For this reason, we take into consideration some variables that help us analyze if legitimacy theory stands behind environmental reporting in the case of Romanian entities and so we consider that the most exposed and largest companies are trying to maintain the "social contract" with the society in which they activate using environmental reporting as a tool for advertising themselves.

LITERATURE REVIEW

In this part, we take an overview of the literature which has analyzed factors that can explain differences regarding environmental reporting for different companies.

In their studies, Brown and Deegan (1998) and Patten (2002) conclude that the more an organization is exposed to the public (investors, users, media, etc.), the more it would be willing to provide all possible information on various aspects, including environmental information to maintain the social contract with the society in which it operates.

In the last two decades, there were some studies elaborated by Patten (1991), Cormier and Magnan (2003), Cormier et al. (2005), Belkaoui-Riahi

(2001), and Watson, Shrives, and Marston (2002) which consider that the intensity of the work carried out represent an essential factor of the quality level of the environmental reporting. The more intense is the activity carried out by the entity, the more increased is the risk of appearing more in the forefront of the media, thus being inclined to provide as much information as possible to the stakeholders to maintain the social contract with the stakeholders.

Wilmshurst and Frost (2000) surveyed chief finance officers from a selected sample of the top 105 listed Australian companies for 1994–1995, from environmentally sensitive industries (chemical, mining and resources, oil gas and petroleum, transport/tourism, manufacturing, construction, and food and household). The survey analyzes the perceived importance of specific factors in the decision to disclose environmental information. The results of the survey suggest that management gives most consideration to shareholders' information needs and legal issues when disclosing environmental information. The results provide limited support for legitimacy theory as an explanatory factor of environmental disclosure in management's decision process and suggest that "the greater the perceived importance of shareholders' information needs and community concerns, the higher the level of environmental disclosures that were observed within the annual report" (Wilmshurst & Frost, 2000, p. 22).

Arcay and Vasquez (2005) analyze the relationships between voluntary disclosure and factors like corporate characteristics and the governance structure of the firm for a sample of Spanish firms listed on the Madrid Stock Exchange. The results show that the firm's size is positively related to voluntary disclosure.

Boesso and Kumar (2007) examine factors that could drive the voluntary disclosure practices of companies in Italy and in the United States. The study analyzes the annual reports of 72 companies in order to determine the volume and the quality of voluntary disclosures. The study shows that factors such as company emphasis on stakeholder management and market complexity affect the volume and the quality of voluntary disclosures.

Kelton and Yang (2008) examines the association between corporate governance mechanisms and disclosure transparency. Results suggest that corporate governance mechanisms influence a firm's Internet disclosure behavior (IFR), and that the association between corporate governance and IFR varies with firm size. Mashayekhi and Mashayekh (2008) suggest that high-quality environmental reporting can attract foreign investors. Other studies conclude that large firms in the term of exposure and visibility would report more relevant and informative disclosures (Elsayed & Hoque, 2010;

Naser, Al-Hussaini, Al-Kwari, & Nuseibeh, 2006) to gain and maintain their legitimacy.

Reverte (2009) analyzes whether variables like firm and industry characteristics, as well as media exposure, are potential determinants of corporate social responsibility (CSR) disclosure practices by Spanish listed firms. The results show that firms with higher CSR ratings present a statistically significant larger size and a higher media exposure, and belong to more environmentally sensitive industries, as compared to firms with lower CSR ratings. Profitability does not explain differences in CSR disclosure practices between Spanish listed firms.

Cheung, Jiang, and Tan (2010) address the question whether transparency matters among Chinese listed companies. The results show that there is a positive and significant relation between company transparency and market valuation. Also the study reveals that overseas listed companies tend to disclose more on a voluntary basis.

Rankin, Windsor, and Wahyuni (2011) analyze the way that internal organization systems, external privately promulgated guidance, and European Union emissions trading system (EU ETS) trading influence Greenhouse gas (GHG) reporting. The results show that firms that disclose more credible information are more likely to be large and in the energy and mining, industrial, and services sectors. Galani, Gravas, and Stavropoulos (2011) investigate the level of environmental reporting in corporate annual reports for Greek companies that have implemented a set of environmental accounting practices and analyzes the relationship between various firm characteristics and environmental disclosures. The results show that the level of environmental reporting in annual reports is positively correlated with corporate size. Milanés-Montero and Pérez-Calderón (2011) analyze environmental reporting and performance for Dow Jones Sustainability (DJS) Europe Index companies. They conclude that legitimacy theory explains the relationship between the quantity of environmental information reporting and the environmental performance in non-environmentally sensitive industries, the level of environmental reporting being higher for better environmental performer companies.

Boubaker, Lakhal, and Nekhili (2012) analyze the determinants of Web-based corporate reporting by French listed firms. The results indicate that large-sized firms used the Web to disclose information to their shareholders.

Manetti, Thorne, and Mahoney (2013) present the results of a survey analyzing the factors that determine 221 Canadian entities to follow independent Global Reporting Initiative (GRI) guidelines in choosing to report social and environmental aspects. The study revealed that Canadian firms issue standalone reports because of the "need to correctly communicate with their stakeholders in order to ensure or convince them that the firm is acting in right way and is leader in this sector for CSR policies and practices" (Manetti et al., 2013, p. 24). Iatridis (2013) analyzes the quality of environmental reported information and the association between company practices and the environment. The findings show that company attributes, such as large size, the need for capital, profitability, and capital spending, are positively associated with environmental disclosure quality.

Mosene, Burritt, Sanagustín, Moneva, and Tingey-Holyoak (2013) explore the relevance of institutional influences on environmental reporting practices for the wind energy sector in Spain. They analyze sustainability reports for the period 2005–2009 from seven main wind energy companies facilitated a longitudinal comparison of the levels of compliance with Global Reporting Initiative indicators of sustainability. Results show that the disclosures have been minimal and their lack of effectiveness and unreliability mean they are not conducive to the notion of increasing transparency in this sector. Although the findings are not consistent with established research that electricity companies needed to legitimize their behavior by taking coercive regulatory concerns into account when establishing wind farms, the results show that "companies seek to initialize their credibility in the eyes of society, in the wind energy sector by responding to pressure from society on governments to encourage non-fossil fuel alternatives in the face of growing social outrage over the need for action over climate change" (Mosene et al., 2013, p. 210).

Murguia and Bohling (2013) analyze multinational mining companies operating in Latin America. The analysis is based on a content of Alumbrera's Sustainability Report from 2009 to 2011 reports. The chapter argues that "sustainability reporting can only play a role in improving a company's reputation if the quality of the reported data is good enough to answer community-raised contentious issues."

In our country, the existing studies reveal almost the same results as we can observe at international level. Jindrichovska and Purcarea (2011) focus their study on CSR in two countries: Czech Republic and Romania. The study considers that although the standard of environmental reporting is based on the same principles in both countries, the particular approaches differ. Also with regard to Romania, a more systematic regulatory approach may be adopted for environmental reporting. Although Budeanu and Thidell (2006) consider that despite the incipient stages of public disclosure of environmental information, Romanian entities are ready to catch up with Western practices (Ienciu, Muller, & Matis, 2011) reflecting that the quality of voluntary environmental information reported by Romanian listed companies compared with Hungarian companies for the period 2006–2008 is incomplete and irrelevant (the level of environmental reporting in this case being very low). The study sustains that the legitimacy theory is the most adequate for explaining and defining environmental reporting within Romanian companies because companies are looking only for those aspects that can ensure a positive image and a good place in the society. We can also remark, within Romanian literature, researchers like Dumitrana (2005), Cretu (2004), Caraiani and Jianu (2007), Lungu, Caraiani, and Dascalu (2008), and Todea, Stanciu, and Joldos (2010) who present conceptual aspects regarding environmental accounting and suggest the low level of Romanian companies regarding environmental reporting and environmental performance.

We consider environmental disclosures corporate needs to legitimize activities within an organization (Hogner, 1982) and we analyze if legitimacy theory, expressed by public pressure and size, explains environmental reporting in the case of Romanian companies listed on the stock market.

RESEARCH METHODOLOGY

The present study is a quantitative research that analyze if legitimacy theory can explain environmental reporting for companies listed on the Bucharest Stock Exchange (BSE). In this regard, we formulate the following hypothesis:

> **Hypothesis 1.** Legitimacy theory, expressed by public pressure and size, explains environmental reporting in the case of Romanian listed companies.

To test this hypothesis, we took into consideration some variables that express the public pressure and size such as

- the category on the stock exchange (a company may be listed in Category I, II, or III) *(BSE_C)*;
- the sales percentage intended for export (here was analyzed especially the opening of the entity outdoors) *(Ex)*;
- the size of the entity expressed by three variables: total assets (*TA*), turnover (*Turn*), and number of employees (*No_e*).

The sample consists of 64 entities listed on the BSE in the first, second, and third tier from seven areas of activity that may impact the environment: agriculture, forestry, and fishing; the extractive industry; the manufacture industry; production and supply of electricity, thermal energy, gas, water; water distribution, sanitation, managing waste, recyclable materials recovery activities; construction; transport and storage; food industry, hotels, restaurants; the repair, retail, maintenance and installation of machinery and equipment; and printing and reproduction of recorded media. The distribution of the companies is presented in Table 1.

Like other studies (Cormier et al., 2005), we exclude from the sample entities that activate in sector with low or no impact on the environment like financial activities, real estate, renting and business activities, education, other work activities, social and personal, information technology, media, mortgage finance, research and development, and telecoms. While some studies demonstrate that the sector of activity determine the level of environmental reporting (*S_A*) (Deegan & Blomquist, 2006; Halme & Huse, 1997; Milne & Patten, 2002) Deegan and Gordon (1996) consider that environmental sensitivity of the industry influence the level of environmental reporting. Also, the sensitivity of the industry influences the development of environmental management procedures (Frost & Toh, 1998). These firms are more likely to report environmental information and to develop environmental procedures than firms that activate in less environmentally sensitive industries, because, more likely, stakeholders need environmental information in their decision-making process. So we consider the sector of the activity as a control variable.

Table 1. Sector of Activity.

		Frequency	Percent	Cumulative Percent
Valid	Extractive industry	3	4.7	4.7
	Manufacture industry	44	68.8	73.4
	Energy, gas, water	1	1.6	75.0
	Construction	6	9.4	84.4
	Maintenance and installation	4	6.3	90.6
	Hotels, restaurants	3	4.7	95.3
	Transport and storage	3	4.7	100.0
	Total	64	100.0	

For assessing the dependent variable that is environmental disclosure *(EnvRep)*, we use the content analysis of 2010 annual reports and we develop a disclosure index (DI) on the following groups of information:

- d1. Non-financial information regarding environmental objectives, management, policy, and other aspects that can reflect environmental performance. This indicator can bring value "1" if the company reports this kind of information or "0" otherwise.
- d2. Key Performance Indicators regarding environmental impact (water, air, soil). Such indictors are stipulated by Global Reporting Initiative,[1] DEFRA,[2] and other organizations. The indicator can bring value "1" if the company reports such indicators or "0" otherwise.
- d3. Financial indicators such as environmental costs, provisions. The values can be "1" if company reports this information or "0" otherwise.

This method for quantifying environmental information allows integration of different types of information into one single figure comparable between companies.

So, our environmental DI is calculated as follows: EnvRep = $\sum_{i=1}^{n} di/m$, where n is the number of element disclosed, m is the number of possible elements to disclose, and di is the group of elements disclosed.

The independent variables are presented in Appendix A.

ANALYSIS AND RESULTS

From Table 2 (Appendix B), we can observe that most of the Romanian companies listed on the BSE (71, 9%) report only one of the categories presented above, and most of all non-financial information regarding environmental objectives, management, and policy (d1).

Table 2. Descriptive Table of Environmental Disclosure.

		Frequency	Percent	Cumulative Percent
Valid	Minim (0)	5	7.8	7.8
	0.33	46	71.9	79.7
	0.67	5	7.8	87.5
	Maxim (1)	8	12.5	100.0
	Total	64	100.0	

From 64 companies, only 8 companies report all types of environmental information, while 5 of them do not report any kind of environmental information. The Romanian companies do not report environmental information using some national or international guidelines, the main source of environmental information being the annual report. Forty-four environmental informational cases were presented in the annual reports of the entities (generally in section 1.1.6), which shows that annual reports are the main sources of information of the entities of Romania. Also, the entities' sites (for those that have one) and the explaining notes to the financial situations represent relevant sources of information regarding the environmental impact. We could also see that the analyzed entities do not emit a separate environmental report or sustainable report, which is a common behavior for numerous entities of European countries. Most of the exposed environmental information are not correlated with environmental performance, which raises again the issue of objectivity regarding these information.

The analyses of our research hypothesis help us identify the independent variables included in the regression model that will be tested in the case of environmental reporting for the Romanian companies listed on the BSE. The regression equation we are suggesting in order to explain the level of environmental reporting within the Romanian companies would be as follows:

$$F(\text{EnvRep}) = \lambda_i + \beta_1 \times \text{BSE\_C} + \beta_2 \times \text{Ex} + \beta_3 \times \text{TA} + \beta_4 \times \text{Turn} + \beta_5 \times \text{No\_e} + \beta_6 \times \text{S\_A} + \varepsilon_i$$

where λ_i is the constant; β_i is the model coefficients; ε_i is the error term; BSE_C is the category on the stock exchange; Ex is the sales percentage intended for export; TA is the total assets; Turn is the turnover; No_e is the number of employees; N_R is the net result; N_R_S is the net result per share; and S_A is the sector of activity (Table 3).

The regression model was analyzed using SPSS, version 17.00, and we apply the stepwise method for determining the variable that could explain the variation of the environmental reporting in the case of Romanian companies (Table 4).

The model above shows the existence of a direct link, of medium intensity between environmental disclosures and size of the company (expressed by turnover) that allows us to conclude that the more intense is the activity carried out by an entity, the more it is exposed to the polluting risk, to the risk of appearing more in the forefront of the establishment and the media,

Table 3. Descriptive Statistics.

	N	Minimum	Maximum	Mean	Standard Deviation	Variance
Environmental Reporting (EnvRep)	64	0.00	1.00	0.4145	0.25993	0.068
The percentage of exports (Ex)	64	0.00	88.03	15.8663	26.85379	721.126
Number of employees (No_e)	64	26.00	25,058.00	1171.2188	3168.76702	1.004E7
BSE category (BSE_C)	64	1.00	3.00	1.7656	0.46264	0.214
Total assets (RON) (TA)	64	15,311,746.00	3.20E10	9.8084E8	4.08538E9	1.669E19
Turnover (RON) (Turn)	64	4,805,673.00	1.40E10	5.7393E8	1.95645E9	3.828E18
Sector of activity (S_A)	64	3.00	9.00	4.7656	1.54038	2.373

Table 4. Regression Results.

	Coefficients (β)	t-Value	p-Value	VIF
(Constant)	0.647	5.838	0.000	
Turn	545SE-11	3.901	0.000	1.074
BSE_C	−0.170	−2.871	0.006	1.074
Ex	0.002	2.293	0.025	1.000

Notes: Model summary – $R=0.617$, $R^2=0.381$, adjusted $R^2=0.350$, $F=12.319$, $p=0.000$, Durbin–Watson = 1.944.

being thus determined to provide as much information as possible regarding its impact on the environment to the users. Also the statistical analyses reflect a correlation between environmental reporting and public exposure (expressed by the BSE category and the percentage of exports), which conclude that the more an organization is exposed to the public (investors, users, media, etc.), the more it would be willing to provide all possible information on various aspects, including environmental information. So we consider that legitimacy theory, expressed by public exposure and size, is the main argumentations for providing environmental reporting in the case of Romanian companies, so our hypothesis can be validated.

CONCLUSIONS

In this study, we analyze environmental reporting differences of Romanian listed companies and we bring legitimacy theory as a background for explaining these variations.

We conclude that like in 2006–2009 periods, in 2010 the quality and quantity of environmental information reported by Romanian company still suffer from irrelevancy and incompleteness. The factors explaining the variation of environmental reporting in the case of Romanian listed companies are the export sales percentage, the BSE category, and size of the company which demonstrate that the more exposed and large companies tend to disclose more environmental information to respond the pressure and to maintain their legitimacy. The Romanian entities provide disclosure strategies to maintain and restore the line with the stakeholders, so legitimacy theory is the main argumentations for providing environmental reporting in the case of Romanian companies. The most exposed companies are trying to maintain the "social contract" with the society in which they activate using environmental reporting as a tool. Environmental reporting is correlated with the opening of the entity outdoors and with the intensity of the work carried out by the company; the more expose or intense is the activity that the entity is caring out, the more increased is the risk for the entity to pollute, the risk of appearing more in the forefront of the media, thus being inclined to provide as much information as possible to users.

This study is a research of some particular entities from Romanian listed on the BSE. As a future research, we try to extend the sample including companies from other developing countries. In this study, we test legitimacy theory using public pressure and size as independent variables. For future research, we try to identify other factors that can express legitimacy like corporate governance characteristics or media reports regarding some bad news.

ACKNOWLEDGMENTS

This chapter is part of the research project POSDRU/89/1.5/S/59184 "Performance and excellence in postdoctoral research within the field of economic sciences in Romania," Babeş-Bolyai University, Cluj-Napoca being a partner within the project.

NOTES

1. GRI Guidelines, 2011; Retrieved from https://www.globalreporting.org/Pages/default.aspx
2. Environmental Key Performance Indicators, Reporting Guidelines for UK Business Retrieved from http://www.defra.gov.uk/publications/2011/03/25/environmental-kpi-guidelines-pb11321/

REFERENCES

Arcay, M. R. B., & Vasquez, M. F. M. (2005). Corporate characteristics, governance rules and the extent of voluntary disclosure in Spain. *Advances in Accounting*, *21*, 299–331.

Ashforth, B. E., & Gibbs, B. W. (1990). The double-edge of organisational legitimation. *Organisation Science*, *1*, 177–194.

Belkaoui-Riahi, A. (2001). Level of multinationality, growth opportunities and size as determinants of analysts ratings of corporate disclosures. *American Business Review*, *19*(1), 115–220.

Boesso, G., & Kumar, K. (2007). Drivers of corporate voluntary disclosure: A framework and empirical evidence from Italy and the United States. *Accounting, Auditing & Accountability Journal*, *20*(2), 269–296.

Boubaker, S., Lakhal, F., & Nekhili, M. (2012). The determinants of web-based corporate reporting in France. *Managerial Auditing Journal*, *27*(2), 126–155.

Brown, N., & Deegan, C. (1998). The public disclosure of environmental performance information – A dual test of media agenda setting theory and legitimacy theory. *Accounting and Business Research*, *29*, 21–41.

Budeanu, A., & Thidell, A. (2006). Voluntary environmental reporting in Romania. *Environmental Engineering and Management Journal*, *5*(3), 487–508.

Buhr, N., & Freedman, M. (2001). Culture, institutional factors and differences in environmental disclosure between Canada and the United States. *Critical Perspectives in Accounting*, *12*, 293–312.

Caraiani, C., & Jianu, I. (2007). Contabilitatea verde – O perspective a schimbari in contabilitate. *Contabilitatea, Expertiza si Auditul Afacerilor*, *4*, 21–26.

Chatterjee, B., & Mir, M. (2008). The current status of environmental reporting by Indian companies. *Managerial Auditing Journal*, *23*(6), 609–629.

Cheung, I.-L., Jiang, P., & Tan, W. (2010). A transparency disclosure index measuring disclosures: Chinese listed companies. *Journal of Accounting And Public Policy*, *29*, 259–280.

Cormier, D., & Magnan, M. (2003). Environmental reporting management: A continental European perspective. *Journal of Accounting and Public Policy*, *22*(1), 43–62.

Cormier, D., Magnan, M., & Van Velthoven, B. (2005). Environmental disclosure quality: Do firms respond to economic incentives, public pressures or institutional conditions? *European Accounting Review*, *14*(1), 1–37.

Cormier, D., Magnan, M., & Van Velthoven, B. (2005). Environmental disclosure quality in large German companies: Economic incentives, public pressures or institutional conditions. *European Accounting Review*, *14*(1), 3–39.

Cretu, F. (2004). The cost-benefits analysis, instrument supporting the administration of environmental externalities. *Contabilitate si Informatica de Gestiune*, *9*, 89–98.

Deegan, C. (2002). The legitimising effect of social and environmental disclosures – A theoretical foundation. *Accounting Auditing and Accountability Journal*, *15*(3), 282–311.

Deegan, C., & Blomquist, C. (2006). Stakeholder influence on corporate reporting: An exploration of the interaction between WWF-Australian and the Australian minerals industry. *Accounting, Organizations and Society*, *31*, 343–372.

Deegan, C., & Gordon, B. (1996). A study of the environmental disclosure practices of Australian corporations. *Accounting and Business Research*, *26*(3), 187–99.

DiMaggio, P. J., & Powell, W. W. (1983). The iron cage revisited: Institutional isomorphism and collective rationality in organisational field. *American Sociological Review*, *48*, 147–60.

Dowling, J., & Pfeffer, J. (1975). Organisational legitimacy: Social values and organisational behaviour. *Pacific Sociological Review*, *18*, 122–36.

Dulacha Barako, G., Hancock, P., & Izan, H. Y. (2006). Factors influencing voluntary corporate disclosure by Kenyan companies. *Corporate Governance: An International Review*, *14*(2), 107–126.

Dumitrana, M. (2005). Environment and environmental costs. *Contabilitate si Informatica de Gestiune*, *13–14*, 113–115.

Elsayed, M., & Hoque, Z. (2010). Perceived international environmental factors and corporate voluntary disclosure practices: An empirical study. *The British Accounting Review*, *42*, 17–35.

Frost, G., & Toh, D. (1998). A study of environmental accounting within the New South Wales Public Sector. *Accounting Research Journal*, *11*(2), 400–10.

Frost, G. (2007). The introduction of mandatory environmental reporting guidelines: Australian evidence. *Abacus*, *43*(2), 23–45.

Galani, D., Gravas, E., & Stavropoulos, A. (2011). The relation between firm size and environmental disclosure. *International Conference on Applied Economics*, 179–186.

Gray, R. H., Owen, D., & Adams, C. (1996). *Accounting and accountability*. London: Prentice Hall.

Gray, R., Kouhy, R., & Lavers, S. (1995). Corporate social and environmental reporting: A review of the literature and a longitudinal study of UK disclosure. *Accounting, Auditing and Accountability Journal*, *8*(2), 47–77.

Halme, M., & Huse, M. (1997). The influence of corporate governance, industry and country factors on environmental reporting. *Scandinavian Journal of Management*, *13*(2), 137–157.

Hogner, R. H. (1982). Corporate social reporting: Eight decades of development at US steel. *Research in Corporate Social Performance and Policy*, *4*, 243–50.

Holland, L., & Foo, Y. B. (2003). Differences in environmental reporting practices in the UK and the US: The legal and regulatory context. *The British Accounting Review*, *35*, 1–18.

Hooper, K., & Xu, G. (2012). From legitimacy by character to legitimacy by image. Ethics and accounting practices in New Zealand. *Managerial Auditing Journal*, *27*(8), 754–773.

Iatridis, G. (2013). Environmental disclosure quality: Evidence on environmental performance, corporate governance and value relevance. *Emerging Markets Review*, *14*, 55–75.

Ienciu, A., Muller, V., & Matis, D. (2011). Environmental reporting within the Romanian companies. *International Journal of Energy and Environment*, *5*(1), 123–131.

Jindrichovska, I., & Purcarea, I. (2011). CSR and environmental reporting in the Czech Republic and Romania: Country comparison of rules and practices. *Accounting and Management Information Systems*, *10*(2), 202–227.

Kelton, A., & Yang, Y. (2008). The impact of corporate governance on Internet financial reporting. *Journal of Accounting and Public Policy*, *27*, 62–87.

Larrinaga-Gonzalez, C., Carrasco-Fenech, F., Caro-Gonzalez, F. J., Correa-Ruiz, C., & Paez-Sandubete, J. M. (2002). The role of environmental accounting in organisational change: An exploration of Spanish companies. *Accounting, Auditing and Accountability Journal*, *14*(2), 213–239.

Lungu, I., Caraiani, C., & Dascalu, C. (2008). Accounting information from traditional towards socioeconomic and environmental requirements. *Accounting and Management Information Systems*, *26*, 22–40.

Manetti, G., Thorne, L., & Mahoney, L. (2013). *Motivations for issuing standalone CSR Reports: A survey of Canadian firms*. Paper session presented at the 36th European Accounting Association 2013 Annual Congress, Dauphine, France.

Mashayekhi, B., & Mashayekh, S. (2008). Development of accounting in Iran. *The International Journal of Accounting*, *43*(1), 66–86.

Meyer, J. W., & Rowan, B. (1991). Institutionalised organisations: Formal structure as myth and ceremony. In W. W. Powell & P. J. DiMaggio (Eds.), *The New Institutionalism in Organisational Analysis*. Chicago, IL: University of Chicago Press.

Milanés-Montero, P., & Pérez-Calderón, E. (2011). Corporate environmental disclosure and legitimacy theory: An Europe perspective. *Environmental Engineering and Management Journal*, *10*(12), 1883–1891.

Milne, M. J., & Patten, D. M. (2002). Securing organizational legitimacy: An experimental decision case examining the impact of environmental disclosures. *Accounting Auditing and Accountability Journal*, *15*(3), 372–405.

Mosene, J., Burritt, R., Sanagustín, V., Moneva, J., & Tingey-Holyoak, J. (2013). Environmental reporting in the Spanish wind energy sector: An institutional view. *Journal of Cleaner Production*, *40*, 199–211.

Murguia, D., & Bohling, K. (2013). Sustainability reporting on large-scale mining conflicts: The case of Bajo de la Alumbrera, Argentina. *Journal of Cleaner Production*, *41*, 202–209.

Naser, K., Al-Hussaini, A., Al-Kwari, D., & Nuseibeh, R. (2006). Determinants of corporate social disclosure in developing countries: The case of Qatar. *Advances in International Accounting*, *19*, 1–23.

Nyquist, S. (2003). The legislation of environmental disclosures in three Nordic countries – A comparison. Business strategy and the environment. *Swedish University of Agricultural Sciences*, *12*, 12–25.

O'Dwyer, B. (2002). Managerial perceptions of corporate social disclosure: An Irish story. *Accounting, Auditing and Accountability Journal*, *15*(3), 406–36.

O'Donovan, G. (1999). Managing legitimacy through increased corporate environmental reporting: An exploratory study. *Interdisciplinary Environmental Review*, *1*(1), 63–99.

Owusu-Ansah, S. (1998). The impact of corporate attributes on the extent of mandatory disclosure and reporting by listed companies in Zimbabwe. *The International Journal of Accounting*, *33*, 605–631.

Patten, D. M. (1991). Exposure, legitimacy, and social disclosure. *Journal of Accounting and Public Policy*, *10*, 297–308.

Patten, D. M. (2002). Media exposure, public policy pressure, and environmental disclosure: An examination of the impact of TRI data availability. *Accounting Forum*, *26*, 152–171.

Rankin, M., Windsor, C., & Wahyuni, D. (2011). An investigation of voluntary corporate greenhouse gas emissions reporting in a market governance system. Australian evidence. *Accounting, Auditing & Accountability Journal*, *24*(8), 1037–1070.

Reverte, C. (2009). Determinants of corporate social responsibility disclosure ratings by Spanish listed firms. *Journal of Business Ethics*, *88*, 351–366.

Suchman, M. C. (1995). Managing legitimacy: Strategic and institutional approaches. *Academy of Management Review*, *20*(3), 571–610.

Sumiani, Y., Haslinda, Y., & Lehman, G. (2007). Environmental reporting in a developing country: A case study on status and implementation in Malaysia. *Journal of Cleaner Production*, *5*(3), 34–56.

Todea, N., Stanciu, I., & Joldos, A. (2010). Environmental accounting – A tool used by the entity for determining environmental costs. *Annales Universitatis Apulensis Series Oeconomica*, *12*(1), 207–217.

Watson, A., Shrives, P., & Marston, C. (2002). Voluntary disclosure of accounting ratios in the UK. *British Accounting Review*, *34*, 289–313.

Wilmshurst, T., & Frost, G. (2000). Corporate environmental reporting. A test of legitimacy theory. *Accounting Auditing & Accountability Journal*, *13*(1), 10–26.

APPENDIX A: DESCRIPTION OF THE INDEPENDENT VARIABLES

Independent Variables	Definition of Variable	Quantification System
The category on the stock exchange *(BSE_C)*	The entity may be listed in Category I, II, or III	Number of the category
Sales percentage intended for export *(Ex)*	Percentage of exports within total sales	Percentage of exports within total sales
Total assets (*TA*)	Total assets	Total assets
Turnover (*Turn*)	Turnover	Turnover
Number of employees (*No_e*)	Number of employees	Number of employees
Sector of activity (*S_A*)	The sector in which the entity activates	We have seven sectors of activity marked with a number between 1 and 7

APPENDIX B: ENVIRONMENTAL REPORTING DISCLOSURE INDEX (DI)

No.	Symbol	Company Name	d1	d2	d3	DI
1	ARS	AEROSTAR S.A.	1	0	0	0.33
2	ALR	ALRO S.A.	1	0	0	0.33
3	ALT	ALTUR S.A.	0	0	0	0.00
4	ALU	ALUMIL ROM INDUSTRY S.A.	0	0	0	0.00
5	AMO	AMONIL S.A.	1	0	0	0.33
6	ATB	ANTIBIOTICE S.A.	1	1	1	1.00
7	ARM	ARMATURA S.A.	1	0	0	0.33
8	AZO	AZOMURES S.A.	1	1	1	1.00
9	BRM	BERMAS S.A.	1	0	0	0.33
10	BIO	BIOFARM S.A.	1	0	0	0.33
11	SPCU	BOROMIR PROD SA BUZAU (SPICUL)	0	0	0	0.00
12	TEL	C.N.T.E.E. TRANSELECTRICA	1	1	1	1.00
13	CBC	CARBOCHIM S.A.	1	0	0	0.33
14	BCM	CASA DE BUCOVINA-CLUB DE MUNTE	1	0	0	0.33
15	CEON	CEMACON SA ZALAU	1	0	0	0.33
16	CMCM	COMCM SA CONSTANTA	0	0	0	0.00
17	CMF	COMELF S.A.	1	0	0	0.33
18	CMP	COMPA S. A.	1	0	1	0.67
19	ENP	COMPANIA ENERGOPETROL S.A.	1	0	0	0.33
20	COFI	CONCEFA SA SIBIU	1	0	0	0.33
21	COMI	CONDMAG S.A.	1	0	1	0.67
22	CGC	CONTOR GROUP S.A. Arad	1	0	0	0.33
23	DAFR	DAFORA SA ind	1	0	0	0.33

***Appendix B** (Continued)*

No.	Symbol	Company Name	d1	d2	d3	DI
24	ELJ	ELECTROAPARATAJ S.A.	1	0	0	0.33
25	ELGS	ELECTROARGES SA CURTEA DE ARGES	1	0	0	0.33
26	ELMA	ELECTROMAGNETICA SA BUCURESTI	1	0	0	0.33
27	EPT	ELECTROPUTERE S.A.	1	0	0	0.33
28	RMAH	FARMACEUTICA REMEDIA SA DEVA	1	0	0	0.33
29	ECT	GRUPUL INDUSTRIAL ELECTROCONTACT S.A.	1	0	0	0.33
30	IMP	IMPACT DEVELOPER & CONTRACTOR S.A.	1	0	1	0.67
31	MECF	MECANICA CEAHLAU	1	0	0	0.33
32	COS	MECHEL TARGOVISTE S.A.	1	0	0	0.33
33	MEF	MEFIN S.A.	1	0	0	0.33
34	MJM	MJ MAILLIS ROMANIA S.A.	1	0	0	0.33
35	OIL	OIL TERMINAL S.A.	1	0	0	0.33
36	OLT	OLTCHIM S.A. RM. VALCEA	1	1	1	1.00
37	SNP	OMV PETROM S.A.	1	1	1	1.00
38	PEI	PETROLEXPORTIMPORT S.A.	0	0	0	0.00
39	PREH	PREFAB SA BUCURESTI	1	0	0	0.33
40	PPL	PRODPLAST S.A.	1	0	0	0.33
41	RTRA	RETRASIB SA SIBIU	1	0	0	0.33
42	ROCE	ROMCARBON SA BUZAU	1	1	1	1.00
43	RRC	ROMPETROL RAFINARE S.A.	1	1	1	1.00
44	PTR	ROMPETROL WELL SERVICES S.A.	1	0	0	0.33
45	RPH	ROPHARMA SA BRASOV	1	0	0	0.33
46	TGN	S.N.T.G.N. TRANSGAZ S.A.	1	1	1	1.00
47	SNO	SANTIERUL NAVAL ORSOVA S.A.	1	0	0	0.33
48	COTR	SC TRANSILVANIA CONSTRUCTII SA	1	0	0	0.33
49	STZ	SINTEZA S.A.	1	0	0	0.33
50	SRT	SIRETUL PASCANI S.A.	1	0	0	0.33
51	SOCP	SOCEP S.A.	1	0	0	0.33
52	ART	T.M.K. – ARTROM S.A.	1	1	0	0.67
53	TRP	TERAPLAST SA	1	0	0	0.33
54	MPN	TITAN S.A.	1	0	0	0.33
55	TBM	TURBOMECANICA S.A.	1	0	0	0.33
56	TUFE	TURISM FELIX S.A. BAILE FELIX	1	0	0	0.33
57	EFO	TURISM, HOTELURI, RESTAURANTE MAREA NEAGRA	1	0	0	0.33
58	UAM	UAMT S.A.	1	0	0	0.33
59	UCM	UCM RESITA S.A.	1	0	0	0.33
60	VESY	VES SA	1	0	0	0.33
61	APC	Vostalpine VAE APCAROM SA	1	0	0	0.33
62	VNC	VRANCART SA	1	0	0	0.33
63	SCD	ZENTIVA S.A.	1	0	1	0.67
64	ZIM	ZIMTUB S.A.	1	0	0	0.33

DOES PROFESSIONAL ACCOUNTING QUALIFICATION MATTER FOR THE PROVISION OF ACCOUNTING SERVICES?

Sergeja Slapničar, Maja Zaman Groff and Neža Štumberger

ABSTRACT

Purpose – *The purpose of the chapter is to contribute to the discussion as to whether some sort of regulation of professional accountants is warranted, by analysing whether professional qualification of accountants affects the provision of accounting services.*

Methodology/approach – *A survey method is used. From a sample of 96 accountants providing accounting services in Slovenia, we estimate the structural equation model and measure competences, knowledge, service mix, customer loyalty and litigation risk.*

Findings – *We find that professional qualification is positively associated with competences. Competences, in turn, are positively associated with knowledge and wider service product mix, but not with customer loyalty and litigation risk.*

Accounting in Central and Eastern Europe
Research in Accounting in Emerging Economies, Volume 13, 255–277

ISSN: 1479-3563/doi:10.1108/S1479-3563(2013)0000013016

Research limitations – *The respondents are practicing accountants. Their self-evaluation of their knowledge should be treated with caution in terms of the absolute values of assessed knowledge as they are inevitably subjective. For other variables, more objective measures are used.*

Research implications – *In the absence of accounting profession regulation, the quality of financial reporting may be particularly vulnerable in micro companies. Although answering the question of whether provision of accounting services should be subject to regulation is not straightforward, the results of our study provide some guidance for regulatory decision making.*

Keywords: Professional qualification; accountants; competences; small and micro firms

INTRODUCTION

Due to the public interest element of the services provided, the accounting profession is strongly regulated. In the accounting context, the International Federation of Accountants (IFAC) defines the public interest as 'the common benefit that all citizens share from the services provided by the accountancy profession' (IFAC, Public Interest Framework, 2010, p. 4). In the IFAC definition, the 'public interest' is related to the interest of all individuals and groups in the quality of financial reporting, the comparability of reports, fiscal prudence, contributions to corporate governance and organisational performance.

An important aspect of profession regulation relates to the requirements needed to practice a profession. Of the three accounting-related professions – accounting in the strictest sense (i.e. book-keeping and reporting), auditing and tax consulting – auditing is most regulated and monitored. Moreover, European Union (EU) legislation regulates only the auditing profession as requested by the Directive of the European Parliament and the Council on statutory audits of annual accounts and consolidated accounts (2006/43/EC). Regarding the approval of statutory auditors and audit firms, member states must appoint competent authorities that may be professional associations but must be subject to a system of public oversight. The Directive stresses specific requests regarding educational qualifications, examination of professional competence and practical training needed for approval to carry out statutory audits.

On the contrary, the accounting-related regulation, specifically the Directive on the annual accounts of certain types of companies (78/660/EEC) and the revised Directive of the European Parliament and of the Council on the annual and consolidated accounts of certain types of companies, banks and other financial institutions and insurance undertakings (2003/51/EC) contain no specific conditions related to professional qualifications of financial statement preparers. For professionals carrying out accounting services in the strictest sense, such as book-keeping and financial reporting, EU legislation does not specify any requirements regarding education and practical training, membership of professional organisations or examination of professional competence. In short, the legislation does not direct the national authorities of the member states to regulate this area.

The legal system significantly influences the organisation of a profession and the requirements to practice a profession in a given country. Altintas and Yilmaz (2012) examined the relationship between the legal system and the accounting profession in common law and code law countries and report that the accounting profession, including professional certification, is significantly affected by the judicial system. In the common law countries, on the one hand, the professional titles chartered accountant (CA) or certified public accountant (CPA) prevail, and the professionals who have obtained a professional certification perform both auditing and accounting services. In the code law countries, on the other hand, the accounting profession is not as harmonised and depends on national legislation. In these countries, accounting and auditing professions have been developed as separate professions with different professional titles (Altintas & Yilmaz, 2012).

In the policy position chapter, *Regulation of the accountancy profession*, the IFAC asserts that professional accountants contribute, inter alia, to the growth of individual companies, assist governments in achieving their goals and promote financial market performance. The IFAC suggests that the regulation of the accounting profession is necessary to ensure that appropriate quality is provided in the accountant services market (IFAC, Regulation of the accountancy profession, 2007). However, it is not surprising that the absence of EU legislation regulating the accounting profession in the strictest sense has led to a high diversity of national regulation in different member states. Recently, the FEE (Fédération des Experts-comptables Européens – The Federation of European Accountants) has released the results of a survey which detail the structure, organisation and other specifics of the accountancy profession across 30 European countries. The survey report outlines different education and qualification requirements, registration conditions and reserved activities (Fee survey on the structure and organisation of the accountancy profession across 30 European countries, 2012). The results of the survey reveal that services provided by professional accountants include preparation of financial information, tax services, statutory audit and other assurance services, services in the areas of non-financial reporting, sustainability and corporate social responsibility, strategy and management consultancy and corporate governance, and that the rules regarding the delivery of these services vary considerably across Europe. Three main conclusions reached are (1) depending on the country, all or only parts of the accountancy profession are regulated; (2) where regulatory requirements exist (in the form of education and qualification requirements, professional titles and/or membership of professional organisations), the rules vary from country to country and (3) only for statutory audit services has harmonisation been achieved at the EU level (FEE, Key features on structure and organisation of the accountancy profession across 30 European countries, 2012).

Scott and Walt (1995) report that accountancy firm customers often have difficulty assessing the quality of professional services. Taking into consideration the highly competitive market and limited ability of customers to assess the quality of service providers, it is possible that formal education, competences and experiences of an accountant may not be the first determinant of choice, but rather subservience to customer interest and low price.

The aim of our study is to contribute to the discussion as to whether some sort of regulation of professional accountants might be warranted. Although the current trend in the area of financial reporting of small and micro firms in the EU is towards an increased simplification of financial reporting (Directive 2012/6/EU),[1] the impact of such a measure on the quality of financial information remains unclear. Professional initiatives have been taken to address the growing concerns of the accounting profession regarding the quality of financial reports prepared by practitioners with a wide variety of educational background and experience offering accounting services to small and micro firms in the non-regulated markets.

The country of our analysis is Slovenia, where, as a result of these initiatives, the Slovenian Chamber of Accounting Services has prepared a draft Accountancy Profession Act. The Accountancy Profession Act is intended to regulate the profession of accountants, preparers of financial statements, and includes requirements regarding professional qualification. In the chapter, we examine whether accounting professional qualification matters for the provision of accounting services by studying its impact on accountant's competences, knowledge, services provided (product mix), litigation risk and customer loyalty.

The chapter is structured as follows. In the next section, we discuss the importance of financial reporting of small and micro firms and describe the Slovenian setting, the organisation of the accounting profession and the professional certification programmes. The following section discusses the methodology, including the sample and the measurement of variables. Thereafter, the results of the study are presented and the final section concludes with discussion.

INSTITUTIONAL SETTING AND THE RESEARCH MODEL

Financial Reporting of Small and Micro Firms

Research related to financial reporting quality predominantly focuses on large public companies. In this sector, such research is highly relevant because of the importance of financial information for various categories of users and the stability of financial markets in particular. As financial statements of small and micro firms do not serve a comparable variety of users, financial reporting of small and micro firms is often neglected by researchers. This is not to say, however, that high financial reporting standards are not equally important in this sector. Small and micro firms have a significant collective impact on national economies in the EU. In 2012, a total of 20.7 million small and medium-sized firms were registered in the EU, accounting for more than 98% of all registered firms. Among these, 92.2% were firms with fewer than 10 employees. It was estimated that small and medium-sized firms would account for 67% of total employment and 58% of gross value added in 2012 (Annual report on small and medium-sized enterprises in the EU, 2011/12).

Given that the owners of small and micro firms may efficiently control their firms not only with accounting but also with alternative control mechanisms and that they are actively involved in management as compared to large firms, the quality of financial reporting in this sector is of primary importance to banks, tax authorities and potential investors. High-quality financial reporting allows more efficient resource allocation and, ultimately, potentially lowers financing costs (as a result of reduced risks and reduced information asymmetry between the external finance providers and owners).

Characteristics of the Slovenian Market in Accounting Services

In Slovenia, the Company Act requires all large and medium-sized firms to present audited financial statements. In addition to yearly statutory audits, financial reporting of these firms is subject to different forms of control, such as audit committees and other governance mechanisms, tax authorities and potential public oversight of the incumbent auditor. In contrast, with the exception of periodic tax audits, the financial reporting of small and micro firms is not supervised. Currently no requirements related to professional qualification of accountants are mandated by Slovenian legislation. Consequently, the provision of accounting services is carried out by practitioners with variable educational background and experience.

Due to the nature of the service (a highly specialised service) and related cost, small and micro firms tend to outsource accounting services to professionals employed in accounting firms specialising in the provision of accounting services for small businesses. In Slovenia, these accounting firms have a relatively short history. Until the 1990s, the Slovenian economy comprised a network of large conglomerate companies. In the absence of small private businesses in the former socialist regime, the function of accounting was primarily financial reporting to the state. The establishment of the first accounting firms in the early 1990s was followed by rapid growth of this sector and coincided with the development of entrepreneurship. This growth continued during the restructuring of the Slovenian economy (throughout the 1990s) and persisted with an increasing number of emerging small and micro businesses in times of economic expansion.

Today, the Slovenian market in accounting services is highly competitive. The evidence of the Agency of the Republic of Slovenia for Public Legal Records and Related Services (AJPES) reveals that in December 2012, there were 4665 registered providers of accounting services in Slovenia (AJPES, 2012).

The two professional organisations of accountants in Slovenia are the Slovenian Institute of Auditors (Institute) and the Chamber of Accounting Services (Chamber). The Institute and the Chamber promote the accountancy profession by developing professional standards and promoting ethical conduct. They also represent and protect the interests of their members. Membership of either of these professional organisations is not obligatory. Both organisations offer professional qualification programmes resulting in the professional title of certified accountant.

To enrol in the programme offered by the Slovenian Institute of Auditors, the candidate must have obtained at least a three-year college degree from a relevant field of study. Additionally, he/she must have at least two years of work experience in high-level accounting-related positions in a large or medium-sized company or in a managerial position in a firm providing accounting services. The training consists of 154 hours of study and includes courses in accounting, auditing, corporate finance, quantitative methods, business communication and commercial, labour, obligation and tax law. The professional examination consists of a written examination and final thesis presentation and defence.

Professional education training at the Chamber of Accounting Services is offered to candidates who have completed a college programme in a relevant field of study and have at least three years of work experience in accounting, or have obtained a university degree and have at least two years of work experience in accounting. The programme consists of 104 hours of study and is built on four thematic sections: (1) accounting and accounting regulation, (2) taxation and contributions, (3) commercial, labour, obligation and tax law, (4) management and business communication. The examination comprises a written examination (theoretical and practical examination with an integrated case study) and an oral examination defending the case study.

The research question addressed in this chapter is whether professional qualification of accountants affects the provision of accounting services. We propose that professional qualification is positively associated with higher competences and that professional qualification and competences positively affect the provision of accounting services via broader knowledge. As

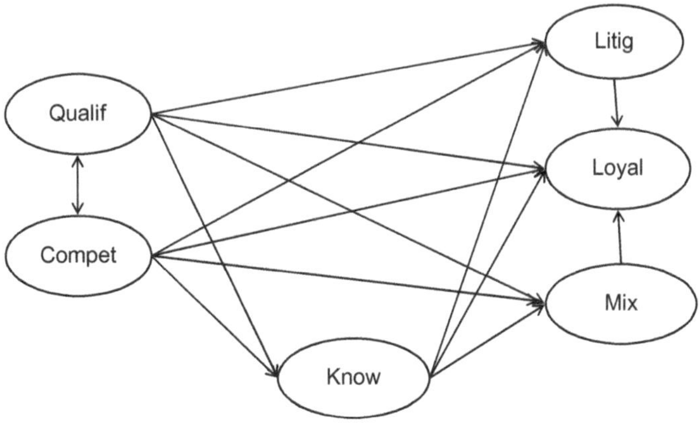

Fig. 1. Research Model.

accounting service quality is perceptual, we measure it by three available objective criteria: the service mix provided, customer loyalty and litigation risk. We present these relationships in the following research model (Fig. 1).

METHODOLOGY

Sample

We sampled the practicing accountants listed in the Catalogue of Accounting Firms, available on the official website of the Slovenian Chamber of Commerce (2012). The Catalogue provides a list of persons with a professional qualification gained either from the Chamber of Accounting Services or from the Slovenian Institute of Auditors. The total number of qualified accountants is 107. We invited all to participate. The same number of accounting firms that employ no professionally qualified accountants was randomly chosen from the AJPES online database. In total, 214 practicing accountants were sent an invitation to participate via an e-mail with a link to an on-line questionnaire. We received 96 completed questionnaires, a response rate of 44.9%. Of the respondents, 31 were not qualified and 65 were qualified. Of the respondents, 75.3% were female, 13.5% completed only secondary school, 55.2% completed a two- or three-year college programme, 29.2% finished a three- or four-year university degree programme and 2.1% obtained a master's degree. Of the respondents, 24% were sole proprietors, 60.4% were employed in an accounting firm with 2–5 employees and the rest employed 6 employees or more.

Variable Measurement

Professional qualification: We measure professional qualification (Qualif) of an accountant as a dummy variable, whereby 0 indicates that the accountant has no formal professional qualification and 1 indicates that the accountant has completed either Institute or the Chamber programme. Given our research question, we do not distinguish between these two professional qualification programmes.

Competences: An accountant may also acquire competences (Compet) from formal education, continuous professional training and from professional magazines and journals that present contemporary trends and the current regulatory changes and standards and their practical solutions. We measure these three aspects of competences with separate indicators. Formal education (Educ) is measured on a scale from 1 to 5 (1 represents completed secondary school, 2 and 3 represent two- and three-year college programmes, 4 represents university degree and 5 represents master's degree). Continuous professional training (Train) is measured by the number of professional training hours per year. The magazine and journal variable (Magaz) is measured by the total number subscribed to (the range is from 0 to 5).

As the quality of accounting services is difficult to measure and as self-evaluation of service quality may not be reliable, we measure instead self-assessed level of knowledge of various accounting or related areas and three outcome variables related to service provision: litigation risk, customer loyalty and service mix.

Knowledge: We measure knowledge (Know) of nine areas related to national and international accounting standards, various types of legislation (labour, financial, obligation, company), taxation, financial analysis, auditing and asset valuation (see the questionnaire in the appendix). The respondents indicated on a 5-point Likert scale how they assess their knowledge in a specific area (1 – very poor to 5 – very good). Measurement items for the construct were determined on the basis of semi-structured interviews with three experts (practicing accountants) and the authors' own experience. We believe that we have identified the conceptually necessary dimensions of knowledge that add up, rather than co-vary, in the formation of the construct.

Both competences and knowledge are formative constructs. Formative constructs are complex and multi-componential constructs formed by their components (Diamantopoulos & Winklhofer, 2001; Rossiter, 2002). The components are based on theory and expert opinion to capture the substance of the construct. They do not have to be unidimensional with regards to the construct, which means that they do not necessarily co-vary. It would be inappropriate to delete any of those items in the pursuit of factorial unidimensionality (Rossiter, 2002, p. 308). We follow this reasoning in forming the constructs knowledge and competences. This perspective is not widely recognised in the accounting literature, but it is gaining relevance in the marketing literature (Diamantopoulos & Winklhofer, 2001; Rossiter, 2002).

We base the selection of the three outcome variables on specifics of accounting services.

Litigation risk has been recognised in auditing literature as one of the proxies of audit failure (Francis, 2004; Palmrose, 1988). As litigation risk is highly relevant in areas where practicing professionals are required to perform their services in line with strict legislation and professional standard rules, the selection of this variable is relevant in the context of accounting services. Errors, mistakes and delays in financial report submissions to tax authorities represent a risk for a customer. Errors in accounting service provision may occur due to inadequate training or negligence. Errors and delays in financial reporting may result in financial penalties for the customers. The customer in turn may enter into legal litigation against the accountant. Material errors may jeopardise the existence of both the accounting and the customer's firm. We measure litigation risk (Litig) by the number of litigation incidences recorded against the respondent.

Loyalty: As shown by previous research, *customer loyalty* is a direct or indirect consequence of service quality (Cronin, Brady, & Hult, 2000; Olsen, 2002; Zeithaml, 2000). Given that there are no legal limitations to the accountant–client relationship (as opposed to audit–client relationship), customer loyalty can be considered as a viable outcome variable in an accounting service quality study. We measure loyalty (Loyal) of customers to the accounting service provider as a percentage of revenues derived from regular customers in total revenues. All variables used in the model are standardised due to different measurement scales.

Service mix: Taking into consideration the specifics of accounting services, service mix was selected as the third outcome variable in our study. The larger the service mix offered to the customers, the more complex the needs the accountant has to deal with. As accounting information for various users is interconnected (i.e. management accounting projections influence reported values of some assets in financial reports), offering additional services may result in an enhanced base-line service, that is book-keeping and reporting. Furthermore, additional services (from tax consulting to management consulting) may improve the customer's decision making. We therefore assume that a wider range of services is indirectly associated with a higher quality of overall services. Service mix (Mix) is measured on an ordinal scale that lists 15 different services.

Analysis

We estimate the proposed path model in Fig. 1 with a partial least squares (PLS) approach to structural equation modelling (SEM) (Lohmöller, 1989; Wold, 1982, 1985). SEM is a system of equations that allows the simultaneous modelling of relationships among multiple independent (exogenous) and dependent (endogenous) constructs; independent variables in one equation become dependent variables in the other. SEM analysis has various advantages over multiple regression analysis and is consequently gaining popularity among accounting researchers (Smith & Langfield-Smith, 2004). There are two essentially different SEM estimation methods: the covariance-based method (estimated with software packages such as LISREL, EQS and AMOS) and the variance-based method (estimated with a software package SmartPLS; Hair, Ringle, & Sarstedt, 2012; Ringle, Wende, & Will, 2005). Unlike the covariance-based method of SEM estimation that minimises the difference between sample covariances and those predicted by a theoretical model on the assumption of normal multivariate distribution (Chin 1998), PLS estimates the model using an iterative ordinary least squares (OLS) regression-like procedure, and is less restrictive on distributive characteristics of the variables. PLS is a prediction-oriented approach that focuses on endogenous target constructs in the model and aims to maximise their explained variance. By focusing on explaining the variance in the endogenous variables, PLS places emphasis on prediction. In parallel with SME analysis in general, its popularity has been increasing over the last decade and it has become a well-recognised method among accounting researchers (see Lee, Petter, Fayard, & Robinson, 2011, for an overview).

PLS may be thought of as an intermediate procedure between OLS and principal component regression. A bootstrap approach is used to determine the distribution of the PLS estimators of regression coefficients and to calculate mean confidence intervals.

The decision for the PLS rather than the covariance-based SEM approach is based on our relatively modest sample size, the use of formative constructs for latent variables and non-normal data which PLS is better equipped to deal with (Hair, Sarstedt, Ringle, & Mena, 2012; Vandenbosch, 1996).

RESULTS

Descriptive Statistics

ANOVA analysis reveals that all three items measuring competences are higher in the subgroup with professional qualification. However, only the magazines' variable differs significantly; completed formal education level and on-going professional training are surprisingly not significantly different between the two subgroups. Also the values of all the items that constitute the knowledge variable were higher in the subgroup with professional qualification, but significant differences were found only in the knowledge of the Slovenian accounting standards, financial law and auditing-related knowledge. The power of finding significant differences is small due to high standard deviations in the subgroups and the low number of observations. The results reveal that of the nine categories; the respondents' self-assessed knowledge related to taxation and contributions is highest. Taxation and contributions-related knowledge were even found to be higher than that of the Slovenian accounting standards. This clearly demonstrates that the core activity of accounting in small and micro firms is reporting to tax authorities. The two subgroups significantly differ also in the number of services rendered to the customers, but not in the incidence of litigations. Although the difference is not significant, it is quite striking that the accountants without professional qualification report higher loyalty of customers (Table 1).

The open-ended question referring to respondents' opinions regarding the introduction of mandatory professional accounting qualifications resulted in 75 answers expressing strong statements in favour. One of the respondents, for example, wrote:

> I strongly support the regulation that would set minimum entry criteria for the profession of practicing accountants. Also, the law should define criteria to maintain professional qualification i.e. the period of knowledge examination every five years and, for example, obligatory professional liability insurance. There should be a public register with the list of accountants that fulfil the criteria.

Another respondent stated:

> The proposal to regulate this profession comes at least 10 years too late! I am amazed that the state allows entrepreneurs to be so unprotected in the area of financial reporting. Entrepreneurs who trust the accounting firm in good faith do not realize that it is completely unverified, and inevitable consequences follow. However, as both, entrepreneurs and accounting firms are small, it seems that nobody cares.

Moreover, many of the respondents without professional qualification would support the introduction of mandatory professional qualification, yet feel that it should be more accessible in terms of price and that the two private institutions should no longer dominate in offering these programmes.

Measurement Model

A formative latent variable is a linear combination of its indicators. For an inbound measurement model, PLS determines the composite variable

Table 1. Descriptive Statistics.

	Qualif	Mean	Standard Deviation	Standard Error Mean
Train	0	40.89	38.888	8.2323
	1	47.83	47.990	7.2600
Magaz	0	1.94*	0.892	0.1602
	1	2.55*	0.919	0.1140
Educ	0	2.45	1.150	0.2065
	1	2.86	1.059	0.1313
Q4 (the Slovene accounting standards)	0	3.77*	0.817	0.1492
	1	4.34*	0.567	0.0702
Q5 (labour law)	0	3.52	0.724	0.1301
	1	3.63	0.782	0.0970
Q6 (taxation and contributions)	0	4.10	0.831	0.1492
	1	4.17	0.840	0.1041
Q7 (financial laws)	0	3.39*	0.844	0.1515
	1	3.78*	0.780	0.0968
Q8 (the European company law)	0	2.13	0.846	0.1519
	1	2.52	0.970	0.1203
Q9 (status law and the law of obligations)	0	2.97	0.948	0.1702
	1	3.12	0.976	0.1211
Q10 (asset valuation)	0	3.74	0.855	0.1535
	1	3.60	0.965	0.1197
Q11 (auditing)	0	2.58*	1.089	0.1955
	1	3.46*	0.937	0.1161
Q12 (IFRS)	0	2.52	0.926	0.1663
	1	3.03	0.984	0.1220
Litig	0	0.16	0.454	0.0816
	1	0.18	0.429	0.0532
Loyal	0	94.68	8.428	1.5136
	1	89.71	19.320	2.3963
Mix	0	8.84*	3.436	0.6171
	1	11.12*	2.349	0.2913

*$p < 0.05$.

scores as the weighted sum of its indicators, whereby the weights represent regression weights (see Table 2). The validity of a formative variable is evaluated differently than reflective variables. It is ensured if content, predictive and nomological validity are ensured. Content validity is provided if the degree of agreement about characteristics representing a construct is high. We believe that our measurement of both competences and knowledge captures the construct's essence. Predictive validity refers to the

Table 2. Outer Weights.

	Qualif	Compet	Know	Litig	Loyal	Mix
Qualif	1					
Educ		0.331				
Magaz		0.739				
Train		0.363				
Q10 (asset valuation)			0.081			
Q12 (IFRS)			0.239			
Q4 (the Slovenian accounting standards)			0.207			
Q5 (labour law)			0.115			
Q6 (taxation and contributions)			0.145			
Q7 (financial laws)			0.196			
Q8 (the European company law)			0.138			
Q9 (status law and the law of obligations)			0.168			
Q11 (auditing)			0.171			
Litig				1		
Loyal					1	
Mix						1

explanatory power of the latent variable. The explained variance of competences is 12.5% and knowledge 38.7%. All constructs have relatively large explanatory power for service mix as they explain 36.4% of variance. Furthermore, the predictive validity of the parameter estimates is estimated via a cross-validated redundancy index or so-called Stone-Geisser Q^2 test (Geisser, 1974; Stone, 1974). Although PLS models lack the index that can provide the goodness of fit statistics of variance–covariance based structural models, Tenenhaus, Vinzi, Chatelin, and Lauro (2005) and Vandenbosch (1996) argue that next to validity of constructs the significance of the variance explained (R^2 values) and the sign of the redundancy indexes (Q^2 values) for all constructs provide an assessment of model fit. As shown in Table 3, the redundancy for all latent variables is positive and satisfactory. Nomological validity refers to predicted behaviour of the construct within the model. Nomological validity is satisfied if structural relationships are consistent with other studies that have been measured with validated instruments. Positive associations between professional qualification, competences and knowledge in our study correspond to an alternative approach in the recent study of Zaman Groff, Štumberger, and Slapničar (2012) in which the authors find positive associations between

Table 3. Explained Variance and Redundancy Index.

	R^2	Redundancy
Qualif	n.a.	n.a.
Compet	0.125	0.055
Know	0.387	0.029
Litig	0.029	0.002
Loyal	0.035	0.019
Mix	0.364	0.091

Note: n.a., not available.

Table 4. Correlation Matrix.

	Qualif	Compet	Litig	Know	Loyal	Mix
Qualif	1					
Compet	0.353*	1				
Litig	0.025	−0.021	1			
Know	0.359	0.602*	−0.136	1		
Loyal	−0.140	−0.151	−0.184	−0.058	1	
Mix	0.366	0.495	−0.087	0.548*	−0.092	1

*$p < 0.05$.

professional qualification and competences of an accountant *as perceived by the customers* (Table 4).

Structural Model

We present the results of the structural model in Table 5 and Fig. 2. The estimated path coefficients indicate the strength and the direction of the relationships among the specified constructs. The statistical significance of the path coefficients is assessed using a bootstrap procedure with 1000 replacements. In line with our expectations, we find that professional qualification is associated with competences ($b = 0.364$, $p < 0.001$). We have tested also the reverse relationship (Compet affecting Qualif) and, for the sake of brevity, we report only the results from Qualif to Compet. The results are robust and do not significantly change any other relationship in the model. The reverse relationship is logical as enrolment into professional

Table 5. Structural Model.

	Original Sample	Sample Mean	Standard Error	T-Statistics
Qualif→Compet	0.364*	0.371	0.089	4.084
Qualif→Know	0.117	0.106	0.101	1.153
Qualif→Litig	0.044	0.045	0.108	0.410
Qualif→Know	0.117	0.106	0.101	1.153
Qualif→Loyalty	−0.088	−0.089	0.087	1.009
Qualif→Mix	0.186*	0.181	0.092	2.030
Compet→Know	0.491	0.510	0.084	5.852
Compet→Litig	0.091	0.099	0.159	0.574
Compet→Loyal	−0.124	−0.102	0.147	0.843
Compet→Mix	0.250*	0.239	0.096	2.596
Litig→Loyal	−0.180	−0.164	0.135	1.330
Know→Litig	−0.178	−0.180	0.166	1.070
Know→Loyal	0.027	0.030	0.145	0.189
Know→Mix	0.302*	0.315	0.107	2.810
Mix→Loyal	−0.029	−0.030	0.083	0.354

*$p < 0.05$.

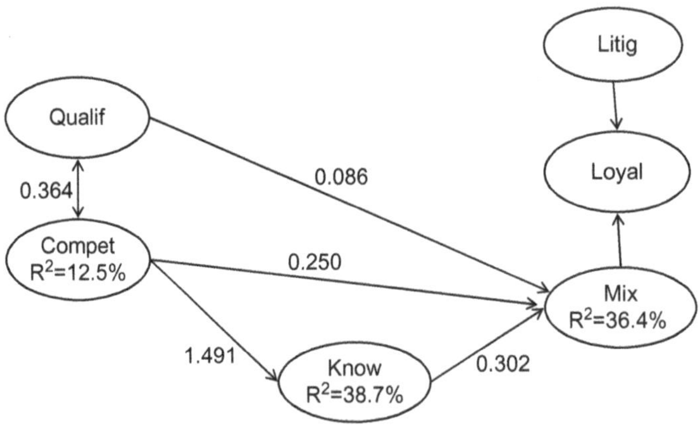

Fig. 2. Results of Estimated Model.

qualification programmes requires a certain minimum education level. Furthermore, we find a positive and very strong relationship between competences and knowledge ($b = 0.491$, $p < 0.001$). The results suggest that there is no direct relationship between professional qualification and knowledge beyond the one captured by competences. Competences are suggested to be the core variable in our research model; the professional qualification contributes to them, but not exclusively. Formal level of education, continuous professional training and professional magazines also add to the competences. Knowledge is significantly related to service mix ($b = 0.302$, $p < 0.01$) as are competences ($b = 0.25$, $p < 0.01$). It is interesting that professional qualification positively impacts service mix after controlling for competences and knowledge ($b = 0.186$, $p < 0.05$). This implies that during professional qualification programmes, skills needed for a larger service mix are gained beyond those captured by competences.

As already reported, the overall model shows that a large proportion of knowledge and service mix variance is explained by professional qualification and competences ($R^2 = 38.7\%$ and 36.4%, respectively). Contrary to our expectations, neither professional qualification, competences nor knowledge influence the other two output variables in the model: litigation risk and customer loyalty are not found to be explained by the predicted variables. Results are robust if we control for the accounting firm size in the model (for brevity not reported).

DISCUSSION AND CONCLUSION

The ultimate goal of the accounting function is to provide high-quality financial information for internal and external financial information users. To achieve this goal in the segment of accounting firms, providing services to small business, sustainability in the form of service quality should be ensured. With the aim of contributing to the discussion as to whether some sort of regulation of professional accountants is warranted, we study whether professional qualification of accountants affects the provision of accounting services rendered by professional accountants primarily to small and micro firms. We are interested in the aspects that distinguish accountants with professional qualification from those without it. We conjecture that professional qualification results in better competences and knowledge which in turn impact the three variables related to service provision: service mix, litigation risk and customer loyalty.

We find that professional qualification is positively associated with competences. We, however, do not find a significant relationship between professional qualification or competences and litigation risk, nor between professional qualification or competences and customer loyalty. Regarding the litigation risk, we find a very low incidence of litigation, which may not fully reflect the true state of errors, misstatements or delays. Regarding customer loyalty, on the other hand, we find a very high proportion of regular customers in both subgroups. It may well be that a certain type of accountant attracts a certain type of customer. As well as the determinants under analysis, the price of the service is probably a very important determinant of customer loyalty.

A limitation of our study is that the respondents in our study are practicing accountants. This limits the choice of construct content and measurement: we are not able to observe service quality as such. Measuring service quality along its identified dimensions (Parasuraman, Zeithaml, & Berry, 1985, 1988; Scott & Walt, 1995) is not reliable if self-evaluated by the accountants. Also, respondents' self-evaluation of their knowledge should be treated with caution in terms of the absolute values of assessed knowledge. However, the fact that we compose the construct with nine substantive items and that we find differences among qualified and non-qualified accountants provides reasonable assurance that the construct knowledge has a meaningful measurement. The other formative variable, competences, is measured by more objective means (education level, hours of continuous professional training and journal/magazine subscription). It is interesting to observe that competences have a very large explanatory power in comparison to professional qualification. This finding implies that on-going professional training from various sources is the most warranted, after completion of formal and professional qualification. The finding that competences and professional qualification are strongly interrelated suggests that professional qualification has a long-lasting positive effect on competences renewal.

Our study suggests that professional qualification does matter for the provision of accounting services. However, although it reveals some important relationships between professional qualification, competences, knowledge and service provision-related variables, the findings do not conclusively support the regulation of the profession as they do not report its positive effects on two important service provision-related variables: litigation risk and customer loyalty. In our model, the only affected variable related to service provision is service mix. A higher service mix implies that in addition to book-keeping, an accountant is able to provide several accounting-related services to the customer. It may therefore be that professionally qualified accountants operate on the submarket of small and micro firms that require more sophisticated services, and that those without professional qualification predominantly serve the firms that engage accountants only to provide financial reporting-related services. Considering the current EU trend towards further simplification of financial reporting of micro firms, our findings suggest that in the absence of accounting profession regulation, the quality of financial reporting of these companies may be particularly vulnerable.

In general, our findings support the need for a more fundamental understanding of the consequences of a non-regulated market of accounting service provision to small and micro firms. Future studies could usefully apply a different perspective and explore a more direct relationship between professional qualification, service quality as perceived by the customers and earnings quality.

NOTE

1. The Directive 2012/6/EU was adopted as one of the outcomes of the EU initiative for boosting Europe's economy. It was intended to reduce administrative burdens, especially for micro companies, in the areas of company law and accounting.

REFERENCES

Agency of the Republic of Slovenia for Public Legal Records and Related Services – AJPES. (2012). Retrieved from http://www.ajpes.si/prs/rezultati.asp?podrobno = 0&tip = 0&maticna = &davcna = &naziv = &ulica = &h_st = &naselje = &obcina = &posta = &dejavnost = 69.200&Sektorizacija = &Oblika = &status = 1&MAXREC = 10

Altintas, N., & Yilmaz, F. (2012). The accounting profession: A descriptive study of the common and code law countries. *Journal of Modern Accounting and Auditing*, *8*(7), 932–950.

Annual report on small and medium-sized enterprises in the EU. (2011/12). *EU SMEs in 2012: At the crossroads*. Brussels: European Commission.

Chin, W. W. (1998). The partial least squares approach to structural equation modeling. In G. A. Marcoulides (Ed.), *Modern methods for business research* (pp. 295–336). Mahwah, NJ: Lawrence Erlbaum Associates.

Cronin, J. J., Brady, M. K., & Hult, G. T. M. (2000). Assessing the effects of quality, value and customer satisfaction on behavioural intention in service environments. *Journal of Retailing*, *76*(2), 193–218.

Diamantopoulos, A., & Winklhofer, H. M. (2001). Index construction with formative indicators: An alternative to scale development. *Journal of Marketing Research*, *18*, 269–277.

Directive of the European Parliament and of the Council 2006/43/EC on Statutory Audits of Annual Accounts and Consolidated Accounts of 17 May 2006, Official Journal of the European Union L 157, 9/6/2006.

Directive of the European Parliament and of the Council on the Annual And Consolidated Accounts of Certain Types of Companies, Banks and Other Financial Institutions And

Insurance Undertakings (2003/51/EC) of 18 June 2003, Official Journal of the European Union L 178, 17/7/2003.
Directive 2012/6/EU of the European Parliament and of the Council amending Council Directive 78/660/EEC on the Annual accounts of certain types of companies as regards micro-entities. Official Journal of the European Union, 21/3/2012.
Fee survey on the structure and organisation of the accountancy profession across 30 European countries. (2012). Brussels: Fédération des Experts-comptables Européens.
Francis, J. R. (2004). What do we know about audit quality. *The British Accounting Review*, *36*, 345–368.
Geisser, S. (1974). A predictive approach to the random effect model. *Biometrika*, *61*, 101–107.
Hair, J. F., Ringle, C. M., & Sarstedt, M. (2012). PLS-SEM: Indeed a silver bullet. *Long Range Planning*, *45*, 139–151.
Hair, J. F., Sarstedt, M., Ringle, C. M., & Mena, J. A. (2012). An assessment of the use of partial least squares structural equation modeling in marketing research. *Journal of the Academy of Marketing Science*, *40*(3), 414–33.
International Federation of Accountants. (2007). *IFAC policy position paper #1: Regulation of the accountancy profession*. New York: IFAC.
International Federation of Accountants. (2010). *IFAC policy position paper #4: A public interest framework for the accountancy profession*. New York: IFAC.
Key features on structure and organisation of the accountancy profession across 30 European countries. (2012). Brussels: Fédération des Experts-comptables Européens.
Lee, L., Petter, S., Fayard, D., & Robinson, S. (2011). On the use of partial least squares path modeling in accounting research. *International Journal of Accounting Information Systems*, *12*(4), 305–328.
Lohmöller, J. B. (1989). *Latent variable path modeling with partial least squares*. Heidelberg: Physica-Verlag.
Olsen, S. O. (2002). Comparative evaluation and the relationship between quality, satisfaction and repurchase loyalty. *Journal of the Academy of Management*, *30*(3), 240–249.
Palmrose, Z. (1988). An analysis of auditor litigation and audit service quality. *The Accounting Review*, (January), 55–73.
Parasuraman, A., Zeithaml, V., & Berry, L. (1985). A conceptual model of service quality and its implications for future research. *Journal of Marketing*, *49*(3), 41–50.
Parasuraman, A., Zeithaml, V., & Berry, L. (1988). SERVQUAL: A multiple-item scale for measuring consumer perceptions of service quality. *Journal of retailing*, *64*(1), 12–40.
Ringle, C. M., Wende, S., & Will, S. (2005). Smart PLS 2.0 (M3) beta, Hamburg. Retrieved from http://www.smartpls.de
Rossiter, J. R. (2002). The C-OAR-SE procedure for scale development in marketing. *International Journal of Research in Marketing*, *19*, 305–335.
Scott, D. R., & Walt, N. T. (1995). Choice criteria in the selection of international accounting firms. *European Journal of Marketing*, *29*(1), 27–39.
Slovenian Chamber of Commerce – Catalogue of Accounting Firms. (2012). Retrieved from http://www.gzs.si/katalogi/zacetna_stran_kataloga.asp?kat=006
Smith, D., & Langfield-Smith, K. (2004). Structural equation modeling management accounting research: Critical analysis and opportunities. *Journal of Accounting Literature*, *23*, 49–86.
Stone, M. (1974). Cross validity choice and assessment of statistical predictions. *Journal of the Royal Statistical Society, Series B*, *36*, 111–133.

Tenenhaus, M., Vinzi, V. E., Chatelin, Y., & Lauro, C. (2005). PLS path modeling. *Computational Statistics & Data Analysis*, *48*, 159–205.

Vandenbosch, M. B. (1996). Confirmatory compositional approaches to the development of product spaces. *European Journal of Marketing*, *30*, 23–46.

Wold, H. (1982). Soft modeling-the basic design and some extensions. In K. Jöreskog & H. Wold (Eds.), *Systems under indirect observation II* (pp. 1–53). Amsterdam, The Netherlands: North-Holland Press.

Wold, H. (1985). Partial least squares. In S. Kotz & N. L. Johnson (Eds.), *Encyclopedia of statistical sciences* (Vol. 6, pp. 581–591). New York: Wiley.

Zaman Groff, M., Štumberger, N., & Slapničar, S. (2012). The influence of professional qualification on customers' perceived quality of accounting services and retention decision. Retrieved from http://papers.ssrn.com/sol3/papers.cfm?abstract_id=2188578

Zeithaml, V. A. (2000). Service quality, profitability and the economic worth of customers: What we know and what we have to learn. *Journal of Academy of Marketing Science*, *28*(1), 67–85.

APPENDIX: QUESTIONNAIRE

1. **Please indicate whether you have obtained any professional accounting qualification:**
   - ☐ I have obtained the professional qualification from the Chamber of Accounting Services.
   - ☐ I have obtained the professional qualification from the Slovenian Institute of Auditors.
   - ☐ I have no professional qualification.

2. **How many hours of continuous professional training per year do you undertake on average? ______**

3. **To which of the following professional magazines or journals do you subscribed and read regularly?**
   - ☐ Iks (book-keeping and accounting magazine)
   - ☐ Revizor (Auditor)
   - ☐ Obrtnik (Entrepreneur magazine)
   - ☐ Davčni bilten (Tax bulletin)
   - ☐ Pravna praksa (Legal practice)
   - ☐ None of the above

4. **Please evaluate your knowledge in the following areas on a scale from 1 to 5:**

	Very poor	Poor	Modest	Good	Very good
Q4. The Slovenian accounting standards	1	2	3	4	5
Q5. Labour law	1	2	3	4	5
Q6. Taxation and other contributions	1	2	3	4	5
Q7. Financial laws	1	2	3	4	5
Q8. European company law	1	2	3	4	5
Q9. Status law and law of obligations	1	2	3	4	5
Q10. Asset valuation	1	2	3	4	5
Q11. Auditing	1	2	3	4	5
Q12. IFRS	1	2	3	4	5

5. **Please tick the services that you provide to your customers (several answers are possible):**
   - ☐ Book-keeping
   - ☐ Financial analysis
   - ☐ Tax consulting
   - ☐ Financial consulting

- ☐ Budgeting and control
- ☐ Information for business decision making
- ☐ Implementation of accounting information systems
- ☐ Administration (issuance of invoices, etc.)
- ☐ Execution of payment transactions for customers
- ☐ Maintenance of accounting records
- ☐ Administrative support for employment arrangements
- ☐ Administrative support for contract stipulation
- ☐ Support in new business development
- ☐ Consulting on restructuring of the firm
- ☐ Auditing

6. Have you ever been the subject of litigation arising from your error or delayed service which resulted in financial penalty to your customer?

- ☐ Never
- ☐ Once
- ☐ Two times
- ☐ Three times
- ☐ More than three times

7. Please indicate the percentage of your total revenue that you receive from your regular customers? _______

8. Please give your opinion regarding the introduction of mandatory professional accounting qualifications by the law. (Open-ended question)

9. Please indicate your formal education level:

1. Secondary school
2. College (2 years)
3. College (3 years)
4. University degree
5. Master's degree

10. Please indicate your gender:

- ☐ Female
- ☐ Male

ASSESSING ACCOUNTING STUDENTS' ACADEMIC PERFORMANCE: A CASE STUDY ON ROMANIA

Carmen Giorgiana Bonaci, Răzvan V. Mustaţă, Alexandra Muţiu and Jiří Strouhal

ABSTRACT

Purpose – *We propose a research design involving the use of Bloom's taxonomy both in facilitating the teaching–learning process and in the educator assessing students' final grades. The latter are compared with students' self-acknowledged grades. Testing is done by considering a sample of accounting students enrolled for the Controlling course in Romania.*

Methodology/approach – *The employed research methodology relies on two instruments: a questionnaire and the examination process. Cluster analysis is used in analyzing students' grades. Determinants of students' academic performance are discussed by using factor analysis.*

Findings – *Comparing students' self-acknowledged grades with those assessed by the educator, we document the necessity of further work in*

Accounting in Central and Eastern Europe
Research in Accounting in Emerging Economies, Volume 13, 279–319

ISSN: 1479-3563/doi:10.1108/S1479-3563(2013)0000013017

enhancing students' ability to better assess their academic performance. Questions belonging to the application and analysis levels seem to be preferred by students.

Practical implications – *We raise a series of theoretical questions in the area of examination performance. The obtained results in relation to the assessment of accounting students' academic performance and its determinants offer useful insights for accounting educators.*

Originality/value of chapter – *Our chapter tests the use of Bloom's taxonomy in the context of an emerging country's educational system that lacked consistency and faced significant challenges throughout history. We also consider two measures for students' academic performance as perceptions upon what should be the same result of the teaching–learning process. The chapter addresses the evolutions and particularities of the Romanian academic environment in the area of economics, developing a brief analysis meant to position the testing of the proposed research design.*

Keywords: Accounting students; examination performance; Bloom's taxonomy; self-acknowledgment

INTRODUCTION

Accounting students' academic performance represents an important component of the educational process, since it should represent a reflection of students' knowledge, and also an indicator of their intellectual abilities and skills. Chia (2005) even documents that graduate's academic performance represents a significant indicator of future initial job interviews. We must also make reference to Vroom's (1964) expectancy theory, which provides a useful conceptual framework for understanding a student's motivation to strive for academic success (Harrell, Caldwell, & Doty, 1985). Furthermore, by using the within-persons decision-modeling approach, Stahl and Harrell (1981) documented that a student's motivation to strive for academic success is positively correlated with the student's actual behavior (academic performance). The manner in which educators, through the evaluation process, are assessing students' academic performance is therefore extremely important in motivating their future behavior. Moreover, we believe that students should also develop the ability to self-acknowledge their academic performance and gain awareness of their actual status. As a saying goes, *we almost always get what we measure*, the assessment process of students' academic performance should be very carefully considered.

As it is also said that *beauty lies in the eyes of the beholder*, it might be a difficult task to reconcile students' self-acknowledged academic performance with that assessed by the educator. Our chapter therefore analyzes and compares the two reflections of students' academic performance by considering a sample of third year accounting students and the Controlling course. Students' self-acknowledged grades (SSAGs) were obtained with the help of the questionnaire, while their final grades as assessed by the educator were those attributed to them through the final exam for the Controlling course. Bloom's taxonomy was used in developing the examination process that generated students' final grades as assessed by the educator, after previously being used within the teaching–learning process during the semester. Other students' characteristics obtained through the questionnaire were used in order to develop cluster analysis.

The question therefore being posed by our study is what would be the best manner in which we could approach the examination process of accounting students' academic performance? In order to find a suitable answer, we must first think about the outcome, and that would be a *faithful representation* of students' academic performance. Correctly reflecting accounting students' knowledge and their intellectual abilities and skills would represent useful input when considering their future behavior that can represent better academic performance for the following academic years (when considering undergraduates) or a suitable career orientation (when considering graduates). Our chapter proposes the use of Bloom's taxonomy within the evaluation process based on its role of providing the classification of the goals for the educational systems, which we think should also be considered when assessing the output of the educational process in terms of students' academic performance. We further analyze how students' final grades are formed based on the taxonomy's levels.

Our chapter proposes the use of Bloom's taxonomy in order to asses accounting students' academic performance. Since the taxonomy is supposed to provide the classification of the goals for the educational systems, it would only be natural for us to also use it when assessing the results of the educational process. Students' self-acknowledgment is also a component of their behavior that can be analyzed and considered within the educational process. Analyzing and comparing accounting SSAGs with those assessed by the educator can bring some insights in this direction.

The results of our chapter could be useful to accounting educators when considering the evaluation process.

Our chapter further develops a review of literature on accounting students' academic performance (section two) in order to acknowledge the state of the art when it comes to this significant component of the educational process. A synthesis of the evolutions and particularities of the Romanian academic environment in the area of economics (section three) is presented with the purpose of positioning the analysis developed in our chapter. A distinctive component (section four) of the chapter explains the research design, which was used in its development. Within the following part of the chapter (section five), we perform the proposed research design and interpret the obtained results. Some concluding remarks, which synthesize our findings, are presented within the final part of the chapter (section six) together with some research limitations and perspectives.

LITERATURE REVIEW ON ACCOUNTING STUDENTS' ACADEMIC PERFORMANCE

Up-to-date literature considering academic performance in accounting rarely focuses on the examination performance by itself, while in most of the cases emphasizing its correlates. If we look at studies being developed few decades ago, we can find support for multiple-choice testing as an alternative to the traditional "problem" or essay test used for evaluation of academic achievement in accounting courses (Collier & Mehrens, 1985), while also encouraging the development of objective test items for use in the classroom. We must nowadays mention Guney's (2009) study discussing the idea of examination structure, noting that students do care about the way the examination questions are asked, and pleading for a rigorous and pedagogic preparation of examination questions in accounting. Guney (2009) documents that some students show their ability and intellect better in multiple-choice examinations, while some on essay-type examinations. That is why he argues for the use of various formats of examinations that should have the role of mitigating the adverse consequences of a typical exam structure on a specific group of students.

If we are to make a review of how *academic performance* is being *measured* within literature and emphasize the exact term being used, we can conclude that it is through marks (Guney, 2009; Jones & Wright, 2010), grades (Gracia & Jenkins, 2003; Lewis, Shimerda, & Graham, 1983;

Ramburuth & Mladenovic, 2004; Schleifer & Dull, 2009), scores (Fordham & Hayes, 2009; Gardner, Milne, Stringer, & Whiting, 2005; Koh & Koh, 1999), points (Kealey, Holland, & Watson, 2005), and examination results (Bartlett, Peel, & Pendlebury, 1993; Chia, 2005; Duff, 2004; Hartnett, Romcke, & Yap, 2003; Lancaster & Strand, 2001; Lane & Porch, 2002; McDuffie & Smith, 2006; Naser & Peel, 1998; Paisey & Paisey, 2004; Tho, 1994). Jones and Wright (2010) use marks on two questions on the final examination dealing with consolidation accounting, Ramburuth and Mladenovic (2004) use aggregate final grades, Lewis et al. (1983) use grade-point average, and Schleifer and Dull (2009) use a grade-point average scale (4 for an A, 3 for a B, 2 for a C, 1 for a D, and 0 for an E). In accordance with the purpose of each study, authors may consider students' academic performance for one or more years, while looking at one or more subjects (accounting or others). For example, Gracia and Jenkins (2003) use total grade points achieved in all modules studied by each student in the previous academic year, while Koh and Koh (1999) use scores obtained in all the subjects for each of the three years of an accountancy degree program in order to capture a better assessment of their overall academic ability than one or two subjects, and to track their performance over time. Other studies using examination results make reference to the common final exam (Lancaster & Strand, 2001), module performance (Paisey & Paisey, 2004), assessment task (Hartnett et al., 2003), assessment test (Bartlett et al., 1993), and quiz scores (Fordham & Hayes, 2009) or percentage of total points earned on three interim tests and on the final exam (Kealey et al., 2005).

A significant number of studies that were developed over time can be included in the body of literature considering the determinants of academic success in accounting. Therefore, *academic performance* is, most of the times, analyzed as being the *dependent variable* within studies considering correlates of academic performance in accounting. Once again, studies vary in accordance to their main objective, looking at a particular accounting subject or more, at academic performance for different periods, and taking into consideration a series of determinant factors (Bartlett et al., 1993; Duff, 2004; Fox, Stevenson, Connelly, Duff, & Dunlop, 2010; Gardner et al., 2005; Gracia & Jenkins, 2003; Guney, 2009; Hartnett et al., 2003; Jones & Wright, 2010; Kealey et al., 2005; Koh & Koh, 1999; Lancaster & Strand, 2001; McDuffie & Smith, 2006; Naser & Peel, 1998; Paisey & Paisey, 2004; Phillips, 1998; Ramburuth & Mladenovi, 2004; Schleifer & Dull, 2009; Tho, 1994; Watson, Apostolou, Hassell, & Webber, 2007).

First explanatory variables of accounting students' academic performance to be considered in literature comprised educational, demographic, and/or financial characteristics variables (Bartlett et al., 1993; Tho, 1994). Primarily developed in the United States, the substantial literature considering the determinants of academic success in accounting focused on gender, prior knowledge of accounting, academic aptitude, and mathematics, producing largely inconclusive results (Duff, 2004). Phillips (1998) notes that in accounting education research, cognitive style and ability have received the greatest attention when assessing performance. A review of accounting education literature by Watson et al. (2007) includes a discussion of learning styles and technology (Tho, 1994). For example, McDuffie and Smith (2006) address the particular use of an audit reporting system as a teaching aid and its impact on students' performance. Koh and Koh (1999) investigate the impact of six variables (namely, gender, prior accounting knowledge, academic aptitude, mathematics background, previous working experience, and age) on the performance of students in a three-year accountancy degree program. Lancaster and Strand (2001) investigate academic performance and student perceptions regarding the cooperative learning format. Further studies consider a blend of data from demographic, attitudinal, and behavioral sources, effectiveness of accounting students' approaches to learning being often considered (Booth, Luckett, & Mladenovic, 1999; Byrne, Flood, & Willis, 2002; Duff, 2004; Gardner et al., 2005; Gracia & Jenkins, 2003; Hartnett et al., 2003; Paisey & Paisey, 2004; Tan & Choo, 1990).

We will furthermore mention a few particular approaches and factors considered when analyzing accounting students' academic performance. Paisey and Paisey (2004) focus on two aspects of student attendance, namely, the reasons why some students do not attend classes, and the issue of whether attendance improves academic performance, documenting a clear positive relationship between attendance at classes and subsequent academic performance. Gardner et al. (2005) look for associations between levels of communication apprehension and students' abilities to advance in their studies or average levels of academic performance, but fail to document it.

As previously mentioned, studies can also be grouped by considering a certain accounting subject when analyzing academic performance. This is the case for Naser and Peel (1998) and Kealey et al. (2005), who focused on determinants of student performance in a Principles of Accounting course. Naser and Peel (1998) examined the impact of a number of new attitudinal variables on examination performance, documenting that student perceptions of factors associated with class size, the attributes of the lecturer, student effort, and the complexity of the course are associated with student performance in a first level Principles of Accounting course. Meanwhile, Kealey et al. (2005) document that critical-thinking skills contribute significantly to explaining the cross-sectional variation in student performance in an Accounting Principles class. A more particular factor such as paper color was also considered by Michael and Jones (1955) and further analyzed by Fordham and Hayes (2009).

Guney (2009) also develops a classification for the determinants of academic performance in accounting employing student-oriented endogenous factors (e.g., age, gender), as well as student-exogenous factors (e.g., quality of teaching, examination structure). And finally, we will refer to the recent studies on accounting students' academic performance. Schleifer and Dull (2009) consider metacognition as an important aspect of self-regulated learning and therefore having potential as a learning skill or attribute that can serve to improve accounting education and performance. Fox et al. (2010) consider the impact of a student peer-mentoring program on first-year undergraduates' academic performance, while Jones and Wright (2010) extend previous work by combining the effect of cognitive style and the use or non-use of two versions of a hypertext learning aid and their interaction on student performance in Advanced Financial Accounting.

While considering literature on accounting students' academic performance, we must also mention those cases when *academic performance represents an explanatory variable* or a determinant factor for another considered dependent variable. It is mostly the case of studies in job search, such as Chia (2005) and Lewis et al. (1983). Chia (2005) investigates the effects of academic performance, extracurricular activities, and emotional intelligence of potential accounting-major graduates on the outcomes of their respective interviewing activities and the number of final job offers given by the multinational Big 5 public accounting firms. His results document that the number of initial job interviews is affected by both a graduate's academic performance and level of participation in extracurricular activities.

Overall, the above presented studies approach academic performance even though the criterion of success being defined differently in each case, as Gammie, Jones, and Robertson-Millar (2003) also comment on previous academic performance that was documented to be a statistically significant indicator of university performance. Therefore, in many cases, due to the limited information supplied in the studies in relation to the precise specification of the independent variables, it is difficult to compare the predictor variables.

Our study proposes the use of Bloom's taxonomy in assessing accounting students' academic performance. Bloom's taxonomy has received considerable international recognition within the evaluation community (Lewy & Bathory, 1994). This was mainly due to the fact that the taxonomy was soon after its introduction used within seminars at the United Nations Educational, Scientific, and Cultural Organization (UNESCO) and the Organization for Economic Cooperation and Development (OECD) (Athanassiou, McNett, & Harvey, 2003, p. 535). A review of literature indicates a growing awareness of the taxonomy's potential usefulness and richness among college and university level educators (Athanassiou et al., 2003, p. 537). The taxonomy can be used in developing the curriculum design process, students' assessment process, and instruction evaluation. Until recently, the taxonomy has been largely used within the teaching process, Stokes (2008) documenting how authors of 24 accounting textbooks used verbs at the lower levels of the cognitive domain.

THE ROMANIAN ACADEMIC ENVIRONMENT: EVOLUTIONS AND PARTICULARITIES IN THE AREA OF ECONOMICS

Before explaining the research design applied in developing our chapter, we consider it useful to briefly position the analysis from a temporal and geographical point of view. We will therefore further present a synthesis of the evolutions and particularities of the Romanian academic environment in the area of economics.

The first regulations to mention how accounting should be conducted in the Romanian Principalities[1] and that public accounting should be regulated, date from 1831 and 1832. These would be the organic norms that represented the milestone regulations in the governing process at that time. It is only 40 years later, after the War of Independence in 1877–1878, that we can speak about the fundaments of a modern economy, marking the beginning of the Romanian accounting thinking (Tiron-Tudor & Muţiu, 2007, p. 212). The history of Romanian commercial schools starts in 1888 when a small number of graduates of the commercial school met and put the basis of *the society of commercial and financial schools graduates* (General Review of Commerce and Accounting (*ro. Revista Generală de Comerţ şi Contabilitate* – RGCC), 1916, p. 35). Writings dated in 1907 mention that in that year, two commercial school graduates organizations existed that later merged into creating *the Body of the High Commerce Schools Graduates*. It was this organization that fostered the initial work on the regulation of the accounting profession (RGCC, 1916, p. 176). The Academy of High Commercial and Industrial Studies was set up in Bucharest in 1913, which was to become a university in 1930. It was between 1933 and 1939 that the Romanian accounting school developed through promoters such as Spiridon Iacobescu, C.G. Demetrescu, and Ion Evian. That period is characterized through the development of scientific controversies, the scientific debate being launched by professors Spiridon Iacobescu and Alexandru Sorescu in their work *General commercial accounting course*, followed by the work of professor Ion Evian, *Theories of accounts (ro. Teoria conturilor)* (1940). Their work generated debates, which had a beneficial effect on Romanian accounting research, creating a stimulating environment for Romanian academics. Accounting became more diversified as the economy grew and accounting developments increased dramatically.

After the Second World War, accounting was impacted in a way that did not have any precedent. A new reform was imposed through the Soviet accounting system, a monist system based on rules and not on professional judgment, created only for Controlling and used only for statistical purposes. Therefore, the term "accounting" was replaced, according to the Soviet model, with "bookkeeping" and concepts like "plan" and "planning" became more in fashion, being present in more and more writings. A new list of accounts for socialist enterprises, inspired from the Soviet model, was introduced as mandatory for all Romanian entities. The censure imposed through the transformations taking place on a political, economic, and social level, together with the exclusion of professor Evian[2] from the academic environment, contributed to the death of scientific debates (Calu, 2005). The idea of practice prevailing theory was encouraged and scientific debates taking place during students' workshops started to focus on narrow situations being faced by enterprises. Inductive research rather than deductive research was promoted (Calu, 2005). Since 1948 the Romanian accounting environment was therefore absent of academic dialog and its fruitful debates, becoming completely "devoted" to the soviet economic system until 1989. Year 1990, representing the first year of liberty from an economic, social, political, and cultural point of view, also brought significant transformations in terms of accounting regulations and practice. The 1990–1993 period was an intermediary one between the old system and the newly desired accounting system inspired by the French one. The initial reform was followed by the Romanian program of developing the accounting system in Romania, carcfully conducted starting since 1997 in collaboration with the Institute of Chartered Accountants of Scotland and funded by the

Know How Fund for Romania. This period is characterized by the openness of the accounting toward the international reality. The reform of the economic universities that started in 1998 was centered on the idea of having the university as a high research center that provides applicable research results. The strategic objectives of the economic universities were focused on developing and amplifying research results from universities that were obtained in previous periods and to reach the targets imposed by the European Union in order to be able to integrate the national economic system into the European one.

Through the Bologna common declaration, Romania undertook the task of aligning its educational system to the European Union's standards until 2005. This could only be done by creating big university consortium resulted through the merger of many universities within a unitary system and by adopting educational programs that are adapted to economic realities. The Bologna declaration (1999) materializes the *Magna Charta Universitatum* adopted in 1998 in Bologna by European universities, as well as the *Sorbonne Declaration* (1998), including multiple purposes such as creating the *European university space*, developing a compatible European educational systems and reorganizing university studies in order to have compatible qualifications in different countries and adapt them to the needs expressed in the market. One of the main objectives of the university education reform aimed the development of human resources and adaptation to the requirements of medium- and long-term economic development. Universities in Romania therefore started the process of adapting their curricula to the standards imposed by the European Union in order to adapt their educational offer to the labor market in our country, as well as in Europe. This also brought significant challenges for the Romanian academic environment in the area of economics, the main preoccupations in accounting education being linked to offering programs that fulfilled the international standards and to providing the necessary education for an accounting graduate.

In order to fulfill such educational needs, the Association of Economics Faculties in Romania (AFER) was founded in 2005, having as main objective to support the ongoing development of academic education with the help of The Chamber of Financial Auditors of Romania (CAFR) and The Body of Expert Accountants and Authorized Accountants of Romania (CECCAR) (Mutiu & Matis, 2010, p. 180). In 2006, these institutions started to work on improving the Romanian accounting academic system by implementing the International Educational Standards (IESs) in the curriculum of faculties of economics, and additionally by working on competencies aimed for bachelor and master's degrees in the accounting specializations. The ongoing process of accounting education's development in Romania has been observed in time by the World Bank and United States Agency for International Development (USAID) who played an active role by monitoring this process. The World Bank's Reports on the Observance of Standards and Codes (ROSC) issued in 2003 and 2009 noted that Romania has done considerable improvements and offered recommendations for future developments. Regarding education and training, the 2009 ROSC report states that universities (except for the Academy of Economic Studies in Bucharest) should enhance their accounting and audit curricula and seek for their graduates exemptions from examinations by international accounting qualification providers (World Bank, 2009, para 100).

Diaconu (2008) analyzes the success of the curriculum's alignment with the IESs by using a matrix to compare the educational curriculum of selected universities by name and supposed content of the disciplines with the international requirements. The study took into consideration all the disciplines included in the curriculum, including the optional and facultative ones. The analyzed universities were the most representative ones in Romania in terms of number of students, history, infrastructure, and research projects. His conclusions point out that the Babeş-Bolyai University held the first place within the classification, with an 83% of cohesion, followed by the Academy of Economic Studies with 78%, Transylvania University Brasov with 65%, and Romanian-American University in Bucharest with 57% of cohesion with IESs. The Babeş-Bolyai University, through its Faculty of Economics and Business Administration (FSEGA), therefore succeeded to become the number one faculty within the country in terms of accounting curriculum development. Having an accounting curriculum almost harmonized with IESs represents a great achievement for its students (Mutiu & Matis, 2010, p. 182).

Our chapter brings support to the reform process, which we still consider to be ongoing, by focusing on the factors that impact the outcome of the educational process in the particular case of accounting students and their teaching–learning process.

RESEARCH DESIGN

Developing the analysis of our research project involves the use of two distinctive instruments: a questionnaire and the examination process that will further be described.

In order to develop the analysis that was aimed through our study, we implemented a *questionnaire* on a sample of accounting students. Choosing the students was done based on our intention of continuing our research in the area of accounting students' academic performance by considering the same group of students who were investigated a year ago when considering a different course (Financial Accounting). This group comprises students within a three years accounting program of Babeş-Bolyai University in Cluj-Napoca, Romania. We therefore aimed a group of 389 students in their third university year, at the end of the first semester. The questionnaire was only administered to a number of 367 students who took the final exam in Controlling during the 2009 winter exam session period. We finally ended up in using a number of 316 questionnaires for this study. We eliminated those questionnaires that either were missing a significant number of filled questions (which we considered to be 10 out of a total of 29) or had no response for the last question of the questionnaire. This last question required students to self-acknowledge their grade for the Controlling final exam, which they had just taken.

The questionnaire was implemented after a 14-week period of educational activities comprising courses and seminars. Controlling courses and seminars were structured during the semester based on Bloom's taxonomy. Students were required to read the materials assigned for the classes and to do not more than three problems or exercises per week as homework. The scope of the seminar was to check the comprehension of the material assigned to be read and to apply the theory to a specific situation. Courses were designed to exercise students' abilities to analyze, synthesize, and evaluate a given case study.

A particularity of our study is that implementing the questionnaire was correlated with students' actual examination through written final exam during the exam session period. Students attending the final exam in Controlling were presented with two sets of documents. Each set was stapled and comprised A4 format white paper and a cover page. The cover page presented a series of distinctive elements such as name of the course, research project, date, and so on. One set comprised the exam questions and its cover page included a small red square (20-cm side). The other set comprised the questionnaire and its cover page included a small blue square (20-cm side). The cover page for the exam questions required students to fill in their personal information (name) in a particular designed space, while the cover page for the questionnaire did not ask for students' identity. Moreover, students were instructed that the questionnaires were anonymous in order to ensure the objectivity of their answers. Students were allocated separate time required for responding to the exam questions and for filling in the questionnaire. This information was clearly explained to them after handing the two sets of documents. At the end of the allocated time, students were asked to place their questionnaires in a distinctive set that was separated from that of the exam documents.

As previously mentioned, the questionnaire was formulated in such a manner that did not allow for the identity of the respondent to be reviled. Still, in order for us to be able to develop our analysis, we needed to correlate each student's questionnaire with its corresponding exam documents, which reflected the academic performance. This had to initially be done without students knowing of it with the purpose of maintaining their objectivity. This was the reason for posting a particular code on the cover page of students' exam documents in a manner that would not receive students' attention. The same code was posted on the questionnaire set of documents. When distributing the two sets of documents to students, each student received the two sets bearing the same code. This allowed us to match each student's questionnaire with the corresponding exam documents. The information obtained through the questionnaire was not used until the beginning of the next semester when students were told about the used code system and asked for their written acceptance in order for us to use the information they had provided within our research project. All students within our sample gave their approval in order for us to use the information they provided through the questionnaire and also their examination information for Controlling.

Questions within the questionnaire were formulated in relation to a series of determinants of accounting students' academic performance as identified through literature. The questionnaire was structured on two distinctive components. The first component comprised 11 questions that had a general character. The second component comprised 18 specific questions asking students to relate to the particular Controlling course. The final question within the questionnaire asked students to self-asses their grade for the Controlling final exam they had just taken and express it in accordance to the Romanian grading system (grades ranging from 0 to 10, where 10 represents the maximum possible grade). Their answers to this final question actually represented SSAG, which we used in developing our study.

As previously mentioned, Controlling courses and seminars were structured during the semester based on Bloom's taxonomy. It was the taxonomy that also helped us structure the exam questions for the above-mentioned Controlling final exam. Students' *examination process* was therefore in deep correlation with the way students learned during the semester. Our arguments for using Bloom's taxonomy refer to its structure that offers a very clear tool of testing students' knowledge and abilities on a continuous basis, while generating clear feedback on what they have to do further in order to develop their learning process. We also consider that grounding the teaching and evaluation process on Bloom's taxonomy gives educators a basis of comparison between the effective level being achieved during the semester and the goal of the educational system. We will further outline some main aspects related to Boom's taxonomy.

In 1956, a committee of college and university examiners published the classification of educational goals under the name of *Taxonomy Educational Objectives: The Classification of Educational Goals. Handbook 1. Cognitive Domain.* The editor of the material was Benjamin S. Bloom from the University of Chicago. The committee's scope was to build a taxonomy of educational objectives, which would provide the classification of the goals for the educational systems. "It is expected to be of general help to all teachers, administrators, professional specialists, and research workers who deal with curricular and evaluation problems. It is especially intended to help them discuss these problems with greater precision" (Bloom, 1956, p. 1). This is referred to as the original taxonomy. After 45 years, the taxonomy was revised. We developed our research based on the original taxonomy.

The original taxonomy of educational objectives related to cognitive domain is structured on two levels: knowledge and intellectual abilities and skills. The first level, knowledge, "involves the recall of specifics and universals, the recall of methods and processes, or the recall of a pattern, structure, or setting" (Bloom, 1956, p. 201).

The second level, intellectual abilities and skills, refers to organized modes of operation and generalized techniques for dealing with materials and problems (Bloom, 1956, p. 201). Materials and problems can have different natures: some of them may require special information and techniques, and some may require general information, which can be assumed to be part of the individual's general fund of knowledge. This level refers to the mental process of organizing and working with the materials and problems in order to achieve a purpose. In order to be able to work with information, this level is based on five sublevels:

1. *Comprehension of material and problem*: comprehension represents the lowest level of understanding. It is related with the ability of understanding what is being communicated and conveying the idea further without necessarily connecting it with other ideas or materials.

2. *Application*: this refers to the ability and skills needed to apply general rules, procedures, and methods called abstractions to a specific situation. To be applied, abstractions need to be remembered first.
3. *Analysis*: this implies to break the material and problem into parts and to analyze them separately and then in correlation with other factors. The scope of this phase is to understand how the initial material was build.
4. *Synthesis* represents the process of combining the material's parts using a new structure, clearer than before.
5. *Evaluation* represents the process of judging the materials for a given purpose. Usually, this phase requires quantitative and qualitative judgments and very often the given purpose is not indicated by the material and has to be identified by the evaluator.

Our study assesses accounting students' academic performance by using an evaluation grid that was structured based on the above presented taxonomy. The content of the discipline was divided into four main parts: marginal analysis, cost–volume–profit analysis, budgeting, and activity-based costing. We tested each part's content based on students' knowledge and their ability to comprehend, apply, analyze, and synthesize. We used closed and open questions and also multiple choice questions, therefore applying various formats of examinations, as advised within literature (Guney, 2009). Open questions approached theoretical aspects and problems whose calculation needed to be detailed by students in order to be graded. The last level within Bloom's taxonomy was tested by using a case study where students had to reach a certain conclusion, which also had to be presented in writing and argued for. The maximum grade that could be obtained (10 points) was structured by considering the taxonomy's five levels (comprehension – 2.25 points, application – 2.25 points, analysis – 2.25 points, synthesis – 2.25 points, and evaluation – 1 point).

After developing the two methodological instruments that were described above, we proceeded with implementing our analysis. Descriptive analysis was performed for the whole sample of students. Correlation analysis was used when considering the two reflections of students' academic performance (students' final grade as assessed by the educator and SSAG). Both descriptive analysis and correlation analysis were also performed on clusters in order to obtain more insights on students' academic performance. The obtained results are presented within the following part of our chapter.

Beyond analyzing students' academic performance, we have also developed a detailed analysis of what we may consider as determinant factors of this performance. Using the information we gathered through the questionnaire, factor analysis was employed in this regard. The total number of questions and therefore elements initially being considered is 29. Another element that can be added when considering students within our sample is their gender. Considering the fact that some of the questions being used comprised sub-questions, we ended up by considering a number of 35 distinct elements for the analysis being developed. Through the developed factor analysis, only 27 questions and namely 32 elements were retained. In order to identify determinant factors of students' academic performance, we have used principal component analysis (PCA), and as for factor scores, the Anderson-Rubin method has been used. Moreover, the developed factor analysis employed 176 valid questions among the total number of respondents.

DEVELOPING THE ANALYSIS AND INTERPRETING RESULTS

Based on previously mentioned methodological aspects, we have further implemented the analysis aimed through the development of this study. This analysis is based on two distinctive dimensions. The first one refers to students' academic performance and the other refers to a series of answers that were offered by students through the questionnaire that was implemented after their examination process through the final exam for Controlling. It was based on these answers that we developed cluster analysis, which allows us to look at students' academic performance more coherently, and in a more detailed manner.

Therefore, the answers that were provided by students through the implemented questionnaire represent the basis for our developing of seven distinctive clusters. The first cluster actually comprises our entire population of students participating in our research project that includes 316 cases (students) being observed. The following clusters are built based on a series of factors that are considered by literature as determinants of students' academic performance and therefore were used in formulating questions within the implemented questionnaire. We will further present the factors determining each of the considered clusters. The second cluster can be called the *gender cluster* due to the fact that it groups respondents based on their gender. Results point the fact that our sample population is mainly formed out of females, representing 86% of the respondents. Another cluster considers students' previous high school characteristics, separating students who went to a high school with economic profile, therefore having previous encounters with accounting disciplines. We therefore separated students who went to a high school with economic profile from those who did not based on the answers they provided. The results being obtained based on this separation show a relative balance between the two sub-clusters.

Another aspect that was analyzed through one of our questionnaire's component is whether students already had some previous working experience in the field of accounting. Two sub-clusters have therefore been created, the first comprising students with previous working experience in the field of accounting. This time results show a major unbalance, the number of students having no previous working experience in the field of accounting being significantly higher. Considering the same topic of accounting practice, students were also asked whether they intend to develop a career in the field of accounting after graduating. This time, almost 90% of our respondents declared they have this intention for their future professional development.

The following two clusters refer to students' attitude toward the accounting specialization to which they currently belong. The first cluster looks at how students became part of the accounting specialization and separates those students who became accounting students as a result of their own wish from those who were determined to do so by their close company or were even "victims" of the faculty distribution process. We can notice that 257 students out of the total 316, meaning 83.44% of them, declared to have chosen the accounting specialization based on their own wish. Our last cluster looks at students' satisfaction related to the accounting specialization at the moment of the questionnaire's implementation. Results show that those declaring to be unsatisfied with the accounting specialization they currently belong to only represent 9.71%. This value is lower than that representing students who did not initially wish to become accounting students (16.56%), suggesting that some of the students have come to be satisfied with the accounting specialization even if this was not their first option when faced with choosing their future specialization, as they were in the past.

We should also mention the fact that out of the total 367 questionnaires that were implemented, we only ended up using 316. This was due to some questionnaires being incompletely filled and eliminated from the analysis, as explained in "Research Design" section. Moreover, as Table 1 shows, the number of cases being analyzed when considering different clusters might also differ from the total number of questionnaires finally being kept

Table 1. Students' Academic Performance Analysis.

Clusters		Correlations	Values				Percentage				Cases
	Bloom comp.		Min	Max	Mean	SD	Min	Max	Mean	SD	No.
Panel A											
	Pearson	0.567^{**}									316
	Spearman	0.589^{**}									316
	SAFG		0.250	9.450	4.934	2.203					316
	SSAG		2.000	10.000	7.487	1.303					316
	Comprehension		0.000	2.250	1.084	0.683	0.00	0.63	0.20	0.110	316
	Application		0.000	2.250	1.266	0.632	0.00	1.00	0.26	0.122	316
	Analysis		0.000	2.250	1.306	0.690	0.00	0.75	0.25	0.113	316
	Synthesis		0.000	2.250	1.095	0.580	0.00	1.00	0.23	0.127	316
	Evaluation		0.000	1.000	0.181	0.202	0.00	0.32	0.03	0.043	316
Panel B											
Gender	Pearson	0.365^{*}									42
Male	Spearman	0.351^{*}									42
	SAFG		0.250	8.470	3.953	2.091					42
	SSAG		3.000	10.000	7.238	1.494					42
	Comprehension		0.000	1.875	0.875	0.552	0.00	0.63	0.21	0.133	42
	Application		0.000	2.250	1.019	0.656	0.00	1.00	0.27	0.158	42
	Analysis		0.000	2.250	1.047	0.736	0.00	0.50	0.23	0.136	42
	Synthesis		0.000	2.070	0.842	0.482	0.00	0.71	0.23	0.153	42
	Evaluation		0.000	1.000	0.169	0.212	0.00	0.32	0.04	0.068	42
Gender	Pearson	0.608^{**}									262
Female	Spearman	0.617^{**}									262

	SAFG		0.250	9.450	5.132	2.211					262
	SSAG		4.000	10.000	7.561	1.235					262
	Comprehension		0.000	2.250	1.120	0.705	0.00	0.59	0.20	0.106	262
	Application		0.000	2.250	1.312	0.628	0.00	1.00	0.26	0.114	262
	Analysis		0.000	2.250	1.367	0.671	0.00	0.75	0.26	0.109	262
	Synthesis		0.000	2.250	1.143	0.589	0.00	1.00	0.23	0.123	262
	Evaluation		0.000	1.000	0.188	0.204	0.00	0.23	0.03	0.038	262
Panel C											
Prior economic high school	Pearson	0.509**									146
	Spearman	0.408**									146
	SAFG		0.250	8.770	4.705	2.156					146
	SSAG		2.000	10.000	7.465	1.303					146
	Comprehension		0.000	2.250	1.056	0.651	0.00	0.59	0.20	0.108	146
	Application		0.000	2.250	1.166	0.628	0.00	1.00	0.26	0.142	146
	Analysis		0.000	2.250	1.276	0.709	0.00	0.61	0.26	0.120	146
	Synthesis		0.000	2.250	1.050	0.566	0.00	1.00	0.23	0.132	146
	Evaluation		0.000	0.900	0.156	0.178	0.00	0.32	0.03	0.045	146
No prior economic high school	Pearson	0.616**									170
	Spearman	0.635**									170
	SAFG		0.700	9.450	5.131	2.230					170
	SSAG		3.000	10.000	7.505	1.306					170
	Comprehension		0.000	2.250	1.109	0.710	0.00	0.63	0.20	0.113	170
	Application		0.000	2.250	1.351	0.625	0.00	0.67	0.26	0.101	170
	Analysis		0.000	2.250	1.332	0.673	0.00	0.75	0.25	0.108	170
	Synthesis		0.000	2.250	1.134	0.591	0.00	0.81	0.22	0.123	170
	Evaluation		0.000	1.000	0.203	0.219	0.00	0.23	0.04	0.041	170

Table 1. *(Continued)*

Clusters	Bloom comp.	Correlations	Values Min	Values Max	Values Mean	Values SD	Percentage Min	Percentage Max	Percentage Mean	Percentage SD	Cases No.
Panel D											
Prior professional experience	Pearson	0.524**									73
	Spearman	0.621**									73
	SAFG		0.700	9.450	5.274	2.047					73
	SSAG		2.000	10.000	7.863	1.283					73
	Comprehension		0.000	2.250	1.117	0.605	0.00	0.42	0.20	0.090	73
	Application		0.250	2.250	1.379	0.589	0.00	0.62	0.27	0.104	73
	Analysis		0.000	2.250	1.408	0.647	0.00	0.50	0.26	0.096	73
	Synthesis		0.000	2.250	1.177	0.559	0.00	0.56	0.22	0.091	73
	Evaluation		0.000	1.000	0.191	0.217	0.00	0.14	0.03	0.034	73
No prior professional experience	Pearson	0.573**									243
	Spearman	0.578**									243
	SAFG		0.250	9.225	4.832	2.241					243
	SSAG		3.000	10.000	7.374	1.290					243
	Comprehension		0.000	2.250	1.074	0.705	0.00	0.63	0.20	0.116	243
	Application		0.000	2.250	1.231	0.641	0.00	1.00	0.26	0.127	243
	Analysis		0.000	2.250	1.276	0.700	0.00	0.75	0.25	0.118	243
	Synthesis		0.000	2.250	1.070	0.585	0.00	1.00	0.23	0.136	243
	Evaluation		0.000	1.000	0.178	0.198	0.00	0.32	0.03	0.045	243
Panel E											
No future professional accounting activity	Pearson	−0.030									32
	Spearman	0.018									32

	SAFG		0.250	7.970	3.342	1.736					32
	SSAG		5.000	10.000	6.906	1.201					32
	Comprehension		0.000	1.875	0.712	0.600	0.00	0.63	0.19	0.151	32
	Application		0.000	1.950	0.885	0.577	0.00	1.00	0.28	0.188	32
	Analysis		0.000	2.075	0.820	0.563	0.00	0.61	0.23	0.141	32
	Synthesis		0.000	2.070	0.820	0.493	0.00	0.51	0.25	0.131	32
	Evaluation		0.000	0.300	0.103	0.112	0.00	0.14	0.03	0.039	32
Future professional accounting activity	Pearson	0.600**									284
	Spearman	0.616**									284
	SAFG		0.250	9.450	5.114	2.180					284
	SSAG		2.000	10.000	7.552	1.299					284
	Comprehension		0.000	2.250	1.126	0.680	0.00	0.59	0.20	0.105	284
	Application		0.000	2.250	1.308	0.624	0.00	1.00	0.26	0.112	284
	Analysis		0.000	2.250	1.361	0.682	0.00	0.75	0.26	0.110	284
	Synthesis		0.000	2.250	1.12	0.582	0.00	1.00	0.22	0.127	284
	Evaluation		0.000	1.000	0.190	0.209	0.00	0.32	0.03	0.043	284
Panel F											
Personal option for accounting specialization	Pearson	0.544**									257
	Spearman	0.584**									257
	SAFG		0.250	9.450	5.157	2.167					257
	SSAG		2.000	10.000	7.622	1.253					257
	Comprehension		0.000	2.250	1.145	0.670	0.00	0.59	0.21	0.105	257
	Application		0.000	2.250	1.312	0.623	0.00	1.00	0.26	0.114	257
	Analysis		0.000	2.250	1.388	0.662	0.00	0.75	0.26	0.111	257
	Synthesis		0.000	2.250	1.118	0.586	0.00	0.59	0.21	0.108	257
	Evaluation		0.000	1.000	0.191	0.213	0.00	0.32	0.03	0.044	257

Table 1. *(Continued)*

Clusters	Bloom comp.	Correlations	Values Min	Values Max	Values Mean	Values SD	Percentage Min	Percentage Max	Percentage Mean	Percentage SD	Cases No.
No personal option for accounting specialization	Pearson	0.542**									51
	Spearman	0.584**									51
	SAFG		0.625	8.820	4.122	1.987					51
	SSAG		3.000	10.000	6.862	1.280					51
	Comprehension		0.000	2.050	0.864	0.665	0.00	0.63	0.19	0.131	51
	Application		0.000	2.250	1.131	0.598	0.00	0.76	0.28	0.151	51
	Analysis		0.000	2.250	0.989	0.703	0.00	0.42	0.21	0.109	51
	Synthesis		0.000	2.070	1.005	0.546	0.00	0.71	0.26	0.138	51
	Evaluation		0.000	0.400	0.131	0.110	0.00	0.11	0.03	0.030	51
Panel G											
Negative attitude for accounting specialization	Pearson	0.035									29
	Spearman	0.044									29
	SAFG		0.250	6.875	2.965	1.475					29
	SSAG		4.000	10.000	6.931	1.412					29
	Comprehension		0.000	1.725	0.527	0.519	0.00	0.37	0.15	0.118	29
	Application		0.250	1.950	0.793	0.488	0.11	1.00	0.29	0.174	29
	Analysis		0.000	2.000	0.822	0.593	0.00	0.67	0.26	0.176	29
	Synthesis		0.000	1.525	0.704	0.479	0.00	0.56	0.24	0.165	29
	Evaluation		0.000	0.500	0.117	0.158	0.00	0.27	0.04	0.068	29
Positive attitude for accounting specialization	Pearson	0.599**									287
	Spearman	0.614**									287
	SAFG		0.250	9.450	5.133	2.168					287
	SSAG		2.000	10.000	7.543	1.28					287

Comprehension	0.000	2.250	1.141	0.673	0.00	0.63	0.21	0.108	287
Application	0.000	2.250	1.313	0.626	0.00	1.00	0.26	0.115	287
Analysis	0.000	2.250	1.355	0.681	0.00	0.75	0.25	0.106	287
Synthesis	0.000	2.250	1.135	0.575	0.00	1.00	0.22	0.123	287
Evaluation	0.000	1.000	0.188	0.206	0.00	0.32	0.03	0.040	287

Notes: Panel A comprises the whole sample of students being analyzed. SSAG, students' self-acknowledged grade; SAFG, students' assessed final grade.
**Correlation is significant at the 0.01 level (two-tailed).

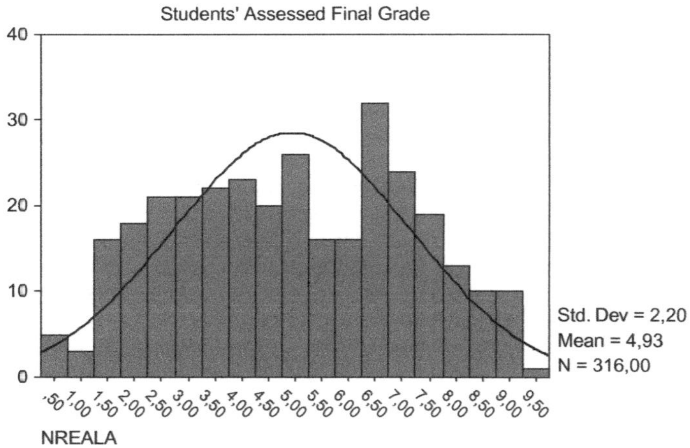

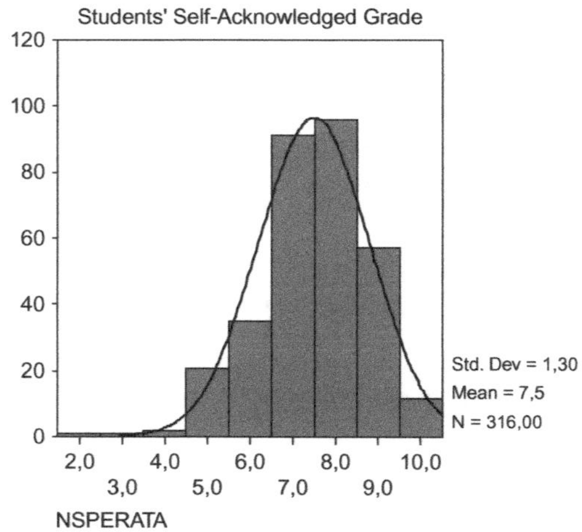

Panel B groups respondents based on their gender. SSAG, students' self-acknowledged grade; SAFG, students' assessed final grade.
*Correlation is significant at the 0.05 level (two-tailed).
**Correlation is significant at the 0.01 level (two-tailed).

Panel C divides students into two categories as follows: the first category comprises students who went to a high school with economic profile previous to university and the second comprises the other students. SSAG, students' self-acknowledged grade; SAFG, students' assessed final grade.
**Correlation is significant at the 0.01 level (two-tailed).
Panel D considers whether students have previous working experience in the field of accounting. SSAG, students' self-acknowledged grade; SAFG, students' assessed final grade.
**Correlation is significant at the 0.01 level (two-tailed).
Panel E groups students based on their intention of pursuing a future career in the field of accounting after graduation. SSAG, students' self-acknowledged grade; SAFG, students' assessed final grade.
**Correlation is significant at the 0.01 level (two-tailed).
Panel F considers whether students are part of the accounting specialization as a result of their own choice or as a consequence of other determinant factors (the influence of their environment or the result of the faculty distribution process). SSAG, students' self-acknowledged grade; SAFG, students' assessed final grade.
**Correlation is significant at the 0.01 level (two-tailed).
Panel G considers students' grouping into two categories based on their satisfaction degree related to the accounting specialization they are part of. SSAG, students' self-acknowledged grade; SAFG, students' assessed final grade.
**Correlation is significant at the 0.01 level (two-tailed).

for analysis within the study. We refer here to clusters comprising less than the 316 students due to eliminating those students who did not answer the question that actually represented the factor that helped us establish a certain cluster. For example, 12 students forgot to mention their gender when answering the questionnaire. As a consequence, Panel B only comprises a number of 304 students.

Moving forward, another aspect that should be discussed is students' academic performance. We have appealed within our study to using two distinctive instruments in order to measure academic success or performance. On the one hand, we used students' final grade as assessed by the educator (the SAFG variable) and on the other their self-acknowledged grade (the SSAG variable). We meanwhile consider that both instruments being used in measuring students' academic performance actually represent two distinctive perceptions upon what should be the same result of the teaching–learning process. We therefore question and analyze these two perceptions on the evaluation process while also making use of Bloom's taxonomy. The obtained results are interpreted in correlation and based on variables obtained through the implemented questionnaire.

A first step of our study would be to analyze the correlation degree between the two grades used in measuring accounting students' academic performance while also considering cluster analysis. We furthermore analyzed the manner in which students' final grades as assessed by the educator were formed when considering the levels of Bloom's taxonomy. We therefore calculated the *percentage* representing the weight of each level of Bloom's taxonomy in generating students' final grade (SAFG).

We might say that some of the obtained results are unexpected and reflect particularities of the analyzed environment. First, when referring to the whole group of students being analyzed (Panel A), we may be expected a high level of students' subjectivity in assessing their self-acknowledged grade to make it difficult to establish a correlation between their assessment (SSAG) and that of the educator (SAFG). Obtained results document that such a correlation exists and records a medium level. The analyzed correlation could not be documented for the group of students who were not planning on pursuing a future career in the field of accounting (Panel E) and also for the group of students who presented a negative attitude toward the accounting specialization as being unsatisfied with it (Panel G). When looking at the graph that reflects grades' distribution for the two considered measurement instruments of accounting students' academic performance (SAFG and SSAG), we can conclude that students' expectation for their grades as based on their self-acknowledgment is higher in comparison to the actual grade being granted by the educator. This for sure we kind of expected as a result of the comparison. When considering students' final grades as assessed by the educator, our sample records a mean grade of 4.93, while the mean for SSAGs is 7.50. We consider the difference between the two calculated means to be significant because the evaluation process measures grades on a scale from 0 to 10. The obtained results therefore identify a significant need for educators to work on improving students' ability to acknowledge their own academic performance.

When analyzing students' final grades as assessed by the educator, we notice that none of the students received the maximum grade (10). Meanwhile, 12 students responded they were expecting to obtain a 10, as mention through their self-acknowledged grade. The highest grade being granted by the educator was 9.45 and belonged to a female student. Cluster analysis points the fact that the highest grade being granted by the educator to a male student was 8.47, with almost 1 point lower than that granted to a female student. As also documented within literature, the presence of gender differences with respect to performance may have implications on students' career choices, course enrolment, and the use of knowledge, and so on (Guney, 2009). While accepting the fact that gender can affect the degree of motivation and thus performance, various studies considering this variable generated mixed evidence. Some studies cannot detect any meaningful relation between gender and accounting performance (Gammie et al., 2003; Jackling & Anderson, 1998). Tho (1994) reports that female students outperform male students in accounting, as they are believed to have higher work needs. De Lange and Mavondo (2004) also show that gender may induce different learning strategies for female and male students which can affect their academic performance.

One of the results that contradict our expectations refers to the fact that the maximum grade obtained by students having no previous economic background is higher than that of students who went to a high school with economic profile. This is also true when considering the two groups' mean grade for both SAFG and SSAG. Moreover, the mean final grade as assessed by the educator when considering the group of students who went to a high school with economic profile (4.705) is below the grade required for passing an exam in accordance with the Romanian grading system (5). This once again raises some question marks. Under these circumstances, we consider we should analyze to what extent are the high school and university education systems correlated and how this impacts students' academic performance? When considering alternative explanations, we might assume that students having no previous economic knowledge work and study harder than those who already do (Panel C). Students' distribution in high schools is another factor that must be considered in order to correctly assess what happens in high schools with economic profile.

Students who already have some working experience in the field of accounting seem to outperform those who do not (Panel D). This can be an indicator of the importance of accounting students' involvement in practice. This is also the case when analyzing students' cluster based on their choosing of the accounting specialization and pursuing of a future accounting career. Therefore, those becoming accounting students as a result of their own wish outperform those influenced by other factors (Panel F) and students pursuing a future accounting career outperform those who do not (Panel E). Results also document the fact that students who are unsatisfied with them being a part of the accounting specialization record lower chances of passing the exam (Panel G).

Another dimension of our study focuses on analyzing how students' final grades as assessed by the educator are being constructed based on the levels within Bloom's taxonomy. When analyzing the whole sample of 316 students, results show that students obtain higher points based on analysis (Panel A). Students seem to receive few points when it comes to comprehension and evaluation. While we were expecting students to have difficulties on the evaluation level questions, their having difficulties on the comprehension level questions was unexpected. As an overall conclusion, students earn their grade based on the first four levels in Bloom's taxonomy, while solving problems belonging to the evaluation level seems to be less accessible for them.

When considering gender clusters, we notice that male students base their grade mostly on questions belonging to the application level, while female students equally rely on questions belonging to the application and analysis levels (Panel B). These results documenting that female students find it easier to reach the analysis level questions are consistent with them outperforming male students. Students who went to high schools with an economic profile seem to rely on application and analysis also, while students with no economic background prefer the application level question (Panel C). This is no longer consistent with the later outperforming the former. Previous working experience in the field of accounting does not seem to differentiate students when it comes to grade formation, questions belonging to the application level being preferred by both students who have it and those who do not (Panel D). This is also the case when considering students' satisfaction related to the accounting specialization (Panel G).

Some differences are also found when considering students' intention of developing future careers in the field of accounting and their status of accounting students. More precisely, students planning on pursuing an accounting career and those who became accounting students as a result of their own desire equally rely on questions belonging to the application and analysis levels (Panels E and F). Meanwhile, students who do not plan on pursuing an accounting career and those who became accounting students due to other factors than their own desire mostly rely on questions belonging to the application level (Panels E and F).

Overall, the obtained results show that students mostly base their final grade in Controlling on questions belonging to the application and analysis levels, while evaluation questions are rarely correctly solved. The mean percentage recorded for the evaluation level is only 3%, while the maximum points that could be obtained on this level represent 10% out of the total final grade.

Considering the previously mentioned context of the applied questionnaire, we also started out with the purpose of analyzing the relationship between students' academic performance and corresponding determinant factors from the perspective of three different dimensions: the academic environment, students, and educators. These three dimensions, which actually represent the initial dimensions we had in mind when constructing the questionnaire, were also defined from the point of view of certain specific and general elements (corresponding to questions within the questionnaire). We actually considered that these three dimensions represent main aspects that have a determinant character, be it positive or negative, for any student's academic performance, considering the learning process of any considered discipline within the university educational preparation program.

In terms of the factor analysis being developed, the obtained results document the existence of 12 major determinant factors of students' academic performance. These determinant factors are built based on the responses students offered when answering the questions being comprised within the applied questionnaire. We must underline the fact that determinant factors being identified through the developed analysis determine 67.49% of students' performance. Moreover, the 0.757 value being recorded for the Kaiser–Meyer–Olkin Measure documents a high quality of the developed factor analysis (see Table 2).

Table 2 reflects the results being obtained through factor analysis while also reconciling the therefore documented new dimensions with the ones

Table 2. Factor Analysis Results Summary.

Rotated Factor Loadings	Component Items	% of Variance	Initial Dimension	New Dimension
Factor 1: Class educator's involvement at class	Q15, Q13, Q25, Q24, Q9	17.91	Educator	Educator
Factor 2: Teaching approaches at seminar and course	Q12B, Q21A, Q12A, Q12C, Q22, Q19	8.46	Student	Student
Factor 3: Seminar assistant's involvement at class	Q14, q16, q26, q18	5.79	Educator	Educator
Factor 4: Current attitude toward accounting and its perspectives	Q3, Q5, Q4	5.38	Student	Student
Factor 5: Extracurricular activities and the learning process	Q10, Q11, Q8, Q6	4.83	Student	Student
Factor 6: Intermediate testing – valuation method	Q21C, Q20C	4.05	Student	Student Educator
Factor 7: Communication during the semester	Q18, Q17	3.96	Educator	Educator
Factor 8: Teaching approaches, previous professional experience, gender	Q12A, Q2, Gender	3.65	Student Educator	Student Educator
Factor 9: Attributing scores for homework – valuation method	Q20, Q21	3.38	Educator	Educator
Factor 10: Prior studies, university's prestige and required references	Q9, Q23, Q1	3.18	Student Environment	Student Academic Environment
Factor 11: The learning process	Q7	3.02	Student	Student
Factor 12: Scores for student's class insolvent – valuation method	Q20	3.88	Educator	Student Educator

Principal Component Analysis (PCA)

No. of participants: 276	
No. of questions–elements (initial): 30 (29 + 1)	No. of questions (retained): 27
No. of analyzed items (initial): 35	No. of analyzed items (retained): 32
Total % of variance: 67.49	
Kaiser–Meyer–Olkin Measure = 0.757	Quality: good
Bartlett's test of sphericity: $\chi^2(190)=3228.512$, $\rho<0.000$	
Determinant = 0.000004556	
Eigenvalues over: 1	
Maximum iteration convergence: 25	Iteration convergence: 20
Factor scores: Anderson–Rubin method	

initially being considered. The detailed results of the factor analysis are presented in the appendix.

On the other hand, our initial approach that considered the three dimensions – the academic environment, students, and educators – proves to be a feasible one considering the fact that most of the initial dimensions were also retained through factor analysis. Among the new factors being built through factor analysis, we must emphasize the learning process, the assessment and grading system of students' academic performance, and student–educator communication during the semester.

CONCLUDING REMARKS

We will further synthesize the main findings of our study while also identifying some research perspectives. Results being obtained when comparing SSAGs with those assessed by the educator, even though correlated, represent an indicator showing that further work could be done in order to enhance students' ability to better assess their real academic performance. This, of course, is based on the consideration that grades being assessed by the educator, which are not considered to represent the supreme truth either, should be less biased than those self-acknowledged by students who for sure tend to be subjective. Developing students' ability to better assess their accounting knowledge as well as abilities and skills might be helpful for them when searching for a job that optimizes their characteristics and expectations.

Cluster analysis being performed within the previous part of the chapter was also interpreted by reference to findings of studies dealing with similar aspects. Some question marks are raised upon the Romanian high school education system in the case of economic profile high schools, since results document that students with no economic background seem to outperform those who went to a high school with economic profile.

Our chapter proposes the use of Bloom's taxonomy in order to asses accounting students' academic performance. Since the taxonomy is supposed to provide the classification of the goals for the educational systems, it would only be natural for us to also use it when assessing the results of the educational process. Our chapter tests the use of Bloom's taxonomy in the context of an emerging country's educational system that lacked consistency and faced significant challenges throughout history. When analyzing how students' final grades as assessed by the educator are being constructed based on the levels within Bloom's taxonomy, an unexpected situation is documented, students' actually receiving lower points for the comprehension level questions than for the application, analysis, and synthesis level questions. Since comprehension represents the lowest level of understanding, the determinants of the obtained results should be further investigated. Overall, questions belonging to the application and analysis levels seem to be preferred by students when analyzing their percentage within the final assessed grade in Controlling, while evaluation questions are rarely correctly solved.

We once again relate to Stahl and Harell's (1981) within-persons decision modeling approach emphasizing the importance of students' examination process. Examination performance as assessed by the educator is considered to be a relevant reflection of students' academic performance being used by the majority of studies within research literature. This represents an argument for its consideration and analysis when aiming for the improvement of students' examination process. On the other hand, students' self-acknowledged performance may motivate students' behavior. Considering the fact that there must be a fair representation of students' academic performance, the relationship between students' and educators' perceptions on academic performance should also be considered. Furthermore, the three initially considered dimensions that helped us construct our questionnaire were documented to represent a feasible approach when using factor analysis in establishing determinant factors of students' academic performance.

The main limitation of the study is linked to the inability of demonstrating the advantages of using Bloom's taxonomy through comparative analysis due to the impossibility of experiencing the same setting twice. Implementing the questionnaire at the same time with students' final written exam during the exam session period might also be argued to have impacted their emotional estate and therefore answers. We position our analysis in the context of the educational system of an emerging economy. The brief analysis of the evolutions and particularities of the Romanian academic environment documents early manifestations of the Romanian commercial schools in the second part of the 19th century. Accounting scientific debates starting to flourish in the first part of the 20th century were brutally interrupted under the Soviet accounting system that came with significant transformations taking place on a political, economic, and social level. The reforms that followed the 1989 revolution brought significant challenges for such a country trying to integrate the national economic system into the European one. All these imposed a certain dynamic for the development of the educational system as well. We therefore test the proposed research design and discuss the obtained results in the context of an educational system that lacked consistency and faced significant challenges throughout history. The obtained results offer useful insights in the area of examination performance linked to the validity of the construct leading to the assessment of accounting students' academic performance.

The results obtained by Diaconu (2008) position the Babeş-Bolyai University's educational curriculum quite well in relation to the international requirements. This makes it an interesting setting to be considered when wanting to focus on the assessment of accounting students' academic performance and its determinants. Still, the setting that is used in applying the proposed research design presents the limitation of only considering one generation of third year accounting students enrolled for the Controlling class during their bachelor studies within the Babeş-Bolyai University in Cluj-Napoca, Romania. Replicating the study for different settings would be the main proposed research perspective which we consider could offer more insights on the implications of the proposed research design.

NOTES

1. For a significant period of time (from the 14th century until the end of the First World War), Romanians lived in three separate states known as the Romanian Principalities: Transylvania, Wallachia, and Moldavia. The Principalities had tight language related, economic, social, cultural, and political connections. In 1859, Wallachia and Moldavia were united through the choosing of the same ruler in the person of Alexandru Ioan Cuza, therefore creating the basis of the modern state of Romania. Transylvania joined them only 59 years later (1918), forming the new Kingdom of Romania.
2. Professor of accounting and an important member of the scientific community.

ACKNOWLEDGMENT

The authors thank the participants at the *Writing to Publish in International Accounting Journals Workshop*, Prague 2011, and the *6th International Conference Accounting and Management Information Systems*, Bucharest 2011, for their useful suggestions. A previous version of the chapter was included in the *Proceedings of the 6th International Conference Accounting and Management Information Systems*.

REFERENCES

Athanassiou, N., McNett, J. M., & Harvey, C. (2003). Critical thinking in the management classroom: Bloom's taxonomy as a learning tool. *Journal of Management Education*, *27*(5), 533–555.

Bartlett, S., Peel, J. M., & Pendlebury, M. (1993). From fresher to finalist: A three year analysis of student performance on an accounting degree programme. *Accounting Education*, *2*(2), 111–122.

Bloom, B. S. (1956). *Taxonomy of educational objectives, Handbook 1: Cognitive domain*. London: Longman Green and Co LTD.

Booth, P., Luckett, P., & Mladenovic, R. (1999). The quality of learning in accounting education: The impact of approaches to learning on academic performance. *Accounting Education*, *8*(4), 277–300.

Byrne, M., Flood, B., & Willis, P. (2002). Approaches to learning of European business students. *Journal of Further and Higher Education*, *26*(1), 19–28.

Calu, D. A. (2005). *Istorie şi dezvoltare privind contabilitatea din România*, Ed. Economică, Bucureşti.

Chia, Y. M. (2005). Job offers of multi-national accounting firms: The effect of emotional intelligence, extra-curricular activities and academic performance. *Accounting Education*, *14*(1), 75–93.

Collier, H. W., & Mehrens, W. A. (1985). Using multiple choice test items to improve classroom testing of professional accounting students. *Journal of Accounting Education*, *3*(2), 41–51.

De Lange, P., & Mavondo, F. (2004). Gender and motivational differences in approaches to learning by a cohort of open learning students. *Accounting Education: An International Journal*, *13*(4), 431–448.

Diaconu, P. (2008). Directions of the accounting educational curricula in the Romanian universities and the conformity with IES provided by IFAC. *Proceedings of the International Conference Accounting and Management Information Systems*, Bucharest, 2008.

Duff, A. (2004). Understanding academic performance and progression of first-year accounting and business economics undergraduates: The role of approaches to learning and prior academic achievement. *Accounting Education*, *13*(4), 409–430.

Evian, I. N. (1940). *Teoria conturilor*. Cluj-Napoca.

Fordham, D. R., & Hayes, D. C. (2009). Worth repeating: Paper color may have an effect on student performance. *Issues in Accounting Education*, *24*(2), 187–194.

Fox, A., Stevenson, L., Connelly, P., Duff, A., & Dunlop, A. (2010). Peer-mentoring undergraduate accounting students: The influence on approaches to learning and academic performance. *Active Learning in Higher Education*, *11*(2), 145–156.

Gammie, E., Jones, P. L., & Robertson-Millar, C. (2003). Accountancy undergraduate performance: A statistical model. *Accounting Education*, *12*(1), 63–78.

Gardner, C. T., Milne, M. J., Stringer, C. P., & Whiting, R. H. (2005). Oral and written communication apprehension in accounting students: Curriculum impacts and impacts on academic performance. *Accounting Education*, *14*(3), 313–336.

General Review of Commerce and Accounting (ro. Revista Generală de Comerţ şi Contabilitate - RGCC) (1916), 35, 176.

Gracia, L., & Jenkins, E. (2003). A quantitative exploration of student performance on an undergraduate accounting programme of study. *Accounting Education*, *12*(1), 15–32.

Guney, Y. (2009). Exogenous and endogenous factors influencing students' performance in undergraduate accounting modules. *Accounting Education, 18*(1), 51–73.

Harrell, A., Caldwell, C., & Doty, E. (1985). Within-person expectancy theory predictions of accounting students' motivation to achieve academic success. *The Accounting Review, LX*(4), 724.

Hartnett, N., Romcke, J., & Yap, C. (2003). Recognizing the importance of instruction style to students' performance: Some observations from laboratory research – A research note. *Accounting Education, 12*(3), 313–331.

Jackling, B., & Anderson, A. (1998). Study mode, general ability and performance in accounting: A research note. *Accounting Education: An International Journal, 7*(1), 65–73.

Jones, S. H., & Wright, M. E. (2010). The effects of a hypertext learning aid and cognitive style on performance in advanced financial accounting. *Issues in Accounting Education, 25*(1), 35–58.

Kealey, B. T., Holland, J., & Watson, M. (2005). Preliminary evidence on the association between critical thinking and performance in principles of accounting. *Issues in Accounting Education, 20*(1), 33–49.

Koh, M. I., & Koh, H. C. (1999). The determinants of performance in an accountancy degree programme. *Accounting Education, 8*(1), 13–29.

Lancaster, K. A. S., & Strand, C. A. (2001). Using the team-learning model in a managerial accounting class: An experiment in cooperative learning. *Issues in Accounting Education, 16*(4), 549–567.

Lane, A., & Porch, M. (2002). The impact of background factors on the performance of non-specialist undergraduate students on accounting models – A longitudinal study: A research note. *Accounting Education, 11*(1), 109–118.

Lewis, T. D., Shimerda, T. A., & Graham, G. (1983). What the academic advisor needs to know about job placement. *Journal of Accounting Education, 1*(2), 135–142.

Lewy, A., & Bathory, Z. (1994). The taxonomy of educational objectives in Continental Europe, the Mediterranean, and the Middle East. In L. W. Anderson & L. A. Sosniak (Eds.), *Bloom's taxonomy: A forty-year retrospective* (pp. 174–189). Chicago, IL: University of Chicago Press.

McDuffie, S., & Smith, L. M. (2006). Impact of an audit reporting expert system on learning performance: A teaching note. *Accounting Education, 15*(1), 89–101.

Michael, W. B., & Jones, R. A. (1955). The influence of color of paper upon scores earned on objective achievement examination. *Journal of Applied Psychology, 39*(6), 447–450.

Mutiu, A., & Matis, D. (2010). Faculty of economics and business administration's vision on accounting education issues, published in the *Conference Volume Dezvoltare Durabila: Utopie sau Realitate,* Ed. Alma Mater, Cluj Napoca.

Naser, K., & Peel, M. J. (1998). An exploratory study of the impact of intervening variables on student performance in a Principles of Accounting course. *Accounting Education, 7*(3), 209–223.

Paisey, C., & Paisey, N. J. (2004). Student attendance in an accounting module – Reasons for non-attendance and the effect on academic performance at a Scottish University. *Accounting Education, 13*(1), 39–53.

Phillips, F. (1998). Accounting students' beliefs about knowledge: Associating performance with underlying belief dimensions. *Issues in Accounting Education, 13*(1), 113–126.

Ramburuth, P., & Mladenovic, R. (2004). Exploring the relationship between students' orientations to learning, the structure of students' learning outcomes and subsequent academic performance. *Accounting Education, 13*(4), 507–527.

Schleifer, L. L. F., & Dull, R. B. (2009). Metacognition and performance in the accounting classroom. *Issues in Accounting Education, 24*(3), 339–367.

Stahl, M. J., & Harrell, A. M. (1981). Modelling effort decisions with behavioral decision theory: Toward an individual differences model of expectancy theory. *Organizational Behavior and Human Performance, 27*, 303–325.

Stokes, L. (2008). A preliminary study of learning objectives across the curriculum: An analysis of various accounting textbooks. *Advances in Accounting Education, 9*, 307–326.

Tan, K., & Choo, F. (1990). A note on the academic performance of deep-elaborative and shallow-reiterative information processing students. *Accounting and Finance, 30*(2), 67–81.

Tho, L. M. (1994). Some evidence on the determinants of student performance in the University of Malaya introductory accounting course. *Accounting Education, 3*(4), 331–340.

Tiron-Tudor, A., & Muţiu, A. (2007). The evolution of accounting profession in Romania – A historical approach. *The Balkan Countries 1st International Conference on Accounting and Auditing*. Avciol Basim Yayin, Istanbul, Editor: Association of Accounting and Finance Academicians (AAFA), 207–217.

Vroom, V. H. (1964). *Work and motivation*. San Francisco, CA: Jossey-Bass.

Watson, S. F., Apostolou, B., Hassell, J. M., & Webber, S. A. (2007). Accounting education literature review 2003–2005. *Journal of Accounting Education, 25*, 1–58.

World Bank. (2009). Report on the Observance of Standards and Codes (ROSC) published.

APPENDIX: FACTOR ANALYSIS RESULTS

Qs.	Item	Rotated Factor Loadings											
		Factor 1	Factor 2	Factor 3	Factor 4	Factor 5	Factor 6	Factor 7	Factor 8	Factor 9	Factor 10	Factor 11	Factor 12
Q15PS	Interest shown by class educator during the exposition	**0.86**	−0.11	0.14	0.01	0.03	0.09	0.07	−0.09	0.02	−0.05	−0.01	0.03
Q13PS	Clarity of expositions made by the class educator	**0.82**	−0.10	0.14	0.03	0.02	0.03	0.17	0.04	−0.08	−0.05	−0.04	0.02
Q25PS	Degree of trust in the class educator's professional abilities	**0.73**	−0.10	0.17	0.20	0.10	0.10	0.07	−0.04	−0.06	0.12	0.10	−0.15
Q24PS	Educator's ability to explain the class's utility from a practical point of view	**0.69**	−0.08	0.32	0.06	0.11	−0.06	0.00	0.00	0.03	−0.06	0.06	0.08
Q9MG	Degree of trust in the university's prestige	**0.49**	−0.21	0.09	0.06	0.20	0.00	−0.15	−0.08	−0.07	**−0.47**	0.03	−0.09
Q12BPS	Initial presentation of the topics to be studied for this subject	−0.18	**0.83**	−0.13	−0.03	0.09	−0.03	0.10	−0.02	−0.08	0.04	0.04	0.09

Q21APS	Seminar valuation methods: attributing scores	−0.10	**0.69**	−0.04	−0.08	0.06	−0.01	0.13	−0.03	−0.12	0.08	−0.05	0.38
Q12APS	Information concerning the seminar's topic presented at the beginning of the semester	−0.10	**0.63**	−0.14	0.02	0.16	0.08	−0.11	**0.41**	−0.06	0.08	−0.04	−0.02
Q12CPS	References-related information presented at the beginning of the semester	−0.04	**0.61**	−0.03	−0.02	−0.05	0.01	−0.11	−0.11	0.22	0.16	0.21	−0.19
Q22PS	Promptitude in receiving the valuation process' results for this subject	−0.05	**0.59**	−0.09	−0.11	−0.13	0.07	−0.04	0.06	0.13	0.00	−0.12	−0.21
Q19PS	Main teaching method being used within the class	0.14	**−0.51**	0.12	0.04	0.04	0.20	0.07	−0.06	−0.09	0.32	−0.15	−0.05
Q14PS	Clarity of expositions made by the seminar assistant	0.27	−0.08	**0.81**	0.09	0.00	0.05	0.04	0.06	−0.06	−0.15	−0.06	0.08
Q16PS	Interest shown by the seminar assistant during the exposition	0.31	−0.21	**0.76**	0.00	−0.02	0.13	0.03	−0.09	0.00	−0.11	−0.06	−0.02

Appendix: (*Continued*)

Qs.	Item	Rotated Factor Loadings											
		Factor 1	Factor 2	Factor 3	Factor 4	Factor 5	Factor 6	Factor 7	Factor 8	Factor 9	Factor 10	Factor 11	Factor 12
Q26PS	Degree of trust in the seminar assistant's professional abilities	0.28	−0.11	**0.74**	0.15	0.10	0.05	0.05	−0.11	−0.02	0.03	−0.01	−0.14
Q18PS	Communication with the seminar assistant during the semester	−0.07	−0.05	**0.62**	0.21	0.05	0.07	**0.59**	−0.01	−0.05	−0.06	0.01	−0.03
Q27SS	Assessment of the subject's practical usefulness	0.26	−0.07	0.39	0.22	0.24	0.23	0.04	−0.03	−0.03	0.22	0.18	0.00
Q3SG	Determinant element in choosing the accounting specialization	−0.05	0.03	0.03	**−0.76**	0.04	0.04	−0.14	0.00	0.04	0.12	−0.17	0.11
Q5SG	Current intention of developing a career in the field of accounting	0.06	−0.13	0.27	**0.75**	0.12	0.08	0.00	−0.01	0.05	0.15	−0.14	−0.02
Q4SG	Degree of satisfaction toward the followed specialization	0.18	−0.10	0.16	**0.73**	0.23	−0.02	0.08	0.00	−0.06	−0.15	−0.12	0.11

Q10MG	Request for implication in extracurricular activities during undergraduate years of study	0.10	−0.01	−0.01	0.03	**0.85**	−0.02	0.01	0.02	−0.02	0.07	0.02	−0.03
Q11SG	Implication in extracurricular activities during undergraduate years of study	0.11	−0.01	0.12	0.11	**0.78**	−0.06	0.14	0.10	0.11	0.00	−0.01	−0.03
Q8MG	Competition among students while learning	0.07	0.01	0.06	−0.06	**−0.42**	−0.11	−0.28	0.38	0.04	0.34	−0.02	−0.16
Q6SG	Using the faculty's and/or university's library services	0.11	0.27	0.06	0.36	**0.41**	0.07	−0.01	−0.27	−0.16	0.07	0.01	0.07
Q28SS	Weekly time dedicated to study for this subject	0.09	0.13	0.03	0.16	0.36	0.20	0.35	0.07	−0.10	−0.20	−0.21	0.06
Q21CPS	Seminar valuation methods: intermediate testing	0.11	0.11	0.01	0.06	−0.08	**0.86**	0.10	−0.01	0.07	−0.03	0.02	−0.01
Q20CPS	Class valuation methods: intermediate testing	0.01	−0.13	0.22	−0.05	0.07	**0.84**	−0.06	−0.01	−0.01	0.09	0.06	−0.06

Appendix: (*Continued*)

Qs.	Item	Rotated Factor Loadings											
		Factor 1	Factor 2	Factor 3	Factor 4	Factor 5	Factor 6	Factor 7	Factor 8	Factor 9	Factor 10	Factor 11	Factor 12
Q17PS	Communicating with the class educator during the semester	0.27	−0.04	0.11	0.09	0.16	−0.01	**0.82**	0.07	0.05	0.02	0.01	−0.03
Gender	Respondent's gender	−0.07	0.06	−0.08	−0.23	0.09	−0.05	0.02	**0.73**	−0.06	−0.16	0.32	0.03
Q2SG	Previous professional experience in the field of accounting	0.05	−0.07	0.05	−0.24	0.01	−0.05	−0.19	**−0.58**	−0.12	−0.07	0.34	0.06
Q20BPS	Class valuation methods: scores for homework	−0.15	−0.12	0.11	−0.01	0.05	0.12	−0.09	0.04	**0.78**	0.04	0.20	0.09
Q21BPS	Seminar valuation methods: scores for homework	0.07	0.27	−0.24	−0.06	−0.02	−0.07	0.12	0.00	**0.73**	−0.01	−0.15	−0.03
Q23PS	Volume of references required to be used for this subject	0.11	−0.14	0.14	−0.02	−0.05	−0.12	0.13	−0.02	−0.06	**−0.61**	0.00	−0.23
Q1SG	Previous studies: economic high school	0.06	−0.09	−0.07	−0.24	0.11	−0.11	0.10	−0.24	−0.10	**0.48**	0.31	−0.13

Q7SG	Collaborating and discussing with colleagues during the learning process	0.07	0.08	−0.04	0.02	−0.03	0.09	−0.01	0.05	0.07	0.06	**0.81**	0.07
Q20APS	Class valuation methods: points for the students' involvement	0.00	−0.02	−0.05	−0.01	−0.02	−0.06	−0.02	−0.04	0.07	0.10	0.07	**0.86**
	Eigenvalues	6.269	2.962	2.026	1.882	1.693	1.419	1.385	1.277	1.182	1.114	1.056	1.007
	% of variance	17.91	8.46	5.79	5.38	4.83	4.05	3.96	3.65	3.38	3.18	3.02	3.88
	α (Cronbach's alpha, a reliability test for our analysis)	0.82	0.25	0.79	0.31	0.48	0.71	0.69	−0.19	0.45	0.19	–	–

The bold values in the appendix show those elements (questions from the questionnaire) that together form a factor. For example, the first five elements in the table together form factor 1 in accordance to the obtained results.

ABOUT THE AUTHORS

Nadia Albu is an associate professor of accounting with the Bucharest University of Economic Studies Romania. She has obtained a Ph.D. in 2005 from the same university. She is focusing her research on IFRS application in emerging economies, management accounting, and the accounting profession. Her research has recently been published in *Critical Perspectives on Accounting*, *Australian Accounting Review*, *Journal of International Financial Management & Accounting*, *Journal of Accounting in Emerging Economies*, and *Accounting in Europe*.

David Alexander recently retired as a professor of international accounting at the University of Birmingham, England. He has published many papers in the field of comparative and theoretical financial accounting and reporting, and regularly updates three coauthored textbooks. He continues in an active research, publication, and mentoring role involving colleagues and conferences in a number of countries.

Jaan Alver is a professor at Tallinn University of Technology, head of the Department of Accounting, and head of the Chair of Managerial Accounting. He received his first degree from Tallinn University of Technology and Ph.D. degree from the Estonian Academy of Sciences. He is a member of European Accounting Association (EAA). His research areas are international accounting, financial statement analysis, cost management, accounting history, and accounting education.

Lehte Alver is a professor at Tallinn University of Technology, head of the Chair of Financial Accounting. She received her first degree from the University of Tartu and Ph.D. degree from the University of Vilnius. She is a member of the European Accounting Association (EAA). Her research areas are international accounting, international financial reporting standards (IFRSs), accounting history, and accounting education.

Cagnur Kaytmaz Balsari was born in 1971 in Izmir. She received her bachelor's degree in business administration at Dokuz Eylul University and her MBA at Loyola University in Chicago in 1997. She has completed her doctoral studies at Boston University in 2004 majoring accounting. She is currently working at Dokuz Eylul University Faculty of Business. She is currently serving as an academic advisor to The Chamber of Certified Public Accountants of Izmir (IZSMMMO) and member of the one of the IFRS consultancy committees of the Turkish Public Oversight, Accounting and Auditing Standards Board. Her major research area is capital markets research in accounting. She has published many articles in national and international journals. She has completed a research project in Foreign Direct Investment in Turkey funded by The Scientific and Technological Council of Turkey (TUBITAK). Financial accounting, managerial accounting, financial statement analysis, IFRS, and empirical research in Accounting are among the courses she has been teaching at the university.

Carmen Giorgiana Bonaci holds a Ph.D. granted by the Babeş-Bolyai University, currently being part of the Accounting and Audit Department of the Faculty of Economics and Business Administration in Cluj-Napoca. She is a member of the European Accounting Association and coorganizer of the *AAC 2013 Convention*, *AAC 2011 Convention*, *AAC 2009 Convention*, *and 3rd AAC 2008 Annual Conference*.

Chiraţa Caraiani is a professor at Bucharest University of Economic Studies, Bucharest, Romania and has a Ph.D. diploma in accounting. She has more than 20 years' experience in teaching and researching activity. The disciplines taught in the field of accounting are ıntroduction in accounting, financial accounting, managerial accounting, controlling, accounting for financial market, etc. The research interest manifests in managerial accounting, intellectual capital, social and environmental reporting and accounting, sustainable development, accounting education by publishing various theoretical and experimental studies in national and international journals, and by developing national research projects as manager and team member.

Cornelia Dascălu is a professor at Bucharest University of Economic Studies, Bucharest, Romania and has a Ph.D. diploma in accounting. She has more than 20 years' experience in teaching and researching activity. The disciplines taught in the field of accounting are bank accounting, public accounting, managerial accounting, controlling, accounting for financial market, etc. The research interest manifests in managerial accounting, intellectual capital, social and environmental reporting and accounting, sustainable development, accounting education by publishing various theoretical and experimental studies in national and international journals, and by developing national research projects as manager and team member.

Tatiana A. Garanina is a Senior Lecturer of Department of Finance and Accounting at Graduate School of Management, St. Petersburg University. She has received her Ph.D. from Graduate School of Management. Her research interests are financial analysis and evaluation of company efficiency and profitability; accounting: Russian and international financial reporting standards; intellectual capital evaluation. She is a member of European Accounting Association and European Finance Association. She participated in a short-term Executive Education Program in Harvard Business School.

Olesea Ghedrovici serves as a senior lecturer at the Academy of Economic Studies of Moldova. She received her Ph.D. and master's degree in finance from the same institution. She has been invited as a visiting scholar to conduct studies at Foster School of Business of the University of Washington, Erasmus University of Rotterdam, and Jagiellonian University in Krakow. She served as an assistant consultant at the World Bank office in Moldova in 2009, and at the Ministry of Education and Religious Affairs of Hellenic Republic, in 2012.

Ionel-Alin Ienciu, Ph.D., is a lecturer at Babeş-Bolyai University, Faculty of Economics and Business Administration, Department of Accounting and Audit, Cluj-Napoca, Romania. He has been involved in didactic and scientific activities in the field of audit and accounting convergence, with a scientific interest in the implications of environmental issues for the accountancy and audit of financial situations. He has participated in national and international conferences. His studies have been published in specialized magazines and books. In the past, he was a manager of a doctoral research project, a member in several national research grants, and a postdoc fellow within a project funded through European funds.

Nicoleta Maria Ienciu is a Ph.D. candidate at Babeş-Bolyai University, Faculty of Economics and Business Administration, Department of Accounting and Audit, Cluj-Napoca, Romania. Nicoleta's interests concern the human capital in the field of accountancy and financial reporting and she has participated in national and international conferences. Studies by Nicoleta have been published in specialized magazines and books such as *Journal of Human Resources Costing and Accounting*, *Review of Business Research*, *International Journal of Business Research*, *Audit Financiar*,

Studia Oeconomica, Economia Regională: ipostaze rurale şi urbane. Nicoleta is a member of European Accounting Association.

Mateja Jerman is an assistant professor in accounting at the Faculty of Management, University of Primorska, Slovenia. She received her Ph.D. from the Faculty of Economics and Business, University of Maribor, Slovenia. Her research interests include financial reporting, accounting for intangibles, and earnings management. She is the author and coauthor of scientific and professional papers as well as course books in the field of accounting.

Polina S. Kormiltseva got her bachelor degree from Graduate School of Management, St. Petersburg University with specialization in finance and accounting. She continued her education on master in management programs at Graduate School of Management, St. Petersburg University and successfully got two diplomas – one from St. Petersburg University and another from Global Alliance in Management Education CEMS (ranked no. 3 in FT ranking). Now she is employed by Google and is responsible for marketing issues.

Camelia Iuliana Lungu is an associate professor at Bucharest University of Economic Studies, Bucharest, Romania and has a Ph.D. diploma in accounting. She has 12 years' experience in teaching and researching activity. The disciplines taught in the field of accounting are introduction in accounting, financial accounting, managerial accounting, controlling, international financial reporting standards, etc. The research interest manifests in financial and reporting, managerial accounting, intellectual capital, social and environmental reporting and accounting, sustainable development, accounting education by publishing various theoretical and experimental studies in national and international journals, and by developing national research projects as manager and team member.

Dumitru Matiş, Ph.D., is a full university professor at Babeş-Bolyai University, Faculty of Economics and Business Administration, Department of Accounting and Audit, Cluj-Napoca, Romania, of different accounting disciplines (e.g., basic accounting, financial accounting, advanced accounting, and international accounting). He is the dean of the Faculty of Economics and Business Administration within the same university. He is member of the Chamber of Financial Auditors from Romania and of the Superior Council of the Accounting and Financial Reporting Council of Romania. He is also a member within the Board of the European Accounting

Association as Romania's representative. Author and coauthor of a significant number of research papers and books.

Cristina Maria Morariu is a lecturer at the Bucharest University of Economic Studies, Romania and currently finalized her Ph.D. at the same institution. Additionally she is a member of different scientific committees. Her current research interests relate to recognition, measurement, and disclosure of intellectual capital. Her writing on the topic of intellectual capital has been presented at international conferences and published in academic journals.

Alexandra Muţiu holds a Ph.D. in accounting from Babeş-Bolyai University and she is an associate professor of accounting at Babeş-Bolyai University and adjunct professor at Plymouth State University, NH, USA. She teaches live and online courses in managerial accounting and controlling, mainly using case study method. She is a strong supporter of accelerated learning, being preoccupied in offering a better learning experience for her students. She has a vast international teaching experience gained through teaching mobility grants in Poland, Turkey, Austria, and scholarships in China and the United States. Her research interests are in accounting education and pedagogy.

Sergeja Slapničar, Ph.D., is an associate professor of accounting at the Faculty of Economics, University of Ljubljana. Her research is focused on management control systems and corporate governance. She has published in a number of international scientific and practitioner journals. She was a board member of the Slovenian Agency for Audit Supervision till 2009 and is a supervisory board member or member of audit committees in a number of Slovenian public firms.

Jiří Strouhal is an associate professor at the University of Economics Prague, from where he obtained his Ph.D. in 2005. He holds a certificate of accounting expert from the Czech accounting certification scheme. He is an editorial board member of several referred international journals. He was a member of the Committee for Education and Certification of Accountants of the Union of Accountants, is currently president of the Chamber of Certified Accountants Czech Republic, and acts as a consultant of financial accounting issues for the Czech Statistical Office.

Neža Štumberger is a practitioner and graduate student of accounting at the Faculty of Economics, University of Ljubljana. In her research work she examines the quality of accounting services from various aspects. She is employed in an accounting firm, providing services to small and micro firms.

Liis Talpas has a BA and MA from Tallinn University of Technology and is currently a Ph.D. student at the same university. She is an Estonian Authorized Public Accountant and a member of the Estonian Board of Auditors. Her research areas are international accounting, international financial reporting standards (IFRSs), and financial reporting of small- and medium-sized entities.

Secil Varan was born in 1977 in Izmir, Turkey. She received her bachelor's degree in business administration in 2000, and earned her master's degree of finance at Dokuz Eylul University, Izmir, Turkey in 2008. She has completed her doctoral studies at Dokuz Eylul University in 2012 majoring accounting. She was assigned as an assistant professor Dr. at the Department of Logistics Management, Maritime Faculty, Dokuz Eylul University on January, 2013. Her major research area is corporate governance and capital markets research in accounting. Financial accounting, cost and managerial accounting, financial management, and investment and financial analysis in Maritime companies are among the courses she has been teaching at the university.

Maja Zaman Groff, Ph.D., is an assistant professor of accounting and auditing at the Faculty of Economics, University of Ljubljana. She has recently published in various international scientific and domestic practitioner journals. She was a member of the board of the Slovenian Association of Accountants, Treasurers and Auditors and a member of the Council of the Slovenian Institute of Auditors. She has focused her research on auditing and corporate governance related topics and is an audit committee member in a number of Slovenian public companies.